OUT OF THIS WORLD THE STORY OF

OUT OF THIS WORLD THE STORY OF

MUSE

OUT OF THIS WORLD THE STORY OF

BY MARK BEAUMONT

OMNIBUS PRESS

LONDON / NEW YORK / PARIS / SYDNEY / COPENHAGEN / BERLIN / MADRID / TOKYO

Cover designed by Fresh Lemon
Picture research by Sarah Bacon

ISBN: 978.1.84938.368.4
Order No: OP53350

Exclusive Distributors
Music Sales Limited,
14/15 Berners Street,
London, W1T 3LJ.

Music Sales Corporation,
257 Park Avenue South,
New York, NY 10010, USA.

Macmillan Distribution Services,
56 Parkwest Drive
Derrimut, Vic 3030,
Australia.

Every effort has been made to trace the copyright holders of the photographs
in this book but one or two were unreachable. We would be grateful if the
photographers concerned would contact us.

Typeset by Galleon Typesetting, Ipswich
Printed by Gutenberg Press Ltd, Malta

A catalogue record for this book is available from the British Library.

Visit Omnibus Press on the web at www.omnibuspress.com.

Introduction

ON first encounter, Muse were the most forgettable band I'd ever met.

Huddled awkwardly around a table in a dank under-arches café a few yards from the west London offices of their PR company sometime in the brittle January of 1999, it was only their second interview with a professional music journalist (their first was with my *NME* colleague James Oldham, for their earliest publicity biog) and the first that would be printed nationally (in *NME*'s new bands section, then titled 'On'), and their lack of media training trembled their teacups, stuttered their tongues. Three fidgety, flush-cheeked posh kids from the West Country, they seemed utterly incompatible with the music they were supposedly making: most notably the lead track from their second EP, 'Muscle Museum', which had dive-bombed the *NME* stereo a few weeks earlier and enthralled us all with its March Of The Diplodocus bassline, its Moroccan snake-charming guitar, and a chorus so grandiose in its falsetto massiveness that it seemed to explode from the speakers like a volcano beneath a Notre Dame full of burning Queen albums.

This, surely, was music made by giants; 80-ft cast-iron rock giants in fact, with the larynxes of screeching harpies, guitars of steaming brimstone and testicles of pure granite. And yet, mumbling nervously into their Diet Cokes were these three fidgety, flush-cheeked posh kids from the West Country. A tiny, sharp-featured and restlessly angular 20-year-old called Matt Bellamy was clearly the spokesperson, jabbering and stuttering his way through the allotted half hour at breakneck pace, as though nerves and media inexperience were prompting a severe attack of verbal gastroenteritis. Bassist Chris Wolstenholme (Wolstenholme? I mean, how public school *was* this band?) seemed friendly and charming enough, sitting ponderously aside adding details and trivia where necessary, while boyishly shy but smiley drummer Dominic Howard, judging from his

total contribution to the interview, might well have been born mute.*
Could it really be that this molten eruption of operatic rock, this
Radiohead-to-the-power-of-Wagner, this first burst of The New Music,
could have emanated from these – well – *students*?

The interview itself was painfully anodyne. They'd met at school, won
a Battle Of The Bands, carried on playing pubs around Teignmouth for a
couple of years until they landed a deal with a minor indie label,
blah-blah-blah. Were they shameless Radiohead copyists? The influence
was there, but they were a completely different band. How did they feel
about being signed by Madonna's label, Maverick? They've also got the
Deftones and Matt liked the Deftones. How did they respond to rumours
of Matt's tearaway teenagedom back in Teignmouth? Well, um, he'd been
a bit of a bad boy but they didn't want to go into that.

We supped our soft drinks, we counted the minutes, we plodded
unstimulated through the 'On' piece motions. And, all questions duly (and
dully) covered, all basic points of history divulged and any hint of an
interesting, controversial or inflammatory quote masterfully avoided, I
thumbed off the tape and informed Muse that they had just delivered me
quite possibly the most boring interview I'd ever conducted.

My words, one suspects, may have been taken to heart.

Because, my oh my, how all that was about to change.

* * *

We downed vodka with roomfuls of groupies in Moscow. We got so
drunk in Austria that we didn't realise we'd left Matt in Graz until we got
to Vienna. We ploughed the gin palaces of Pigalle and fought back crowds
of grabbing arms at the stage door of the Barcy. We started a photoshoot,
unannounced and unscheduled, in Red Square, only to be chased back to
a speeding people-carrier within 10 minutes by hordes of clamouring

---

* Indeed, Dominic's early forgetability factor would be driven home to me a few weeks
later: having raced across the lawns of Reading University chasing the opening riff of
'Muscle Museum' when Muse were supporting Gene on the 1999 university tour, I found
myself, post-show, in Gene's dressing room, being asked by their drummer Matt if I'd
enjoyed the support act. "They're going to be massive," I replied, and thankfully so, since
I'd failed to recognise Dominic standing a foot away from me in a woolly hat, listening
intently to my reply.

Russian girl-fans who'd unexpectedly spotted us there.* We talked of naked, mushroom-fuelled hot-tub sessions in Richmond recording studios. We did the sights of London together, from a virtual meteor ride in the Science Museum to a playback of 'Absolution' in the Planetarium (complete with celestial star show) to admiring the waxy rear of Kylie Minogue in Madam Tussauds.

Over the decade following that damp January disaster of an interview I regularly rode the back bumper of Muse's starship to success, interviewing them at pivotal stages in their rise and watching them rapidly expand as a live act, outgrowing the theatres like a toddler outgrows its cribwear, bulging the roofs of arenas across Europe and finally bursting free into the stadiums they were born to call their own.

At the earliest stage it was clear this was a band too big for their venues. On those early *Showbiz* support tours and small headline shows they raged like some gargantuan rock beast trapped in too small a cage; Matt would end each show in a destructive frenzy, smashing guitars, frisbeeing cymbals across the stage (coming close to beheading Dom at one memorable Paris gig) and rolling around on the floor spewing feedback as if in musical outrage at not having the stadium budget his music deserved. By the time second album, *Origin Of Symmetry*†, took them to the Academies, Apollos and Zeniths, the orbs came out; dozens of inflatable white planets filled with silver ticker tape launched into celestial flight during 'Bliss'.

Come *Absolution*'s arena invasion the orbs began to fall from the sky, strafed by ticker tape cannons and holographic lasers. Come the festival headline extravaganzas of *Black Holes And Revelations* they'd grown firework waterfalls, future-flash enormo-screens, a guitar that seemed to change colour depending on Matt's mood and third-century organs that lit up like the spaceship from *Close Encounters* with each note. That Muse still felt cramped by their surroundings was most evident in Dom's drum riser – a neon rendition of a satellite that was so big that the arena stages were too small to allow them to fit wings to it, leaving it resembling a

* This event was actually caught on camera by Muse's long-time documentary film-maker associate Tom Kirk and included on DVD 2 of the 'Hullabaloo' Live DVD release in 2002 – you might just be able to catch a snippet of my interview with the band as we speed off into the chilly Moscow afternoon.
† My own personal platinum disc for which I ferreted excitedly from a courier box in late 2001, a nod of thanks for three years of stout support.

massive dot-matrix blender. There were even plans to erect a huge aerial transmitter mast in the centre of the auditorium on the *Black Holes . . .* European tour in order to extend the stage set (themed around the HAARP installation in Alaska, which conspiracy theorists believe to have been built as part of a governmental mind-control scheme) right out into the audience, but the £1 million price tag put them off.

And so, inevitably, there was Wembley Stadium – their coming of age, their bursting from the arena cocoon, the full unfurling of their stadium band cloaks. Here the three of them rose, back to back in a plume of smoke from a platform in the centre of the pitch, before strolling into a sensory blitzkrieg. Enormous antennae shot lasers into the stratosphere. The giant orbs had evolved, pulsing spectrums of light from up in the stands, overlooking the stage like a council of gigantic alien brains, or floating around the arena dangling acrobats from their undersides. And the stage itself assaulted the eyes; one huge video screen blazing out warped and pixellated phantoms of the band or films of lap dancing she-droids or devastated futuristic cities of delusion. It was the Muse spectacle as it was always meant to be experienced, a show as monumental as their music had always been. It was, you felt, Muse coming home; Muse *exhaling*.

At Wembley Stadium that balmy June evening in 2007, Muse were the least forgettable band I'd ever seen.

* * *

And the interviews? Such interviews! The secret lizard people running the government! The 11th planet on a collision course with ours, from whence life on our planet had arrived on its last pass by Earth! The hallucinations of Martian landscapes! The jet packs, the governmental mind control, the 9/11 conspiracy theories, the Cydonian knights, the blatant calls to revolution! Just as his music grew bolder and more bombastic and his stage show became a blinding space-age monolith of technology, Matt Bellamy's interviews became ever more wild and intriguing as he expounded on internet conspiracy theories, corruptions political and religious, and ideas about the make-up of the universe that he'd pieced together from disparate scientific facts linked with his own brilliantly skewed sense of logic.

Far from that dull, mumbling teenager in the west London café of 1999, Matt Bellamy had grown into a man intent on questioning everything, on peeling away the lies and rumours that bombard us daily to expose his own personal truths about the political, religious and scientific universe we inhabit. And then on taking hallucinogens and diving in to truly *experience* it. Part truth campaigner, part mad scientist, part sci-fi geek, part psychedelic visionary, Matt was a whole new evolution of the rock star gene; fiercely intelligent and Wagnerian of vision, mind-warping concepts and worldview-challenging theorems would spew from his lips at a breakneck rate, impossible for the listener to process and comprehend at once and always overflowing the interview time we were allotted and the word lengths I was commissioned. Often it felt like trying to interview the entire internet on random search.

In trying to capture this dizzying experience within these pages, the quotes herein are largely previously unprinted segments of interviews I've conducted with Muse covering their entire career, charting Matt's development from media-shy mutterer to one of music's most fabulous and fascinating personae and revealing perhaps an untold side of Muse's rocket ride to the opera-rock stratosphere. It's an epic story of tragedy, adventure, mysticism and glory, so strap in tight, Muse go supermassive in T minus ten, nine, eight . . .

Mark Beaumont, June, 2008

Chapter One

TAKE a stroll, one autumn afternoon, out along Teignmouth's ornate Victorian pier – past the peeling Aunt Sallies, the coin shunts and the go-kart track on the site of the old Pavilion, to the rusting old telescope shackled to the seaward end. Twist a coin in the slot and peer north-east, away from the mouth of the Teign and the port, along the railway's route through the Parson's tunnel, towards the two stacks of rock, vaguely human in shape, rising from the crashing waves on the eastern cape of Dawlish.

To the locals they're known as the Parson and the Clerk, and they say the devil Himself planted them there.

The legend runs something like this: some centuries ago an ailing Bishop of Exeter retired to Dawlish in the hope that the sea air might restore his failing health. A local priest, however, saw this as a chance to weave his way into the old man's affections and claim the bishopric for himself when the former passed away. With his clerk as a guide the priest made the perilous trip across Haldon Moor daily to make his entreaties to the bishop until, one night in a violent storm, the pair found themselves lost on the moors, miles from the right path. "I'd rather have the devil himself, than you, for my guide!" yelled the priest, at which precise moment a horseman rode by and offered to lead them out of the storm. After a few miles they arrived at a brightly lit mansion in the grip of a bacchanalian feast; the home, it transpired, of their horseman host. For several hours the two caroused with the outlandish guests, guzzling wine by the flagon, partaking of the ungodly pleasures of painted ladies and whirled into wild, distorted dances to warped, contorted music until, near dawn, news arrived at the mansion of the death of the old bishop. Desperate to grasp his promotion at the earliest opportunity, the priest raced to his horse along with the clerk and their guide, but their horses refused to move. For some minutes the furious priest set about his steed with spur and whip, thrashing the poor beast half to death, crying "the devil take the brutes!"

7

The guide heard him, turned and, with a sudden glint of red in his eye, hissed "thank you sir" and "gee up". And away sped the horses with the priest and the clerk on their backs, straight over the cliffs at Dawlish and into the sea.

They say the two stone stacks out beyond the cliffs are all that's left of the pair, turned to stone by Beezlebub for their greed and ambition, slowly eroded by the accusing surf.

Mysterious horsemen. Religious corruption. Demonic possession. Supernatural transmogrification. And weird, wild musical hedonism.

It's the sort of story that might, on his arrival in this soiled yet sleepy corner of the Devon coastline, turn an impressionable 10-year-old's head.

* * *

When the Bellamy family moved to the close-knit community at Dawlish (population: around 13,000) from Cambridge in 1988 to be closer to dad George's parents, you suspect they quickly sparked a few local legends of their own. George Bellamy, word spread, used to be a rock star: in 1961, as a predominantly country-and-western singer aged 20, the Sunderland-born guitarist answered an advert placed in *Melody Maker* by legendary impresario Joe Meek, a celebrated songwriter, producer and eccentric famed at the time for his hit-making nous, inventive production techniques using distorted and compressed sounds beaten out of household objects, and a morbid fascination with the occult. Meek hired George as the rhythm guitarist in his latest project, instrumental combo The Tornados.

Joe Meek used The Tornados as in-house backing musicians for many of his productions, playing with the likes of Billy Fury and Marty Wilde at his Holloway Road studio, but they also released singles of their own. Their 1962 debut, 'Love And Fury'/'Popeye Twist', had failed to chart and its follow-up 'The Breeze And I', followed suit, but George was clearly a lucky charm for the band: within four months of his audition The Tornados' third release, 'Telstar', became a huge hit. A keyboard-led tune in the vein of a space age Morricone (it opened with the fuzz and bleeps of an imagined satellite), written by Meek in July 1962 and inspired by the satellite that broadcast the first TV pictures across the Atlantic, 'Telstar' topped the UK singles chart for five weeks, made The Tornados the first British group to reach number one in the US Hot 100 and went on to sell five million copies worldwide over the next six months. In the space of a month in 1962, The Tornados became serious competition to The Shadows as the UK's premier instrumental guitar band. 'Telstar' would also go on to heights of pop notoriety by becoming Margaret Thatcher's favourite song. And George became a global pop star.

His days in The Tornados were tempestuous, not least because of Meek's bizarre and often violent working methods. When he wasn't introducing George to the mysteries of the Ouija board, he was acting the schizophrenic task-master: at one session that didn't meet Meek's expectations, the band fled the studio as he launched into a characteristic tirade, only for Meek to throw a weighty tape recorder down the stairs after them, knocking out the bassist. The tours were equally eye-opening, taking in summer seasons at Butlins and one memorable gig in Manchester with Rolf Harris and The Beatles at the height of Beatlemania that erupted into a girl-screaming riot, complete with a police invasion of the venue. In the midst of the chaos, George walked into Rolf Harris' band's dressing room to find a scene of the utmost debauchery, as the band were all making out with women in riot gear. The whereabouts, at this point, of Jake The Peg's extra leg are sadly unrecorded.

Fame's fleeting spotlight didn't linger too long on George Bellamy however. In 1963, bassist Heinz Burt – who owned the shotgun that Meek, depressed and facing a mountain of debts, used four years later to murder his landlady and shoot himself – left the band to pursue a solo career, and The Tornados, hobbled from capitalising on the Stateside success of 'Telstar' thanks to being contractually obliged to stay in the UK as Billy Fury's backing band, began two years of plummeting chart positions and dizzying line-up changes that left George disillusioned. He left the band and 'enjoyed' a brief solo career, releasing a couple of EPs that went almost entirely unnoticed. His record-producing company, Sound Venture, and his label, SRT, failed to take off, and that was the end of George Bellamy's rock'n'roll dream.* Only a houseful of classic records (which he keenly collected for years), pianos and guitars marked him out as a one-time chart player. OK, so he wasn't exactly Bono, but for a

---

* Apart from re-recording 'Telstar' with several original members of The Tornados in 1978 and playing the local Devon pub circuit with a band called Rough Terrain in the late 1990s.

region whose only famous residents before that had been John Keats 200 years before, a hardcore porn star called Layla-Jade, a man called Donald Crowhurst, who'd lied about sailing single-handed around the world, and a fisherman called Wesley who was in a Norwich Union advert, he was something of a local celebrity.

And his wife, Marilyn? Word was she was a mystic who could talk to the dead.

Belfast-born Marilyn Bingham had moved to the UK in the 1970s, meeting George – who by this time was working as a taxi driver in London and had a daughter by a previously failed marriage – within hours of stepping off the boat. Back then, the only particularly unusual thing about this unassuming red-headed Irish lass was an obsession with the music of Queen, but after the pair married and moved to Cambridge to start a family – first son Paul, and then, on June 9, 1978, Matthew – Marilyn began to develop an interest in the occult.

By the time young Matt was five years old, family evenings once he was in bed were spent around a Ouija board, with Marilyn and George (now working as a plumber in Cambridge) channelling the spirits through the board while Paul wrote down the letters as they were spelt out. For four years Matt knew nothing of his family's secret dabblings, other than that his mother was superstitious; one of his first memories is of spinning around on the spot with a bucket and spade in his hands, letting go and smashing a household mirror, only to be informed by Marilyn that he'd cursed the family for seven years.* Then, aged nine, he walked in unexpectedly on one of their late-night Ouija board sessions. The boy was shocked and intrigued but, rather than scare their youngest son with horror stories and warnings of terrifying possessions or fiendish summonings, his parents sat him down and calmly explained to him the process, theory and theology behind their contacting the spirits of the dead.

Matt Bellamy, nicknamed 'Bells', was a hyperactive, even troublesome child; intently curious, endlessly questioning and emotionally open (his first love, he claims, was his babysitter, with whom he fell in love after she saved him from choking as a child). At primary school he learnt to

---

* Matt's most vivid memory from his early years is having his trousers pulled down in a supermarket when he was six and having to run home half naked.

effortlessly recite the alphabet backwards, and he remembers as a youngster inviting some calling Jehovah's Witnesses into the house to try to 'help them' work out why they were trying to convert people to a belief system they hadn't even questioned themselves. Even at the age of four, when his uncle, rumoured to be a member of the SAS, was shot dead in Belfast, Matt was astute enough to distrust what he was being told by the media about his family's tragedy. The newspapers said he'd died in an IRA ambush but Matt took care to note that no one was ever arrested and IRA involvement was never properly established. The impact on the boy grew more profound as he got older; by the time he was 10 he was asking questions about it but nobody knew any answers – for the rest of his life he would distrust society and its organisations, forever questioning the validity of what the newspapers were telling him.

This spiritualist revelation in his family, then, was a new source of fascination, a new crowbar on the hinges of the unknown.

And it became, over the years to come, something of a dangerous obsession.

Matt joined the circle, taking his brother's role of letter marker and, for four years, until the family crumbled, they summoned spirits together, both in Cambridge and in their new environment of coastal Devon – a rich seam for the spiritually inclined, with its myths of devil horsemen and cursed clergymen. They spoke to 18-year-old World War II victims, to dead family members and friends who passed on intimate and personal details that were 'unspeakably real' and, during one séance in 1990, to a spirit that predicted the first Gulf War a full year before hostilities commenced. The most memorable message Matt received from the board read, 'He who seeketh knowledge seeketh sorrow.'

When he enrolled at Teignmouth Community College in 1989 aged 11[*], Matt would regale his schoolmates with his Ouija experiences and spent his spare time furiously consuming books on the occult and spiritualist practices. Recognising that his mother was showing signs of becoming a full-blown medium – mouthing the letters as the marker slid towards them, finishing words before the spirits themselves would – in his early teens Matt and his brother urged her to take the next step towards full

---

[*] The school was then known as Teignmouth High, but changed its name to Teignmouth Community College during Matt's time there.

spiritualist contact with the other side and stop using the board altogether, instead communicating with the spirits directly. Seeing that her sons were developing an unhealthy obsession with her abilities, and perhaps herself frightened that the spirits had already started speaking through her, telling stories about their lives from her very own lips, Marilyn Bellamy insisted they stop all séances immediately, fearful of losing her family to chaotic, uncontrollable forces.

But not before she delivered one telling prophecy.

One evening in his eleventh year, Marilyn Bellamy sat her youngest son down and, in a slur that made him think on reflection that she might have been a little drunk, told him that she had seen the future and that he was going to be a rock star.

Kind of famous, kind of scary, kind of mysterious, kind of mad: whatever rumours and legends surrounded the Bellamy family when they first arrived in Dawlish in 1988, one thing was sure.

Somehow, this clan was charmed.

* * *

Turn your telescope back down the coastline, along the length of the railway to the seafront at the very mouth of Teignmouth Pier itself, and you will find a far more deceptive divide than that between this life and the next. On the southern side of the Teign estuary, like the surfside pleats of Dartmoor's rolling skirts, lies Teignmouth harbour, lolling with fishing boats, moored yachts and ferries taking tourists across the river to the chocolate-box town of Sheldon, with its waterside inns and peeling beach huts. In summer its shore-side bars, ice-cream sellers and gift shops make Teignmouth a popular short break retreat for city dwellers from London and the Midlands, but the chintzy, retiree-friendly exterior disguises a darker underbelly.

In the 17th century, Teignmouth harbour was a haven for smugglers. And in the early 1990s, to the detriment of the northern side of the Teign estuary, it still was.

For, on the north side of town, when the sun went down and the tourist crowd took their day-trip summer buzz back to town with them, a seedy underworld of drugs and violence was thriving. Like Torquay without the nightlife, in winter Teignmouth became a ghost town in which the retirees and the teenagers were opposing armies. Both were terrified of the gangs of jaded 25-year-old drug dealers hanging around the gambling machines in the arcades or outside Hot Bananas and Monty's nightclubs, chatting up their 14-year-old clients; ex-cons in souped-up motors looking to enforce their control over their meagre turf. The ships brought the drugs that the alcoholics sold to the teenagers to get in their knickers and buy the Capris that they'd burn along the seafront, hunting the rock kids to beat up.

There was no avoiding them. Aside from the fact that there was nowhere else for the self-respecting truant to hang out than down on the promenade, the only cash machine in town was directly across the road from the arcade used as their dealing base. So barely a withdrawal went by without another incident: the kid who got a brick in the face for the crime of having piercings, or the time one Dominic Howard – a drummer kid into guitar music who hung out with the local longhairs at Teignmouth Community College – got attacked out of nowhere. He just went to get some money out one night, heard a cry behind him of, "You just call me a waaaanker?", and felt hot hands on his shoulders. Dominic learnt early: born on December 7, 1977, in Stockport near Manchester, he moved with his parents to Teignmouth when he was eight years old and, by the time he was 11, he'd been inspired to take up drums after seeing a jazz band performing at TCC, discovered indie-rock music and was immediately branded a target. Before he'd even reached his teens, Dom had discovered that, for the youth of Teignmouth, the town was all about drugs and fighting. After all, once winter descended, there was simply nothing else to do.

No wonder Matt Bellamy avoided hanging out on the seafront on his arrival. At home, after all, was the allure of the Ouija and a newly emerging obsession: the intricacies of the piano keyboard. As a small child Matt had shown little interest in the piano, besides clumsily plonking out the notes to the theme from *Dallas* at the age of three; he was very adept at this – his brother would sit him by the TV while a programme's theme tune was playing, then carry him to the piano, where the tiny Matt would pick out the notes to the song, prompting his brother to shout to his friends, "He's a machine!" Clarinet lessons at the age of nine faltered because Matt was too difficult to teach and then, when he was 10, his father played him the haunted blues of Robert Johnson and another light turned on in the boy. Perhaps it was the supernatural story of Johnson

13

earning his guitar virtuosity by selling his soul to Satan at the crossroads that burrowed into his occult-obsessed mind, or maybe he was stolen away by Johnson's furious fingering itself, but he would later claim that this was the first time that music had ever moved him. Similarly, the piano panache of his dad's Ray Charles records enraptured him, and music became Matthew Bellamy's second major passion.

Fascinated by the mathematics and emotions it could create, without ever taking a lesson he began to pick out tunes on the household piano, learning Ray Charles tracks by ear.* These jazz classics were technically complex and free-form, yet Matt relished the challenges of copying them and found strong encouragement from his family – his brother, hearing him master a number of blues and jazz numbers, would ask him to work out melodies to songs by The Wedding Present and The Smiths.

And so Matt was launched down a dual path of musical influences that would create a magical dichotomy in his musical tastes. The intricacies of jazz piano would, as he hit his teenage years, lead him to develop an interest in classical music, an even more difficult and complex form for his inquisitive mind to pick apart and master. During his schooldays, Matt's favourite piece of music became Hector Berlioz's 'Grande Messe Des Morts', a mass written to commemorate the dead of the French Revolution, depicting the pain, terror and aftermath of Judgement Day. The 90-minute piece was so exhausting and intense that, on its first performance in Paris in 1837, it made several chorus singers pass out and members of the congregation weep uncontrollably. For Matt musically, with its grand sweeps, mighty emotions and other-worldy themes, 'Grande Messe Des Morts' was Ground Zero.†

On the indie side, Matt was drawn to equally dark and intense material. He was clearly a kid seeking to suck the anger and emotion out of his rock music (and was far too young and distanced from Britain's major clubbing capitals to be even remotely affected by ecstasy culture and the baggy trends of The Happy Mondays or The Stone Roses), so from the melodic guitar angst of Morrissey and Gedge in the late '80s he had embraced (via

* Matt's brother had received guitar, singing and piano lessons but not taken well to them, so Matt's parents opted not to bother Matt with formal musical training.
† Over the next few years Matt's classical tastes would expand to include Chopin, Rachmaninov, Spanish guitar virtuoso Adres Segovia and South American orchestral composer Villa-Lobos.

a flirtation with Midlands 'fraggle' noise popsters Ned's Atomic Dustbin)
the burgeoning US grunge and rock-rap movements of the early '90s,
listening to a lot of Rage Against The Machine, some US hip-hop, Sonic
Youth, Dinosaur Jnr and compulsively spinning Smashing Pumpkins'
Siamese Dream and Nirvana's *Nevermind*.* Full of serrated guitars, anguished
yowlings and irrepressible hook-lines, *Nevermind* was a pivotal record
in Matt's life; it showed him that music could be violent, intense and
devastating but at the same time tuneful, immediate, life-affirming and
meaningful. It showed him that music could be an outlet for the more disturbing and troublesome emotions, a release, and in years to come he
would credit Nirvana as showing him that rock could save him from being
the nasty, violent person he could have become. As formative records go,
it was a doozy.

Meanwhile, the possibilities of the fretboard frenzy he'd first experienced in the music of Robert Johnson continued to excite him. But while
many teenagers lose themselves in the aimless metal fripperies of so many
guitar-licking rock poodle-heads, Matt looked elsewhere for inspiration,
finding the same fascination in the technical pizzazz of Jimi Hendrix as he
did – after several trips to Greece and Spain as a pre-teen – in the wild
arpeggios of the flamenco guitarists. And yet he'd still never picked up a
guitar, instead, he'd painstakingly mimic these disparate styles – rock,
flamenco, classical, grunge – on his family's piano, eventually making his
first stage appearance in a school talent contest at a prize-giving evening
aged 13, with a boogie-woogie piano act.† As a result of his performance
Matt got his first ever groupie, kissing a girl who was impressed by his
playing. For the first time the teenage Bellamy realised that music was a
short-cut through the teen-sexual quagmire, that girls loved a rock star.

Rock geologists might here point out that the building blocks for Matt
Bellamy's future musical endeavours were already in place. A love of
crunching guitars. A fixation on sky-scraping virtuosity. The doomy
bombast of the classical crescendo, the seared lyrical poetry of the

---

* Less publicly, Matt was also a fan of 70s prog widdlers Rush.

† Matt's performance, even then, was so impressive that word of a new teenage piano
prodigy in the area reached a local studio owner by the name of Dennis Smith. Dennis
thought Matt was too young for representation at the time so made no approach, but
when Matt contacted him a few years later he remembered his name, of which more
later.

emotionally damned. And a fever to explore the unknown that's all around us, be it musical, mental or metaphysical.

Matt Bellamy's core components were laid out ready. He just needed an intense personal trauma to meld them.

★ ★ ★

George and Marilyn Bellamy split up in 1991. No reason for their separation has ever been offered in print, nor has one been sought. Were you to question Marilyn, one suspects, she might tell you it was simply foretold.

The split, understandably, was devastating for the family. George moved to Exeter to pursue his plumbing career while Marilyn, Paul and Matt moved into Teignmouth proper to continue their lives as seamlessly as possible. After a year without contact with their father, arrangements were made for the two sons to visit George every couple of weeks in Exeter*. Paul's girlfriend took his father's place at the Ouija board sessions (which were by this time reaching their troubled and disturbing peak) and life, as best it could, went on. Matt, then 13, believed at the time (as many teenagers undergoing parental separations do) that he was emotionally unaffected by his parents' split, that he simply felt nothing about it, a void. He even went as far as to claim he was happier without his dad in the house, as it meant he could invite people over without permission and could largely do what he wanted. But to all around him it was clear that the combined assault of puberty and divorce hit Matt Bellamy hard.

Once mischievous and hyperactive, Matt suddenly became quiet, introverted and prone to troublemaking. At home he struggled to maintain a close relationship with Marilyn, who'd been affected very badly by the split: they argued incessantly, grew distant from each other. Matt's grandmother, who lived nearby, was a stabilising influence and, when tensions at home reached unbearable levels, the three of them went to live with her permanently, despite the fact that his grandmother was already a little mentally befuddled with age. Plus, Matt's life instantly became harder financially: his family life had been comfortable, verging on middle class, but at his grandparents' home money was tighter. The family fragmented, the unknown was upon him.

---

* Although, as the years passed, Matt would see his father only once or twice a year.

Outside the home the change in Matt was even more stark. Although Matt sees his schooldays as no more traumatic than anyone else's – playing sport, having girlfriends, etc – it was a cold and troubled period of his life; he shaved his head, played truant regularly and began mixing with the harder elements of his peers. He started taking soft drugs – marijuana and magic mushrooms – and wearing UMBRO tracksuits. His early attempts at holding down a job were foiled: at 10 Matt would get pocket money as a fetcher on upper-class pheasant shoots, earning 50p for each pheasant he retrieved, often having to break the necks of those that hadn't been killed by the bullet; and at 13 he got a paper round but was knocked down by a car in his first week. He recovered but then got bitten on the arm by a dog as soon as he went back, so he gave up and turned towards the criminal margins.

There were rumours of his involvement in alcohol-fuelled fights (although largely as a bystander). He began growing his own marijuana in his mum's attic and, whereas he'd previously avoided the seafront, now he began hanging out there with his new hard-nut schoolmates, picking fights, drinking beer, playing football (Matt was a skilled defender), looking for trouble. When he wasn't sneaking into the Single Parent's Club in Winterbourne every Monday and Tuesday, he'd hang around outside the arcades drinking cider and trying to meet girls who would always go off with the Capri-driving lads; inside the arcades he'd wear slip-on shoes, having found out that the slot machines would always pay out the jackpot of £1.50 if you sent a jolt of static electricity through the keyhole with a 10 pence piece.

One memorable night, Matt and a few friends broke into an outdoor swimming pool to go dive-bombing after hours, only to find themselves in the glare of a police helicopter's spotlight and the recipients of official cautions. At school, when he turned up, he became argumentative with teachers, constantly challenging their authority or undermining their control with sneered asides, and he was always late; when he left TCC aged 16 Matt was given an award for having more late marks than any other pupil at the school, a total of 365.

Like the arcade drug dealers he'd once despised, Matt Bellamy was turning into one of Teignmouth's problem children: for the time being he was indulging in the usual teenage scrapes but, unchecked, he was only a few years away from buying his first Capri and being caught forever in the closing nets of coastal delinquency. He was becoming, social services might have noted, a textbook ne'er-do-well.

In reality, however, Matt Bellamy was simply in the midst of upheaval and looking for answers. He needed to know who he was, why his life had so dramatically changed and what reasons, in this world or the next, could have prompted such an unexpected juggling of his life. At school he took up drama, joining improvisational residential drama courses perhaps as a conduit for expelling through fictional characters the frustration and emotions he found impossible to tackle in himself. At home, his pleas for his mother to truly fulfil her potential as a medium were perhaps driven by a belief that the spirits might provide him with explanations for his confusion or wisdom to guide him forward, and when the Ouija board sessions stopped Matt became disillusioned with the occult. He came to believe that rather than contacting the dead, the board was merely a tool with which the user made contact with an element of their subconscious, that it was a part of yourself that you were too frightened to connect with that was moving the marker, sending yourself messages from suppressed corners of your psyche. This opened up a realm of questions and possibilities to the teenage Bellamy, who suddenly became obsessed with trying to understand the universe around him: the forces, conscious and unconscious, that act upon us; the hidden explanations behind supernatural activity, superstitions and a world we take for granted.

In direct opposition to his previous belief in the spiritual world, he turned to science to help explain the universe. He began devouring science books, learning about the solar system, theories on the origins of the universe and the possible existence of alien life, the first suggestions of string theory. He would soak up every crackpot theory or bona fide scientific breakthrough, filling gaps and linking them all together with his own invented logic. It was an inquisitive approach to the world, a need to scratch below the apparent surface of things, that would become a lasting characteristic.

And, perhaps most pivotal of all, in his need to express his troubles the best way he could, music became an undeniable need in him. So, at 14 years old, Matt Bellamy picked up a guitar.

It was his brother's guitar he picked up at first, a Marlin copy of a Fender Stratocaster that was too big for him, so he hacksawed whole chunks off the body and neck.* Quickly abandoning this mauled instrument for a nylon-stringed acoustic, he tuned the strings to an E chord and spent his evenings playing along with Robert Johnson records. And his first role as a guitarist, ironically, was using his instrument to summon the dead.

Matt discovered that three of his female friends were dabbling in witchcraft and, since he fancied one of the girls, he agreed to be their fretboard wizard. At night he'd accompany the trio to 'haunted' houses, forests and graveyards, watch them as they unpacked their potions and spell-books and play suitably spooky, twisted guitar licks while they cast their spells and summoned their demons. Matt reports no ghoulish sightings or ghostly visitations from these expeditions, certainly nothing as otherworldly as he was used to from his Ouija experiences, but if this was a step back theologically, it was a huge leap in the right direction for Matt's musicianship. With his interest in the classical works of Chopin, Rachmaninov and Berlioz intensifying, Matt's ambitions were to one day join a jazz group or an orchestra, a goal that was thwarted when he realised he wasn't very good at reading music. Then, at the age of 15, he saw a video of Jimi Hendrix burning his guitar at Monterey in 1967 and decided that rock was the way forward for him. *Siamese Dream* had proved to him that hard rock music could still include interesting structures and unconventional arrangements, but this was something altogether more inspiring. That burning guitar told Matt Bellamy that his music should be about chaos.

And not a moment too soon. Inspired by but, due to its isolated south coast location, dislocated from the UK's dizzying music scene, with opportunities for a stratospheric career in business being pretty much capped at local shop ownership and with enough soft drugs flying around to stun a semi-pro funk band, in the early 90s Teignmouth naturally developed a thriving music scene of its own. Admittedly this consisted largely of semi-pro funk bands and Pink Floyd-style prog outfits, but still there was an explosion of local bands forming, original songs being

* It's been claimed that, when his parents bought him his first amp for Christmas, as if foretelling the fate of many future pieces of musical equipment, Matt managed to break it within five minutes.

19

written, a sense of excitement building, a feeling that something special was beginning to happen in Teignmouth.

One young prophet remarked that it felt as if a muse had descended.

* * *

The truth behind the formation of Rocket Baby Dolls is an enigma wrapped in a mystery locked in a conundrum, buried under a massive pile of failed Teignmouth bands.

First, according to a myth that no one involved can confirm or deny, was Teignmouth College school band The Magic Roundabout. A shadowy bunch, this lot; we can be fairly sure that Dominic played drums but it's uncertain whether they ever performed live or were ever even a 'band' at all. What we can be sure of is that Matt Bellamy became more and more adept at the guitar thanks to growing his fingernails and taking flamenco guitar lessons, in which he would race ahead faster than the teacher would tell him, mastering complex techniques but skipping simpler lessons, which left him technically impressive but with gaping holes in his basic skills. He also had a knack of learning songs by ear, and flitted between the growing numbers of school bands throughout his early teens, largely as a keyboardist, without ever settling firmly on any one.

Music, it seemed, was saving him from a future as a drug-blasted fuck-up: he stopped getting drunk by the sea and instead went to rehearse at friends' houses. He turned to minor-league promoting, hiring out spaces on the Broadmeadow industrial estate for £3–4 an hour, where he'd put on concerts for whichever band he was in that week, along with other local bands. These nights became the epicentre of the Teignmouth music scene, attended by every local musician worth his salt. One group that played alongside Matt's was called Carnage Mayhem – the most popular and accomplished of the TCC school bands at the time, they would also hire out the leisure centre to put on nights where the coolest Teignmouth kids would come to smoke spliffs and talk up the scene. Carnage Mayhem were an inspiration to Matt to improve at the guitar in the hope of eventually being asked to join a good band. And they also just happened to include, on drums, Dominic Howard.

Matthew Bellamy and Dominic Howard met on The Den, a patch of grass in Teignmouth town centre where the different tribes of the town would congregate to cast distrustful glares at each other. Matt was hanging out with the sporty types, Dom was with the cool kids. But Matt was uncomfortable with his social clique and he wandered over to Dom in his shell suit, introduced himself and asked him to teach him more on guitar. There may more likely have been light drizzle than thunderclaps that day, but rarely has there been a rock meeting more momentous.

Matt and Dom had actually attended the same primary school but didn't know each other, despite sharing friends. Now, however, cresting 15, they became acquainted although, at first, they seemed irreconcilable opposites. Dom was the long-haired jazz rocker whose parents saw his drumming as a hobby that would never lead anywhere – his interest in music as a child extended no further than messing around on his sister's keyboard when he was five and drumming on anything he could find. One of his earliest memories is of catching a fish and hitting its head on the ground until its eye popped out, an event about which he feels no little shame. Matt was the tracksuited wide boy with the flat-top haircut and danger in his snarl, who just happened to be a secret piano prodigy on the sly. But they were both out-of-town kids (Dominic's family moved from Stockport to Devon, where his mother had grown up, in 1985) and they bonded over a shared love of melodic hardcore music. When Dominic wangled Matt, to whom he'd given lessons in 'cool', an audition for Carnage Mayhem in 1992, there was an immediate connection. Playing together they recognised an inventive, experimental streak in each other, and Dom convinced Carnage Mayhem to let Matt join as guitarist.

When Matt told his father he'd joined a band, on one of his fortnightly visits to Exeter, George Bellamy gave him a sage piece of advice forged from hard-earned experience. "Enjoy it while you're young," he said, "and get laid." At this stage it was industry advice that Matt most learnt from his father; as a youngster he didn't 'get' 'Telstar' but, as his musical career developed, he came to appreciate it as a forward-thinking record, one that had perhaps drawn him towards more atmospheric styles in his own songwriting.

Monumental as Matt's arrival would eventually prove to be, at the time it spelt the end for Carnage Mayhem. Matt and Dom insisted on playing half hour sets of Primus-style wonky punk riffs and covers of indie thrash pop bands such as Ned's Atomic Dustbin. Indeed, the first gig Matt ever saw, with Dom in tow, was that very band in Exeter around this time; Matt remembers moshing the night away while Dom passed out during support act Kinky Machine. Another gig was The Senseless Things, both bands being lumped together as 'fraggle' alongside Mega City Four and The Levellers, due to their raggle-taggle punk guitars and their dread-locked, scruffy hair reminiscent of UK TV puppet show *Fraggle Rock*, and the sounds they made were, they happily admit, not very pleasant. So, shortly after Matt joined his new band they agreed that they needed a name to reflect this. Carnage Mayhem was ultimately deemed not extreme enough; Youngblood was taken on briefly but soon discarded too. So they settled, towards the end of 1992, for a moniker that didn't radiate quite so many sunshine vibes: Carnage Mayhem became Gothic Plague, a name that was actually suggested by Dom's sister.

The first confirmed performance by Gothic Plague was on December 21, 1992, at Teignmouth's Meadow Centre; 'Entrance one pound' read the hand-written flyer, 'Behave!!!'. They played at the bottom of a bill that included Bagpuss Shot Kennedy, Avqvod Zoo and Fixed Penalty – a band that featured, on drums, a lanky, hairy figure by the name of Christopher Wolstenholme.

Gothic Plague were a band out of time. Their name allied them with 70s goth metal acts. They were developing the virtuosity of a young Rachmaninov. And – as Britpop was gathering pace across the UK with the release of Suede's eponymous debut album, the generational ennui of Blur's *Modern Life Is Rubbish* and the long-laboured ascendance of Pulp with their breakthrough hit, 'Babies' – down in their dislocated corner of Devon, playing gigs for mates in the TCC's sports hall's boxing ring that passed for a stage, they were widdling and scronking away with all the punk experimentalism of an 80s jazz hardcore band; enraptured by Nirvana, Sonic Youth and fraggle, but utterly un-interested in the foppish alt.revolution taking place in London. Matt claims that the band didn't even listen to any of the Britpop records, so distanced did they feel from the London-centric scene. Indeed, over the next 18 months Matt and Dom shed – or indeed, frightened off with their experimental punk meanderings – any musician that might dare to play with them. A large number of bassists and guitarists rotated through the band before dropping out, leaving Matt and Dom, by the time they'd hit 15 years of age, not just best friends but a formidable guitar and drums duo, the bane of all bassists and singers with the gall to take them on.

So it's perhaps no wonder that Gothic Plague didn't blaze too dazzling a trail across Teignmouth's rock firmament. As 1994 dawned, in-band arguments had become so vehement that the last bassist and singer in Teignmouth that wanted anything to do with Matt and Dom had left in extremely acrimonious circumstances (there were, they would later explain, "all sorts of fights"). Gothic Plague were in pieces, Matt and Dom now reduced to a two piece. Without a bassist, and a good seven years before The White Stripes would make such a slight to the Gods of rock line-ups acceptable, they folded the band. Because who would ever want to play with them? Surely that would have to be a bassist prepared to withstand any amount of musical mauling, who had no interest in copying the credible musical trends and styles of the age, and who wouldn't be embarrassed to be in a band with a faintly ludicrous name. But where would they find such a man?

And yet Matt and Dom stuck at it, playing and recording their first attempts at original material in a school rehearsal room in spare hours, with Matt reluctantly taking up vocal duties. Within weeks they caught word that the drummer from the rival school band who would rehearse in the room next door, Fixed Penalty – a group who described themselves as 'post-rock' but were actually skater kids largely playing Mega City Four and Wonderstuff covers, long after those bands had split up – had been thrown out for admitting he liked Status Quo. And he was up for learning to play bass. The perfect man for the job.

Christopher Wolstenholme (nicknamed 'Cheers' by his sister and mum when he was young, although he has no idea why), like Matt and Dom, wasn't originally from Teignmouth at all, which immediately made him part of their out-of-towner gang. He was born on December 2, 1978, in Rotherham, South Yorkshire, and moved to Teignmouth with his parents at the age of 11. Like many of Teignmouth's youngsters during those band-saturated times, Chris began his musical voyage as a guitarist after he was asked if he wanted to take up the instrument in school music class, sticking with it until he discovered that you could throw a stick into the TCC dining hall and hit a dozen wannabe Johnny Marrs before it hit the ground. So he learnt to play drums and spent some months uncomfortably filling the kit stool for Fixed Penalty, until his shameful denim-loving musical tastes were exposed.* So when Matt and Dom approached

---

* Status Quo were not the full extent of Chris' musical shame: the first record he ever bought was 'The Birdie Song' by The Tweets.

him to join a band with them, it was with what he describes as "a great spirit of sacrifice" that he agreed to learn bass. The first time he picked up a bass guitar was two days before he, Matt and Dom agreed to play together.

The three-piece were still a very raw proposition: while Matt and Dom's 18 months in Gothic Plague had seen them grow remarkably accomplished at their instruments for kids of 15, Chris, in the year below them, was still very new at the bass. Their first rehearsals took place in the TCC music rooms, and the trio were offered full use of them largely because, they thought, the music teacher, Miss Bird, fancied Chris and Dom, although she hated Matt. They were inevitably clumsy affairs but, after so long trying to muddle through as Gothic Plague while all around them were losing faith and leaving, this new group felt to the threesome to be an exciting fresh start. And while they felt no kinship musically with the Britpop scene, they were certainly inspired by it creatively. It was time, they decided, to cast off the Senseless Things cover songs and begin writing their own material.

Over the next few weeks, Matt, Dom and Chris set about honing their sprawling punk experiments into more digestible (but still pretty nasty) chunks of raucous riff rock, while getting to know each other as a band. They clicked both musically and personally – Chris shared Dom's warm, unassuming nature and Matt's ardent, serious enthusiasm for melodic bombast – and the three spent almost every waking hour together, either plotting their world take-over between lessons for their imminent GCSEs or rehearsing every evening, while Matt's songwriting took on an angsty rock tone. The first song they wrote together was entitled 'Small Minded', an attack on the dismissive attitudes of the Teignmouth populus by three soulless kids of the computer age trying to make a human contact through music. The themes of their future were evident even then, as raw and unrefined as the music itself.

Yet somehow this felt like a pupal stage, a band waiting to be something greater. Having gelled as an albeit ramshackle punk trio as the summer approached, they spotted notices around town for a Battle Of The Bands contest to take place in February – £10 entry to play six songs – and decided that, as the first time the three of them would ever perform live together, this could be their chance to relaunch themselves as a new force to be reckoned with on the Teignmouth scene. They realised that their lack of technical ability and tightness could be outweighed by an outrageous onslaught of attitude, flam and recklessness. They would take the Teignmouth 1994 Battle Of The Bands contest and throttle every ounce of punk-rock vigour out of it.

But first they needed a new identity. Gothic Plague had been too medieval, too prog metal, too Norwegian to suit their new mean, lean riffage machine. They needed a far sexier, glammier, Manic Street Preachers sort of a name.

The night before the contest Matt happened to chance upon a Japanese soft-porn movie on Sky and the name of the film caught his eye: it was an anime called *Rocket Baby Dolls* about a group of girls with super powers fighting swarms of monsters invading Tokyo. Rather than shooting the monsters, however, they 'love' them to death.

So Gothic Plague were burnt on the punk-rock pyre. Long live Rocket Baby Dolls.

★ ★ ★

There could only have been a couple of hundred people at Broadmeadow Sports Centre for the Teignmouth Battle Of The Bands 1994 contest, but every muso in Devon no doubt swears blind that they were there when Rocket Baby Dolls took the stage for their debut live performance.

They certainly cut a memorable figure. After what felt like an endless parade of semi-pro Jamiroquai-style funk bands in torn flares and Pink Floyd-aping progsters flapping their lengthy fringes towards the judges' table, these three snotty young punk kids, just turning 16 and driven to the gig by their mate Tom Kirk, strutted on stage in sharp black threads and carelessly applied make-up in a nod to the goth-glam look of Marilyn Manson. They picked up guitars that were barely in tune, snarled a sneery "'ello" and set about thrashing the living hell out of their instruments, the PA and what remained of the audience's eardrums.

Punk riffs flew like doodlebugs. Drums rattled and clattered like continuous thunder. Glittery mascara flew from the stage in hot, sweaty globules. The tunes, if there were any, were buried under several tons of enthusiastic widdling, grandiose posing and flurries of feedback, as Rocket Baby Dolls took their philosophy of attitude over ability to its ear-splitting extreme. They looked like The Cure, sounded like a psychopathic Rush and, after 20 gob-smacking minutes, they closed with a cover of

'Tourettes' – a track from Nirvana's final album, *In Utero*, and thus not exactly one of their more restrained or melodic numbers – at the end of which Dominic set about destroying the drum kit, prompting a stage invasion that saw Matt, Chris and 50 invaders smash up all of the onstage equipment (which wasn't even their own – it had been hired in for all of the bands to use).

With Matt being physically dragged off the stage, still playing, and the rest of Rocket Baby Dolls and their trash-hungry mob storming off the stage to the colourful abuse of the other bands, heading out to the car park to graffiti ROCKET BABY DOLLS in spray paint over the equipment-hire van, the judges peered awestruck over the wreckage of the stage and had no choice but to declare Rocket Baby Dolls the out-and-out winners. For "taking the piss".

Shocked (they'd caused chaos at the competition largely as a protest and a statement, they never thought they might actually win) and invigorated by their success, Rocket Baby Dolls realised there might just be a future in this rock'n'roll business after all. The following month they booked a gig at Dawlish Sports Centre, where they'd play in the corner of a roller disco to a gathering support of friends and schoolmates.

But if Matt, Chris and Dom were taking their band seriously, they wanted the rest of Devon to do the same. And Rocket Baby Dolls, as a moniker, sounded too frivolous, too novelty for a serious rock band. They wanted something shorter, snappier, something that would fit on the posters in big, bold letters. They wanted something that reflected the feeling that new songs were somehow falling out of the sky on a daily basis, and the sense Matt had that he had somehow 'summoned up' this band, the way mediums could summon up inspirational spirits at times of emotional need.

So, only a week after the Battle Of The Bands that birthed them, Rocket Baby Dolls became Muse.*

And Muse had some serious improving to do.

* * *

* Other suggestions for the origins of Muse's name include the three 'witches' Matt played guitar with, and an art teacher who'd explained the meaning of the word to Matt and Dom at school.

If their inaugural gig as Rocket Baby Dolls was an untidy triumph, the two years that Muse spent becoming serious professionals were, by contrast, a disheartening slog. Matt and Dom reached the end of their compulsory schooling in June 1994, and their GCSE grades were impressive, with Matt and Dom achieving As in drama and art respectively; Matt's impressive showing in drama was less to do with the Christmas tree he'd played in an infant school production and more to do with his portrayal of a southern bluesman in a school play, performing a moving monologue and a Robert Johnson song. Even though Chris still had a year to go at the school, they could no longer make use of the school boxing ring in which to stage their gigs and were thrust out of TCC's cosy band scene into a local Devon gig circuit that boasted next to no proper venues – and certainly none that would book bands that were under 18. Hence, over the years to come, they were forced to beg for gigs anywhere they could get them. Often this meant playing in pubs and working men's clubs in mid-afternoon, playing their frenetic punk racket in a corner of a saloon bar while old men played dominos over a pint and their grandchildren ran around slapping off the band's pedals at unexpected moments – a living, snivelling, belching Alan Partridge sketch. Since they no longer played covers and because their songs weren't exactly AOR family-friendly fare, they were often cut short and told never to come back. St Austell's Working Men's Club in Cornwall would become a regular Muse haunt in the years before they were signed, but the Devon scene, it transpired, didn't look too favourably on ambition, passion or vitality.

Muse needed to appeal to a world outside the south coast pub-funk circuit, and that would take hard graft.

Over the summer after leaving school Muse played only one gig, at Totnes Pavilions, before Matt, Dom and schoolmate Tom Kirk (who would become Muse's ever-present video documentarian) enrolled at Coombeshead College in Newton Abbot in September to study for A-levels. The biggest influence on Muse's future output that can be gleaned from their regular schooling was the effect that taking an A-level in media studies had on Matt; being taught the processes and prejudices behind the media clicked with his long-held belief that you couldn't trust everything the newspapers told you, confirming in his mind that the public was being fed one-sided information, like a religion. As he entered adulthood, Matt would come to believe that the best way to change the world would be for every child to be taught media studies, forcing them to question the 'truths' being imposed upon them.

Otherwise, their time at Coombeshead was most productive musically: the college boasted its own recording studio, and Matt was on the music technology course (which included the opportunity of having Muse gigs assessed professionally by teacher Mike Prouse). Immersing themselves in these college opportunities, Muse entered a period they'd later describe as very dark and introverted, making music solely for themselves and not caring what anybody else thought of it. Yet, as the best band at the college (other than a bunch of chancers from nearby Ashburton who went by the stomach-turning moniker of Dripping Womb), Muse gained a strong following among the student population. They became regular Ace Faces at the local indie venue The Cavern Club, a converted pub that would host hardcore gigs and where Matt, Dom and Chris would often be found hiding in the corner by the mixing desk, nervously sipping at underage pints behind chin-length hair, and it was here that they wangled their first proper-venue slot that October with the help of a ramshackle demo.

The Cavern's promoter, Ronnie Kerswell, was impressed by their first performance there and encouraged Muse, after a warm-up gig at Teignmouth's Jolly Sailor pub in November, to enter another Battle Of The Bands contest at the Cavern early in 1995. The band were firm favourites; throughout the contest the judges placed them second in every heat to ensure they went through to the next round but didn't win each heat prize, since they were such a shoo-in to win the final prize of a brand new guitar and strings. On the way home from the semi-final, however, their place in the final ensured, Dom bizarrely managed to break his hand punching Tom Kirk's bicycle seat, putting him out of drumming action for the next three months and ironically leaving Kerswell himself to win the final with a comedy DAT-based two-piece called Kindergarten Sluts. Slightly ashamed to have won almost by default, Kerswell gave Muse the top prize anyway.

Before Dom's bike-battling accident, however, Muse made their first gigging foray out of Devon. Deciding that if the music industry wouldn't come to them they should bring the Muse mountain to the metaphorical Mohammad, in February 2005 they hired out Kentish Town's Bull & Gate – a north London pub venue famed for hosting debut London gigs for the vast majority of major bands when they were still unsigned. The band paid for dozens of their friends and family to make the 200-mile trip with them, and played to an enthusiastic audience of mates and absolutely nobody else. They swore they'd never play London again, but if the gig did Muse no good in getting a record deal, it certainly boosted their confidence, made them feel less like a local Teignmouth band and more like a proper touring outfit.

After a few months out of the gig circuit while Dom's hand healed, in May of 1995 Muse made a four-song demo taped in Chris' house, featuring now long-discarded early songs 'Backdoor', 'Sling', 'Feed' and 'Jigsaw Memory'. These crude punk-pop songs formed *This Is A Muse Demo*, a tape that already featured the current Muse logo on its cover and curiously accredited the songs as being 'copyright Geobell Music'*, possibly a hint that George Bellamy had helped with the recording. The tape was distributed to local contacts by their first manager, Phil Korthals (a fan of the band from Teignmouth in his early twenties who helped get the band reviews in local papers, but with whom they would soon fall out and part company acrimoniously), got the band several gigs in Torquay and Plymouth, at venues such as The New Railway Inn (where Muse would become regular players), The Piazza and The Ark Royal, and helped bag them their first international date in Le Charleston Bar in Cherbourg, France that June.

Although it meant a trip to the Continent (albeit little more than a quick hop across the Channel), essentially this was another disheartening pub gig, playing to disinterested drinkers who, if they paid any attention at all, would demand they play Queen covers or shout at them to turn their amps down. The bar turned out to be a dockside pub inhabited that night by about 20 gay sailors and skinheads, but there was a sinister undercurrent to the venture: the organiser was using the band as a cover to smuggle cigarettes back to the UK, which Muse were unaware of until they'd finished the gig, packed up the gear and headed back to the van, only to find all available space taken up by 200,000 cigarettes and crates of beer and wine. The ferry journey home was a particularly cramped one.

That gloriously hot summer of 1995, when the young men of Muse weren't sneaking onto the tankers arriving in Teignmouth port and jumping off the ends into the sea, was otherwise spent becoming fervent

* A rare copy of *This Is A Muse Demo* fetched £500 when auctioned on eBay in 2005; Dominic or Dom himself made a bid.

festival-goers. Having made their first foray to the Reading Festival in August 1994 – where Matt was particularly inspired by Jeff Buckley, the first artist to make him feel comfortable with the idea of singing in falsetto – June 1995 saw them head, ticketless, to Pilton for their first Glastonbury experience. Dom recalls trudging from the train station to the site, where he spent hours circling the perimeter fence until he chanced upon a bloke with a portable drill and some wood, making himself a ladder. Joining the crowd of people watching this most enterprising of Glastonbury crafts, they then followed the man over the fence and celebrated getting in for nothing in the foulest of fashions. Another, somewhat muddier year, Matt somehow managed to lose his shoes while moshing to Weezer*, and spent the rest of the weekend risking trench foot by wading barefoot through the ankle-deep mud. The Portaloos near their tent had been tipped over, covering their sleeping quarters with effluent and leaving them no choice but to take plastic bags inside their tent and use them as disposable lavatories. Amazingly, the experience didn't put them off festivals and Reading 1996 was a particularly poignant one for Muse. Watching Rage Against The Machine playing on the main stage, Dom turned to Matt and said, "When we're headlining that stage, then we'll know we've made it."

For the next 11 years, as their successes mounted and the venues expanded, Matt and Dom would occasionally ask each other if they've 'made it' yet. "Not until we've headlined Reading," was always the response.†

It seemed at the time an impossible dream. But it would turn out to be a very tangible prophecy.

★ ★ ★

Throughout 1996, the process of becoming better musicians turned out to be arduous: Matt spent less time singing with the band and more time

---

* Matt might have got these events confused as Weezer played Glastonbury in 1995, when the festival was basked in glorious sunshine.
† Chris' first festival experience was at Reading 1995, the day after he got his GCSE results. He had a deal with his parents that he would get more money to spend at the festival the higher his grades – £15 for an A, £10 for a B and so on. Although worried he'd have to survive the entire weekend on £20, Chris did well enough in his exams to survive the weekend comfortably.

playing long, improvised pieces of complicated music, inspired by his interest in classical music, determined to become a full-on guitar and piano virtuoso, while the gigs they booked at nearby pubs (such salubrious venues as The Beer Engine in Crediton and The Pirate in the coastal surfer's town of Falmouth) in order to play for their mates were as much to try out the meaty new rock tunes they were beginning to carve out. Tunes that boasted both a granite rock crunch that cut refreshingly against the frivolities pop of Britpop and the stodgy plod that characterised many of the post-Oasis bands of the era, and a soaring melodicism reminiscent of the best moments of early Radiohead.

Songs like 'Cave' and 'Overdue' were among the first to evolve from their riotous (but formless) ruckus. 'Overdue' was a rough-hewn tune that grew from a brooding arpeggiated verse to a wild falsetto screech of a chorus hook by way of serrated bursts of hacksaw lead guitar, not too far removed from choice cuts from Radiohead's *The Bends* album or their forgotten pre-*Bends* gem 'Pop Is Dead'. 'Cave', meanwhile, was a better pointer of where Muse were heading musically – even in its raw state in 1996, this riff-smothered funk-pop thrash oozed epic vision and pomp, particularly when Matt's vocals lifted off into a Thom Yorke warble on the line 'Come in my cave', climaxing in an operatic vocal chord tremelo that would one day become Matt's trademark.

These new songs were strong enough for the Cavern promoters to offer Muse the headline slot on their stage at the Exeter date of the Big Top Trip tour, which saw summery Britpop trio Dodgy take a circus tent around the country in which to hold their shows. The unsigned bands stage was given to local promoters at each show to pack with the best local acts, and Muse by this point were popular enough to close the night. It was to be their first festival headline slot, and it was a slot they felt most comfortable in.

And if these tracks showed the promise bubbling within the young Muse, a few months that he took off from the band in the summer of 1996 to go travelling across Europe exposed Matt to further inspiration. On Aegean islands and in the Spanish heartlands Matt's eyes and innards were opened – he fell in love with the local beauties and felt the passion of the regional music consume him. He came home with his head filled with slinking Greek laika melodies and dark Germanic moods, a combination that was already escaping from his fingers in the form of the Mediterranean snake-charming opening to 'Muscle Museum', a song conceived on the Greek islands about the internal struggle of your soul and your body not allowing the other what it craves.

Ironically, though Muse felt so distanced from any scene or movement in alternative music, they were indeed mining a similar musical vein to contemporaries whom they wouldn't be aware of for some years. In Chester, similarly inspired by the rock bombast of *The Bends* and also a band with a keen sense of the experimental, Mansun were starting to put out their first few EPs, while at UCL in London, a group of four students with a desire to make chiming Big Music (without, admittedly, Muse's volcanic guitar squeals) were beginning to rehearse under the unassuming moniker of Coldplay.

It would be several years before these bands would form the first credible post-Britpop wave of UK guitar music, and there were still pitfalls for Muse to dodge yet.

Not least the dissolving of their fanbase. As their two years studying at Coombeshead College came to an end, the following they'd built up among the student population disappeared overnight, as all of their fans left Devon to go to university. Rather than follow their friends to college or into full-time employment, they took part-time jobs in order to carry on with the band. Chris took work in a local guitar shop for £90 a week, and also worked part-time on an ice-cream van and as a golf caddie. Dom did odd jobs on building sites and school canteens, worked as a dresser for graduation students and had a stint packing Spice Girls T-shirts in a factory, while Matt drew the shortest employment straw, scraping a living working for a firm that cleaned caravans and toilets on a local camp site as well as for a painting, decorating and demolition company, for whom he once demolished an entire shopping centre. By day they grafted; by night they rocked out.

Come November, the band felt confident enough to return to Coombeshead and use its studio to record their first semi-professional demo, an 11-track collection of the tracks they were playing live at the time, known today as the Newton Abbot demo.* Among the tracks were

---

* Most of these would end up as B-sides to singles from debut album *Showbiz* and be played live occasionally as fan-friendly rarities, including 'Jimmy Kane', 'Agitated' and 'Ashamed', the riff of which has been used as the outro to 'New Born' and 'Showbiz' live.

rough, self-recorded versions of future album track 'Sober' and B-side 'Twin', then titled, comically, 'Balloonatic'. The one known copy of this demo was on cassette tape, with the other side of the cassette filled with a compilation of various bands by the tape's previous owner; the original compilation track-listing for the taped-over side was scribbled out.* Those tracks included The Prodigy's 'Breathe' and Smashing Pumpkins' 'Tonight'.

No one knows how many copies of the demo were made, who they were handed out to or what deals, if any, were struck on the back of it, but having filtered by word-of-mouth through the Devon hardcore scene in July 1997, 'Balloonatic' became the first Muse track to be officially released to the public when it appeared on the Lockjaw album *Helping You Back To Work Volume 1*, a hardcore demo compilation from a label set up by the members of UK punk band Tribute To Nothing. Whether any official permission was given for its inclusion among tracks by the charmingly named likes of Choke TV, Leech Woman and Hydra is uncertain, but Matt would later claim to have never known that 'Balloonatic' had ever been released under that name.

So, ignorant of the tiny steps Muse were making towards success and with the hardships of lavatory sanitation and the strains of struggling around an unappreciative pub circuit hanging heavy, Matt slipped back towards his old tearaway ways.

At 18, after two years of making the lengthy slog to Exeter from his grandmother's house in Teignmouth for college, Matt moved into Exeter full time to live with a painter and decorator friend. Living in Exeter gave Matt more opportunities to see live music, and he used it to dabble in electronica, waving glowsticks around at gigs by the likes of The Orb, Orbital and Aphex Twin. The music, however, simply didn't speak to him. They ran their own initially successful decorating firm, and his friend's dad owned lots of cheap property so let the two of them rent a flat as an office and living space. Using their meagre decorating skills, they spent all their spare time turning the flat from a derelict hovel into a pleasant, if colourful, abode: situated above a pornographic bookshop on Forth Street in a seedy side of town, it reminded Matt of the flat from

---

* The demo surfaced in 2007 on an internet auction site and saw a collective of Muse websites club together to raise the £740 needed to secure its purchase for sharing on the sites.

Trainspotting. Powders and mirrors and needles and tinfoil were constantly strewn around the place and the pair would have house-callers all hours of the day or night – junkies using the flat to shoot-up heroin or gangs of party kids intent on doing lines of cocaine until dawn. Matt's friend, it soon became apparent, wasn't making his living merely from decorating; he was a drug dealer with plans for expansion.

The experience disgusted Matt Bellamy – he was a child of hash and the mushroom, and the depths of desperation that he saw in the people turning up at his flat to score cocaine and heroin put him off harder drugs altogether. Although they enjoyed some wild nights out together – once memorably being thrown out of Exeter club Timepiece for moshing too violently to Blur's 'Song 2' – their decorating business foundered due to the drug-dealing sideline, and he eventually ended up in prison.

Matt also fell in with a minor-league car theft ring, stealing crap cars and selling them on for a small profit. After making a few quid, however, it was a career path Matt was scared away from after stealing an Escort from a scrap yard owned by a local hard-man. He sold it on for few hundred pounds, only to have the bruiser turn up at his house saying he'd burn it down with his family inside unless Matt handed over £500. Matt gave him the van that Muse were touring in at the time and swore off grand theft auto for good.

After all, Matt had way too much to lose. Aside from being in Devon's most promising new band he'd also developed a deep relationship with a Teignmouth girl, whom he'd been seeing since he was 15.* So Matt had stability, independence, self-belief and, most important of all, a truckload of talent.

Now all he needed was a break.

* * *

If you want to get to Sawmills studio at high tide you need to wait for the boat to come and fetch you. It chugs you along the tidal creek on the west bank of the River Fowey in Cornwall, under overhanging reeds and

---

* At one particularly mischievous point in his Exeter days Matt convinced all of his attached friends that it would be really good for their various relationships if they all slept with prostitutes. His friends complied but Matt refrained, only to watch some of his friends' relationships fall apart as a result.

branches, and moors you a few long steps from the front porch of the 17th-century water mill, lovingly converted into one of the most technologically advanced, if romantically remote, recording studios in the UK. The Stone Roses recorded here, as did Supergrass, Oasis, The Verve and Robert Plant, and, to a struggling teenage Muse, it was the closest thing to a local eldorado they could imagine.

Its founder and owner, Dennis Smith, was well known as a south coast music industry impresario – he not only ran Sawmills but also dabbled in band management when an appropriate act caught his ear; he'd notoriously wangled a production deal with a fledgling Supergrass. And when Matt Bellamy contacted him in 1995 for advice on getting studio time, after a few days of racking his brains he remembered where he'd heard the kid's name before: Matt Bellamy, the young piano prodigy from Teignmouth Community College his mechanic had told him about after catching his impressive performance on the boogie-woogie piano at a school talent contest back in 1991. And now he had a fully fledged rock band? Smith couldn't resist checking this out.

Catching their live show for the first time at The Berkeley Centre in Camborne in October 1995*, Smith was impressed by their spirited performance and the rough-hewn material that the formative Muse were bashing out at the time, but thought that the songs still needed knocking into shape. Bonding with the band over a shared love of Primus, Smith became a regular at the pub and working men's club gigs that Muse played in 1996, their first important industry contact and a valued advisor. Bypassing their then-manager, Phil (who was rather inexperienced in dealing with industry contacts), Smith kept in close contact with Matt and his guardians – his mother and his grandmother – receiving a message every couple of weeks from Matt, who was keen to keep in touch with the one experienced hand being held out to Muse from the darkness.

Over the course of 18 months, during which Smith followed Muse's progression and improvement at dozens of gigs, he encouraged them to forget dreams of playing America or even London for the time being and

* There is some confusion over whether Smith saw this gig before Matt contacted him, as he claims to have been tipped off to the band by a local journalist who had interviewed him at Sawmills some months before.

concentrate on creating a local buzz, promising that he'd work with them as soon as he felt he'd seen the 'magic show' that proved they'd done the necessary growing up. His advice was astute – when Muse made a second trip to the Big Smoke to play their first proper gig at the Bull & Gate in June 1997 they played to only one paying punter, and when Phil organised their first label showcase, with Parlophone early in 1997, it led to nothing.

It was a full 19 months after Smith first saw the band, at a gig at Exeter Cavern in March 1997, that Smith felt he was certain he'd discovered one of the decade's greatest young UK rock bands and was ready to become more involved. He offered Muse the same agreement that he'd offered Supergrass some years earlier: he'd allow them to use the recording studio at Sawmills when it wasn't in use by other bands to put together some demos, on the proviso that if they were to get signed on the back of the recordings, they'd pay Smith back for the studio time.

And so, for five days in the autumn of 1997, Muse took the boat out to Sawmills to piece together their first professional demo, with Sawmills engineer Paul Reeve at the production desk. The more senior Sawmills producer, John Cornfield, was busy working with Supergrass at the time, so Smith gave Reeve, an engineer with experience of playing in local bands The Change and Blueskin, his first chance to prove himself at production with the fledgling Muse, reportedly because Smith thought that Matt and Reeve had similar singing styles. The 10 tracks they recorded included the live staples of 'Overdue' and 'Cave', both versions differing from the ones they would eventually re-record for their debut album. The demo version of 'Overdue' is almost two minutes longer, featuring a slow bridge where the album version ends, leading to an additional run through the chorus, while 'Cave' (originally entitled 'Nova Scotia' before it was recorded) is a far rougher cut than the final version. Additionally they laid down 'Coma', an early track that was uncharacteristically poppy (exposing, perhaps, their musical naivety at the time), and 'Escape', a drastically different take on the version that would eventually appear on their debut album.

Enthused by the recordings, Smith's mind was made up – these songs had to see the light of day. And Smith was perfectly positioned to help them. He had already set up a production/publishing company, Taste Media, in 1996 with ex-A&R man Safta Jaffery, through which the two of them could help to (unofficially) manage Muse. Having worked as a record company executive at Dick James Music/Decca Records and Magnet Records, Safta had all the right industry contacts and hard-nosed experience of the ins-and-outs of A&R, territorial licensing and making records. Safta was the business arm of Taste Media, a tough negotiator with impeccable connections in the UK and international music business, and he was also, through his management company, SJP, working as manager to many top producers including Ron Saint-Germain (Tool, Bad Brains), John Cornfield (Supergrass), Michael Brauer (Coldplay, Jeff Buckley) and John Leckie, who'd worked with The Stone Roses and Radiohead. Crucially, Safta was also an enthusiastic fan of the band and certain he could help them become massive. Dennis also had his own indie record label, Dangerous, on which he offered to release the above four tracks. Hence, after a few months of polishing and nervous anticipation, Muse's first release, 'The Muse EP', was issued on May 11, 1998, with only 999 hand-numbered copies printed, featuring artwork created by Dom of three photocopied sections of his face collaged into one rather wonky visage.*

While the vitality and verve of 'The Muse EP' was enough to win over the casual listener, in retrospect it sounds like a band awkwardly finding their way around the recording studio and its techniques. It showcases a band that were a fraction of what Muse would soon become and should, most fairly, be considered as a pointer to the far superior tunes that the band were writing, even around the first EP recording sessions. And lyrically it fails to capture the churning intelligence and questioning nature that Matt Bellamy was developing.

'Overdue' crudely appears to tell the story of a relationship falling apart due to errant young lust, with the additional bridge finding Matt singing, "You should've been there when I was aroused", while 'Escape' reads like the ramblings of a schizophrenic character unable to control his violent inner psyche, or a veiled reference to his parents' divorce ("Why can't you just love her/Why be such a monster/You bully from a distance"). The

---

* A demo release entitled 'Sawmills Promo' was released simultaneously with the same track listing, except that 'Escape' retained its former title of 'Escape Your Meaningless'. A fake 7″ was also fraudulently produced by a forger, with the same barcode as used on the CD release.

theme of 'Cave' was the result of Matt's reading, the cave motif taken from the assertion in the popular war-of-the-sexes tome *Men Are From Mars, Women Are From Venus* that men often hide in metaphorical caves during times of stress, but even this was flimsy theology when you consider that Matt, aged 16, was already reading books on the future evolution of human kind, including Matrix-like theories that we will eventually all be wired into some sort of man-made heaven scenario, which we would invent for ourselves individually. It would be some years before Matt found the confidence to dissect such outlandish ideas in song.

The EP sold slowly at first, creeping out of shops as word gradually spread of the wired rock eruptions vaulting out of the south coast. But, with the band booked to play a breakthrough set at the In The City music conference in Manchester that summer, Safta and Dennis had tricks up their sleeves. Tricks that, within a year, would see Muse whisked around the globe in a flurry of lures and chequebooks. 1998 would prove to be the year of the Great Muse Goose Chase.

DOMINIC HOWARD

(Printed by kind permission of IPC Media)

What's your earliest memory?
"I don't remember much about living in Manchester, just little bits like going to Sunday School with my sister for some weird reason. Moving to Devon, that's when I first start having memories, but my earliest memory is actually when I was one, funnily enough, which sounds like a lie but is actually true. I was sitting on a beach in Spain and my dingy popped while I was sitting in it. I have a vivid memory of sitting in it while it popped. It was on the beach, not in the water."

Your parents weren't very musical were they?
"Not so much, they'd listen to music around the house but they never played and were never that passionate about music. I'd certainly always been into music and I found a picture of when I was three or four dressed up as Adam & The Ants, all punked up with a guitar and playing it left-handed so it was upside down, so I was quite impressed! So I was

clearly into music from an early age and at least had the thought and the idea that I could pick up a guitar and try to strum it and play it. That obviously stuck with me and continued through the next 10 years. The fact that I had this guitar, I must've played it quite a bit, but it was probably both guitar and drums at the same time but I didn't play the guitar too much. I only really got serious about playing music when I started playing drums when I was 13, after seeing some kind of jazz band that was playing at school and being extremely blown away by the drummer and what he was playing onstage and how the music made me feel, I guess it really made a mark."

GLEN ROWE, MUSE TOUR MANAGER 2000–2003

"Have you heard about Dom breaking his arm as a child? Well, the story goes from [Dom's sister] Emma that they were out in a park at some family do and they were playing catch and Dom, just throwing a tennis ball, breaks him arm!"

Do you know anything about Chris' childhood?
"Chris is quite guarded about his childhood actually. He has got a little sister and he grew up being the big brother to his little sister and being a father figure for his mum. Chris is quite angry that his father died, because I think he loved his dad and never got to have that special time with him. It is quite guarded. I think he had the perfect Devonshire childhood from the outside looking in. I'm sure there was some sort of torment in there, but he's really close to his mum."

COLIN STIDWORTHY, SCHOOLMATE AT TEIGNMOUTH COMMUNITY COLLEGE

"I was in the same year as Matt and Dom, but never had anything to do with Chris cos he was in the year below. I probably knew Matt the best as he was in my music class. He was quite an intelligent lad, always had an answer for everything. I seem to remember that he would always antagonise one of our teachers, Mrs Lancaster, I'm not sure why but they just never got on. On reflection, it was probably because he was always talking or hand-drumming on his knees.

"Matt was never much of a sport man, in football he was always played in defence, and you hoped that he never got near the ball. Give him a musical instrument and he was impressive; give him a ball to kick and he was useless. In his music class Matt came to life, he seemed to be able to play any instrument, but I remember him being really good on the piano. I'm not sure if he had had lessons out of school but he was very good, better than anyone else in the class; he just had the knack of picking up an instrument and being a natural. We would be given tasks to play simple tunes on the instruments but spent most of the time listening to Matt play. Our music teacher, Mrs Bird, seem to recognise this and I think was a big influence in helping Matt and the band. Apart from lessons, the music block was generally closed, but Mrs Bird would often open it up and let the band practise during lunch times and after school. When they were practising at school I never would have guessed that they would be where they are now, they were just a couple of lads that had music in common. There were a few other bands in our year but Matt, Dom and Chris just had that extra determination and natural talent that nobody else had."

SAFTA JAFFERY, TASTE MEDIA

How did you first come to hear about Muse?
"Dennis introduced them to me. Dennis and I had been friends a long time and, because Dennis had the studio and I had the producers, and Dennis didn't have business relationships at top level or business experience, which I had because I'd been in the business a long time, we set up Taste Media in '96. When we formed Taste Media I knew about Muse because Dennis had told me. We had Taste Media up and running and we had a couple of other artists signed on it; nothing came of the other artists and Muse were our third signing. When Dennis was doing the EPs it was with me in the background, because I suggested it was a good idea to do it through Dangerous. We were very much involved in it. Taste Media obviously became known as Muse's label, but later on we also signed Shed

Seven and One Minute Silence. We released the last Shed Seven record after they were dropped from Polydor, and also other bands called Serafin, signed to Elektra in the US, and Vega 4, signed to Capitol Records in the US, who all had major territorial deals similar to Muse's."

How did you get on with the band?
"I got on well with them as they – particularly Matt – were respectful of my experience and thus followed my advice, but I was always the guy who had to say no, if you see what I mean. I was the guy who would say no to the band and I knew that that would come back and bite me later on, but someone had to in those early years, to make the economics work. Dennis is this gentle giant and so somebody had to play the bad guy, so we decided early on that I was going to play the part of the bad guy, so, for example, I made all the deals whenever the band wanted to fly business class and we couldn't afford it, I was the guy who said, 'No, you can't.'"

Were they an easy band to manage?
"Matt could be quite difficult at times but they were fine; the good thing was that they were an intelligent band, and they were always pushing the boundaries. Sometimes you're managing a band and you're telling them what they should be doing. The great thing with Muse was that they were very co-operative and always looking to lead the way. I enjoyed that, because I haven't had that with some other bands that I've worked with. You're always sort of leading them and I always think that it should be the other way around. Matt always wanted the best and he always asked a thousand questions; although that sometimes made life more difficult, in the end that was why we got such good results. He came up with the stage concept. That was all him and I'm not gonna take any of that away from him. He's a pretty restless soul. He'd be one of these people I'd be on the phone to for hours. He'd call about whatever it might be and you'd have to give him reasons from every direction. It was quite exhausting to be honest; I had two young children at home whom I almost never saw for five years. My wife Nadia used to say, 'You're married to that band; you're not married to me.' I'd spend hours and hours on the phone, and I'd have two suitcases ready to leave at the drop of a hat to go around the world to deal with whatever issues required addressing."

PAUL REEVE, PRODUCER

How did you first hear about Muse?
"I was working at Sawmills. I've known Dennis since I was a kid really; I was a singer and I've known him since then. I had a studio in London, working with bands, and I was in a band myself, and when I came back to Cornwall I went to see if I could get into Sawmills. I did bits and bobs of work there with local bands, three or four projects, and that was probably the first time I'd been given an album to produce from beginning to end. About the third project I got involved with was Muse."

Didn't Dennis put you together with Muse because he thought you had a similar singing voice to Matt?
"I think he felt there was a commonality in the music, definitely. When I played it to my mum she thought it was me! I wish, mother, I wish!"

How did you first meet them?
"They were teenagers when I first knew them, and I think except for Chris they were out of work, just dossing about and stuff. They were kinda typical teenagers. Obviously Matt's always been quite an intense kind of chap, but the other two were very typical lads. I found them interesting and likeable and I have done throughout. The first thing we did together became 'The Muse EP', and then the next batch of work we did together became 'The Muscle Museum EP', which I still think is a splendid bit of work. And that was the beginning of *Showbiz*; most of those recordings went on to *Showbiz* and we went on to turn that into a whole album with the great John Leckie."

What were they like in the studio?
"This was before they'd done any proper touring so there were some technical issues in their playing. They were inspiring. The day I drove home after recording 'Unintended', it must've been a while ago because it was on a cassette in my car, it was sunrise and I remember thinking, 'If other people don't think this is good then I don't know what I'm doing.' I've always found that a very moving piece of music and I still do, it's absolute genius. The whole experience was very heartening, to see that when you do actually come across something that stands head and

shoulders above other things, it stands a fighting chance. That whole experience was brilliant. We were quite experimental, we tried some things, we were quite close musically. I got involved in singing on some of the stuff and tried to point Matt towards instruments that he hadn't necessarily been interested in. We certainly had a good, close relationship for a couple of years in the studio. I found them easy-going because there was a commonality, although there was some intensity there."

How did you see them develop?
"In the early days I saw the sort of progression that you do see from bands when you put them in somewhere like Sawmills and they haven't previously really done a proper recording. Doing something with a proper engineer and producer in a proper studio, and you take it home and think 'Shite!' It's a real eye-opener. So I did see, because of that, some real progress. However, there's no substitute for going on tour. When they came back off their first proper tour they were like a different band, especially in the rhythm section, there was no comparison."

Chapter Two

AND so it came to pass that, in 1998, the rock cooled. With the hugely publicised race for number one between Blur and Oasis in 1995 acting as a false fanfare to both bands' creative free fall (although that of Oasis wouldn't arrive for two more years, with 1997's massive-selling but cocaine-bloated *Be Here Now*), indie felt cheated and Britpop slumped. The chirpiness of Sleeper, Echobelly and Space had begun to twang the nerves of the nation's back teeth; even critically acclaimed albums deserving the edict of 'post Britpop classic' – The Boo Radleys' *C'Mon Kids*, Gene's *Drawn To The Deep End*, Suede's *Coming Up* or Pulp's *This Is Hardcore* the following year – failed to match the sales expectations and chart glories of guitar pop's mid-90s peak, and all of these bands declined towards their inevitable termination of contract. As a balm, the label rosters and charts instead became filled with Oasis-endorsed dad-rock bands such as Hurricane No. 1, Stereophonics, The Seahorses and Kula Shaker; bands with the hair and trousers of alternative musicians but whose music was alternative to nothing. Even Travis, a howling great balls-out rock act in 1998, would see the error of their ways and become the prime exponents of AOR slush-rock with 1999's *The Man Who*.

So the music industry that convened in Manchester for 1998's In The City music conference* was a safe-minded but uncertain one. British music was becoming stale, and the first flushes of the internet downloading revolution were starting to pinch. Those A&R men, managers, label executives, journalists and PRs knew they needed to find a fresh and exciting direction for UK rock, but had no idea what form it might take. The kids seemed to be hooking into the quasi-prog rock quirkiness of Chester's Mansun and the dark, ambiguous perversions of Placebo, but there was no definable scene around them.

---

* An annual event since 1992, the brainchild of the sadly departed Factory records supremo Tony Wilson.

The music press, meanwhile, were backing grotty squat noiseniks like Campag Velocet, Tiger and The Lo-Fidelity Allstars, who would clearly sell about 15 records between them. In alternative music terms the only album that had achieved stone cold, across-the-board international acclaim and success in the previous year or two was Radiohead's *OK Computer*, a dislocated, cold-souled record fascinatingly at odds with the past 20 years of rock music, throbbing with pre-millennial ennui and technological disenfranchisement. It was the musical equivalent of the gawky loner geek at school who used to be into hair-rock but discovered computers and made his first million in the internet boom by the age of 17. Ideally industry figures would turn up at ITC 1998 and find all 500 of the attendant bands making records like that – although, obviously, the studio techniques of *OK Computer* were way out of the reach of the average band from Lincoln with a garage and a four-track. They had more chance of finding every band made up of ferrets playing skiffle songs on xylophones.

No, the music industry queueing for conference accreditation at Manchester's Midland Hotel that year was the most confident headless chicken ever known. They needed to be blinded by the New Thing, but they couldn't conceive what the New Thing might look like.

* * *

The New Thing arrived at Manchester's Crown Plaza hotel that mid-September morning unaware and uncaring what sort of state the UK music business was in. Sticking to Safta Jaffery and Dennis Smith's advice, Muse had spent the spring and summer of 1998 stuck firmly in their own Devon-based world, playing at insalubrious hotel bars and university canteens in Torquay, Ashburton, Exeter and Plymouth, straying from their decision only to concentrate on building a local fanbase by playing as far afield as Matt's old stamping ground of Cambridge in February and a showcase to a smattering of interested labels at London's Water Rats in April (none of whom remained particularly interested after the gig). The highpoint of their year to date – aside from the (largely unnoticed, press-wise) release of 'The Muse EP' – had been bagging a slot at the Soundwaves Festival in Plymouth that August, a seafront stage that found Muse in nervy mood, premiering a new track called 'Hate This And I'll Love You', despite Matt being so frustrated by the technical failure of a new pedal he was trying out – a Pro Co Rat – that he spent a good five minutes of the set kicking it around the stage.

Despite its low profile, 'The Muse EP' had been submitted by Jaffery to the In The City selection panel in the hope of the band getting noticed as part of the conference's In The City: Live Unsigned competition. Aside from ITC itself being the UK's premier opportunity for new bands to be seen by all of the industry's prime movers and shakers in one place (most major rock bands have played an early set there; Oasis, Idlewild, Catatonia and Stereophonics had all been through in previous years), the unsigned band contest had gained a huge amount of A&R kudos when one of its earliest finals had seen Kula Shaker pitted against Placebo, both of whom went on to significant mainstream success. So while much of In The City consists of an aimlessly scurrying anthill of A&R men, agents, managers and music hacks racing randomly between the 50 venues around Manchester that present ITC showcase gigs, each following their own agenda, chasing whatever snippet of hype they might have overheard during the daytime industry-panel discussions or from the next (strangely over-occupied) cubicle in the Midland bar lavatories the previous night, the final of In The City: Live Unsigned was a must-attend event for all delegates.

Muse had been granted a headline slot on September 13 at a venue called Collier, a converted church hall that wasn't likely to attract many passing industry stragglers due to its no drinking or smoking policy. And while the rafters were rammed at the showcases of bands such as Coldplay and Doves that year, Muse nonetheless drew a respectable crowd of intrigued insiders on the back of next to no hype, and played a sturdy set, although the pressure of the event inevitably left them feeling disappointed with their performance.

The music industry looked at Muse that night and felt decidedly . . . undecided. They rocked, sure; they had a certain Jeff Buckley-meets-Radiohead timeliness about them, yes (although more like Radiohead circa *The Bends* than *OK Computer*, and that was *so* 1994), but in an era when only a sure-fire platinum seller of the future would do, they seemed too ragged, too meandering, too unconventional, too risky. And Muse looked at the music industry and felt out of place, a little disgusted even. In the bar of the Crown Plaza that night, Muse observed the industry hog-fest at its most virulent, drugged-up and stuffed with bullshit, and decided there were games here that they didn't want to play. When Nik

Moore from Work Hard PR, who had been at their gig that night, approached them to offer his services as publicist for free with the proviso that they would keep him on if they became successful, they agreed with thanks. When a representative from Zomba record label expressed an interest in them playing for his US paymasters, they were intrigued and excited by the offer. But when they heard that they had been chosen as one of the best three bands of the conference and selected to play the In The City: Live Unsigned final, they opted not to turn up. They didn't want to "overdo it, play to a business audience", they'd later claim.[*] "And the live thing was a bit of a shambles." In the event, shonky indie novelty act Younger Younger 28s went on to win the competition that year.

Muse left In The City 1998 as they had found it; big, a bit scary and containing no labels interested in signing them, although there were glimmers of interest here and there, enough to draw the band back to London in October to play more showcases at Camden's Monarch and Falcon pub venues. Recoiling from the industry glitz and gall – albeit with a new sense of confidence that they really were among the best new bands in the UK – they returned to the drudgery of the Devon circuit, next stop the Plymouth Cooperage.

Yet their experiences at In The City had given Muse a fresh angle on the way they would record and release their music. They wanted as little as possible to do with the crushing major label treadmill they'd seen so many other bands at ITC desperate to clamber on, so with Safta's ideas and intuitive planning, Matt, Dom, Chris and Taste Media agreed that they would produce the records themselves and then license the music to record companies for promotion and distribution. They had access to top producers and they had a studio for free, so what was to stop them? And best of all, it meant they would have no contact with A&R departments trying to guide them towards the trends of the day, or label bosses telling them what sort of songs they should write to shift the most units. No pliable puppets, Muse: they would be their own bosses, write their own rules.

And besides, where Britain's pursuit of Muse's signatures had slowed to a crawl, America's was just about to escape the traps.

* * *

* In my first interview with them for *NME* the following year.

CMJ is like In The City on crack. New York's annual music conference, held in October, the College Music Journal showcase event has got three times the number of venues and five times the number of bands as the UK event, and takes over all of downtown Manhattan and parts of Williamsburgh in Brooklyn for five days a year; the streets fill with thousands of margarita-stewed attendees barging and baying to gain access to the hottest, most over-guest-listed gigs and fighting over taxis across town to catch the more far-flung hype bands. Amid CMJ's sprawling chaos it is every man, and every artist, for himself.

Unlike its UK equivalent, the US music industry convening on the Lower East Side in October 1998 knew exactly what they were looking for. They were looking for mid-teen rock. Nu metal was breaking huge in the States, with the likes of Korn, Limp Bizkit and Slipknot selling many millions of albums to disenchanted, hormone-addled early teens. America's youth was in the grip of an Upper Body Rock revolution; all the industry needed was a more mature, intricate version to keep the nu-metal kids buying rock records past puberty.

To several US labels, then, 'The Muse EP' sounded like a salvo of salvation. A pounding rock blast with hints of System Of A Down's prog metal tendancies, and Radiohead-meets-Nirvana guitars? This was intelligent Upper Body Rock in excelsis, and Safa played the EP to several US industry players on a business trip that autumn.

A slot at CMJ was hastily arranged for Muse on October 31 at famed Lower East Side alt.rock haunt the Mercury Lounge on Houston, playing alongside fellow UK rockers Feeder. On their arrival, Muse got their first nibble on the major label pie as Zomba courted them with possibly their first-ever free dinner. Unfortunately for Zomba, however, word of Muse's potential had spread fast around CMJ 1998 and, with them officially classed as a 'hot tip', the Mercury Lounge's faux-elegant back room was rammed with label hotshots for their set, most notably an A&R scout called Nanci Walker from Columbia records, similarly enthused by the EP. A storming, if technical fault-riddled set gleaned almost entirely from the demos recorded with Reeve at Sawmills the previous year, found Matt's virtuoso guitar playing and ardent vocal squeals turning heads and chequebook pages alike, and garnered them two major footholds on their future success.

The first came courtesy of producer John Leckie, who was also in the crowd at the Mercury Lounge that night. Something of a music production legend, Leckie had worked very sparingly with rock bands during the late 90s, being incredibly selective with his projects following a career that few could equal for glitter factor. Having started out as an in-house engineer and tape operator at Abbey Road in 1970, just as The Beatles' strange hold on the studio came to an end with their split, he worked on albums by all of the solo Beatles (including George Harrison's *All Things Must Pass* and John Lennon's *Plastic Ono Band*), Pink Floyd (working on the legendary *Dark Side Of The Moon*) and Mott The Hoople. On going freelance as a producer in 1977 he became a top production player of the post-punk era, working with The Adverts, The Fall, Magazine, Simple Minds, Human League and XTC throughout the 1980s, culminating in his helming of *The Stone Roses*, widely acclaimed as one of the greatest British debut albums ever recorded and the record that sparked off the 90s Madchester generation. When he followed this by working on shoegazing classic *A Storm In Heaven* by Verve (as they were then), it was clear that Leckie was a man capable of moving with the sonic times, and through the 90s the awards rolled in: a *Music Week* award for Best Producer in 1995, a Q Award for Best Producer in 1996 and a Brit for Kula Shaker's *K* in 1997. That he had also produced Radiohead's *The Bends* album, however, would prove to be both a blessing and a curse for Muse in the coming years.

John Leckie had been managed by Safta Jaffery since 1985 and had long been aware of Muse through Safta's recommendation, catching a few London gigs towards the end of 1998, building up a passing relationship with the band. After the Mercury Lounge gig, the renowned producer made the band a promise. If they could ever afford him, he'd work with them.

Buoyed but a little bewildered by their first experience not just in America but in the eye of the US industry maelstrom, Matt, Dom and Chris returned to Devon at the start of November as changed men, out of sync with their ordinary home lives. If the A&R guys buying them drinks and dinners at CMJ had had no idea of the world from which Muse had come, their colleagues and friends back at their guitar-shop jobs in Torquay had even less concept of what was happening to them, of the stories they were telling. Back home they had steady girlfriends (aside from Dom), grotty flats littered with drugs, and bosses demanding they work extra overtime to make up for the time they'd missed. In New York City they'd had free meals, drinks on tap, the rock world at their feet.

Then, only a few weeks later, came foothold number two. Columbia records wanted to fly them to Los Angeles to play a showcase gig for the label heads.

And Muse's world went supernova.

★ ★ ★

They flew into LAX around Thanksgiving 1998. They were met at the airport by a limo and taken to the first of many "fake meals", lavished with expensive wines and undercooked meats. In balmy Los Angeles, Muse were tempted with every lure and bribe available to the opulent, excessive and flashy US music business – an industry not averse to throwing casual offers of girls, drugs and money at impressionable young bands in return for their shaky signatures. A few days earlier Matt had been cleaning toilets in a freezing caravan park in early British winter; this, he reasoned, was another world entirely.

The Columbia showcase gig, to the label's credit, was organised some way outside of Hollywood's seductive sleaze and steam – an hour down Santa Monica Boulevard in Santa Monica, a sanitised and gentrified mall and motel paradise on the US West Coast, playground of the movie industry, its boardwalk overrun with plastic surgery addicts clutching toy dogs and its multi-million dollar beachside condos just up the coast at Big Sur. And that day the story of Muse was rewritten as a tale of two piers: from the murky, faded seaside glamour of Teignmouth pier, which had born witness to their adolescent growing pains, their fate was to be sealed at a gig on Santa Monica pier on November 23, shaded from the Californian sun by black drapes and watched by an expectant crowd of US rock moguls, makers and shakers.

The gig was a raging success, with one Columbia executive, Tim Devine, allegedly moved to tears by the performance, and Rick Rubin – for whom the gig had been scheduled at 11 a.m. so that he could take time out from producing Tom Petty to see the band – declaring to Safta that Muse were the 21st Century Beatles. With Rubin asking Muse and Taste Media to stay in town for a few more days to hang out with them, the Columbia contract was all but on the table – Devine just had to talk to his boss, Donnie Ienner, who had to talk to his boss, who had to talk to the MD, who'd need to see the band showcase for himself . . .

Later that day, Muse began packing up their travel bags at their hotel for their afternoon flight home, confidently assuming that after a few months of contract ironing they would be signed to Columbia by early 1999. And they might be to this day had they booked an earlier flight out. But on his return to the hotel, Safta found a message from Guy Oseary, Madonna's partner in both relationship (at the time) and in running Maverick Records. Originally seen as something of a vanity project, Maverick was riding the wave of a few early successes after having signed Alanis Morissette, The Prodigy for the US (just as they hit number one on the *Billboard* chart with *Fat Of The Land*) and (much to the interest of Muse) coolest of the nu metal bunch, The Deftones.

Having been keeping tabs on Muse since Safta sent him the 'Muse EP' and getting wind of the industry buzz around them at CMJ, Guy – the creative A&R end of the Maverick partnership; throughout their relationship with the label Muse would never once meet Madge herself – had heard that the band were in LA and was amazed to hear that they were without a UK or US deal. Knowing he had to move fast as the Columbia claw was closing, he insisted to Safta that the band stay in LA for a few more days to play for Maverick, offering to pay for accommodation, limos all over town and new first-class flights home, whatever it took. That Muse were in town on Columbia's dollar bothered him not an ounce; if they didn't play a closed showcase for him the very next day, he told Safta, he'd just have to fly them back out to LA the following week.

The Muse camp thought the offer over for a second – another 72 hours in sun-drenched LA, the chance to work with the man who signed The Deftones and maybe get Madonna's autograph for Matt's brother, who had been a massive fan when he was younger. And most importantly, rather than munching down overpriced meals with A&R underlings, now they were actually talking directly to the man who makes the decisions, who could sign them in a second if he wanted to, and to a label with only around 15 acts, so they'd be guaranteed priority status. Plus, Maverick didn't seem to them to be the sort of label that would drop a band after their first album through poor record sales. They were a little dazzled and baffled by their Los Angeles experience – Matt was having great fun but didn't think their music warranted the intense attention. He found the US interest amusingly fake, hilariously unnatural. They were bemused by it all, but they certainly weren't in a hurry for it to end. So they agreed to book a rehearsal room to showcase for Maverick the next day and began unpacking in earnest.

It was a motley bunch of dealmakers that gathered the next day to watch Muse showcase. Dennis and Safta were joined by Steve Sessa, the LA attorney recently hired to represent the band's contract dealings, Oseary and one Steve Jones from The Sex Pistols, invited by Oseary more for punk kudos than for his enthusiasm for the band – he spent the set chewing gum and looking bored and was never introduced to them. Not that Muse would have been particularly star-struck; they were a little bleary-eyed that day themselves, having wasted no time the previous night, finding they were still in LA, in diving back into corporate hog heaven. Representing the Columbia lobby chasing Muse's signatures, Rick Rubin and producer George Drakoulis (producer of such diverse acts as The Wu-Tang Clan and Primal Scream) had rolled by in Rubin's classic Bentley at 2 a.m., straight from the studio where he was producing the new Tom Petty album, and whisked them off to Sunset Strip to drink until the even smaller hours.

So, tentatively, and with the inherent awkwardness that comes with performing in a small room to an audience of five who could make or break your career, a heavily jet-lagged and hungover Muse began their set. They got through 'Cave' and 'Muscle Museum' before Oseary stopped them. "You don't need to play any more," he said and offered them a deal. He'd later describe the experience as "extremely powerful and beautiful". Despite Oseary clearly being enraptured with the band, and ready to do business without any concerns that the UK market had failed to show much interest in them, Muse and their management begged him to hear more of their planned six-song set. He asked to hear 'Cave' and 'Muscle Museum' again and confirmed "we can do business".

That business was wrapped up within a month. Beating off half a dozen less determined bidders, Maverick flew Muse back out to LA to sign a two album co-label record deal with Taste for the US, Canada and Mexico on Christmas Eve 1998 – while many labels might have baulked at the idea of sharing the rights to a band's music with several rivals around the world, this wasn't an issue for Oseary since he had a similar deal with The Prodigy, and that had worked well for him. So according to plan, Muse still had control over the recording and production of their music for the world's biggest music market. They couldn't have dreamed for a better Christmas present.

The big one out of the way, Muse flew back to the UK to start filling in the rest of the globe.

* * *

With news of Muse's near-instant signing in the US, Safta – working as Muse's worldwide A&R and manager on behalf of Taste Media, had little trouble mopping up licensing deals via his contacts in the rest of the world's territories. Last on the list was to secure a deal in the UK and, with all of the major labels having already passed (although the band played a showcase for Parlophone records at the Princess Charlotte on January 11, 1999, their first gig of the year), he had to look further afield. He turned to Mushroom Records, a label based in Australia but whose UK division had been set up by Korda Marshall (formerly of Infectious and before that RCA) in 1997, largely to represent Australian bands in Britain. However, in the early 90s Korda landed Mushroom lucrative deals with proto Britpop combo Ash and Nirvana producer Butch Vig's successful glam-rock band Garbage, and the offshoot's remit broadened to encompass dis-covering talent and signing it to the label. As a Devon boy himself (and an acquaintance of Dennis Smith from their pre-record industry days), Korda had been following Muse's progress for some years and had been among the label heads to turn them down twice previously as, like Safta and Smith, he had been keen for the band to develop a grass-roots following first. The sudden interest from Maverick and the enthusiasm for the band expressed by his Australian counterpart, Michael Parisi (who'd been among the lucky recipients of one of Safta's 'Muse EP' packages), however, forced his hand, and Mushroom UK signed a co-label three-album licensing deal with Taste for the UK, Ireland and Australasia.*

The other major territories toppled like dominoes. For France they signed to Naïve; for Germany, Switzerland, Austria and Eastern Europe they were bagged by Motor/Universal. Indeed, only one package was sent by Safta to Germany – addressed to his long-standing friend Tim Renner at Universal and Tim's wife, Petra Husemann, at Motor. Husemann thought they had the sort of Radiohead-ish teen angst that would work well in Germany and wanted to see the band play live.

---

* Some local press reports later claimed, probably erroneously, that Mushroom signed Muse before CMJ.

Hence Muse's first tentative jaunt of the UK in January 1999 – stretching their touring legs around such legendary but tiny British toilet venues as the Manchester Roadhouse, the Hastings Crypt, a rammed Duchess Of York in Leeds and the Tunbridge Wells Forum. Famous for once actually being a public toilet, the night Muse played the last named on January 15 was the night that Nik Moore of Work Hard, who had been handling the band's publicity for free since In The City, was invited down to see the band and told there was another PR company interested in working with them. Shortly afterwards, Muse switched to the highly respected Bad Moon PR under the guidance of Anton Brookes, who had done press for Nirvana and The Happy Mondays. A matter of months after that they switched again, to the new and unproven Impressive PR, under the reins of ex-Arista publicist Mel Brown, an enthusiastic witness of the band's CMJ show. Other gigs were at Bedford's Esquires and the good old Exeter Cavern, supporting whoever would have them along the way, and the tour was interrupted halfway through to fly to Hamburg to play for Universal/Motor at the Logo Club on January 19. Blown away, Husemann and Renner signed the deal with Muse that night, cursing their luck that they could only get the rights to the territories they did. Safta and Dennis stopped at four deals for the time being, keen to have four dedicated teams working on the band rather than just one – it wouldn't be until the autumn of 1999 that they would begin to seal deals for Japan and Scandinavia.

The UK tour, to promote their second release, 'Muscle Museum EP', on Dangerous, was a landmark for Muse. Their first as a signed band, they suddenly had a big, white rented van, a tour manager, a booking agent and the Madonna stamp of approval behind them. They even had a road crew of sorts, although this was a fairly motley bunch of local Teignmouth mates and layabouts, including a gypsy stoner guy they'd found sleeping rough who claimed he'd been living on Cornflakes and water for three weeks, whom they took on as their monitor technician out of sheer sympathy. Their gigs in America had made them realise that, actually, they might not be too bad a band after all, but the leap from playing their own gigs to college mates and their growing fanbase in Devon, to industry showcases full of A&R men or support slots for bigger bands whose fans weren't interested in them, made them more introverted, playing to themselves rather than to the audience. This was all thrillingly, terrifyingly real, and happening dizzyingly fast. They knew that to make the most of the opportunities ahead of them, they'd better shape up, and fast.

So rehearsals were taut and gigs were intense, with an average 10-song set list of 'Overdue', 'Cave', 'Uno', 'Instant Messenger', 'Sober', 'Fillip', 'Rain', 'Muscle Museum', 'Unintended' and 'Showbiz'. By the time the 11-date tour wrapped up at University Of London Union with a support slot to moody Swedish rockers Kent, having played almost as many gigs in one month as they'd previously played in a year, Muse had become a tight and tremendous rock proposition. Matt's vocals were becoming glass-shattering shrieks of falsetto fury, his guitar playing volcanic and worthy of a man with twice his number of fingers. Chris and Dom had turned into a thunderous rhythm section, making contemporaries like Coldplay look like the cack-handed shambles they were (back then). Muse had become one of the country's most accomplished and exciting new rock bands.

And not a moment too soon. Because the spotlight, having turned violently their way, had just been switched on.

* * *

January in rock is the indie chancer's theme park. With the major acts having shot their promo load in the Christmas rush and the nation's consumers largely penniless for a month, the huge commercial acts lay low and the more astute major labels leap on the opportunities provided by lower than usual sales and plentiful 'Bands To Watch This Year' magazine polls to grab one of their lower-priority acts a shifty Top 10 hit amid the sales lull. Around this time, Welsh rockers Feeder made a fine art out of the crafty January hit single and the tactic, becoming an indie standard in the 90s, has produced such flash in the pan 'careers' as the Electric Six, White Town and Babylon Zoo.

And there, but for the grace of Lamacq, went Muse.

The 'Muscle Museum EP' was intended to be a fairly quiet release, a stop-gap gathering up of the remaining six tracks recorded during 1998's Paul Reeve sessions at Sawmills before recording began for the debut album (and before their various big bucks distribution deals kicked in, allowing them to produce vastly more copies of their records). As with 'The Muse EP', only 999 copies were made, plus some CD-Rs not including 'Muscle Museum 2' and un-numbered copies for press and radio, each hand-numbered and largely sold from January 11 in Devon record stores or at the gigs. A low-key release, intended to stir up a bit of hype and interest, to remind the UK that had passed them by at In The City that Muse were still here, and making some real industry noise.

Thing is, a song like 'Muscle Museum' just doesn't want to be kept quiet. Named from the two words surrounding 'muse' in a dictionary and featuring a brand new method for recording a guitar solo without a guitar (concentrating on the epic widdle-fest he was planning for the end of the chorus, Matt accidentally missed a chord during recording and had to sing the solo instead; by singing it into a Marshall amp it sounded just like a guitar, only more ghostly, shrill, manic and human – the technique was used on several tracks on 'Showbiz' and, to this day, Matt needs a heavily distorted microphone onstage in order to recreate the effect live), 'Muscle Museum' was the band's killer pop hit, and they knew the release couldn't help but make a splash. The swirling Egyptian tomb-raider of a riff; the knowing indie wink of the lyric, "I have played in every toilet"; the exotic bass throb; the chorus that exploded like Vesuvius – even in this raw demo state it was monumental. Louche, mysterious and assured, yet powerful enough to knock fillings out at 50 paces, its Freudian dissection of the battle between conscience and basic human desire sounded like the perfect ultraviolent antidote to the AOR stool, rock becoming prevalent in those post-Oasis times.

The final track on the EP was a truncated one-and-a-half minute acoustic version entitled 'Muscle Museum 2', doused in the sounds of rain and with Matt's plaintive vocals far back on the horizon of the mix; and sandwiched between the two was not so much a clutch of B-sides as a demo'd preview of the debut album to come. First up was 'Sober', re-recorded with Reeve from the Newton Abbot demo version: a funky, frenzied celebration of fine liquor and its healing effects in the event of emotional turmoil ("Matured for years and imported/Into my glass you poured it/And you're the only reason that I remain unfrozen"). One of the first examples of Matt at his most histrionically falsetto vocally and wildly free form in his guitar playing (there are several moments when he sounds like he's playing guitar with a hammer or a cattle prod rather than a plectrum), it made a startling impact.

'Uno', eventually to be Muse's first 'proper' single, followed, initially trembling its way through a sombre and sinister Latino tango before the hypercharged rock chorus grabs its partner by the throat and spins them around the dancefloor with furious resentment: "You could have been number one . . . And we could have had so much fun/But you threw it away." Already here, linking this with 'Sober', a theme of anger and rejection was looming, and fans would later speculate that 'Uno' was about the same person (a jilting ex of Matt's perhaps, or an early band associate unwilling to put the work in) who also came under fire on 'Hate This And I'll Love You' and the later 'Hyper Music'.

Matt's fragile emotional state is more directly linked with the fairer sex on 'Unintended': still deep in the same relationship he'd had since he was 16, he admits that 'Unintended' was written at Sawmills, spewing out almost accidentally after a phone conversation with his girlfriend – an unintended love song in the plainest of terms. Over an elegant, near classical acoustic guitar arpeggio, and with Paul Reeve supplying backing vocals, he pours out his heart about how his latest love could be the one to help him get over a previous shattered relationship, if only he'd let her. Though they'd been unable to perform it live for much of 1998, due, according to Matt, to their lack of a keyboard player (in 1999 they concocted an electric version for live dates), it would be Muse's big, tear-sodden ballad moment for years to come, and to follow it with the slight 'Instant Messenger', concerning finding love in internet chatrooms and allegedly named after Muse's old touring van, seemed almost perverse. ('Instant Messenger' became 'Pink Ego Box' for its release on a later B-side after internet provider AOL legally objected to its automated voice saying "you've got post" being sampled on the track.)

When 'Muscle Museum EP' first aired in the *NME* office, such was the volume of ears perked that I was promptly dispatched to interview the band for the underwhelming 'On' piece, giving them their first burst of national publicity that February and placing them firmly in the alternative world's spotlight. But perhaps a more pivotal event occurred that day before the University Of London Union show, when Matt strolled the quarter of a mile across Tottenham Court Road from ULU to the Radio One building on Great Portland Street and handed a copy of 'Muscle Museum EP' to the receptionist, telling them to pass it on to DJ Steve Lamacq.[*]

Helmsman of the BBC's indie-radio Mecca, *The Evening Session*,

---

[*] This almost certainly wouldn't have been the first copy of the EP Lamacq had received, since Muse's radio plugging was then being handled by the late Scott Piering, who had first introduced the DJ to the band.

Lamacq's patronage was the holy grail for all aspiring rock bands in the 90s. The indie John Peel, Lamacq is an avid, nay pathological new-music hunter, who devours every demo and scours every support slot for a new band to wax maniacal about on air. So while so many national broadcasters are merely slaves to a playlist, Lamacq got 'Muscle Museum EP', listened to it and obviously loved it. While all around were snuffling up 30 seconds of the title track, hearing a serrated indie-rock howl, fiery chugging guitars, angsty lyrics and an explosive, emotive chorus and decrying Muse as a Xerox of *The Bends* era Radiohead – a comparison that would first niggle, then annoy, then plain anger the band over the next few years[*] – Lamacq instead heard grand musicianship, intense fragility and the heady clunk of cold, hard tunes. To the band's amazement, Lamacq started playing tracks from the EP on air within weeks, then invited the band into the studio to record a prestigious session on February 17. Before they knew it, he was offering them the opening slot on the Radio 1 *Evening Session* Tour that May, below riotous punk hopefuls 3 Colours Red and all-girl US glam rockers The Donnas. Of the hundreds of bands crossing Lamacq's radar every week, he'd pinned his colours to Muse's lapels.

With both national music press and the nation's prime alternative radio show backing the record, it sold out almost instantly, and reached number three on the *NME* Indie Singles Chart. A big deal back when the *NME* Indie Singles Chart existed. Muse, in their own little way, had arrived. Now it was time to hit the road and tell the UK about it.

* * *

Heaven knows what mad gig-booking drugs Muse's agent was on in 1999, but they were about to tour like there wasn't just a gig tomorrow but there was a gig the day after that, and the day after that and every day until the end of time. Thankfully for the band, their live appointments were unveiled gradually; had anyone told them, having just returned from their first-ever UK tour, that from this point on they would be touring for at least 18 months solid with a matter of months off to write and record their first two albums, you suspect a defence mechanism might have kicked in –

---

[*] And of which I myself was guilty; my 'On' piece that month included the line, 'If there was a National Sounding Like Radiohead Championship they'd be on the expert judging panel alongside Radiohead and another band who sound exactly like Radiohead.'

particularly for Chris, who had just discovered that his girlfriend Kelly was expecting their first child. Instead, Muse eased into their future as one of the UK's most hard-touring bands with a wide-eyed naivety. They were told where they were playing and who they were playing with; they went where they were told and they played.

First. Through February 1999 Muse were support act to Britpop fops Gene (a tour on which I first saw Muse play at Reading University, the gig at which the first-ever video recording of a Muse show was taken). Still in their little white van, this jaunt around the UK's universities and mid-sized venues – Colchester Arts Centre, the Brighton Centre and Bristol Anson Rooms, at which gig the very last copies of 'The Muse EP' and 'Muscle Museum EP' had sold out – felt like an extension of their January tour, only this time they were playing bigger halls to uninterested fans of another band, themselves dwindling in numbers, as an added feature to the main event. With their furious rock finding little favour with fans of Gene's elegantly turned louche-pop, they once again turned inward, playing for themselves, Matt ripping up stages and throwing himself and his guitar around wildly to make up for the cross-armed reception or to dazzle the disbelievers. Yet the headliners were so impressed that they asked Muse to support them at the Forum in London a month after the tour ended and again two weeks later at the Astoria theatre, on a day when they managed to squeeze in a second show at Sound Republic in Leicester Square. These were by far the biggest venues they'd yet played – apart from Chris, who had somewhat bizarrely played with Status Quo during one of their soundchecks in Plymouth in 1997. (Rick Parfitt was too ill to soundcheck and Chris' college mates, whom he was visiting at the time, included Status Quo's keyboard player's son – he volunteered Chris to fill in for Parfitt for the check, playing 'Don't Waste My Time' to Chris' immense delight.) And big venues, giving their monster sounds space to roar and rampage the way nature intended, suited Muse perfectly. Nervous and insecure they might have been, but playing big halls felt strangely like coming home.

Second. In May, after a couple of warm-ups at Harlow Square and Tun-bridge Wells Forum, the Radio 1 *Evening Session* Tour kicked off at Cardiff University for a six-date trot east, through Birmingham, Manchester, Shef-field and Portsmouth (where Muse's seven-song set was broadcast live on Lamacq's show) to its explosive demise at the London Barfly, where Muse premiered a new instrumental track – a bluesy riff-rage of a song tentatively entitled 'Hyper Music'. Befitting their new status as big shed players (albeit in the support slots), Muse were granted by Taste Media the rock-star status symbol of a proper tour bus for the first time and, rolling like a headliner now, Muse performed like one, stealing night after night from The Donnas and 3 Colours Red with their bombastic passions.

Third. Having made the trek east, the day after the *Evening Session* tour ended Muse turned around, hooked onto the Feeder tour as support and went back again, zig-zagging across the UK for nine dates, via their second gig at the Portsmouth Pyramid Centre in a week. By the time they wound up at the Sheffield Leadmill on May 30 for a fortnight off after three solid weeks of touring, they were changed men – both emotionally and physically. Hitting the high falsetto note in 'Cave' had taken its toll on Matt's throat, and his voice box was literally shrinking as a result of the nightly strain. Later, doctors examining it would remark that they'd never seen vocal chords like his in a man before – they looked exactly like those of a woman.

In the months between these tours, Muse weren't slacking. In March they flew back to LA to play another showcase for Maverick at the Viper Room, who were keen to show off their new signing to their US team. Not that the gig was a raging success: the legendary venue (outside which River Phoenix famously died of a drugs overdose) had an audience of around 20 that night, and it was the day after the Oscars circus had rolled through town, leaving in its wake a city bruised and hung over. Muse themselves had hit the Oscars party circuit straight off the plane – when their bus pulled up at their hotel, a flurry of photographers raced to get their pictures, unsure who they were but assuming anyone rolling up to a Hollywood hotel in a band bus on Oscars night must be pretty famous. Bemused and amused by their first paparazzi experience, the band decided to live up to the lie and were ferried around various celebrity bashes by Maverick all night, mingling with the A-list and knocking back cocktails like Best Actor winners. So by stage time the next evening, Muse were a racked, wrecked threesome, exhausted by a combination of high living and jet lag.

Back in England between tours, though, the party had to stop. Muse had an album to record and some serious money behind them in order to make it. So, obviously, they called in a favour . . .

* * *

John Leckie brought many things to Muse's debut album, *Showbiz*. An inflated sense of grandeur and focus. A crunching rock punch. An intense culture of experimentation. A classicist's insistence on using analogue tape when modern digital equipment was lying about all over the place. But ask Muse what they remember him bringing most and they'll name two things – good weed and Hitler's microphones.

Now say what you like about the Nazis, they certainly made good microphones. Under instruction to make Hitler sound like the voice of God during his radio broadcasts, German technicians invented the condenser microphone, designed to make the voice more powerful. In the 1970s, Leckie went to Germany and bought hundreds of them in various styles (his collection is now worth a considerable amount), so when Matt wanted his vocals on 'Sunburn' to emulate the edgy keyboard sound from a DJ Shadow track he was listening to at the time, Leckie brought out an antique microphone used by the German army in tanks – strapped around the neck, it picks up throat vibrations and makes the wearer's voice sound rather like Linda Blair in *The Exorcist*. Edgy isn't quite the word for the effect it had on 'Sunburn'. Plain terrifying comes closer.

Over an initial three weeks of recording at London's RAK studio and final sessions at Sawmills in April, Leckie and Muse pieced *Showbiz* together efficiently and economically, working as co-producers. Having made the sudden leap from painting and decorating to minor pop star faced with life-changing decisions on a regular basis, Matt was intent on making sure nothing went awry and that control of Muse and their music didn't slip away from the band – so sure was he that the band would end up getting shafted if they were only interested in making the music that he went as far as making sure he never missed any meetings, particularly in the US, whether the topic was sleeve art, promo photos or the tiniest detail concerning the creative side of the band. So when it came to producing the album, Muse couldn't hand complete production responsibility even to a man as experienced as Leckie; they needed to be hands-on with the recording of the songs, since they had strong views about how they wanted them to be recorded and arranged. Matt could already see the difference between recording and playing live: the latter was a performance, whereas the former is something to be constructed and honed, like a sculpture. And he wanted every line and curve of his first sculpture to flow perfectly.

From the 50 songs that Muse had in their repertoire as they entered the studio, the four of them whittled the number down to 12, choosing the least progressive of the songs to record for the album, and also those less concerned lyrically with their home town and its traumas than more recent numbers about the wider world to which they'd so recently been exposed. Since they were recording as only a three-piece, Muse were keen to experiment, and Leckie, as a bit of a mystic on the side, was open to unusual suggestions. Between them they played around with whatever instruments they could lay their hands on: Mellotrons were used instead of guitars to make sounds akin to huge choirs of voices, while Matt was suddenly itching to get back to playing the piano again. He'd barely touched the instrument for years while Muse were building and honing their guitar-based set list, but recently he'd been listening to a lot of early 20th-century piano music, emotional but technically complex composers such as Rachmaninoff, and he had a head full of ivories. So when 'Sunburn', written and demo'd while the band were in the studio*, didn't sound right when played on guitar, Leckie suggested that he switch to the studio piano to work it out. Hence the delicate opening tinklings of 'Showbiz' were born and a stellar canon of sonic supernovas was begun. Indeed, Matt's rediscovered interest in the piano would go on to heavily influence the songwriting for Muse's second album, *Origin Of Symmetry*.

*   *   *

It sounds tiny now; now that we know what they're capable of. Tinny, brittle and light on air-punching rock tunes, it now sounds like a test run, a warm-up, a training level. But at the time, *Showbiz* sounded like a meteorite storm from the blue.

The lilting piano refrain of 'Sunburn' is an instant Muse calling card. It's no mistake such classicist stylings open their debut album as the song is practically their manifesto, their statement of intent: gently and with seductive familiarity, it takes our hand and invites us to peer into the mighty abyss that links the grandiose old world of classical music with the thunderous new world of rock. Both equally powerful and bombastic but a universe apart in terms of grace, delicacy and preciseness, 'Sunburn' was where they locked horns. Where most rock bands used strings and classical

---

* The demo version of 'Sunburn' had drastically different lyrics based around the somewhat supernatural couplet, "When you're dead and gone/I'll still feel your glow".

influences to embellish their more sombre moments (most hard-rock albums by this time had to have one token 'Nothing Else Matters' song), here Muse did something new and unthinkable – they threw both pomped-up styles full force at each other and basked in the blast from the fusion. From song one on album one, this ethos would come to define their work.

The lyrics to 'Sunburn' suggest feelings of worthlessness and guilt, as though Matt wrote it remembering how he felt in America, being chased by record labels for music he felt wasn't worth the attention yet – "Come waste your millions here/Secretly she sneers/Another corporate show/ A guilty conscience grows". But if Muse inwardly felt like a waste of Maverick's money, musically they disproved it instantly with the loping, prehistoric bassline and agitated Aegean arpeggios of song two – the Paul Reeve recording of 'Muscle Museum', now with added beefy drum overdubs. While Bellamy would later claim that the song was in some way about people in the future no longer needing physical bodies, this is difficult to decipher from the lyrics, as indeed are hints of his claims to the song being a battle between the mind and the loin (aside from in the line, "Too long trying to resist it"). Instead, what comes through most plainly – perhaps due to Matt's relative inexperience in writing lyrics – is a thinly veiled snipe at the haters back home: "I have played in every toilet/ But you still want to spoil it/To prove I've made a big mistake". But any lyrical fudging and incongruity is more than made up for by the sheer massiveness of the tune itself – a chorus like a stack of Giza pyramids toppling into the Grand Canyon. Which, again, would become a Muse trademark.

A fillip is defined as an embellishment or stimulus that excites or arouses, and the track 'Fillip' certainly does the job. Frivolous and jaunty, while still rocking like the proverbial mutha, it trips along poppily in a US collegiate rock style for two minutes (Muse were probably trying to emulate the tuneful post-grunge of Foo Fighters, but ironically turned out something very similar to early Radiohead tracks such as 'Anyone Can Play Guitar' or 'Pop Is Dead'). At which point the Mansun mask slips and the hidden prog song beneath is exposed, as we enter a fairly pointless minute-long dreamy/dreary plod with Matt wailing aimlessly in falsetto, which marks 'Fillip' as *Showbiz*'s first less-than-thunderous track, despite a cracking gallop back through the good bit again at the end.

Delving into his Robert Johnson collection for influence, Matt's first tender and affecting ballad on *Showbiz* comes with the bluesy 'Falling Down' – a forerunner to their cover of Nina Simone's blustery 'Feeling Good' on album two and an excellent chance for Matt to indulge his every Jeff Buckley crooner fantasy, which he attacks with an emotive gusto belying his youth. The stately tone and Albert Hall friendly arrangement, meanwhile, disguises the meaning of the song, partly involving Matt's inclination to blow up Teignmouth (population 15,000) for making him feel alienated and unwanted in his youth: "I'm falling down/And fifteen thousand people scream/They were all begging for your dream/I'm falling down/Five thousand houses burning down/No one is gonna save this town . . . you would never hear me sing/You wouldn't let me begin". Rarely in rock does something so savage sound so saintly.

'Cave''s larynx-feminising roar followed, re-recorded with Leckie from the version on 'The Muse EP' and all the more brutal in its Neanderthal sentiment and epic in its elongated chorus howl. Its succinct rock wallop is contrasted by the album's title track, a brooding five-minute epic that sounds like thunderclouds gathering for the first two minutes – a tribal thud of distant drums, a tremulous rattle of bass – while Bellamy hisses and moans about the dark sides of our personalities that we hide from the world: "Controlling my feelings for too long/Forcing our darkest souls to unfold . . . and pushing us into self-destruction". Then the storm breaks in claps of chugging bass and searing vocal acrobatics, and 'Showbiz' lifts off like it's being performed by some Norse god of warfare, complete with a guitar solo that sounds like it's being played by an epileptic Ted Bundy, and a terrifying closing yowl from Bellamy.* Mighty – no wonder the track closed almost every set Muse played that year.

Album-wise, after all, you can only follow it with a ballad to help you recover your breath – this time 'Unintended', Leckie choosing not to add anything at all to the Paul Reeve original version other than a brisk tightening up and mixing (unsurprisingly perhaps, since it bore close resemblance to ballads Leckie had himself produced for Radiohead). After which begins an unnecessarily extensive exhuming of bit players from 'Muscle Museum EP' and 'The Muse EP'; 'Uno' is thoroughly deserving

---

* This is actually the highest recorded note that Matt Bellamy has ever sung, a G#, and the song also has the greatest range of three and a half octaves.

of its place on *Showbiz* for its almighty Godzilla waltz and desperate senti-ment, and, in an album context, the slightly muscled-up 'Sober', as a straightforward hard-rock song, adds welcome melodic beef to the latter half of the record. But even the drastic reworking done on 'Escape' – the added vocal effects and synthetic strings – can't stop its slower sections paling in comparison to 'Unintended' and 'Falling Down', and its heavier central section resembling a shameless clone of The Smashing Pumpkins; and chopping around the arrangement of 'Overdue' (slicing out the mid-tempo bridge and adding a final chorus) doesn't stop it sounding like one superfluous rocker too many. Chris would later claim that the best Muse songs were the ones that sounded great with little alteration and that the more they worked on songs in the studio the worse they got; certainly the more extreme surgery conducted on these two tracks added to the sag at *Showbiz*'s end.

The closing track, 'Hate This And I'll Love You' – the album's third ballad, albeit a chest-bursting one in the vein of Pink Floyd's most bom-bastic 'slowies' – in retrospect sounds like a practice run for more hard-hitting apocalyptica that the band would achieve on later albums. With Matt sounding weary of a relationship in which he's cast as the underdog ("You're making me feel/Like I was born to service you/But I am growing by the hour") over the chirrup of cicadas, the track builds from a mournful waltz on synth and guitar to several crescendos of doomy, Wagnerian rock redolent of 70s prog's more epic excesses. As a closing track it summed up *Showbiz* perfectly: mighty, ambitious, impressively proportioned but slightly out of focus and imperfect, still merely a hint of what Muse were capable of. While many debuts offer the pinnacle of a band's capabilities – 12 great pop songs slaved over for five or six years, an achievement they'll disappointingly fail to match when required to write their second album in six months – *Showbiz* sounded like a band with the grandest of musical aspirations but some way from fulfilling their potential. In a business in which many new bands live or die by their debut album, Muse had made a taster, a showreel of the band they might become. It may have been the best album they could have made at the time, but in the late 1990s – when the concept of allowing a band to grow and develop over three or four albums was laughed at by the record industry as a 70s throwback and bad business sense – to fail to be the best and change the world right from the off was risky indeed.

Recording on *Showbiz* was completed by mid-May 1999 and, as the band ferreted away in the first fortnight in June, mixing the record and working on the artwork and promo designs, Taste Media set about releasing their first 'proper' single – i.e. an unlimited release on an established label. But which would they choose? A quick scan of the track listing and there was only one real contender . . .

* * *

'Uno' was released on June 14, amid a flurry of press interest. A smattering of articles around the release of 'Muscle Museum EP' had now become something of a torrent, the music press' radar tweaked by the buzz that had been building around the trio and the rather snazzy promo CDs of the single – pressed in a semi-transparent design that would become a trademark of Muse promos for the entire campaign. So suddenly, alongside the interest they'd already seen from *NME*, their record was *Q* magazine's Single Of The Week and positive noises were being made in reviews and interviews in *Kerrang!* and *Melody Maker*. On a short tour of the UK's least glamorous venues – the Wolverhampton Varsity, Southampton's Joiners Arms, the Chelmsford Army & Navy and so on – to promote the single and warm-up for their flurry of festival dates, Matt was introduced to the concept of the 'phoner', as *Dazed & Confused* contact him in his tour bus bunk while in Manchester.

It's one of Matt's first batch of press interviews and he's cautious and wary about how much of himself he should reveal, so he naturally becomes a spout of essential, harmless trivia. His singing is influenced by Jeff Buckley and Deftones. He finds it easier to knock out dark songs than happy ones. He considers Bach, Palestrina and choral music to be "godlike". His favourite drink is champagne and he loves gourmet food. He never writes a song down as he composes them, he just remembers them if they're good enough. Muse is basically the reason he lives. Yes, he likes Radiohead, in fact, alongside Nirvana they're the band that means the most to him from the 1990s, but he doesn't think Muse are just a copycat Radiohead band. No, he's not met Madonna yet – in fact, Dom doesn't even think she knows she's signed them.

The press punch was minor, but it made its dent. On June 21 Muse were in Wolverhampton when they heard that 'Uno', with barely any radio play outside of *The Evening Session*, had charted at number 73. The chorus cry of, "You could've been number one" may have been thwarted, but the alternative nation's interest had been sparked: four days later, when Muse stepped out onto the New Bands Stage at Glastonbury Festival at 1 p.m. on a sweltering hot afternoon – not exactly the most prestigious of slots at the UK's most legendary annual hippyfest – they were met by the sight of slam pits full of early convertees down the front and, behind them, roughly 3,000 curious indie fans craning their necks to see what all this Devonshire Radiohead fuss was about. The attention, and 'Uno''s chart position, was a major confidence boost to Matt, Dom and Chris and it coasted them through a sprinkling of festival dates in Germany – at Neubiberg's Southside festival and the Hurricane festival in Scheessel – to a riotous gig at London's 100 Club, which Matt would later claim to be one of his favourite Muse gigs ever. Three days later, and still buzzing, their Glastonbury experience was repeated at Scotland's T In The Park, a packed and expectant tent won over by the ferocity and grandeur of Muse's rock ambition.

The crowds were expanding. The press was imposing. The charts were cracking. The tours kept on coming. And, slowly, things began to get ever so slightly out of control . . .

* * *

On July 15, Muse's huge family home of a tour bus rolled into Portsmouth to start a seven-date joint headline tour with Anglo-Dutch punk-pop band Cay, with whom Matt claims to have been already well acquainted by this time, having played with them many times, although details of these previous dates are lost in the mists of time. The band on board smoking dope and listening to Nirvana, Travis, the Deftones and Tom Waits were excitable (they'd just returned from their second show in France, at the 500-capacity New Morning club in Paris for a radio event), but tense. It was to be a claustrophobic tour – the cram of bodies into the tiny venues to see them meant that Matt had never played so close to the audience before, particularly at the Birmingham Foundry, a glorified corridor where Muse played on the foot-high stage crammed into an alcove next to the bar – and one fraught and askew with tensions, with the trio them-selves on opposing mental time-frames. Appreciating the opportunities opening up to them, Matt was so keen to make sure he didn't mess the shows up that beforehand he was withdrawn, incapable of dealing with large crowds, nervous to the point of nausea. All of that dissipated the second he hit the stage, wrenched out in vital and violent performances – guitars were lobbed across stages, drum kits demolished, injuries narrowly avoided. After the shows Matt was far more relaxed and exuberant, but by then Chris, whose girlfriend was by this point extremely close to childbirth, would often be making his excuses and leaving for the frantic drive back to Teignmouth for the night.

Plus, for the first time there was the almost constant presence of a journalist from the music press, to report any misdoings or salacious comment that might slip out. Their naivety was exposed that very afternoon, with Chris telling a journalist from the *Portsmouth News* that Teignmouth was a dreadful place to live as a teenager, dead in winter, full of tourists in summer and catering only for the needs of the retired. Within months his words would come back to haunt him in the most comical of fashions.

With drink and dope flowing freely, the tour was peppered with incident. In Birmingham, Matt became convinced that a writer from *Melody Maker* has set Cay's singer Anet up by getting her so drunk before the show that she fell off the stage, and vowed not to let journalists travel with Muse in the future. It was an opportunity missed for the hack responsible, since, on the way to the next night's gig in Leicester, the Muse tour bus broke down and the band performed an impromptu acoustic set in the forecourt of the Leicester Forest East service station to a select crowd of Midlands lorry drivers. At the unavoidable date at the Exeter Cavern the band were the image of professionalism, conducting a US interview after the gig* before Chris fled home to be with his budding family; the very next night at the Liverpool Lomax they seemed a frayed and untamable proposition, with Matt hammering his guitar so hard that all of the strings snapped.

The scent of riot was in the air. And five days later and 5,000 miles away, it kicked off in earnest.

---

* This was filmed by Maverick; the set list was 'Uno', 'Cave', 'Sunburn', 'Falling Down', 'Agitated', 'Overdue', 'Muscle Museum', 'Escape', 'Unintended', 'Showbiz', 'Fillip' and 'Do We Need This?'.

SAFTA JAFFERY

What was the deal between Muse and Taste Media?
"Muse signed a six-album record deal with Taste Media in 1998, just before their appearance at In The City in Manchester. It was agreed that Dennis and I would manage the band, but would do it for free as we had been granted the recording and publishing rights. Muse and Taste together were in control of every aspect of the band's creative and business output, from making the recordings to creating their videos and artwork and setting up the numerous tours. I had devised a system where whenever Muse wanted to make a recording or create a video, each territorial licensee was contractually obliged to contribute their territorial market share percentage, which had been pre-determined in terms of finance to enable the band to realise their ambition on each particular project. Also, each territory provided a guaranteed tour support financial shortfall, enabling the band to tour extensively in each territory whenever the right opportunity presented itself. This model meant that no particular label had to pay out the full 100 per cent of any of the cost, just affording to contribute whenever necessary. This was particularly important as we recognised from the beginning that it would be the live performances through touring that would eventually help Muse find their fans and believers, as the band's recording output in the early days was too challenging and alternative for mainstream radio. And as there were, and still remain today, very few alternative radio outlets available for the band's music to be heard in mainland Europe outside of the UK, the investment would go into touring, recording and creative videos and artwork.

"So I targeted each particular label in each territory where I already had an existing working relationship, and where I knew I'd be trusted as co-partner to break the band. Each territorial agreement was self-contained and not crossed with the other, meaning that if Muse were to find success in one territory, they would immediately reap financial rewards from that one territory and not depend on whether any of the other territories were successful. In a normal worldwide deal signed with a major label for the world rights, typically a band is paid a global advance that's not recouped until all the monies have been recovered by the label, which has to happen before the band is paid any royalties. Most bands, even with platinum status success in the UK, hardly ever recoup the record company investment, as monies are continually ploughed back into trying to achieve success in the other territories of the world!

"Also, all the creative and marketing decisions were taken by Taste and Muse, therefore allowing the band to have total creative freedom in all of their output from the beginning.

This gave Muse an advantage over any other bands around at that time as it allowed them time to experiment with their creative art, and learn to do things in their own way without the usual pressures and compromises that are normally expected when climbing the tall ladder to success. It was a very innovative and original artist-development method that would allow the band time to grow and mature in the most natural way, and that had not been done before.

"Dennis and I were completely instrumental in making the band happen. We were the label, we created everything, we signed a six-album deal with the band and Warners then bought the company off us, with me retaining the name and logo of Taste. After the three albums, because all of the licence deals were up, Warners bought the Muse contract from Taste. After which Dennis and I decided to go our own way, with me then buying out Dennis's interest in the publishing company Taste Music Ltd, as I'm still the band's publisher for the first three studio albums, so my involvement was very serious and still continues and remains active on a day-to-day basis.

"I put Muse with all my mates around the world. All these licensee deals that I did, that was all the stuff I learnt when I worked at Magnet, these were all of the people I already knew. After I left Magnet I set up a producer management company called SJP, which was managing all these producers. Having been in A&R for all those previous years, I fancied getting back into making records again, and that's when Dennis and I decided to team up, because he had the studio down in Cornwall, and because that was one of the studios where a lot of my producers used to enjoy working it made sense for us to do it together. Also, Dennis needed someone in London who had the contacts. He didn't really know the business side, as he'd never done it before, so I was the guy who'd done it for real and had the business relationships, and that's why we made a really good team. The band had the closer relationship with Dennis, so when he brought me in it all worked really well from everyone's perspective."

Whose idea was it to license the music out to different labels in the various territories?

"That was my idea, because having been in the business for as long as I had, for a band like Muse who weren't radio-friendly, I knew we could only break them through touring, and if we had made a worldwide deal with one label then we wouldn't have got the real shot at breaking the band internationally in the way we managed to do. So it was my idea to do the licensing thing. So I said, 'Let's do this territorially and build the deals heavy on tour support', because I knew we wouldn't get them on radio. All the deals I did were three-album licence deals with reversion rights after a certain term period and they were also all individual territorial deals.

The Maverick one was interesting because that was the one that never took off.

"The Maverick deal was good because when I took Muse to see Columbia records there was this girl called Nanci Walker, who now works at Universal Music in LA, and if it hadn't have been for her we wouldn't have got started. It's because of her enthusiasm that we were flown to Los Angeles. We did that Santa Monica Pier showcase, and the reason why it was done in the morning that day was because Columbia wanted Rick Rubin to see the band. He was mixing Tom Petty at the time, that was the only time he could come out, that's why the showcase was done at 11 a.m. on the Santa Monica Pier."

Where exactly did that gig happen?

"It was actually on the Pier itself. It was an indoor venue, there was a little building on the Pier – it had a roof on it, but it wasn't like a traditional gig, they had to bring in a PA and stuff. It was just Columbia's sense of humour to put us on there."

How was the American experience different from England, where there was no particular interest at In The City that year?

"It was a time when Britpop had just peaked, and everyone had decided guitar bands were over. So even though Muse were one of the three bands that everybody thought were the best at In The City, none of the A&R people could get excited about them. And I took everybody to see them, even after In The City, when we did the show at the Barfly, and then we did another one at the 100 Club. I took everyone I had contacts with at A&R but nobody got it, they all looked at me saying, 'This would never happen.' That's why I said to Dennis, 'Let me go to America cos we're not gonna get arrested here; let's go to America and let's see what happens.' So I went off to America with all these packages and I got a really good response out there. People got it there because the Deftones and bands like that were happening over there; [Muse's] sound was more in tune with what was going on in America. It was too hard-edged and sophisticated for here. In America the A&R people seemed to get it – I really got some good reactions from the A&R meetings."

You were practically ready to sign up with Columbia before Maverick rolled up, right?
"Yeah, what happened was, when we did that Santa Monica Pier showcase, Rick Rubin thought they were great. He actually came up and whispered in my ear and he said, 'They're absolutely fucking brilliant – you've got the 21st-century Beatles.' That's what he said to me. And then he said, 'Can you guys stay in town, cos I wanna hang with you.' We were due to fly out later that afternoon. So, the other guy who was there from Columbia was a guy called Tim Devine, and Tim was the head of A&R at Columbia so, Tim having seen Rick Rubin's reaction said, 'OK, we'll change the flight and you guys can stay for another couple of days.' So when I went back to the hotel there was a message there waiting for me from Guy Oseary, who was one of the A&R guys I'd seen on my original American trip, and Guy said, 'I know you guys are in town – you've got to showcase for me,' and I said, 'We can't, we're here on Columbia's time and money,' and he said, 'Well if you don't showcase for me I'm gonna fly you back again next week!' and I thought, 'Oh fuck, I don't wanna do that, we've just come all this way.' So I said, 'Let me get back to you', and so I called Tim Devine and said, 'Look, we're gonna do another label showcase, are you OK with that?' and he said, 'No, we're not OK with that, you're here on our money.' So I said, 'Supposing I get the other label to pay for all the extra hotel rooms for the couple of days . . .' and he still wasn't happy about it, but I'd just made a decision [that] we're gonna do it. So I called Guy back and I said, 'All right, this is the deal – if you pay for the hotel rooms and fly us back business class, we'll do it!' So he agreed to it and the next day we did the showcase for Maverick. He turned up with

Steve Jones and stopped them after the second or third song and said, 'This is why I got involved in the music business – you guys are the shit. You guys are great.' It was at a rehearsal room. The next day he called me, saying, 'Look, you've got the best band in the world, I really wanna sign the band. I know you've got Columbia interested but I guarantee I'll give you anything you want. This is my lawyer's number.' So I took the number and gave it to my lawyer over there and they literally gave us everything we asked for. It was unbelievable for a band that nobody wanted. When I told him that it was only gonna be for America he wasn't happy, but he said, 'If that's the only way I'm gonna get it, I'll do it.'"

So did all the territories slip into place after that?
"The other ones did and actually the UK was last, because the next deal I did was with Tim and Petra at Motor Music, which went through Universal in Germany. Tim again had been an old mate of mine, whose background was Polydor records Germany A&R for a long time, so I'd made records with him back in the day. He'd already known I'd been working with the band and he'd already expressed interest, so that was the next deal that we did. And after that there was this new label in France called Naïve, they were a completely new independent label set up by Patrick Zelnik, who had ran Virgin France for 18 years, and their head of A&R was Frédéric Rebet, who had previously worked at Sony Music, where I had worked on some projects with him, and again they gave us the deal we asked for. So we did Naive and then we did Benelux, I signed them to Play It Again Sam in the Benelux territories and again I did that directly, with Kenny Gates and Leo Van Schack. And then we were gonna sign to a label [in the UK] called Disco Valante – remember them? It was run by Andy Ferguson – he managed the Undertones – and Julian Palmer. But they were attached to Sony, so every time they sent me a deal memo it was like 55 pages long and was completely different to what we'd talked about. Also at the time I was negotiating a deal with a guy called Michael Parisi, who was then the head of A&R at Mushroom in Australia. He loved the band, he thought they were fucking brilliant and he thought Korda [Marshall] was completely wrong for turning them down. And I said, 'All right, forget the UK, I'll do the deal with you for Australia.' So I was actually in LA that time and Korda was flying through LA from Australia. I met him at the Sky Bar at the Mondrian and we were talking

about the deal for Australia, then he turned around and said, 'What about the UK?' And I said, 'You didn't want the UK.' And he said, 'Well I want it now.' And I said, 'Korda, I know you, you'll change your mind next week!' So I wrote out the terms on a napkin and I made him sign it. I've still got that napkin, and that was the deal. And he resented me for it, cos the deal he gave me was fantastic for us but expensive for them. And that was pretty much the contract – the lawyers had to then work off the napkin. That's how it ended up in the UK. Thank God to be honest – I knew Mushroom were our best bet and Korda was the the right partner to be with, cos he totally got it once he was on board."

How was Showbiz *financed?*
"It was financed through the Maverick deal. It was a two-album firm deal. It was a pretty decent advance and I'd already worked out that it would pay for the first album."

And you chose John Leckie?
"John was already sort of on board. John first saw the band with me at the Water Rats and I'd already played him all the demos. He'd already made a good connection with Matt after the Water Rats show. And he came out to CMJ just to support us really. It was just a question of finding the right label home so we could do it the way John wanted to do it."

Were you happy with the record?
"Absolutely. I think the record came out really well. There was very little input from us – we totally trusted John and the band trusted him, and they went in and did it."

PAUL REEVE

How did you feel about Showbiz *when it was done?*
"I thought it was a good first record. I was in awe of working with John because he was and remains one of my heroes, so that whole experience was as much to do with John as it was to do with the band for me. When the record was finished you can't really hear it for a bit, and when I came back to it I thought it was good. I still think it's a good and powerful

record, and I think it's their most honest record still. I was proud of it, my input into it."

Your input was more to do with the direct pop songs, whereas with John they tended to meander off into more experimental territory, as they continued to do on Origin . . .

"That's my thing, I'm a songwriter and I love the pop song as a form. You're actually quite right, I hadn't noticed that to be honest, and prog, which I suppose is what they are now, is not my thing. Things like 'Uno', things like 'Unintended', to me they are really beautiful pop songs. I can certainly remember a conversation where I convinced Matt that he should record 'Unintended', and in typical Matt fashion he said, 'Oh, I've got shitloads of those!' He thought it was too grown-up. It is slightly out of context with what they were doing, but I love that element of Matt's songwriting and I'm hoping at some point in the future he'll come back to it because, as a pop songwriter, there aren't many around like him."

MATT BELLAMY

"Around that time we were getting waltzed around in limos and private planes and it was way ahead of its time, we'd only sold one record. I thought that was a bit weird, but this definitely could be going some-where. When that all fell through and I went back to painting and decorating it inspired me, made me think that if we can have that effect, even if it's a big bubble, maybe we can do it again. It was a few years down the line when we could afford to go on our own plane ride. Hanging around the limos and planes at 18 or 19 was a bit of an eye-opener, but it wasn't until six years later that I actually got in one I'd paid for myself! A lot of people were saying, 'They're gonna be huge', and I thought maybe, but not on the first album. I think that would have been a dreadful time if we'd hit the big time at the age of 20, with the first album, because it would have been downhill from there."

Chapter Three

EVERY generation, it is said, gets the revolution it deserves.

In the repressive society of the 60s, rebellion meant permissiveness, epitomised by the flower power movement and encapsulated one wet and wanton August weekend in 1969 in Bethel, upstate New York, at the Woodstock Festival on Max Yasgur's farm. Half a million convened there over three days, sick of the buttoned-down rigidity of society and the senseless brutality of Vietnam, intent on getting naked, getting unified, getting down.

In the permissive society of the 90s, however, rebellion meant violence. So the first major re-creation of Woodstock, in 1994, ended up being a boneheaded, mud-flinging wreck of a festival, and by 1999 a post-punk American youth stoked up by the senseless brutality of the first Gulf War, politically lobotomised by a one-sided, pro-war media and high on Limp Bizkit's nu metal nihilism, convened on Griffiss Air Force Base for their own generation's Woodstock. They wanted their own brand of rebellion, just like their parents did, but the freedoms they wanted were to get pissed and destroy.

The event's organisation didn't help matters. Held on a hazardous waste site by promoters intent on making as much money from the weekend as possible (a philosophy in direct contrast to the original festival's counter-culture ideals), ticket prices were high and no outside food or water was allowed on site. After a thorough frisking at the gates, ticket holders had water bottles confiscated before being allowed onto a concrete site with no shade in 100 degrees heat, only to find that the official vendors were charging $4 for a bottle of water, $12 for a pizza and $15 for a bag of ice. When vendors asked the organisers to allow them to lower their prices the organisers refused, claiming this would lead to a loss of profits. The two stages were a huge distance apart and there were insufficient toilets for the numbers on site; as they began to overflow, several were overturned by angry rock fans and nearby water pipes pulled out of the ground. The line-up, meanwhile, was unlikely to provoke too chilled and loved-up of an atmosphere – Limp Bizkit, Metallica, Rage Against The Machine, Megadeth and Korn all took their places beside the Willie Nelsons, Dave Matthews Bands, George Clintons and Bruce Hornbys of the old guard.

When Muse took to the main stage early on Sunday afternoon – the final of three excruciating and expensive days for the crowd – they could see the festival was at breaking point. Rubbish and human waste covered the site, the crowd was chanting and banging drums as if in protest, and in the distance there were outbreaks of fighting. Fires had already been lit, but it would be some hours later that Woodstock '99 disintegrated into chaos, when Limp Bizkit performed knucklehead anthem 'Break Stuff', while singer Fred Durst rode across the moshpit using a slab of plywood wall ripped from a production tower as a makeshift surfboard. During Red Hot Chili Peppers' closing set, an audio delay tower caught fire during 'Under The Bridge' and many more fires sprung up in response, encouraged by the band playing Jimi Hendrix's 'Fire' at the behest of Jimi's half-sister. Sections of the hot and frustrated crowd went on a destructive rampage, tearing down or setting alight toilet blocks and makeshift structures, overturning and looting vendors' trailers and cash machines. The MTV crew were evacuated for their own safety; 38 arrests, four rapes and one death were reported.

The 90s youth generation had gotten the revolution it deserved. Muse, having left the site long before the trouble flared in earnest, would later claim they had great fun at the festival, and joke that John Entwistle's bass lines must have started the riot. But Matt Bellamy would look back at the events of Woodstock '99 and see in its rage and blare a blind and bullish America, lied to and subordinated by its leaders and media, angry and frustrated at being the bottom rung of a society it had no control over, lashing out at some vague concept of 'authority' the only way it knew how.

And it set him thinking. When *NME*'s Stephen Dalton interviewed Bellamy in New York that year, Matt was chomping on a big cigar in a swanky Manhattan hotel, trying out the US megastar dream for size, and he was suddenly seized with dangerous thoughts. A new side to Matt Bellamy began to emerge – a young man unafraid to describe himself as tormented and troubled and plagued by the multitudinous woes of the world. Heavily affected by the events of Woodstock, he'd begun to see a downward spiral in the American culture around him, started to see signs of impending apocalypse. "There's a lot of fear hanging around, which people are trying to deny, but there is. And when that's over, hopefully there will be a positive thing. Either that or extremely negative, hahaha! And it will ALL be over . . ."

★ ★ ★

Though Muse saw no more fear and loathing on their nine-day whistle-stop tour of America that July, they certainly did see several other seditious flaws in America's cultural make-up. The most noticeable: indifference. If you're a new band who haven't played every chicken shack and barnyard in America for two years solid or don't have a major song on radio, a movie soundtrack or a video game, you are nobody. And so Muse found as they played a series of small shows in Boston, Chicago, San Francisco and Chicago, culminating at the WEA Convention in LA, playing to rooms of 30 DJs and industry-vibe chasers, pretty much the only people in any given city who'd have had cause to hear of them. The exception was at East Village indie hangout Brownie's in New York, when Manhattan's industry crowd crammed onto the guest list but then largely failed to show up at the tiny backroom bar to see them. MTV had a table reserved; Anthony Kiedis from Red Hot Chili Peppers hung by the bar. Otherwise there was a smattering of industry support present and two actual paying fans with a sign reading 'Teignmouth'.

The second was that most painful of US touring traditions, the DJ meet and greet. With no one central national radio station in America along the lines of Radio One, the power in breaking bands lies with the local and college radio DJs and it's expected of touring bands to make visits to the main alternative stations in every city they visit to personally thank the DJs there for playing, or for considering playing, their song. Trouble is, nobody told Muse this. Sticking to their written schedule, they turned up at their first radio station on the tour with guitars, expecting to play an acoustic session, only to find not a session studio but a meeting room with lots of food laid out on a long table, populated by a dozen or so radio station workers nibbling on it and ignoring them. When they asked someone where they should set up for the session they were met with a chuckle of, "You're not going to play!" and a grunted thanks for buying the pizzas. It turned out Maverick had wangled the meet-and-greet to make it look as though Muse had bought takeaway for the entire station staff. It only took a couple of embarrassments like this before Maverick were organising for Muse to play their acoustic sessions – by the time they reached LA they were dutifully booked in to play on KCRW Morning Eclectic show; a bootleg of this set has been released under the title 'Muse Live On 89.9 KCRW Radio – The Showbiz Acoustics'. It included unplugged versions of 'Sunburn', 'Falling Down', 'Overdue', 'Uno', 'Cave', 'Unintended' and 'Muscle Museum'.

From the WEA Convention, Muse flew straight to Germany, because Europe was calling. Ever since they'd signed their European deals, the labels concerned had been crying out for the band to come and tour in earnest there, so Muse made extensive plans to do so. It was to be a decision that would gain them much respect and devotion from European crowds, who often felt ignored or short-changed by minimal tours by their favourite British bands, and the benefits were almost immediately apparent. After a stop-off at the Rees Haldern Pop Festival in Germany, Muse arrived in St Malo's Route Du Rock shindig for a day that would become a highpoint of their early career. Only a month and a half before they'd played in Paris at a radio-show gig to 500 awestruck punters; that day, 9,000 people flocked to St Malo to see them. Excited by their almost instant acceptance in France (particularly after their disheartening US experience), over the next year and a half Muse would tour the continent repeatedly, their fanbase exploding in appreciation and adoration for a band that seemed to want to come back and play for them again and again.

Finding Europe to be their playground, the band hit Cologne in Germany for three days of bizarre gigs, from a fifth anniversary party for the label Motor to a Visions after-show party, from a televised party in the streets to a festival actually called Bizarre. They were itching to explore these thrilling new territories more, but first they were needed back home. There was, after all, pressing business to attend to.

* * *

Chris became a father to Alfie Wolstenholme, his first son, in September. When his girlfriend, Kelly, had suggested the name before the birth he'd baulked at it, thinking it sounded like the name of a drug dealer, but when he first set eyes on his son, his cheeky little face convinced Chris he was an Alfie. The birth itself slotted in fairly smoothly with Muse's punishing touring schedule – the only problem it seemed to cause was Chris' late arrival for the band's first-ever set at Reading Festival. Obviously this was something of a landmark for Muse (although still some way short of 'making it' by headlining the Main Stage), but Chris' bandmates were understanding when a train delay on his race up from his girlfriend's side meant that they had to cut back their afternoon set on the Carling Premier stage – the tiny new band's stage, that day swamped with whooping converts from Glastonbury and beyond.

If Chris, aged only 20, was taking an early opportunity to grasp at adulthood and settle down before Muse's career became too hectic (he also stopped drinking too much before shows around this time, to stop himself messing up the songs onstage), his bandmates were using Muse's success to indulge quite the opposite ends of the psyche. What groupies were about at the time were generally shared between Dom (Muse's only single member) and the road crew (many of whom were also enjoying their first taste of touring life), and Dom and Matt were increasingly disposed towards the hedonistic life of alcohol, dope and potential mischief.

And while Chris was busy buying baby toys, Matt was buying the ultimate in boy's toys. With his first major cheque, he bought himself a jet-pack. At least, that's what the press slaveringly called it. In fact it was a paramotor – essentially a paraglider (like a parachute) and a propellor driven by a 50cc engine: when worn on your back it allows you to float upwards from standing up to 10,000 ft, oxygen allowing. Matt had read about such a contraption and always dreamed of owning one in his most Rocketman fantasy moments, so it was his first treat to himself when the money started coming in, at a cost of £6,000. His plan was to fly it over festivals with a huge banner flapping from his back reading 'come and see Muse play', or to take it along on a US tour and fly it into the Grand Canyon – get it up to 8,000 ft, turn off the engine and simply float down into the abyss.

In spare moments between tours for the next few years he'd take the paramotor to Kemble Airfield in the Cotswolds and fly it up to around 3,000 ft, spinning around as he took off and then flying at will, having the best time of his life, feeling like he was on the next step of the evolutionary ladder, a leap ahead of the toilet-trashing sub-humanity of Woodstock. But above 3,000 ft things started going a bit blurry and Matt never found time to complete his lessons. Gradually, scuba diving would take precedence as Matt's favourite extreme leisure activity.

The other Muse business of autumn 1999 was rather more down-to-earth. At a Borderline gig, they'd been approached by an American band also called Muse who owned the rights to use the name for live shows, so Taste Media were locked in trans-Atlantic communications to make sure the US Muse, who were about to break up, would give them rights to the moniker (they did). Safta Jaffery was also deep in negotiations to finalise distribution deals for Muse in Japan and Scandinavia to add to their four existing worldwide deals, and spread their net of global conquest even further. Plus there was Muse's first TV studio performance, for Canal + in Paris, to film (playing 'Uno'), and a minor five-date UK tour to promote the biggest slice of business at hand.

The album version of 'Cave' was released as a single on September 6[*] over two CDs: the first included a remix of 'Cave' and 'Twin', a renamed re-recording of 'Balloonatic' from the *Helping You Back To Work Volume 1* compilation; the second was backed with 'Coma' from 'The Muse EP' and 'Host', a new song that sounded, rather familiarly, like a plea to be released from a soul-sucking relationship (or place). As Muse jetted back to America to begin three weeks of solid promotional interviews to plug their forthcoming debut album (including one gig in NYC, at SOBs), the single quietly garnered Single Of The Week plaudits in the rock press and, charting at number 53, crept up close enough to swipe at the neck of the Top 40.

With almost a year of solid groundwork complete, it was time for the big push. It was, as they say in the more dramatic entertainment circles, showtime.

* * *

On October 4, 1999, Muse's debut album, *Showbiz*, crash-landed in the UK onto a rather desolate rock landscape.[†] Sidestepping direct critical pigeonholing, the record fell between two stools. It had molten riffs and pop hooks, so was it the bastard child of nu metal? If it was, bands like Korn, Limp Bizkit and Slipknot (a riot-inducing bunch of rock freaks

---

* This was the second single release in the UK and France but the first in the US, where three versions of the CD were produced.
† Curiously, it was released earlier in Europe and America, on September 6 in France, September 20 in Germany and the 28th in the US.

dressed in numbered boiler suits and hellish Halloween masks, famed for pissing on each other onstage and carrying dead crows around in jars to sniff when they wanted to get 'in the zone') had made the genre, in the eyes of the mainstream press, at best an icky amusement and at worst a bad joke in a baseball cap. Muse wore black on the back cover and played epic operatic guitar music like 'The Bends', so were they the New Radiohead? If they were, they were four years too late – Radiohead themselves had turned their backs on such crass bombast with *OK Computer* two years earlier and, rumour had it, were in the middle of making an experimental, minimalist laptop album. Alternative music had lost its taste for pompous rock guitars and found solace in nice men on stool-wearing cardigans and woolly hats. The copies of the album sent to journalists were certainly attention-grabbing – the CD was contained between two clear square Perspex sheets held together through the centre by a plastic nut and bolt, with a tiny spanner taped to the front* – but, unsurprisingly, *Showbiz*, while never feeling the full thrust of the critical rapier, was often stung by its swipes.

The moody, black-clad shot of the band on the back cover along with the enigmatic cover painting of a faceless space lady in a white minidress stepping into a volcanic puddle on a distant planet of fire and ice, brought down accusations of pretention and suspicions that the band were closet cybergoths. Some reviewers found Matt's foggy lyrical angst grating, others noted their universal appeal: they were rock enough for the metal kids, tuneful enough for the pop kids and miserable enough for the indie kids. Suede, Nirvana, Mansun and (oh yes) Radiohead were regularly namedropped; the words 'Wagnerian uber-anthems' began their decade-long tenancy in Muse reviews; the ratings rarely ventured too far from the six out of 10 region. *Showbiz* received a grudging semi thumbs-up, approached by wary but intrigued reviewers in the same way you'd approach some kind of pulsating alien roadkill.

Bereft of both the career-killing critical mauling and the gushing universal review-as-fellatio that would have seen them bask in the limelight as press darlings for six months before disappearing to escape the hype, *Showbiz* sloped to number 69 on the first week of release, purchased by every one of Muse's rabid fanbase and pretty much nobody else. Out on a tour of Britain's medium-sized academy venues supporting Skunk Anansie

---

* This item, with spanner included, will fetch around £50 from collectors.

as this news seeped through, the truth of their situation, and the work still ahead of them, dawned slowly on Matt, Dom and Chris. If their explosive live performances were winning them fans and only their fans were buying their record, they were going to have to tour and tour and tour like their lives depended on it. Which, at that unsure juncture on the road to success, it felt like it did.

But even as they were turning the pages of the tour schedules being sent through to them with increasing regularity, tours that now ran on well into the new millennium with barely a break for breath, a few page turns later awaited magical news. Sales figures in France – where *Showbiz* had been on sale for a month already and where cynicism and scene-chasing are not so much part of the reviewer's lexicon – showed that the album was selling five times faster than in Britain, with 35,000 sales and rising. And a similar surge was underway in Germany. On the continent, *Showbiz* was something of a minor sensation.

Enough of the 'building a local fanbase' business; it was time to go and give the European labels what they wanted.

* * *

To say that Muse's various European tours at the close of 1999 and the dawn of 2000 were tempestuous would be understating the case. They were by turns thrilling, fraught, overwhelming, drunken, violent, inspiring and a bloody good laugh. And they very nearly blew Muse's minds.

The first thing that stunned them were the crowds. Great, screaming, swarming crowds. Hooking first onto a short Pavement tour of Germany and then onto a tour of France sponsored by *Les Inrockuptibles* magazine, the band were amazed by their reception. At the Pavement gigs at Hamburg's Logo club, Berlin's Knaack or Munich's Incognito, a sizeable portion of the crowd had turned up to see them rather than Stephen Malkmus' wonky alt.rock crew, while the five-date *Les Inrockuptibles* tour began with rammed venues chanting their name and ended with all-out chaos. Racing over from an acoustic session at Paris' Oui FM on October 11, they arrived at the MCM Café for a televised gig on MC channel to find the venue packed with 500 people, with another 500 baying for entry on the street; the gig itself was a near riot, with fans falling onto the stage in the crush. Similar scenes were repeated at a Virgin Megastore show, where hundreds couldn't gain entrance.

In the midst of all this hullabaloo, perhaps France missed an important evolutionary step in Bellamy's songwriting: several new songs destined for B-sides were played on this tour ('Recess', 'Do We Need This', songs adored only by the most avid of megafans), but the previous night in Toulouse they'd premiered a new track called 'Nature_1', the first example of Matt employing apocalyptic lyrical themes. Addressing a lover, a God, a political figurehead or possibly himself (depending on your interpretation), Bellamy likens the object of this fractured relationship song to an earthquake, a broken dam, a natural disaster. Clearly, having seen a bit of the world, his concerns were becoming global.

The second thing that shocked Muse was their own capacity to crack up. Still very nervous and antisocial before gigs, the added pressure of the increased crowds would occasionally push an increasingly control-freaky Bellamy over the edge. Compounded with the swirl of alcohol, soft drugs and the groundhog day disorientation of the touring life – plus the confusion of trying to fathom what his place in this dizzying new world of rock success might be – Matt began to feel less connected to the outside world.

His vision began to blur on regular occasions, he'd often disappear by himself after gigs – out on the town with fans or back to his hotel room with alcohol – and, when frustrated by mistakes made by his largely inexperienced and sometimes shambolic road crew (mostly old mates from Devon and homeless guys they'd taken pity on), his temper would lash out: one night in Vienna, Matt ran an amp trolley across the floor of the venue at Chris in a wild rage, missed his bandmate and hit the mixing desk, causing thousands of pounds worth of damage. (Muse were banned from hiring equipment in Austria or Germany ever again after this incident.) Most gigs would end with his guitar, his amps and Dom's drum kit being trashed as Matt span through it all like a destructive dervish. He never purposely set out to destroy instruments or equipment but, if the gig had a nasty and destructive vibe to it, he'd often try to wrench the sound of pure rage out of guitars that simply couldn't take the abuse. Much of Muse's equipment never made it back from Europe alive.

And then there was the enormity of it all. On November 16, at the invitation of Anthony Kiedis, Muse supported the Red Hot Chili Peppers at the Bercy in Paris. As indoor venues go, you don't get much bigger than the Bercy – with a capacity of 16,000 and a back wall several light years from the stage – it's the equivalent of a stadium with a roof on and a daunting shed for the most experienced band to play to. For Muse the day was simply bizarre – on the way to Paris from Cologne in Germany (where they'd been playing more shows with Pavement), their tour bus had broken down, spewing petrol smoke, in the middle of a forest, which sent them into Blair Witch-style freak-outs. When they eventually arrived they popped into Flea's (RHCP's bassist) dressing room to say hello, only to find him meditating intently. Then they stepped out onto the biggest stage they'd ever played on, intending to blow the back wall clean off the Bercy with their wildest stage tantrums during opener 'Uno', only to find themselves with lead problems that meant they had to stay rigidly on their spots. Yet this (and the other dates they played with RHCP at Hamburg's Alsterdorfer Sportshalle and Bordeaux's Patinoire) brought out the big band within Muse – if playing to small, uninterested crowds as other bands' warm-up act for most of the year had driven them inward, in front of such huge, largely appreciative audiences as these Muse could let their inhibitions go, be more outgoing onstage and have a laugh, like back in the TCC sports hall. The echo of the arena felt comforting, familiar; they almost felt at home. Had you told Muse then that they'd be headlining the Bercy themselves two albums later, they'd have laughed, but just might have believed you.

At the time, though, the thing they couldn't believe was meeting Dave Grohl. The ex-Nirvana drummer's band, Foo Fighters, were also on the bill at the Bercy, and the starstruck Muse wasted no time in tracking him down after the show. Invading the Foos' dressing room they sat drinking with the amiable rock god for some time – "I'll have to get fucking drunk to be as good as you were tonight!" Grohl memorably exclaimed – before going awol with him for four hours. When they reappeared just in time for their bus call to Bordeaux, Matt was so drunk he was incapable of speech, Chris was falling asleep on his feet and Dom was grinning from ear to ear while swigging from a bottle of Jack Daniel's. It was to be the start of a beautifully unhinged friendship.

If this wild and eye-opening jaunt around Europe took Muse out of this world, however, they were about to be brought right back down to Teignmouth with a bump.

★ ★ ★

They expected to return to Devon that November as homecoming heroes. Local boys done good, the first band ever to launch themselves out of Teignmouth and into the continental big time.

It was, after all, a celebratory week. They'd just played to 16,000 dumbstruck new fans at the Barcy and two days earlier had released their best song as a single: 'Muscle Museum' received a well-deserved double-CD release on November 22. CD1 came backed with a live acoustic version of the lead track plus 'Do We Need This', a sinister three-chord piano and percussion* creeper that launches into Muse's trademark riffmania for the chorus, seemingly about the vacuous nature of celebrity ("She only exists when she's on a screen"); CD2 boasted 'Pink Ego Box' (previous titled 'Instant Messenger') and a climactic crescendo of distortion and clamour called 'Con-Science'. Muse entered into a marathon of single signing for 'Muscle Museum', signing almost all of the vinyl copies, to the extent that an unsigned copy is deemed rarer by collectors. Showing his mischievous and playful side, Matt scrawled Dom's mobile phone number onto several copies of the single in case any of the fans wanted to give him a call; Howard later changed his number after a plethora of giggling voicemails.

With sales of *Showbiz* remaining steady, and sensing that Muse's time was almost upon them, Taste Media/Mushroom gave 'Muscle Museum' a hefty promotional push, making two videos for the song[†]: one a montage of live shows in Europe for the kiddie-friendly pop channels and the other, intended for MTV in America, a rather more disturbing and moody film shot in a rundown Los Angeles school gym during their promotional trip in September by director Joseph Kahn, a director generally known for rap and R&B videos who was then branching out into the mainstream with promos for Bryan Adams and Backstreet Boys. Intended to show everyday people going about their lives before each undergoing a tearful breakdown, it was, according to Matt, "extremely expensive", a sign of Maverick's overhyping and overspending, which was already starting to

---

* Some of which was played by Tom Kirk.

† Not the first time that Muse had made multiple videos – 'Uno' had a total of three promos, one made up of live footage, one featuring a girl lost in a maze of doors trying to find the room where the band are playing, and one of the band standing on Tower Bridge during rush hour as hordes of commuters push past them, a video they'd later describe as "embarrassing".

worry the band. And while its images are somewhat surreal and suggestive (naked girls on beds or toilets were just some of the shots that didn't make the final video), this was tame compared with some of the proposals they turned down from other directors – ideas they considered perverse, such as that of an eight-year-old boy wandering around with a syringe full of milk that he squirts in people's faces, or which they liked but were deemed unsuitable, like the treatment that opened with the band drinking from the nozzles of petrol pumps.

The promos, along with the addition of 'Muscle Museum' to the Radio One C-List (an essential step in breaking new bands in the UK) was thrusting the song to within inches of the charts (it came in at number 43). And while their labelmasters might have wanted a bigger breakthrough by now, Muse were utterly uninterested in numbers and chart positions and arrived back in Devon feeling like low-key heroes and expecting, naively perhaps, to find their hometown basking in their shared glory. But when Muse arrived for a BBC Radio acoustic session in Exeter a week after the Bercy gig on November 24, they were surprised to be greeted with a less than enthusiastic reaction from the local press.

That day, the *South Devon Herald Express*, which had previously ignored the band, carried a picture of Teignmouth mayor Vince Fusco tossing a copy of *Showbiz* into a dustbin.

The Teignmouth cognoscenti, it turned out, had not taken kindly to Chris' comment a few months earlier about their town. As local politicians hungry for photo opportunities generally do, they'd taken offence at the idea that Teignmouth was a boring place for children to grow up and the suggestion in several national interviews that the town was awash with drugs. "Teignmouth is no worse than anywhere else as far as drugs are concerned," Mayor Fusco fudged in the article. "To start being rude about their hometown, where a lot of people helped them with their music shows a lot of ingratitude now they are about to break the big time." One hopes the journalist recording this quote, like those at the most laughable Comical Ali press conferences, could see the drug-laden ships docking over Mayor Fusco's shoulder, but certainly Muse weren't going to be trodden down by such frantic filibustering.

Declining a request to meet with the Mayor, who wanted to shake their hands for a follow-up photo op, they instead played the BBC session to premiere a gran-friendly new track – a heavily rocked-up version of a song written by Anthony Newley and Leslie Bricusse but made famous by jazz chanteuse Nina Simone, entitled 'Feeling Good', played on guitar for this session instead of the piano Matt would employ for later versions. Matt had been trying for some time to write a song like it because it was one of his mum's favourite records, but, unable to match it, he decided to simply rip off the whole thing instead. Nonetheless, their post-metal take on the tune added a tense sexuality and force to the original's smoky sensuality – the sort of reinvention of a familiar standard that can create a modern classic and snatch a legendary tune as a new band's own, in much the same as Oasis did with 'I Am The Walrus' and Jeff Buckley with 'Hallelujah'. The fact that Bellamy sang the song's third verse through a megaphone only added to their sense of graciously defiling the classics.

Not that the local wrinklies were won over with a touch of nostalgic nudging. At a radio promo for a station aimed at OAPs that afternoon, Muse found themselves bombarded with complaints about their attitude and their music when the phone lines were opened to the public: even the DJ himself turned against them, claiming he hated their records while their studio seats were still warm.

Stressed beyond belief and withdrawing within himself more than ever, Matt developed a thumping migraine before Muse's gig that night at Exeter's Lemon Tree. The band had friends and family in the audience and a small army of local fans, and the pressure to live up to the hype was intense. But the crowd were the polar opposite of the phone-in complainants – the venue raged, the B-sides got bigger cheers than the singles and Muse's local support was resoundingly affirmed. So enthusiastic was the vibe that night that Muse even played a Nirvana-esque instrumental in honour of their big night out with Dave Grohl.

The experience was settling for Muse: after this gig, Chris had two weeks to go home and be with his family and Matt began to focus on his new-found success, to understand it. It was a time of extreme flux for Matt, not least residentially – he would soon have to give up the flat in Exeter because every time he came home from tour he'd find a drunkard or drug addict living in his room, whom he'd have to turf out with extreme awkwardness. Meanwhile, his ambitions of recording the second album (half of which he had already written on backstage pianos whenever he could find one at the venues) in the summer of 2000 had already been put on hold, as he didn't want to make a record too similar to the first.

Catching a New York gig by gravel-voiced experimental bluesman Tom Waits, whose work, along with that of Jimi Hendrix and Captain Beefheart, they had been introduced to by John Leckie during the recording of *Showbiz*, had been a huge inspiration for Muse, giving them warped ideas for their second album like using bones as percussion, voodoo instruments and, well, writing better lyrics. Matt was dissatisfied with his lyrics on *Showbiz*, later claiming that they were half real-life experiences and half raw hatred for everything, including himself, inspired by the dark side that he believed to be in everyone: "You can either be a violent person and go out there and kill people," he told one interviewer, "or you can be in a rock band." Ambitious plans were forming, and these theorems needed time to ferment.

Plus, Matt's on-tour reading material was becoming more scientific and colourful. At the point where his lyrics were beginning to leave behind the concerns of the small-town outcast and take on more universal themes, Matt was beginning to read up on the concepts of string theory, dipping into Brian Greene's *The Elegant Universe* and Michio Kaku's *Hyperspace*, stretching his ideas about the physics of the universe far beyond the superstitious constraints of the Ouija board. On Muse's last tour of 1999, supporting dire pomp-rockers Live around the UK and Europe, Matt readjusted himself: adulation was processable; hedonism was, within reason, allowed – the parties thrown by Red Hot Chili Peppers for their crew after every show had opened his eyes to the possibilities of extravagant post-gig shenanigans, and Muse were keen to have that sort of fun on the road rather than simply having a few post-gig beers in a Travel Inn before bed. They started getting fans backstage for the parties, heading out to local bars after the shows, seeing a bit of the towns they were visiting and requesting soft drugs on occasion – at the Munich date of the Live tour, Muse's request to the label to procure them some weed left them with so much hash left over that they had to give it to a very grateful Everlast (ex-House Of Pain dad-rapper) before they left.

Becoming less stressed and nervous as the final tour rolled on through Copenhagen, Stockholm, Oslo and Dusseldorf*, Matt's vision and focus returned as Christmas approached; he was starting to get used to and

* The band broke off from the tour for one night only to return to the UK to play at the Xfest event at the London Astoria.

comprehend his hectic, head-spinning new career, his status as a rising pop star. He was beginning to have the time of his life.

And he was, coincidentally, writing the song of his life too.

* * *

The millennium celebrations in England were a bit of a damp squib. The fireworks weren't as good as those in Sydney, society wasn't thrust back into the dark ages by a global computer meltdown, and the first paying entrants to the Millennium Dome quickly discovered it to be a pretty pointless waste of money, an upturned white wok that no one could work out what to do with for at least five years.

No, the real millennium fireworks went off six days later in the 1,200 capacity Paradiso club in Amsterdam. During a 17-song set – Muse's longest to date – that opened with the searing jazz firestorm of 'Feeling Good' and premiered a quiet, affecting new song called 'Screenager', concerning the distances that technology places between people in a generation enslaved by television and the internet, something quite miraculous happened; something that would launch Muse out of the also-ran indie league and towards the stadium stratosphere.

Out of a squall of feedback rose a snaking guitar riff, one of the greatest known to man, writhing up the neck of Matt Bellamy's guitar as if trying to wriggle clean out of the song. Halfway through its ascending, hook-drenched cycle it ran headfirst into a brick wall of fuzzy bass and pile-driving drums, and faltered as Matt stepped up to the microphone and, in as close to a baritone as he was capable, crooned the words, "I've exposed your lies, baby . . ."

No one, not even Matt himself (having thrown the lyrics together from random phrases that came to him), knew for sure what 'Plug In Baby' was about; his guitars, the dislocation of the internet generation, some kind of Matrix-style alternate future reality where man is pitted against machine, the concept of putting a 'soul' into an inanimate object such as a computer, an analogy for the touring lifestyle – all of these have been suggested by fans, critics or the band themselves. What the crowd at the Paradiso that night, and every other crowd Muse would play to over the next two and a half years of near-solid touring did know, however, was that it was a tune with the size and ferocity of an erupting Krakatoa, and the chorus yodel of, "My plug in baby crucifies my enemies/When I'm tired of giving" was so overwhelmingly catchy that it made them pogo by reflex. In 'Plug In Baby', Muse had not just written their best song to date, they'd hit career gold. From this point onwards Muse gigs weren't just enjoyable, they were unmissable.

The Amsterdam gig – half full of avid fans and half of curious rock kids checking out what all the fuss was about – had originally been scheduled for a 100-capacity venue but was upgraded at the last minute. This was a story repeated in France, where *Showbiz* was becoming something of a chart mainstay, the following week, when their Paris show at Elysee Montmarte sold out, so an extra show at the much larger 3,000-capacity Bataclan was swiftly added to the end of a week of French shows that January. Similarly, in the UK all the tickets for an advertised Muse gig at University Of London Union in February were snapped up so quickly that the band's agent began planning their next step up the London venue ladder, a headline date at the legendary Astoria theatre. *Showbiz* may have been selling steadily, albeit under the chart radar, but word of Muse's onstage brilliance was clearly out.

For Muse, it felt like they were beginning to dip a toe into the big time. Matt could see it in the attention he was getting from fans – the more obsessive girls would start cornering him in the dressing room all night, at first seeming quite normal types, but then bursting into tears when he went to leave, saying they were in love with him and had dumped their boyfriends to be with him.* And the shoulders they were rubbing with were heavily dusted with celebrity too. Booked onto a support tour with post-grunge rockers Bush in Germany for the rest of January, Muse found themselves watching the band from the side of the stage beside Brian Molko and Courtney Love, and, breaking from the tour for a couple of days to fly back to London to support Irish guitar-pop gods Ash at the Astoria, they took the opportunity to stop off at the *NME* Awards at the Mermaid Theatre on February 1 to collect the award for Best New Artists, as voted for by the magazine's readers. Amazed to have beaten the likes of Eminem and Macy Gray and dazzled to be surrounded by a theatre full of their rock heroes, Muse grabbed their award and rushed for the door: in a display of wild rock'n'roll extravagance (although they'd later claim this was the only way they could possibly make it back to Germany in time for

---

* This apparently happened twice.

that night's gig), Taste Media/Mushroom had hired them a private Lear jet full of champagne and a buffet to whisk them back to Germany to continue the Bush tour as soon as possible.

Little did they know that accepting the Best New Band award would very nearly be the last thing they ever did.

* * *

The start of 2000 was life-threatening for Muse, never mind career-threatening. Most of the band had faced near-death experiences that January: something heavy had fallen off of a lighting rig being erected in France and narrowly missed crushing Chris into a mushy pulp, while Dom had almost bought it several times – once when he hadn't realised you have to pedal Dutch bicycles backwards to brake and almost went under an Amsterdam tram, and once at the Astoria show, supporting Ash, when Matt had thrown a particularly vehement end-of-gig strop, smashed a mike stand to pieces, sending shards of it skidding all the way to the mixing desk, and then swung his guitar into the drum kit, almost decapitating the hapless drummer. On their jet-pack flight to glory, death was Muse's co-pilot.

But as Matt, Dom and Chris sat in their eight-seater private flying swig palace on the runway at City Airport bound for Hanover after the *NME* Awards, they had no idea how close they were about to come to being the latest air-crash statistic.

As the plane taxied from the terminal to the runway, the band noticed something odd out of the window. There were sparks coming from the rear starboard engine. The more the plane's engines were revved, the more sparks were blown out until, seconds before the pilot began his acceleration for take-off, the engine burst into flames. For several seconds as the plane accelerated, Muse thought they were going to die, images of mournful black and white shots of themselves on the covers of all the weekly music magazines flashing through their minds.

Thankfully, the pilot noticed the fire (caused by a fuel compression problem) in time to abort take-off, and a shaky but unharmed Muse tottered off the plane and did what any self-respecting band who'd just narrowly avoided death should do. They got in a cab and went straight back to the *NME* Awards after party to get hideously drunk and joke with this writer about how they'd have sold a million albums the very next day if they'd gone down in a jet-fuel fireball.

Private jets? Champagne and finger foods? Scrapes with an early demise? Drinking in the face of extreme misfortune? As true rock'n'roll heroes Muse had proved their worth, and would go on to do so all year. Back in Europe on the Bush tour, I caught up with the band to interview them for *Melody Maker* in Vienna four days later, only to find that Matt had disappeared after the show in Graz (where his madcap rock'n'roll antics went as far as unscrewing the door handle to his hotel room) in Austria the previous night, and not turned up in time to catch the tour bus the 200 miles to Vienna; the band had arrived to find Matt's bunk empty and a message from the singer saying that he was making his way to the gig by train. After the previous night's show, he explained when he eventually turned up, he'd gone looking for the band's tour manager to use his phone but, when he got to the Irish bar they said they'd be at, nobody from the crew was there, so he'd spent the rest of the night drinking with strangers with worrying sympathies for the neo-Nazi Freedom party, which was gaining support in Austria at the time, and bad taste in nightclubs. After a visit to a club playing Supertramp hits, Matt had ended up at a house party until dawn; when we welcomed him to Vienna that afternoon he had been up for 48 hours' solid. The rock'n'roll Force was strong in this one.

That day's photoshoot in Vienna was strange enough – the *Melody Maker* photographer took us to a strange public park full of surrealist statues depicting enormous babies leading tiny businessmen by the hand, men with no faces and flippers handing tea to demons, and women with their heads flipped open to expose dragon's faces beneath. Dizzy from tiredness and not a little freaked out, Matt had a particularly explosive gig that night at the Libro Music Hall, almost decapitating Dom with a cymbal he threw across the stage, destroying his guitar at the end of the 40-minute set and hurling a microphone stand towards the audience, accidentally hitting a security guard on the back of the head. The guard was naturally furious; backstage immediately afterwards, Muse's tour manager was locked in a heated debate with the head of security and Matt was nowhere to be seen – he'd been warned to get out of the venue and head straight to the airport for his own safety.

Two-day benders, attacks on security, wanton destruction of instruments: the strain and frustration of so long on the road needed a release, and that spring Muse found it in going mildly berserk whenever anything went wrong. Sometimes Matt's freak-outs worked in their favour: that May, slotted between Soulwax and Bush at an MTV Five Night Stand show at Shepherd's Bush Empire, Matt felt the crowd was rather lacklustre during their set and so he went on a wild, guitar-flinging frenzy that totally won the crowd over. Other times they almost demolished the band, such as when a short while later a German MTV promoter cancelled their appearance at the German equivalent of these shows at the very last minute and the band trashed their dressing room, building a pyramid in the middle of the floor with smashed bits of fridge, chairs and food. Matt, still angry, went on to smash up his hotel room, causing £3,000 worth of damages, so upset and negative about the experience that he seriously thought about ending the band that night. *NME* ran an article entitled 'Muse: Reaching Burnout' and, while a little premature, that wasn't far wrong.

Similarly, when they appeared on Chris Evans' influential Channel Four chat show *TFI Friday* to promote the February 21 release of 'Sunburn' as a single[*], they hated their performance: the pianist drafted in to play the piano part messed his part up completely, ruining the intro to the song. To add insult to embarrassment, Chris Evans introduced them as "Sunburn, playing their new song 'Muse'". As he left the stage, orange-shirted and snarling, Matt threw his guitar clean over Dom's head into the backdrop and kicked over the monitors in disgust. Such bad behaviour seemed to be far more under control when Muse played 'Screenager' on Japanese radio station Air West and an eight-song session at the Australian JJJ's Live At The Wireless programme in Melbourne that same week, although it's uncertain if the band travelled to Australia to do this set.

Yet even that tantrum might have worked for them. Muse were gaining a reputation as an exciting live prospect because of their wild onstage antics, and also, in my interview with the band in Vienna, Matt began to show another key side to his character – his inquisitive desire to pick apart the secrets behind science, nature and human faith. In the interview, he exposed curious elements of his character: he claimed to have two personalities, one that wanted to connect with people and a more aggressive side that wanted to scream his anger at the girls in the front row waiting to swoon over Gavin Rossdale. He said that he thought a war was on the

---

[*] CD1 came backed with early track 'Ashamed' and a live version of 'Sunburn'; CD2 included 'Yes Please', originally titled 'Crazy Days' on the early demos, and a live take of 'Uno'. A 12″ of three remixes by Timo Maas and Stephen McCreery was also released.

way, that the population explosion had reached the point where conflict was inevitable. But most pertinently, in trying to explain the thoughts behind 'Sunburn', he delved into the secret world of moths, claiming they always use the moon as navigation, so when they hit lightbulbs they believe they've found their idea of fulfilment, of heaven, but it's false and unreal. He likened this to humans venturing into space, an act he believed represented the human race reaching for something beyond what we were meant for to the detriment of our faith and happiness: it's science destroying essential human truths by disproving the existence of heaven. When asked what his personal 'lightbulb' might be, he replied, "Women".

As 'Sunburn' was one of the last songs written for *Showbiz* it was clear Matt was moving beyond the themes of Teignmouth and how boring it is, and now, more comfortable with talking about himself and his songs in interviews, Matt was opening up his unique intellect and imagination for the benefit of the rock press. He even went as far as to dismiss the album they were touring to promote as "a bit faffy and bollocks" (the first hint that the band weren't entirely satisfied with the way *Showbiz* had turned out, having obsessively dissected its flaws, and were keen to make some serious improvements on album two), and joked that because they had Madonna in their back pocket they had "money coming out of our arses". This snotty, shy little Devon ne'er-do-well was turning out to be quite an intriguing rock'n'roll character after all.

Whether it was the *TFI Friday* tantrum, 'Sunburn's' impressive video featuring the band playing the guilty conscience of a light-fingered babysitter, its appearance on the Radio One C-List or Matt's biology-gone-mad Moth Heaven Theory, this single finally saw Muse break into the charts, hitting an impressive number 22, although on its release Matt curiously claimed that it would be better for the band if it stayed out of the charts. The single's success was capped by a sold-out 10-date headlining tour of the UK (taking in the Bristol Fleece & Firkin, the somewhat larger Manchester Academy and Leicester's Princess Charlotte among other venues, on their way to the London ULU show) as the band prepared for their first major go at breaking America.

And though America would resolutely remain unbroken by the end of it, Muse's eyes would certainly have been opened.

* * *

Whatever they got up to on their lost evening with Dave Grohl after the Red Hot Chili Peppers show at Bercy the previous year, they must have made an impression. For in its wake Muse were chosen by RHCP, long-term fans and mentors by now, as the perfect band to open them and the Foo Fighters on a month-long tour of the American arena circuit in March and April of 2000. Though they were only playing a one-month segment of a five-month tour (after 15 years of heavy touring, Red Hot Chili Peppers liked to take it as easy as possible on the road, only playing for three weeks and then taking 10 days off), the significance of the offer was monumental. Not only were they on the road with two of America's biggest and most respected rock bands – a blooding to be proud of indeed – but they were nightly playing enormous venues to 20,000 potential US fans. The breakthrough possibilities were gargantuan.

At first the dates were intimidating in the extreme. Avoiding all of the East and West Coast cities where there were significant amounts of fun to be had during time off, Muse's section of the tour carved a swathe of funky post-grunge rock through the Bible Belt of America, playing such glamor-ously named venues as the Madison Dane County Expo Center, Dayton Ervin J Nutter Center and the Knoxville Thompson-Boling Arena. These were hangars as bland and soulless as their monikers suggested: all-seated venues with security guards patrolling the aisles to keep people in their allocated seats and eject anyone who might dare to have a bit of a mosh. To a not particularly curious audience waiting for the main event, each night Muse would play standing stock still on their spots, rarely indulging in their usual guitar-flinging bouts of insanity.

And yet, each night, the rock fans of middle America were won over; the whoops got louder, the 'yeah!'s more enthusiastic. Keeping their set short and punchy, Muse learnt during this month that they could tailor their set to big rock audiences and pull it off. They found the confidence to really push their performance to the back wall of a huge room, discov-ered the stadium band within. By the time they got to Roanoke, Virginia, they were inspiring such rabid responses that, in a rather friendlier reminder of Woodstock, the crowd literally tore up the floor of the ice rink while they played, and Dave Grohl sent his schoolteacher mother onstage to calm the crowd with her best schoolmarmish tactics.

But it was offstage that Muse got the majority of their tutelage in rock'n'roll. They learnt that their rock heroes were people too – despite only having played one gig with them, Dave Grohl greeted Chris on the first day of the tour by leaping on his back like the oldest of mates, and the Nirvana sticksman became a close drinking buddy of Muse on the tour. He'd come and jam with them, playing drums during soundcheck while his own band looked on in awe (it was such a rare occurrence, and even rarer when they were joined by RHCP to jam on what Matt would later describe as 'alien funk' tunes, a cross between Michael Jackson and Nirvana), and after gigs they'd hit the local bars mob-handed. One memorable night in Dayton all three bands went out after the show and passed a karaoke bar playing a Foo Fighters song, at which point Grohl raced into the bar, shoved the hapless groaner at the mike out of the way and gave a full-on rock rendition to show him how it was done. The bands stayed drinking in the bar until dawn, singing rock standards with the drunken locals and off-duty cops, who couldn't believe their luck. Strangely, through all this Chris, the band's biggest Nirvana fan, could never bring himself to ask Grohl about his old band – he left that up to a rather more shameless Matt.

Otherwise, their first extensive US tour opened their eyes to opposing ends of the moral spectrum. As they were touring the mid-west Bible Belt, many afternoons were spent deep in theological or religious discussion between themselves or with the pious locals, allowing Matt to expound and explore his unconventional views on religion with the zealots trying to convert him to Christianity – one fan even wrote him a 10-page letter explaining how music was merely his attempt to fill the hole in his life that he should rightfully fill with Jesus. A few hours later, meanwhile, the darker side of touring crawled out: every night the Chili Peppers would hold after show parties for the band and their crew, and this inspired Muse to get more involved with the social element of touring, ushering their own fans and crew past the velvet rope. At these parties Muse began noticing 30 or 40 women waiting around for the chance to meet Anthony Kiedis or Flea, and willing to do absolutely anything to achieve their frankly carnal goals. It was Muse's first glimpse of the organised groupie phenomenon – the girls they'd met on their own tours were never so brash or predatory. And when the girls who didn't get picked to meet RHCP turned their attention to the cute English support band, their requests to come back to their bus for 'some pot' seemed fake and uncomfortable (as, incidentally, did the offers of hard drugs that came their way on these tours). The largely attached Muse were approached by girls far more on this tour than ever before and, for now, the sleazier side of the rock circus discomfited them.

By the time their slot on the tour wrapped up at Chattanooga UTC Arena on April 12, America had proved itself a scary but tameable beast. While most British bands find the scope of the world's biggest music market unfeasibly daunting and baulk at the years of touring it might take to break it, Muse relished the challenge. The US press was making favourable noises too, comparing them to Spacehog and Bush, both UK bands who had exploded in the States while keeping a relatively low profile at home. Muse's short jaunt there had showed them they were the sort of band liable to make serious inroads, and plans were made for major, lengthy US tours.

Little did they know that, as events unfolded between Maverick and Muse, it would be another two and a half years before the band would play in America again.

* * *

Back in England, the numbers were getting big. *Showbiz*, after a slow start, was now fast approaching 250,000 sales worldwide due to its flash-fire popularity in Europe and slow-burn appeal in the UK (where it was approaching the 115,000 sales mark), and the gigs were reflecting their rising stature. Having initially been terrified when their agent told them he was booking a night at the Astoria at the start of June, to the point where Matt told his management to cancel it as they'd never fill it, Muse were frankly flabbergasted when they were told the date had sold out and a second night was planned. This sold out too. Muse, it seemed, were a lot bigger than even they thought.

To get there, Muse played a rag-bag of shows around Europe and the UK, hitting Dublin to play with fading Britpop stars Elastica at Temple Bar and Trinity College's annual student ball, and then starting a fortnight's whiz around France and Germany supported by fellow indie punks Idlewild, including a bizarre one-song gig at the Cannes film festival, where they played 'Showbiz' by the side of the Cannes Canal, filmed for the Nulle Part Ailleurs channel. For the gig Matt brought out an unusual guitar: a Gretsch Synchromatic Sparkle Jet with a spinning hypnotic disc stuck to the front. It obviously wasn't worth much in sentimental value to him, since he lobbed it straight off the platform the second he'd finished playing it.

The first proper gig of that tour, at Lille's L'Aéronef on May 16, was notable for opening with a startling new song. Written during sound-checks on the US tour it was a crunching, ricocheting rock monstrosity with a riff that could topple mountains and another example of Matt's new out-of-body lyrical approach: a song about the expansion of the human mind outside of the physical form, rather like the next stage of evolution into a purely spiritual 'space baby' as described at the end of Arthur C Clarke's *2001: A Space Odyssey*. Later it would have a 'Sunburn'-style piano intro added, but for now it was just the pure, raw bones of 'New Born'.* It would open most shows on the tour and it rocked mightily. Indeed, the song added such power to the set that Dom got so carried away in the feedback crescendo of the final song that he destroyed two drum kits onstage at a cost of £3,000 each. This gig also saw the first live performance of 'Darkshines' from *Origin Of Symmetry*.

It was to be a tour characterised by extreme violence towards backline. Not caring what people thought of him onstage and with his hair now gelled into sharp punk-rock spikes, Matt set about his equipment at the end of each set like an abattoir slaughterman in a hurry. At Le Summum in Grenoble, France, he had a second go at destroying that Gretsch Synchromatic Sparkle Jet guitar by throwing it at an amplifier, shearing the hypnotic disc clean off and into the crowd, where it was swept up by an avid fan. And this was far from the end of it.

When Muse got back from Europe and began a celebratory UK tour to announce the release of the last single from *Showbiz* – 'Unintended', on May 30† – they chose as support rising contemporaries Coldplay. Both bands had been slapped heavily with the 'Radiohead copyists' brush – indeed, Muse were becoming increasingly tiresome of the comparison, Matt at one point exclaiming that, "What we're doing is definitely at least 10 years beyond what they were doing when they started" – so the choice was a brave one, but perhaps designed to highlight the extreme differences between the two.

And the differences were stark: while Coldplay went about perfecting

---

* Called 'New 1' on the set lists, while 'Screenager' at this point was called 'Razorblades And Glossy Magazines'.
† The two CDs were backed with 'Niche', 'Recess' and radio versions of 'Falling Down' and 'Hate This And I'll Love You' from the Oui FM sessions.

their slick, arena-friendly stylings, Muse annihilated every stage in sight. At the Sheffield Leadmill Matt stormed offstage for five minutes when a technical problem reared its head, returning in time to pile into the drum kit. At the Wolverhampton Civic Hall, the gig ended with Matt skipping with his guitar lead and then pouring water over Dom, who was lying prone over a smashed-up bass drum, before the three of them wrestled each other off the stage. At one of these shows Matt somehow managed to get himself lodged into one of the large white plastic cones that made up their stage set during his final song rampage and, unable to physically leave the stage at the end of the song, had to slide himself under the drum riser and wait for the venue to empty before being rescued. At the second of their two sold-out nights at the London Astoria, he ended the gig lying on the floor surrounded by the wreckage of several speaker cabinets and lay there for 17 minutes, quite comfortable, until the tour manager came to carry him off.

He was, in retrospect, considering his position. He was playing massive, sold-out shows of his very own. His single, 'Unintended', had just gone Top 20. He was a bona fide rock star.

And he was seriously losing his mind.

MATT BELLAMY

"Playing the Astoria was a big deal the first time. That was when I was still with my first girlfriend, and at the end of the gig we rolled under the drum riser and I was kissing her a little bit. I was hiding and looking at the crowd as they left but there were a couple of psychos down the front who realised I was there, so in the end I had to roll out and say goodbye. That was a celebration of getting to a certain point, the Astoria."

SAFTA JAFFERY

Did you see the band develop over that year?
"Absolutely. The touring developed them. Soon after we made the record, within six months, they'd become better than on record. At the

time when we made the record that was pretty much where they were at. That was their sound, that was what they were like then. But because we had them constantly out on the road, within six months they'd improved so much that they had become better than the record."

Did you see the potential in the new songs such as 'Plug In Baby'?
"I remember hearing 'Plug In Baby' in Paris. Korda was next to me and I said to him, 'That's the song that's gonna take us to the next place.' And he sort of looked at me and he wasn't sure. But I said, 'That's the song Korda, listen to that fucking riff!' They had all these other songs that they'd been trying out for *Origin* . . . once *Showbiz* was sealed and in the can, but 'Plug In Baby' was always the one for me. When I heard that song I just knew that was the one that would open doors at radio."

What was the plan after you set them running with Showbiz?
"Because we had all these sub-territorial deals, we'd sit down with the licensees and plot out what activity the band were gonna do in each territory. The UK was always a priority, but the UK was a slower burner. Radio One were slowly coming round to the band, but things were moving a lot faster in France. What we did with France is we had key journalists fly to the UK very early on when they were doing UK shows, so we already had a lot of the key tastemaker journalists in our pocket. And they started talking up the band in France, and also their live shows were really escalating very fast. Oui FM in Paris in particular really supported the band."

How did you feel about Showbiz *getting a sniffy reception?*
"It was typical of the time to be honest. Everybody had written them off here, everybody had said they were Radiohead rip-offs. It wasn't easy to fire Anton Brookes [press officer at Bad Moon PR]. You can imagine. Anton's a long-standing friend of mine and he kept telling me, 'It will happen. You've got to be patient.' And two singles in I was going, 'Anton, I can't fucking wait any more mate! I've got to get something.' I remember me and Korda sort of cringing over each other going, 'You're gonna have to tell him', and I'm like, 'Thanks Korda.' And we replaced him with Mel [Brown, Impressive PR] and she was at every Muse gig, right at the front, telling me how brilliant they were. And I thought, Mel might not

be as sophisticated or have the same credibility as Anton, but she was gonna be a bull in a china shop, and that's exactly what she was. As soon as we changed to her, the press started to come through."

Was it exciting when the band started taking off in France?
"Well it was hard work, because we were managing the band and we were also the label, so we were doing everything. I was trying to keep all the licensees in tow. America was putting a lot of pressure on me, saying, 'We were the fucking ones who gave you the money to do this in the first place.' So Guy [Oseary] was always on the phone going, 'You've got to come back, you've got to do this, you've got to do that'. But the frustrating thing for Guy was that when things started to happen here in the UK, Maverick was so behind the scenes. I remember turning up at Maverick when we were Gold here and in his eyes they were still this baby band that he'd signed. And he was still giving us this whole plot that we had to do this, that and the other, which didn't really work any more with our global plans."

Did you see any of the pivotal tour with the Chili Peppers and the Foo Fighters?
"That was a great learning curve for the band. It was a great insight for Matt and the boys to see how things are really done and how the other half live, and an insight into touring in America. They came back almost a different band from that experience. And then we started tightening up on the road crew. Dennis and I decided there are two things we can do: we couldn't afford a proper road crew at the beginning because we had no money – it was just mine and his money, so we decided we'd put them out with local guys from Teignmouth whom they knew. To be honest they were a bit of a motley crew, but we got through it. It didn't really hold them back because those early tours were little toilet tours, and the fact they even had a road crew was a bit of a luxury to be honest with you, because most bands didn't even have that. They weren't the best but I think when we did outgrow them we changed at the right time. Things kept going up as they always did."

How did you cope with the costs of Matt smashing things out of frustration?
"Well, Dennis and I were always on the lookout for new endorsements! That one was never easy, but fortunately we had a lot of endorsement

deals going on at the time. We weren't getting too many complaints but there were times when the tour budgets were coming back and I was thinking, 'Fuck, how am I gonna get that one through?' Each licensee for each territory had to pay their part of it. So the French had to pay whenever Muse toured in France. That's the way we devised it, so the band could go out and play all these shows. Everybody always wondered, particularly in the early days because we managed to secure all the key support tours, 'How the fuck did they get that?' I remember the guy who signed the Foo Fighters in America saying, 'I don't know how the fuck you got your band on this support, they're my fucking band and I couldn't get my bands supporting them! How the fuck did you get yours?' "

GLEN ROWE

When did you start working with Muse?
"It was the release of *Showbiz*. I didn't start touring with them until the second album but I did loads of bits and pieces. I did all sorts of festivals. At the time I was working for Zildjian cymbals and I think I heard them on XFM. I don't know how it came about but I thought they were amazing, and I A&Rd them for Zildjian to say, 'This drummer's amazing.' I met Dom and helped him get his drum deals and gradually started doing some bits and pieces with the band, the odd live thing. I was retired from the road at that point. I was working for the Manics and through that I was doing the Zildjian thing, and Dom wanted someone to come out on tour with them who understood drums. I think I officially started on the 'Plug In Baby' tour."

What were they like as people?
"Really quite normal but really close-knit. It was like the first time I remember thinking that Muse were like a classic band, it was like seeing a gang mentality, the fact they were so tight with each other. It was like no band I'd ever met before; and still I work with bands who say, 'We're a gang' but they're not. You know, I have memories of Dom and Matt tickling each other and laughing like fucking schoolkids."

They're very tactile aren't they?

"Really tactile, and I remember thinking that was quite weird at first. Well, probably just thinking, 'Oh that's sweet', but they do spend all their time with each other, even now, as much as they can do. Matt not living here doesn't make it very easy, but it is weird how they really live each other's lives, growing up through Chris' dad dying early . . . lots of things seem to mirror each of their personal lives. And they all help each other. They know when someone's in a bad mood and will take them away in isolation for a little bit while everyone else carries on. For a three piece, three's not really a number for a band, there's usually someone left on their own, but with Muse there never was."

On that tour, weren't they using a fairly amateurish crew, like their mates from Teignmouth?

"Rick was doing front of house. Rick got the job because he was a sound man at the Cavern or at some other local venue, and he got the gig apparently by telling them off. They would smash their gear up even in the early days, and Rick says that he had a real go at them because they smashed up somebody's mikes. You know, 'You've gotta stop fucking doing this, this isn't a playground, this is really serious, you've got to knuckle down and make this work if you wanna be a successful band.' So at that stage they had Rick doing front of house, and one of their local mates called Alan was their T-shirt guy, it was literally them in the back of a splitter bus driving around. They always had the feeling that something was gonna be massive but they never shied away from it, it just seemed like they were going though the notions of what normal bands do. It was really weird, quite an eerie feeling really. Me and Matthew always got on really well, both being Geminis and both hyperactive as children; I could understand what he was going though. His mind races at four million miles an hour, always has. His mum tells these stories about him as a kid, he's always been like this. He hasn't changed a bit, he's a very smart bloke who does amazing things."

What were they like to tour with? A handful?

"In the early days they smashed up their gear through frustration. They had shit techs in the beginning. Dan, one of the guys, would give them a guitar that'd be totally out of tune and Matt would just smash it up, like,

'How am I supposed to even start this?' Or his pedal board would stop working. Because he was trying to do something really technical without having the budget to do it, it was never getting there. The pedal boards were just too complicated, didn't actually work and he got really frustrated, and then we had to slim everything down. Everything got so complicated, so they'd smash everything up and we'd be on the phone to endorsement companies all the time, saying, 'Dom's totally put a hole in his bass drum, actually the whole kit's ruined, [so] can I have another one tomorrow please?' and hiring stuff in. Everything settled when we finally got some good crew, who had to be very military about the operation, because if it wasn't absolutely pristine every night then they were gonna fucking demolish the stage. So when we got some good guitar techs, they knew that if they fucked it up then the gig tomorrow would be twice as hard, so they didn't."

Were you on the US Chili Peppers tour?
"No, but I remember seeing them after they got back from that and that's when they changed gear in their live set. Before that, Matt was quite still and very focused on his singing, but then went away to America and toured with the Foo Fighters and then he was fucking leaping around the stage and going nuts. It was like a breath of fresh air; they saw what they could do and how much fun you could have on stage and that was it, he then became the Matt Bellamy he is now. He took off."

Did you see much of the hysteria, especially in France?
"Yeah. Oui FM were massively into the band. They really championed them and felt they had discovered them for themselves. We turned up to radio stations in fucking Benelux and had 600 people outside, because in certain pockets of Europe Muse were just so cult and kids just absolutely found a connection with Matt. In-stores got really out of hand in Japan and in France. It was strange, because usually a band will blow up in one country, then go somewhere else and it will either be the same level or much smaller. But with Muse it was always up and down in hysteria. You'd go to the country next door and it's just all right, but you go back to that town four months later and it's fucking mental."

Chapter Four

THE hallucinations had started kicking in on the Chili Peppers tour, around about Albany, New York state. Although it wasn't Albany in Matt Bellamy's head. Matt Bellamy was on another planet altogether.

It was a desert planet, wasteland as far as the eye could see, and much bigger than this one as the horizon was endlessly flat and went on forever. Matt was alone, scorched by an icy sun, burning hot, a cloying dryness in his veins. He looked around for shelter but saw none, only a glint of sunlight glancing off something reflective in the distance. Not an earthbound surface though, this was up in the baking blue sky, and being joined by another, and another, a swirling swarm of distant flashes. Then the objects flew closer and he could focus on them. Triangular metal blades, shiny and ultra-sharp. Hundreds of them. He started running, dodging the blades as they flew around him, stabbed at him, pierced the back of his head. But they wouldn't break the flesh on his scalp, they'd somehow pass straight through, directly into his brain, and lodge there just as he'd wake up, back in the real world, his head a pulsing mass of migraine. A migraine that would last until the gig that night, until he started drinking it away.

It was a recurring hallucination, chasing Matt across the US, and it made him start to believe that the arid planet was the real world and Earth itself was just a dream. It stayed with him all through the day, on planes and buses he could never stop thinking about it. In Knoxville, Tennessee, he was introduced to a guy who, he swore was a blade himself, come to stab him. On some remote US cable channel, Matt caught a TV show about psywar – the conspiracy theory that suggests the government is trying to control our minds by using radiation to send pulses of information into our brains through mobile phones or electrical devices – and started thinking he might be a victim, that America was the hub of such covert practices.

A small step away from sleeping in a tin-foil hat, Matt decided to consult a doctor as soon as he was back in the UK and the source of his problem was uncovered. Matt had been living on one cup of tea and copious amounts of red wine every day and, for one eight-day period in the US, he hadn't drunk a drop of water. His doctor told him to drink two litres of water a day and, before he knew it, Matt was back on terra firma.

Yet, although his mind was no longer playing tricks on him, it was certainly throwing out some unusual sparks. As press interviews in the wake of 'Unintended''s Top 20 success became more probing and Matt's sprawling thoughts unravelled in public, a wild array of strange, scary and wonderful insights into this most colourful mind began to emerge. His greatest fear was being impregnated by an alien, giving birth to a freak and having to hide it away while bringing it up (or being buried alive). He had recurring nightmares about his family being in a Nazi concentration camp. He was listening to nothing but Berlioz, which he believed to be the very peak of recorded music; given a time machine, he'd travel back to 1850 to listen to it being written. His idea of heaven was "a Christian ideal of the mind without the body". He had two personalities, one positive and one negative, which he moved between; but he also believed he could download other people's personalities into his own, soaking up their experiences and characteristics. He'd once thrown a TV out of the window, but only to help a hackneyed old industry type live out his rock'n'roll fantasy. He can't listen to the radio in a car as he hates having music he doesn't want to hear played around him but would rather listen to the music in his head; in fact, he's mentally written entire songs without knowing if he'd play them on guitar or piano, and played them first time without rehearsing. He'd watched animal porn on the internet, to see what people were getting up to. His most recent dream was of a massive Muse gig where the likes of Flea from RHCP, Tom Waits and the guitarist from Limp Bizkit guested on songs while covered in blood. The intense feelings he'd experienced over the past year were vastly more interesting than those he'd experienced for the previous 21. He could cook risotto, and his idea of happiness was a secluded tropical beach full of naked women. He doesn't speak onstage because he thinks words would "demean" the songs. He had no fear of looking ridiculous in public as he'd spent a lot of his formative years with a Down's Syndrome sufferer*, and so he didn't worry about what other people thought of him. He admired Al

---

* Matt has never spoken about this person in interviews.

Pacino's character in *The Godfather* for his revenge tactics, but personally he'd have to be paid a million pounds to kill someone. If he was invisible for a day he'd break into Buckingham Palace and torture everyone. Oh, and he wished gravity was lighter so that all the spiders would die.

The spiders, you see, might possibly be from Mars. One of Matt's more madcap theories at the time – one of the first of many that would come to light over the next eight years – was that spiders dominate the universe, able to hibernate forever so that they can survive in space. He believed (or joked convincingly) that space was full of floating baby spiders waiting to land on a planet where the conditions were right for them to come alive and colonise the new territory. Ziggy Stardust, in Matt's strange biological philosophy, might well have been a true story.

How much of this was heartfelt sincerity and how much was mischievous wind-up, brought on by the bemusement of suddenly being a regular music press interviewee is uncertain, but even outwardly Matt was showing signs of unusual behaviour. He dyed his spikes regularly – a luminous shade of electric blue one week, a shock of peroxide the next[*] – and began regularly tracing the veins on his forearms with black ink, even going so far as to ask tattooists to fill them in permanently, although none were prepared to perform the required needlework.

All of this – the punkening of his image, the furious metaphysical concepts pouring out in interviews, the stealing of other people's character traits – was part of a process of wanting to transform into someone, or something, else. Matt was no longer the shy, socially awkward young Devon kid; he was being forced into a very adult world of sex, money, international travel, fame, public criticism and the constant pressure of having to defend or explain his music and himself at every turn. Part of him wanted to protect the childhood Matt by creating a whole new persona for himself, built from scraps of the personalities he came into contact with; part of him wanted to forget that that young, bored and frustrated kid with no discernible character of his own (as he saw it) had ever existed and to grow up, become someone new. Some years later, Matt would claim that he could remember nothing at all of his life from before this point, before that long, hard summer of 2000. He felt as if the child he had been before the age of 22 simply hadn't existed.

[*] Dom was also known to sport a shade of Loreal's Intense Red around this time.

And certainly Muse's work rate was making it easy for him to forget he'd had any other sort of life than this.

* * *

Between June and November of 2000 Muse played around 40 festival dates across the globe, following the sun. It seems an impossible figure, but the late 90s saw an explosion in the festival circuit: where there had once been only a handful of established events to play – Glastonbury, Reading, Germany's Rock Am Ring, Denmark's Roskilde and Spain's Benicàssim comprised most of the circuit until the 90s – suddenly every decent-sized town in Europe had to have one. In Britain alone, as the ill-fated Phoenix festival sank back into its own ashes in 1998, the likes of V, a reborn Isle Of Wight festival and numerous smaller events were rising in its place. So it was becoming standard practice for a band breaking through in their home country and with some label cash behind them to hook onto the festival circuit for the entire summer – indeed, the international promoters began to organise their line-ups together, so that often the same bands played each event, like a massive touring circus around Europe.

Onto such a treadmill stepped a gig-ravaged Muse, now into their 18th month of almost solid touring, and the strain was showing. Not necessarily on the band so much as the crew, ill-prepared for the hard conditions of a festival show or the added chances for rock'n'roll indulgence they offered. Matt later remembered seeing Dom's nude backside running down the aisle and a crew member with a couple of women on his face at various points, but too much indulgence from the crew leads to mistakes on the job, and mistakes on the job lead to Matt smashing stuff on stage . . .

The technical problems grew progressively worse as the summer wore on. The first run of festival shows, from Rock Am Ring through Holland's Pinkpop, Sweden's Hultsfred Festival and Italy's Heineken Jammin fest went smoothly, but the following week, at a Glastonbury warm-up in Torquay's Riviera Centre, Matt's guitar problems had him ramming his instrument repeatedly into his amp and the drum kit while Chris crowd-surfed, still playing the outro bass riff to 'Ashamed', to escape any flying debris. At the Highfield festival in Hohenfelden, Germany (headlined that year by Beck), the joy of having a queue 45 minutes long for their signing session was dampened by a set that saw Matt pushing his amp across the stage at Chris during a closing 'Agitated' and once more diving into the drum kit (a hefty display of rock'n'roll mania for 2.30 p.m.). At that year's Reading festival, where they headlined the Radio One Evening Session stage on the Friday night, Matt found himself plagued by a plethora of technical problems, barely being able to hear anything through his monitors at all. With the crowd chanting "Fuck off Oasis!" to Dom's cheery drumbeat in the pauses between songs (Manchester's most arrogant were playing on the main stage at the time), Matt looked to the wings for help from his crew, and spotted the stoned gypsy guy – his 'monitor technician' – asleep at the side of the stage with a lit spliff in his hand. That particular gig ended with two of Matt's old school friends wandering onstage dressed as policemen, with the word 'MUSE' written in gaffer tape across their buttocks.

The ending of the average Muse gig became the dictionary definition of 'chaotic'. But all of this paled in comparison to the disaster of the Radio One Big Sunday event at Ipswich's Chantry Park. Turning up expecting to play a two-song set to the hordes of hyped-up teeny-boppers who frequent such events, Muse were shocked to be told that they were going to have to mime to a backing track as the event was to be entirely mimed. When they said no, they were told that Mansun and JJ72 – two of the other acts appearing that day – had agreed to mime, so they had no choice. In some sort of compromise, Matt eventually persuaded the organisers to let him sing the vocal live, only for the band to walk onstage to find none of their own instruments set up. So with Chris bashing comically away at a drum kit belonging to Scots AOR rockers Texas and Dom thunking on a borrowed bass, Matt – with no guitar to hand at all – began singing 'Muscle Museum' to the backing tape only to find there was no vocal monitor at all. Worst of all though, when Matt tapped the microphone to see if it was on at all, the sound engineer took this as a cue to stop the backing tape and restart it. Muse walked off before the tape operator could cue up their second song.

Not, it must be said, that Muse weren't having the time of their lives. They were seeing the world with their mates, playing music every day, getting copious female attention, drinking with Coldplay and other contemporaries, living the dream no matter how arduous, frustrating and draining it felt at times. And there were some fabulous moments that summer, too. Being presented with their first gold disc for 100,000 sales of *Showbiz* in the UK, straight after their sizzling performance at that year's

Glastonbury, at which Matt claimed he could feel a connection with his younger self, who had crammed down the front at that same stage some years before, likening the feeling to the final scenes of *2001: A Space Odyssey*. The article in a teen mag slavering over 'gorgeous' Chris (much, one imagines, to the amusement of his girlfriend, Kelly, who was an occasional touring partner to the band until the smoky tour bus was deemed an inappropriate place for little Alfie to spend extended periods). The late-night bender with a couple of groupies around Camden after a Channel 4 recording at the Barfly, which had Matt vomiting all the way to Germany on a flight the next day. And the new songs were flowing thick, fast and fabulous: at Cologne's Bizarre festival on August 18, a storming new tune was introduced to the set with a synthesiser intro like a knackered old Gameboy and a stop-start stampede led by Chris' bass (the song didn't have guitars on it until it was recorded for 'Origin Of Symmetry'). It already sounded like a future set closer, with Matt howling the immortal line, "Give me all the peace and joy in your mind" like a breathless banshee. It was called 'Bliss', and it was to become the song that launched a thousand bouncing moons.

Matt was also starting to play up to his pop-star status for larks. After an initial spate of festivals, he complained to management that he wasn't writing enough songs for the second album (not true, they were coming along quite fine), and since the band had studio time booked in November to start recording, he had better have some time off to write. He even managed to convince them that in order to write the sort of songs he was planning, he needed to go swimming with turtles and sharks somewhere tropical for two full weeks. So in September a fortnight in the Maldives was booked for him. He came back with a tan, a love of scuba diving and only one extra song written – the surprisingly un-tropical mood piece 'Megalomania'.

And then there was Japan. Making their first sojourn to the Far East on August 5 to play two dates at the Summer Sonic Festival at the Conifer Forest in Fujikyu and the WTC Open Air Stadium in Osaka the following day[*], Muse were immediately struck by the place. It was a very Muse

---

[*] The tour was also promoted by the release of an eight-track, Japan-only EP on Muse's Japanese label, Avex, called 'Random 1-8', featuring eight B-sides plus three hidden remixes of 'Sunburn'.

sort of country: big, loud, fast, technologically advanced, full of neon glitz and pixellated glitter. The clothes were sharply cut and futuristically stylish – in tune with Matt's mentality and body size, so he stocked up on a whole new image. The gadgets fascinated him and, with a bit of money now starting to filter in, he splashed out on one of the first mini MP3 players, the size of a wristwatch, on which he began to download all of his music, liking such a small and obscure method of listening to music as he wouldn't be asked to turn it off on airplanes. At the festivals their slots were hellish – in Osaka they took the stage at 10.30 a.m., first on the main stage supporting Reef and Jon Spencer Blues Explosion, while Fujikyu was even worse. There they played at 8.30 a.m. in the beating sun to a swelteringly hot crowd who were exhausted and fainting at the barriers. But this meant that Muse had most of the day to party after the shows and, over this visit and a further four club dates in Nagoya, Osaka and Tokyo two months later, they took full advantage of the opportunity.

Because there were two things that made Japan Muse's major partying capital in 2000. The first was the magic mushrooms. Psilocybin mushrooms were legal in Japan and something that Matt had indulged in before, since Devon was something of a hotbed for their natural growth. As far as Matt was concerned, drugs were all about natural purity: anything grown by nature, such as weed or mushrooms, he'd happily partake in; anything made from chemicals in a mobster's bathtub he steered well clear of. He was interested in exploring the mind and the universe, exposing himself to alien experiences and concocting surreal new theories of the truths behind our very existence. He wasn't that bothered about getting a mild cocaine buzz in order to feel better about himself in social situations. Indeed, as the *Showbiz* tour went on, Matt and Dom had concocted a plan – roughly once a year when their schedule allowed them a few days to themselves they'd fly to Amsterdam, pick up some mushrooms and head to Vondel Park to hallucinate for a couple of days, truly connect with themselves, even looking for the darker elements of their subconscious to confront. And their use may not have been confined to days off judging by Matt's one and only notable between-song utterance all year, which wasn't a "thank you, this next song's called . . .": at the Malmo KB in Sweden, Matt introduced 'Feeling Good' with the puzzling statement, "Sun is like a spoon, like I had could make a good man bad" – possibly a reference to The Smiths' song 'Please Please Please Let Me Get What I Want'.

For Muse, mushrooms enhanced the "surreal and intense" Japanese experience, making the neon brighter, the traffic noises softer, the barging crowds like a sea of welcoming faces. They'd borrow money from their PR to visit drug markets to stock up before mushroom-fuelled trips to temples near Nagoya and Osaka, where Matt remembers finding praying women in white face paint remarkably erotic. Japan for Muse was a seductive swirl of shapes, colours and flesh.

The flesh being the second party incentive. It was a long-held cliché that UK indie bands could be unknown at home but already huge in Japan – Japanese idolisation of Western culture (especially the danger and freedom they perceived in rock bands) meant that the fans there were far more obsessive and enthusiastic, chasing the most mid-table of indie bands down the streets in scenes of screaming fandom resembling *A Hard Day's Night*. Often, though, they hound musicians rather more politely – the same fan might turn up at eight different locations a band might visit in a day, quietly requesting a photo each time or presenting their girlfriends with gifts. Such it was for Muse on that first trip; at one point during the Summer Sonic visit, Matt found himself in a lift with two girls who, suddenly realising who he was, dropped to their knees (in adulation, he insisted, not to administer sexual favours). Elsewhere they found giggling girls around every corner, some more willing than others – at one point Matt and Dom conducted an orgy with nine girls in their hotel room, fuelled by magic mushrooms. Such exploits didn't come without their consequences of course – Matt's six-year relationship with his Teignmouth girlfriend was becoming increasingly frayed as he spent so much time away, and for Dom, the band's resident Cassanova, it meant having the more obsessive groupies follow him around to every gig, unable to accept the flippancy of their encounter.

No such worries for the band themselves, however. They were most definitely moving on. As Muse's mammoth festival schedule rolled on through T In The Park, Greece's Rockwaves, Marseille's Six Fours Open Air Festival, Switzerland's Paleo Nyon 2000, Italy's Independent Days 2000 and countless others – the band often finding themselves on a Groundhog Day of a semi-metal bill, regularly fourth on before Blink 182, Limp Bizkit and the Deftones, in no particular order – back at home Taste

Media/Mushroom was set to release the final single from *Showbiz*. A familiar one though – 'Muscle Museum' got its third release on October 12. Astutely noticing that the four formats of 'Unintended' had had the, um, intended chart effect, 'Muscle Museum''s final push for 'hit' status came in three formats, backed with a motley and largely superfluous array of live tracks ('Agitated' from the Astoria; 'Escape' from the Bercy), remixes (Timo Maas hacked away at 'Sunburn', while the Safta Jaffery-managed Ron Saint Germaine did the business on 'Sober'), the LA-shot video and, most notably, a cover of the title track by Belgian dance act Soulwax under the Two Many DJs moniker.* The single duly reached number 25, finally attaining its rightful place in Muse's burgeoning pantheon as a bona fide Greatest Hit.

And just in time; there was a whole new set of monsters ready to be unleashed.

★ ★ ★

To say that the recording of Muse's second album began in an unconventional fashion isn't even half of the story. Not many recording sessions, you see, involve the band, five days in, naked in the Jacuzzi eating maggots.

It was, of course, the mushrooms' fault.

November 2000 and, after the last of their live appointments for the year on a five-date tour of Australia (where Muse were asked to present an award at a major televised ceremony, Australia's equivalent of the Brits, during which Matt accidentally swore on live TV) and a final cluster of shows in Scandinavia, Muse had a whole fortnight off before they were due at Ridge Farm Studios, a 17th-century building set in 13 acres of rolling rural grounds in deepest Surrey, to record 'Plug In Baby' as the first single from the second record. Taste Media had planned for the whole album to be produced by John Leckie again, but they were keen to keep Muse's momentum going with the rapid release of a new single. Leckie was away in Africa for the earlier sessions, so the band opted to record the single with Dave Bottrill, whose work the band had admired on Tool's *Aenima* album (a crunching prog-rock record in tune

---

* Muse were slowly becoming obsessed with Belgian music, later citing Soulwax as major influences.

with Muse's ambitions) and experimental Belgian pop band dEus, who were fast become a huge Muse influence. With production credits on rock, prog and indie albums by the likes of King Crimson, Mudvayne and PJ Harvey, Bottrill seemed to be a man able to combine a lightness of touch with a heavy rock thump, and so perfect to record the rockier tracks for Muse.

And rockier they undoubtedly were. Having honed songs such as 'Plug In Baby', 'New Born' and 'Bliss' over a year of extensive touring, Muse had not only built up an impressive global fanbase, they'd also found their real sound. It was harder, heavier, more refined, and they were confident they knew exactly how these songs would work in the studio. Recording *Showbiz* they'd been unsure of themselves, but this time they knew how they wanted it to be. They set up a gig-sized PA and played loud to eradicate any sense of dislocation between the three of them in the studio, and they were so determined that the record would be made by a three-piece that they made sure each of them could hear every take no matter where they were in the building. They employed a Rage Against The Machine recording technique, learned from RATM's guitar tech, who was now working with Matt, of putting clean bass down and then distorted top end bass on top, so that the bass is similar to the guitar: the effect is like having a second guitar at the top end of the bass, making a three-piece sound monstrous. Sure enough, 'Plug In Baby' came together remarkably easily and quickly and, deciding that Bottrill was the perfect man to record the other rocked-up numbers they'd written, Muse found what was to be a single session turning into the recording of almost half of the album. So they set about recording 'Bliss', 'New Born' and 'Darkshines' as well.

And then, on the fifth day of recording, they woke up to find that the field right next door to the studio had blossomed overnight with an immense number of magic mushrooms. And they promptly set about eating them all.

The sessions became somewhat unpredictable. After two or three takes, the tripping band would shrug, strip off and dive into the Jacuzzi, eventually forgetting about recording altogether and spending four days in the hot tub together eating mushrooms, which, in their addled state, looked like maggots. On the third day, Matt fell asleep in the tub and went deaf in one ear. Unsurprisingly, the takes sounded awful and the entire session had to be remixed back at Sawmills with John Cornfield at the desk.

Amazingly, the remix sounded sensational. 'Plug In Baby' was a monumental tune by the time Cornfield was finished with it, a landmark of 21st-century rock music. Mushroom wasted no time releasing it to radio and it crept swiftly up the playlists, as those in the know began spreading news around the press of the incredible comeback that little prog-rock band from Devon were conjuring up. As 2000 wound to a close, Muse had not only wowed the hearts of the UK, the Far East and Europe, selling around 250,000 copies of the single worldwide in the process (it had outsold recent hard-rock efforts by big hitters Marilyn Manson, Korn and Slipknot, and insiders were predicting the album would go platinum by Christmas), but they'd come full circle. They were rock's big buzz band again. And this time they'd deliver in spades.

★ ★ ★

Come January 2001, the production roles were reversed. Now it was Bottrill's turn to be unavailable, off to produce Tool's *Lateralus* album in the US for several months, while Leckie returned itching to get to work on the album's remaining seven tracks. In the *Showbiz* sessions he'd introduced the band to the likes of Captain Beefheart and Tom Waits, and was pleased with the way they'd absorbed these influences in a fiercely modern, post-millennial way. Plus, Leckie's reputation granted him the keys to any studio he wanted to work in, and the band visited several while making their sophomore record. They spent time in Peter Gabriel's Real World studios near Bath (handy for Chris to pop home to Teignmouth during breaks in recording), and on The Astoria, a houseboat moored at Tagg's Island on the Thames near Hampton Court. The boat was originally owned by theatrical impresario Fred Karno, the man famed for discovering Laurel & Hardy and Charlie Chaplin – indeed, Chaplin is said to have attended many parties there. In 1986, Pink Floyd's Dave Gilmour bought The Astoria and converted it into a floating recording studio, and it was here that Leckie brought Muse to piece together the remaining songs.

Despite the satisfyingly frequent airings of 'Plug In Baby' from the studio radio, the sessions were long and draining – the band would arrive at midday expecting to do 12 hours' work but get nothing done until after dinner. Then they'd work until 4 a.m., existing in a weird nocturnal world

that heightened the darkness in the music*, and between band and producer they had some rather crazed ideas for the sessions. Matt was keen to
work with synthesisers in order to recall the synth-dance tracks he used to
like when he was six and, having seen Tom Waits perform live in New
York, during which the veteran blues growler had played animal bones,
Matt had been inspired to try to utilise strange and macabre instruments, to
create a sinister, unhinged mood to the album. He asked Leckie if they
could use bits of metal as percussion and if he could make a drum kit out of
human skulls, as this would make the sessions more "vibey". Leckie joked
later that it was hard enough to find animal bones near the studio, let alone
human ones, yet animal bones they did find, heading to a nearby butcher's
shop and buying some ribs for Leckie to tune in time to use them as percussion on 'Screenager'. They also picked up some llama claws, which
Leckie, inspired by Muse's dark sense of invention and experimentation,
made the band hang around their necks before each song was recorded
and wander around the room for five minutes chanting, banging the claws,
hitting wind chimes and snapping bubble wrap in order to create an
underlying atmosphere, over which they worked their magic. Matt would
refer to it as "psycho-acoustic", but every sound on the record was original noise, there were absolutely no samples. On one track – the
Rachmaninov-inspired 'Space Dementia' – part of the percussion track is
the sound of Matt zipping and unzipping his fly.

Lyrically, the mood of the album was also taking a sinister turn. Despite
Matt now claiming that the first album was lyrically so bleak that he'd be
embarrassed to put some of the songs on in public and that the new album
was "radiating positivity", the mood and tone of his subject matter was
most definitely not concerning the sun putting his hat on. Matt was
writing lyrics absolutely straight, jotting down whatever came to him and
not thinking about what they might mean until much later, so his ideas of
his own themes were still a little vague. He knew that they were all about
himself at the core, but he felt he had so many different characters writhing
within him that he never knew which one the songs were really about. He
talked of one of the songs being about wanting to devour the peace and
contentment of other people, and of another about being so envious of

---

* Dom and Matt kept up this time-keeping for some weeks after the sessions finished,
unable to sleep until 5 a.m. each night.

what someone else had that he wanted to steal their very essence to get it, to kill them and absorb their soul. He spoke of part of him wanting to blow up the world and another part wanting to be in love with everyone. He claimed that stagnation was death, that when you stay too long in a job, a relationship or a place it hobbles you as a person, and that these songs were about reduction and purity, about removing the distractions that stop you being yourself.

He also spoke about the way that times of change and unrest in his life made him want to write music more, since it was the only real constant in his life, and hence that June he would give up his flat in Exeter and move into a temporary flat in Islington, north London, with Dom and Tom Kirk, which would act as a very makeshift home since its only furnishings besides the regulation landlord set-up consisted of a piano and a laptop. Although Matt later admitted to feeling like the typical wide-eyed Devon kid lost and adrift in the Big City, he and his flatmates planned to move cities every six months to keep the creativity alive: next stop San Diego.

Murder, envy, destruction, lust, dislocation: these were the emotional themes driving the record, but the cerebral influences behind the album's thinking gave these human traits a distinctly alien and scientific hue. Three books Matt has dipped into during the previous year had lit sparks in his ever-curious mind. Mark Ward's *Virtual Organisms* likened the birth of artificial life to a new species, an event as monumental as the beginnings of human life itself – basically arguing that robots are human too. These ideas of future evolution and the fuzzying of the line between man and machine had already come up in 'Plug In Baby' and 'New Born', but it was the other two books, Michio Kaku's *Hyperspace* and Brian Greene's *The Elegant Universe*, which gave Matt's new vision its creative cohesion.

Here comes the science part. Concentrate. These books and various scientific magazine articles introduced Matt to the concept of string theory: very rudimentarily, the theory that the universe at its smallest and greatest extents is made up of minuscule or gigantic vibrating strings, and that our universe itself may simply be a 'bubble' created by two of these super-strings clashing together in a 'multiverse' beyond the edges of space. And they also presented him with a mathematical quandary that truly captured his imagination. His reading gave him the idea that, in the 11th dimension, everything in nature becomes perfectly mathematically symmetrical, a perfect sphere; that indeed our universe would not be able to exist without the symmetry deeply embedded in it. If such symmetry exists, goes one strand of the argument, then the universe must have been created by a sentient being.* To whit: were you to discover the origin of that symmetry, you will have found God.

This is, however, some way outside of provable scientific fact. Over the coming years Matt will often point out that his more outlandish theories are the result of him reading the odd chapter here and there of various different scientific books and creating his own theories to fill in the gaps between them, and this is a prime example. Greene's book states that, while any additional dimension to our known four (three spatial dimensions plus time) would have to be curled-up and microscopic in order for us to have been unable to detect it, string theory requires 10 dimensions in order to be mathematically workable – the tiny vibrating strings would have to be able to move within nine special dimensions plus time for the equations to reach conclusions within reasonable probabilities. In 1995, physicist Edward Witten proposed an 11-dimensional universe in order to create a theory in which the five different and seemingly incompatible strands of string theory were unified into an overall M-Theory, answering many previously unsolved conundrums about the structure and workings of the universe, but certainly at the time that Matt was dipping into these ideas no one in physics really knew what the 11th dimensional theory actually was, beyond a hodge-podge of vague equations and grand concepts. M-Theory provided a framework in which symmetry in all forces in the universe was attainable insofar as all the sums made sense, but in 2001 science was still some way from providing an equation along the lines of $E=MC2xM$-Theory$=GOD$.

Happy to run with the ideas that intrigued him most, however, Matt gleaned two things from these books. One, a new, mind-blowing view of the universe, which shifted constantly between believing we were mere insects in the galactic void and thinking that, actually, we're the most interesting thing to be found in that vast emptiness. And two, they gave Matt Bellamy his title.

Origin Of Symmetry refers to a statement by Michio Kaku that a book about supersymmetry should be called *The Origin Of Symmetry* as it would

---

* An equally compelling contradictory argument, though, is that the universe was born from inevitability; that scientifically it couldn't have existed any other way than it does.

have an equally profound effect on physics as Darwin's *The Origin Of Species* had on biology. It was also the working title of a song that was either dropped from the album or had its title changed.

The final burst of recording for the album occurred in February and took in a tour of cathedrals in Bath & Wells and Exeter in search of the grand, epic and desolate church organ sound on 'Megalomania', the song that would eventually become the album's climactic track. Eventually they found the perfect place: St Mary's Church in Bathwick, and approached the vicar there for permission to play it.

The playing of a church organ usually requires the granting of a licence, but the church was willing to waive the necessity if Muse could provide them with a lyric sheet, so that they could make sure they weren't handing their blessed instrument over to any of those nasty rock devil worshippers they'd heard had been going around burning churches in Norway. At the time, the lyrics weren't written – and when they were they would detail the pessimism and frustration Matt could feel in the breakdown of his long-term relationship and, for a while, would be called 'Go Forth And Multiply', after the instruction in the Bible that angered Matt as it suggested that humanity's only purpose on Earth was to have sex and reproduce, and he felt we had a higher purpose. So, thinking better of telling the church the truth about the song, Matt quickly scribbled out some nice, positive lyrics for the church heads to read and permission was duly granted for the knock-down fee of £350. Whether it was lying to men of God, the dark Latino import of the piece he was playing or the fact that the song would later take on an even more anti-church stance, Matt would later describe the recording of 'Megalomania' as one of the darker moments in his life.

Yet when I caught up with Muse on The Astoria towards the end of recording they seemed in fine spirits. Buoyed perhaps by the *Telegraph* reporting half a million sales for *Showbiz*, Matt was enthusing about the joys of MP3 and downloading free music from Morpheus, now that Napster had been shut down. He detailed his metal-blade hallucinations and mushroom benders for the first time and revealed he'd written a new song called 'Thoughts Of A Dying Atheist', about someone's last moments and how they'd surely want to go back and live the most hedonistic life imaginable (the title had been another working title for 'Megalomania', but this new song was perhaps more telling of his current relationship difficulties and his yearning to indulge in the rock-star life himself, and hence it wouldn't see the light of day for another couple of years). He also expanded on the evolutionary ideas brought up in 'Plug In Baby' and 'New Born', claiming that if we were looking to evolve with science we'd genetically produce humans who can breathe other atmospheres, live in space or fly. Verbose, imaginative and occasionally a bit crackpot, he was fast becoming the most fascinating and unpredictable interviewee in rock, a full-blown musical eccentric, a unique rock'n'roll nutjob. A superstar.

As mixing and mastering of the record got underway at the legendary Abbey Road studios in north London, Muse broke away from working on the record that February only to play two radio sessions: the first at Capital Radio in Leicester Square for XFM on February 12 was plagued with technical problems again, although Matt managed to keep his cool when his guitar broke at the intro to 'Plug In Baby' and he was noticeably out of tune for the first-ever live performance of a sprawling falsetto meta-opera entitled 'Micro Cuts'*; and the second at BBC Radio's Maida Vale studios, where they relied more on tried-and-tested older material. It had only been three or four months since they'd last played live, but they found that having been playing so tightly in the studio they couldn't loosen up so easily for live shows.

Meanwhile, over the three months leading up to the new album's release on March 5, 'Plug In Baby' had crept onto the Radio One B-List and its startling video was cutting a swathe through MTV – Muse's best yet; in sci-fi shirts and vertical haircuts they play in a modernist bedroom infected with the dismembered heads, limbs and torsos of robo-supermodels, spewing robotic tentacles from the gaps where their innards should be (they were meant to be futuristic mechanised porn dolls that had fallen apart).

To the casual observer, Muse had returned with a first single from a new album only five months after the re-release of 'Muscle Museum' had wrapped up the *Showbiz* campaign, seemingly conjuring this mammoth rock hit out of nowhere in a matter of weeks. To those of us who'd been raving about 'Plug In Baby' since we'd first heard it the previous January, knowing that Muse had this killer song up their sleeves that would rocket them into the big league, silence all the 'Radiohead copyist' naysayers and

* This was also the first performance of 'Citizen Erased'.

121

trample all their previous material beneath its mighty boot heel, this was the moment we'd been waiting 12 months for. This was where our passion was to be proved right.

Its two CDs were padded out with the inspired video plus some of Muse's more throwaway tracks: 'Nature_1', a pre-'Showbiz' ballad called 'Spiral Static' and old instrumentals 'Bedroom Acoustics' and 'Execution Commentary' – a flamenco-inspired piece and a cacophony of noise and shouting that was used as an outro to 'Showbiz' in live shows respectively. The B-sides were originally intended to be 'Futurism', under the title 'Tasseract', and 'Darkshines', under the title 'Policing The Jackson Funk', but these songs were saved for later releases. Its sleeve swarming with bug-eyed cartoon aliens, the song reached number 11, an unavoidable, inevitable smash hit single.

Appealing far beyond their rabid fanbase to the *Breakfast Show* masses (indeed, the release saw them head out to France again to perform it on the *Nulle Part Ailleurs* show, broadcast on March 2), it made Muse a firm chart concern, one of the UK's most successful alternative bands of the time and promised a second album full of lean and focused hook-drenched pop heaviness.

It couldn't have been more misleading.

★ ★ ★

Origin Of Symmetry, as it poured in all its pomp and circumstance from the mixing desk of Abbey Road, was undoubtedly an album of two halves. When recording the record, Muse had intended it to showcase their more eccentric and hard-rock side, and it certainly achieved that: almost in the style of the prog-rock albums they were being witheringly compared to, it opened with 'side one' (in old money) of largely blistering rock hits and 'side two' of mostly meandering latino/blues/metal/opera experiments that were by turns awe-inspiring, lacklustre and off-puttingly over-the-top. Add in the lyrical themes – science-fiction tales of the next stage of human evolution; the lack of a power figure to look up to, a king or a God; observations of consciousness and whether there is such a thing as individuality; the futility of existence; the pointlessness of morality and goodness in a society that has destroyed the concept of 'heaven' – and the influence of Bach's 'Toccata & Fugue In D Minor' and you had a record that o'erleapt its own ambitions and slightly faltered on the other side. It emerged, remember, at around the same time as the first brilliantly taut and concise EPs from New York's The Strokes, who would invigorate alternative music for the rest of the decade; next to such a lithe indie greyhound, *Origin* . . . seemed almost prehistoric in its stomporific vastness.

Not that you could tell from the opening brace of tunes. Tight, beefy, metallic and imbued with a visceral, ultramodern production by Bottrill and Leckie, the first songs here roared from the speakers like the *Showbiz* band zapped direct into the 25th century. Six bracing minutes long, 'New Born' sounded like a genetic mutation of 'Sunburn', another piano-led album opener of music-box tenderness* that exploded into a riff a million times more heavy, distorted, catchy and devastating. The first of many Muse songs you felt was capable of destroying entire moons if pointed in the wrong direction, it concerned Matt's phobia of evolution, his fears of the loss of human individuality as we career towards a future where humanity is merely a collective of engineered bodies connected via cables and capable of existing in space (Matt had clearly watched *The Matrix* a number of times by now). From the opening riff onslaught to the vocoder outro vocals, which suggest the entire song has just been played by androids, it was clear we were inhabiting new musical territory here: we're not sat in Teignmouth moaning about the townies now, Toto . . .

'Bliss', meanwhile, was a song that snuck out of Matt's childhood subconscience: he knew he'd ripped the 80s synth arpeggios off from somewhere, a children's TV programme perhaps, but had no idea where (it was actually a *Top Gear* game for the Nintendo Entertainment System). But because of the innocent childhood connotations it stood as his favourite Muse song to date and the most positive on *Origin* . . ., despite possibly being the song he'd previously described as being about wanting to devour other people's happiness.

'Space Dementia' is the term NASA give to the intense sense of dislocation, isolation and insignificance that astronauts left in space for a lengthy period of time suffer when looking back at Earth. But Matt brought it back to Earth with a bump: he was the astronaut in this scenario and someone he can't imagine being without represents the distant home

---

* During the Bottrill sessions, Matt's voice was used instead of the piano for the intro but later removed as it seemed too strange, an effect of the magic mushrooms.

planet. It's not stretching the imagination too much to suggest this is probably about the girlfriend he had back in Teignmouth, but fan sites – of
which there were several worldwide by now – certainly stretched their
imaginations in trying to work out the meaning of the opening line, "H8
is the one for me/It gives me all I need/Helps me coexist with the chill".
Did 'H8' refer to getting high, making the song a reference to mushrooms? Did it mean 'hate', as in he wanted his girlfriend to hate him? Or
was it, as Matt himself claimed, a part of a microcomputer that could be
used as a small robot's brain? Whatever, 'Space Dementia' was certainly
the first of *Origin . . .*'s progressive forays, taking in soothing piano refrains,
frenzied hard-rock segments, lilting synth interludes, lifted precisely from
the first movement of Rachmaninov's Second Piano Concerto, and a final
cataclysm of operatic guitar noise, feedback and the zipping and unzipping
of Matt's fly, made to sound like someone chainsawing apart a motorbike.
It began like Liberace luring us into an ornate boudoir and ended like Pink
Floyd's inflatable pig exploding. Monumental.

'Hyper Music' had started life as a bluesy instrumental interlude on the
Showbiz tour; here it grew lyrics (it's original title, 'I Don't Love You', was
maybe too blatant to the song's meaning, along with the chorus cry of, "I
don't love you/And I never did!") and a bilious, driving punk energy. It
was, according to Matt, "sheer negative pain and anger", the exact
opposite of 'Bliss', and it was Muse stretching their claws and discovering
how deeply they could scratch.

The pivotal presence of 'Plug In Baby', with its spectacular reminder of
'New Born''s theme and pop crunch, acts as an essential grounding factor
in the centre of an album straining to fly off into some self-indulgent prog-
metal horizon, but its careening pop genius can only do so much,
considering what follows. 'Citizen Erased' was seven minutes of evil
electronic fuzz dotted with ethereal ELO space-noise sections, and
Bellamy crooning about the agonies of being interviewed all the time
while simultaneously trying not to give too much away or contradict
himself – "Break me in/Teach us to cheat and to lie/And cover up what
shouldn't be shared . . . please stop asking me to describe". A bit rich
coming from anyone with an interest in promoting their records in the
press of course, but as an immaculately melodic pointer to the elaborate
epics Muse would soon be capable of, 'Citizen Erased' was a doozy.

However, 'Micro Cuts' – the song about his hallucinations of flying

A teenage, sensible-haired Muse pondering one of their earliest promo shoots, June 1999.
(JIM DYSON/GETTY IMAGES)

The Tornados, September 1962. George Bellamy, far left.
(LFI)

George Bellamy, left, considers world
domination in one generation's time.
(LFI)

Joe Meek, between rages.
(HULTON ARCHIVE/GETTY IMAGES)

Rocket Baby Dolls on Teignmouth promenade – only the jumpers failed the audition.
(HERALD EXPRESS)

At home with Muse, 1998.
(HERALD EXPRESS)

Sawmills Studio, where the magic
first happened.
(MARK STACEY)

Moody Muse, with only Matt still caught in his 'jumper period'.
(HERALD EXPRESS)

Outside Sawmills taking a break from recording *Showbiz*.
(COURTESY OF RUTH TAYLOR)

Rocking the Kajagoogoo look, 1999.
(ED SIRRS/RETNA)

Onstage at English Riviera Centre,
Torquay, June 21, 2000.
(JOHN WHITEHEAD/HERALD EXPRESS)

Preparing to napalm the English Riviera Centre, June 21, 2000.
(JOHN WHITEHEAD/HERALD EXPRESS)

The Glastonbury debut, June 25, 2000.
(TINA MCCLELLAND/RETNA)

Matt's best Sid Vicious, onstage
at T In The Park, July 2000.
(ANDREW CARRUTH/RETNA)

Celebrating the first of many awards, *Kerrang!* Awards, Lancaster Hotel, August 28, 2001.
(CRAIG BARRITT/RETNA)

Matt wakes up unexpectedly in his pyjamas to find he's at the *Kerrang!* Awards 2002.
(LFI)

Absolution Muse pose for promo shot, September 2003.
(TINA KORHONEN/RETNA)

blades in the desert and his psywar paranoia – marked the point where *Origin* . . . began verging on the ridiculous. With Dom tapping out a stilted classical rhythm, Matt falsettoing wildly throughout like Maria Callas on a bonfire, and what seems to be a full Wagnerian choir somewhere in the background on 'vibes', it took Muse's operatic pretensions into the realms of self-parody and became the sole reason why, in the *NME* office after its release, writers could no longer refer to the band merely as 'Muse' but had to stand on their chairs and wail 'MEEEEYUUUUUSEEE!' at the top of their straining lungs. Only Chris' mighty bass thump, truly coming into its own on *Origin* . . ., stopped 'Micro Cuts' from breaking free from its moorings and floating off into the rafters of the Royal Opera House, insane from the visions.

From here on in the album loses focus, becomes (looking back) an over-egged blueprint of the sharper and more honed Muse they would morph into on their next album. 'Screenager' was remarkably direct in theme – it's about a teenager being brought up more by the television than by a parent, and embracing self-harm because of the ultra-perfect body images they're bombarded with – but musically was a triumph of invention over substance. Played on llama claws, animal bones, bubble wrap, wind chimes and shopping bags (as well as the usual guitars and synths), it rose pleasantly to a chorus refrain that lifted off to nowhere, never quite reaching the soaring heights of 'Citizen Erased'. The semi-funky Dire Straits-gone-metal stylings of 'Darkshines' seemed to sit incongruously with the oxyacetylene blast of the previous rock songs, feeling lightweight, reedy and dated in comparison. The echoing Latino guitar solo, particularly, sounded like something from a Sade album, and the lyrics, about being attracted to a pretty girl with a dark side to her nature, were disappointingly straightforward in such other-worldly company.

It's telling that the sexually charged pomp and pout of 'Feeling Good' – the album's one cover version, included because Matt wanted his listeners to know there was positivity unpinning his music; a new dawn, a new day, a new life – is the stand-out track on the second half of *Origin*. . . . A tightly composed and astutely delivered piece among a sea of billowing ideas and ambitions, it was an example of how powerful Muse could now be when tackling a tune of classic simplicity. The closing 'Megalomania', at the other extreme, showed how bombastic and huge they could sound, with its grand slashes of *Phantom Of The Opera* church organ and God-accusing lyrics.

That closing pair encapsulated the glory and the folly of *Origin*. . . . One was tight of melody, the other mammoth in scope; soon Muse would combine the two and become world-beaters but for now (especially in the wake of 'Plug In Baby' 's magnificent pop hooks) this felt like a sprawl too far. Muse, it seemed, had been given some enormous new winged musical boots and were trying to run in them before they'd learnt to glide.

Bold, ambitious, brazen and ballsy, *Origin Of Symmetry* was Muse gone big. And things, in all senses, were about to get bigger.

GLEN ROWE

Do you remember much about that huge run of festivals?
"These were the days when it was still band and crew on one bus, and I remember there were so many French festivals. They'd call them festivals but it was more like a fucking fête. We'd roll into some tiny town in northern France and there'd be a tiny stage in the middle of the square, but they did every single one of those things and there'd always be 500 people. There was always a pocket, no matter where they went, all the funny gigs where some bands would turn up and say, 'This is a waste of time', but Muse never felt that, ever. They always treated everything as though it was a really important show, even if there were 50 people there. I know it sounds corny, but they really did take pride in trying to make them become the greatest band in the world."

How did you feel when you first heard the Origin . . . *stuff?*
"I remember thinking, 'What are they gonna do as a single after 'Plug In Baby'?' I remember sitting there when I got a copy of the album going, 'There isn't another single on here' apart from 'New Born', and that would be the shittest radio edit of all time, trying to make that into three minutes."

Chapter Four

SAFTA JAFFERY

Whose idea was it to keep them on the road during the Origin Of Symmetry
recording?
"I think it was a joint decision between us all really, the game plan was
always really to go out and find the fans. They were young, you can't do
this with certain bands but they were young. One day we could send them
to Greece, the next day to Spain, the next day to Scandinavia and they'd
be fine, they'd recover. They were in their late teens, early twenties, so to
them it was just a big party. They were just excited to be out. I remember
when they had a few days off and Matt would call up and say, 'What's
happening next?' it's like, 'Fuck's sake Matt, just fucking take it easy!' But
he always wanted something to do and they never complained about
that."

Do you think the second album suffered from not having enough writing time?
"No. Not at all. Because those songs that appeared on *Origin* had already
been written on the road and they were fine with them. The band
recorded the album in parts, so they did the first session with Dave Bottrill
at Ridge Farm. And they recorded them in that particular sequence in that
way – 'New Born', 'Bliss', 'Darkshines', 'Plug in Baby', they did those
with Dave Bottrill and they worked really well. They were left alone, they
did have the time and the freedom to experiment and all that. You've got
to remember Matthew never demoed. He didn't want to do demos. And
if you said anything negative, that was it. The song was scrapped. You
couldn't say anything negative. I had to be very careful with my words, I
learnt that early on."

Were there lost Muse classics?
"Yeah, absolutely, anything negative. You had to be very careful."

Was it your idea to put them with John Leckie the second time?
"Absolutely. It worked really well the first time. Maverick were very
happy with the record and so was everyone else. But after John, Matt
came to me and said, 'We want someone like John but younger', someone
a bit more closer to their age with similar musical tastes really. So that was
a difficult one. I thought, 'Fuck, they've worked with John, now how can

they improve from here?' So when I went looking, I went to America; I knew there had to be someone in America. And again it was Rick Rubin who put me on to Rich [Costey]. I went to LA and I said to Rick, 'Who are the new guys that you are excited by?', and he just looked at me and he said, 'Rich mixes all my records' and just walked out the room. I thought, 'OK, who the fuck is Rich?' And the great thing was when I met with Rich, he was already a big Muse fan. He'd just done this record with Cave-In and Fiona Apple, and he'd worked with some other bands that [Muse] were fans of. But even when I came back with the idea of Rich Costey, they were like, 'No, fuck off, we're not working with him, we want someone a bit bigger.' It took a bit of persuading, then they said, 'All right, well if he really wants to work with us we'll have to do it here in the UK.' So I said, 'All right, he's never worked here before but I'll get him here.' So we booked the Air studios, and fortunately they connected, all went well and the rest is history."

Chapter Five

HAVE you heard, went the whispers, about the moons? Word filtered back from the provinces and from Europe throughout the spring and summer of 2001 of the most bizarre sights greeting crowds at the end of Muse's larger gigs. Besides the now familiar white cones lining the back of the stage, the encore of 'Bliss' would see dozens of huge, inflatable white moons launched from the stage wings, the venue balcony or wherever they could be hidden, bouncing brilliantly around the crowd or onto the stage, emitting a burst of ticker tape whenever they were popped. There was talk of the crew being dressed as ringmasters on occasion, of Muse's stage show expanding at an even faster rate than the size of the venues they were playing. They were packing out the Manchester Academys, Cambridge Corn Exchanges, Paris La Cigales and Amsterdam Paradisos of the mid-table European circuit, but in their hearts and pockets they were already treating them like arenas.*

Have you heard about the weird instruments? They claimed that Dom was leaving his drum kit for a song or two to play what appeared to be a huge African xylophone made from animal bones. Apparently he'd tried bleaching some of the bones from the recording sessions in order to keep them fresh enough to take on tour to play, but they started rotting so he had to leave them at home.

And have you heard about the parties? It seemed the show didn't end with the balloons for some lucky fans. Backstage were held wild masked balls fuelled by magic mushrooms and tequila, or massive lake-side cocktail parties, or frenzied nights of fumblings on the tour bus. Sometime after the recording of *Origin . . .*, Matt had split with his girlfriend of six years – she'd either tired of his constant touring or taken the hints from the tracks

---

* Indeed, when asked midway through the *Origin . . .* world tour where they could see themselves playing in the future, Matt declared he'd end his career playing smoky dive bars like Tom Waits, while Dom envisioned them playing stadiums.

on the album that were painfully pessimistic about relationships (he was quoted as saying he found it impossible to have a steady relationship while on tour so much). Finding himself single for the first time since he was 16, Matt decided to follow Dom's lead and take advantage of the sex and socialising he'd previously felt uncomfortable with. Suddenly, touring became less of a jading experience for him and more like freedom; he'd never really experienced anything outside of Devon before, and this new sense of instability and adventure felt like fun. And yet, there was still a darker side to his excess: when his relationship broke up he felt he'd lost a sense of self, and he felt he wanted to break himself up into as many pieces as possible in order to spread himself around. He felt dislocated from his old friends back in Devon as all he had to talk about these days was his band, so being on the road was the only chance that Matt had to connect with his fanbase, with the people he could really relate to through his music. And he was connecting in the most literal way possible.

He was still uncomfortable with the shallowness of groupie-dom, however, and concocted methods to overcome his aversion. The band began holding masked after-show parties to allow people's inhibitions to drop, helped by the ready availability of mushrooms. Matt would don a white mannequin mask, large gold bow tie and curly blue clown's wig; Dom would disguise himself as a red-helmeted Transformer and Chris would have a weird, yellow Japanese concoction. Matt would, some years later, describe a tried-and-tested method to instigate an orgy: first get all of the party-goers in masks, then start a 'bundle' with your mates that turns into a tickling session involving some girls, and then let nature take its course. Chris, with a girlfriend and son back home and another one soon to be on the way, was never involved in such activities, preferring to hang out with the crew when the parties became too frisky. The 2001 tour was the longest time Chris had ever spent away from his family and, while he missed them madly, he couldn't let himself wallow in homesickness, so he took the role of making the drinks (wine for band and crew, beer for Dom).

Word of these parties spread over the course of 2001, and some fans began following the band on tour purely to be involved in them. The parties occasionally held scary moments for Matt – one fan tried to give him his girlfriend because, "I think she was doing his head in", while others gave him gifts of fattening medicines because they were worried about his weight. He began wearing jewellery given to him by fans, and was forced to change his email address when too many people got hold of it and started sending him long mails about how his music had stopped them killing themselves. During his more 'shroom-addled moments he felt hounded backstage and felt the need to escape, and he made himself a loose rule to hang out with the less-obsessive fans of the band after the shows if at all possible, as much for his safety as his sanity. But what he gained most from this period of extreme indulgence was a firmer knowledge of his 'other', more hedonistic self and a more intimate connection with his bandmates.

The music may have been of a higher class; the behaviour, however, as is the wont of those newly attaining the status of 'rock star', was rather more crudely played out.

* * *

Muse's world tour to promote *Origin Of Symmetry* began on April 4 with a secret show at Exeter's Lemon Grove for around 300 fans, family and obsessives flown in from around the globe, before taking in a swift five-date tour of the UK and heading to the continent in earnest on April 12 for an acoustic radio session at 3FM's Denk aan Henk show. Here they played stripped-down versions of 'Space Dementia' and 'Megalomania' before hitting the Paradiso for that night's gig. Unlike previous tours, this time they were under constant scrutiny via the camera lens of Tom Kirk, their old schoolfriend, who came to visit the band at the Paradiso and happened to have his camera with him. He'd just finished a college course in Brighton and, in their trademark manner of hiring crew and touring mates from their small pool of Teignmouth pals, the band suggested he act as their multi-media advisor, filming them whenever he could. Three days later, when he'd failed to return home from the tour, he was fired from his job in the UK and took to filming Muse full-time for a project that would eventually become the extra material on the *Hullabaloo* DVD.* Tom, metaphorically speaking, has never come home since.

Supported by rising indie hopefuls The Cooper Temple Clause and JJ72, Muse toured a set of roughly 16 songs around the UK and Europe

---

* The DVD featured the author interviewing Muse in Moscow that September.

(taking in France, Germany, Switzerland, Holland, Sweden, Denmark, Spain, Italy, Norway, Luxembourg and Belgium), spanning their two albums with a refined punch. With a more fixed plan to the set list than the random song shuffles of previous tours, gigs would generally open with the revolving trio of 'Micro Cuts', 'New Born' and 'Uno' before piling into 'Showbiz', 'Screenager', 'Feeling Good', 'Sunburn', 'Hyper Music' and 'Unintended' (usually in roughly that order), the main set closing with a mix-and-match of 'Cave', 'Fillip', 'Citizen Erased' and 'Hate This & I'll Love You'. 'Plug In Baby' almost always precluded an encore of 'Muscle Museum', 'Bliss' and sometimes a final 'Agitated'. These more structured sets were a sign of their growing maturity as a live band, developing set peaks and troughs in their show and incorporating the first elements of an arena spectacular in 'Bliss''s bouncing balloon cascade. It was also a thumbed nose to the anti-shows of Radiohead, whom they were still being (innacurately) compared to. With his group's music now sounding so clearly unique, Matt could only put the continued presence of the R-word in their reviews down to the fact that they were both British bands who shared a producer, but concluded that there were no British bands as good as Muse. Indeed, Radiohead's Colin Greenwood caught the band on this tour, hilariously commenting that they needed to "lighten up".

Muse's new maturity didn't stretch to their onstage behaviour though. Having hired a more professional crew this time there were less technical problems to give Matt the red mist, and with the balloon show providing a nightly slash of 'wow' during the encore, he no longer felt the need to be a one-man stadium show. With the help of his new guitar tech (the ex-RATM guy), he'd studied his hero Tom Morello's guitar rack and realised that the less effect pedals you use the more you actually play your instrument, so he was ever more ardent in the technical quality of his performance. But his new-found freedom, relationship-wise, encouraged him to let loose and enjoy himself to such a degree that he still went berserk at the end of the shows anyway, and his bandmates were happy to join in. Matt would claim that he came close to madness onstage, feeling lost and not knowing what was going on; he'd liken it to being a ventriloquist's dummy or John Malkovich in the movie *Being John Malkovich*, when the eponymous actor climbs inside his own brain and sees everyone around him as having his own face. Madness or exuberance, each night on the final chord guitars would fly into amps, drum kits, balloons, hanging cone drapes, backdrops and sometimes Dom's face; one night Matt even tried to trash his piano with his guitar. The drum kit was pulled to pieces at almost every gig and the band would carry each other offstage on their backs or upside down, leaving the crowd to fight to the death over cymbal stands, drumsticks and shards of smashed guitar (or sometimes fully intact ones). It was the best of times, it was the wildest of times, yet most of Muse's wilder moments were saved for offstage.

There were hints of tour bus tequila-fuelled threesomes and wild dressing room trashing sessions, in which they'd spray champagne around the room or lower it down to clamouring fans outside the windows in ice buckets. Band members were known to pass out in lobbies after too many nights of drunken snorkelling in the hotel's Jacuzzi. At a filmed recording of six songs for Madrid radio station Radio 3, Matt, allegedly drunk at 4 p.m., replaced the distorted third verse of one song with the words "fucking fucking fucking fucking little fucking fucking little fucking fucking little fucker, yeah!" and some incoherent mumbling, causing the band to be banned by that station. At a TV appearance in Paris, having now sold 150,000 copies of *Showbiz* in France, the police had to escort them through a screaming crowd of 2,000 people clogging the entire street to the studio doors. In Copenhagan, after a gig in the independent anarchist enclave of Christiana – an island in the centre of the city that's like an extended squat, where Denmark's anti-establishment die-hards live by their own rules, which consist largely of decriminalising and openly selling soft drugs – a *Kerrang!* journalist reportedly witnessed scenes of tour-bus depravity involving copious mushrooms and tequila, and various members of band and crew and around 10 Scandinavian girls in varying states of undress.

The Italian leg of the April/May tour was even more off-kilter. At a show in Milan, finding himself on a larger than average stage, Matt attempted a full circuit of the drum riser between verses, only to fail to make it back to his mike in time for his cue.* In Rome, where the band played a sold-out show at the Palladium, Dom, Chris and Matt spent the afternoon pulling warrior poses, making imperial thumbs-down actions

---

* This may have happened later, at a festival date in Bologna that September.

and reciting lines from *Gladiator* at the Colosseum while getting recognised by tourists from Teignmouth. Later, Matt broke the noise limits of the venue with fiery guitar licks during the show and premiered a new instrumental piece he'd been working on, tentatively titled 'Butterflies & Hurricanes', a tune that would eventually come to represent the most perfect blending yet of Muse's classical, hard-rock and melodic edges.

The next day in Rimini, on April 28, the after-show would prove to be a pivotal one for Matt Bellamy. Rimini is a picturesque seaside town to the north of Italy's Adriatic coast, surrounded by stunning green hills sloping down to the sea, and it was here that Muse pulled up to the cowshedesque Velvet club where they would be playing that night. Matt was in playful mood – he wandered around during the day with a banana on his head and teased out a few of the arpeggiated harmonies of The Smiths' 'Please Please Please Let Me Get What I Want' during soundcheck, later claiming that it was an example of the sort of Morrissey lyric he aspired to writing but wasn't capable of . . . yet.*

The gig was impeccable: Matt's guitar playing was on fire, Dom ended up standing on his drum kit to talk to the crowd, and backstage afterwards Chris ran around drenching everyone within spraying distance with champagne (from the five bottles that Muse demanded on their rider each night, along with a fresh pair of socks, since Matt's feet had a tendency of stinking out the dressing rooms) in celebration of the news that his beloved Rotherham FC had been promoted to the First Division. In the highest of spirits, Muse invited many fans to an impromptu 'aftershow' by the beautiful duck lakes nearby; usually a site reserved for local fishermen but that night the scene of a Muse pedalo party. It's believed to be this night that Matt met a special girl, one he could really connect with and who would eventually draw him back to Italy for good. A few months later he would claim that he'd met a girl who could accept him having fun on tour, could understand his situation and the scrapes it might get him into and that, in relationship terms, he finally had everything he'd ever wanted. Matt was certainly moved by something that night; the next day, as the tour bus rolled on to Vienna for a headline gig at the Libro Music Hall, where I'd watched them support Bush only

* The Smiths were a regular tour-bus favourite at the time, to the extent that Matt began quoting lyrics from 'Half A Person' and 'How Soon Is Now?' in conversation.

15 months before, he took some personal time out to go and ruminate at Beethoven's graveside.

★ ★ ★

The link between fan and band was becoming increasingly strong: Matt would regularly post bulletins on fan sites such as microcuts.net, and a select few fans were even invited to be extras in the next video, for *Origin . . .*'s second single, 'New Born', on May 21 by emailing their details to Taste Media; successful applicants were filmed moshing to the song in a west London warehouse, while Muse' performance was filmed in Prague on a rare day off from the European tour. The location was chosen to fit a tight budget (Prague, like Canada, is very cheap to film in) but the set was anything but, constructed on its side so that in the final promo the band would look as though they were playing on the side of a building to their stunned fans. They didn't, it just looked as though the director had turned the camera on its side, but despite every technical hitch imaginable, the need to morph the two shoots together into one and a deadline so tight that the producer apparently still has nightmare flashbacks every time he hears the tune, Muse thought it was their most successful video to date. They were painted yellow so that their skin would seem golden on the screen, a that director David Slade used with Muse on several occasions.

Meanwhile, the tour rolled on through Germany and Scandinavia, Belgium, Luxembourg and Spain, with Muse occasionally playing afternoon sets for TV or radio shows such as Madrid's RTVE station or Radio One in the UK, before their rapturously received and long-since sold-out evening gigs, playing to thousands of adoring Muse-ites in every city. As the tour rounded up with a triumphant lope back across a smattering of the UK's bigger halls towards two sold-out nights at London's 5,000-capacity Brixton Academy – London's biggest theatre venue and a landmark gig for all bands rising through the rock ranks, representing a gateway to the arena circuit – things couldn't have looked better for Muse. The fan pandemonium of 2000 was converting into long-term adoration; Muse were becoming a band who really meant something to people.

What's more, they were becoming regulars in the upper reaches of the UK singles chart. The plan had been, if 'Plug In Baby' went well, to next release a less obvious single, and sure enough on June 5 the six-minute stormer 'New Born' was put out over a grand total of six formats: CDs 1 & 2 carried the video and a live take of 'Plug In Baby' recorded at the Amsterdam Paradiso at the start of the European tour, plus three new songs. There was an offcut from the Leckie sessions entitled 'Shrinking Universe', which would go on to be used in the trailer for the movie *28 Weeks Later*, and a folkish, upbeat number called 'Map Of Your Head', which though it would have sat oddly on *Origin . . .*, was less throwaway than it first appeared. This song is also credited as an admission of Matt's fetish for white socks; the line "wearing just socks and a phone" was taken by fans to be a reference to posts he'd made on muse-official.com in which he claimed to find girls wearing only a T-shirt and socks to be the ultimate turn-on. Finally, there was an improvised piano doodle called, with appropriate modesty, 'Piano Thing', the sort of virtuoso bout of tinkling that Matt would throw out between press interviews around this time if there happened to be a piano in the room.

Not enough formats for you? Then try the Hyper Music Box featuring all the new songs, the live 'Plug In Baby' plus 'New Born' live and both of the singles videos. Want it on 7"? Why of course, with 'Shrinking Universe' on the flip. A Maxi CD in some territories, you say? OK then, they made a concoction of CD1 and CD2. Still want more? How about a 12" of remixes by Timo Maas and Paul Oakenfold, with you in just a fortnight. Finding their fanbase to be of the completist variety, let it not be said that Muse weren't milking the multi-format release ploy dry, but the tactic was bearing fruit. 'New Born' charted at number 12, having been pressed further into the public conscience all week by a string of shambolic TV appearances that saw Muse back on their old destructive form. They smashed up their rose-draped set at *CD:UK* in retaliation for being introduced by Richie from 5ive (host Cat Deeley jokingly threatened to send them the bill for the damages), drove to Leeds for a gig at the University, partied all night then raced back down to London to play 'New Born' on T4 with humongous hangovers (the song was cut off by the credits halfway through), then rushed straight to Bristol to play another gig. By the time they reached the *Pepsi Chart Show* on the eve of 'New Born''s release, they were so dismissive of the pop TV treadmill that they 'performed' (i.e. mimed for the cameras) with Chris on drums, Dom on bass and Matt not even playing guitar but swinging from a curtain above his amps for the end of the song. There were similar scenes at *Live &*

Kicking, when the set was invaded by some of Muse's body-popping mates and the song ended up in a band bundle that thankfully didn't turn into an orgy.

Whether going about the serious business of international touring or the novelty piss-take of children's television, Muse were riding high. But little did they know it was about to get a little worse before it got a whole lot better.

* * *

When the message came through, Matt probably thought it was another joke from Chris Martin.

As the figureheads of two bands suffering the press brickbats of being cast as 'post-Radiohead', Bellamy and Martin had struck up a close friend-ship: Martin would come round to the London flat that Matt, Dom and Tom Kirk were now sharing (they'd collected sufficient people to party with in London that they didn't need to go to Devon to party any more) to play them demos for songs from Coldplay's forthcoming second album, *A Rush Of Blood To The Head*, looking for a reaction. Matt always thought that he'd never be able to do that, since if anyone had been critical of his demos he'd have wanted to kill them, but then Matt had learnt a lot from Chris about being charming and, in an ironic comment on each other's good nature, the pair spent the summer embroiled in a joke text-message slanging match. Matt would text Chris calling Coldplay "that 'Yellow' band"; Chris would direct his reply to "Mr Pomp Rock Short-Arse". The 'abusive' banter rolled on endlessly; they were the epic-rock Derek & Clive.

So that summer afternoon in Hyde Park when one of Muse's pre-album press interviews was interrupted by phone calls from their management's office to say that they'd been called a "Radiohead tribute band" by a major rival guitar band, Matt no doubt chuckled to himself for a second. Until he scurried off into the bushes to check the details. At some point that summer Matt threw his mobile phone, which had Rage Against The Machine's 'Revolver' as its ringtone, into a river. It may well have been that day, after the news was to give him.

This was no jocular badmouthing from Chris Martin at all. The quote was from Kelly Jones, singer with Stereophonics, an unfathomably popular, plodding, post-Oasis trad-rock band aimed at the stool and slipper dadrock market: the two bands had played US shows and festivals together, yet Stereophonics were exactly the kind of breed under threat of being wiped off the face of the map by Muse's ravenous future rock. At a press conference to launch Stereophonics' 'A Day At The Races' shows – festival-type multi-band events headlined by Jones' crew, which were to have taken place at Donington had not that year's foot-and-mouth outbreak forced the organisers to move the shows to the Cardiff Millennium Stadium – Jones had announced that they'd asked Muse to play on the bill but that their agent had insisted the band be paid £25,000 to perform. "You can get a Radiohead tribute band for less than that," Jones jibed, and a classic tit-for-tat music press spat ensued.

"I wish I could be as cool as him," came Bellamy's response, "and I wish I could write lyrics like him." "He's just a tool, he should get laid more," went Jones' withering riposte. It was a bit rich coming from a band who reportedly demanded £1.7 million to play The Carling Weekend, Matt said, adding that they'd have played the gig for free since they'd got on well during their US shows, only now Stereophonics would have to pay him £2 million and hire him a personal Portaloo for him to support them. Matt was uptight and a bastard, Jones wittily rejoined.

And so it went on for several weeks until the truth of the matter leaked out: there'd been a misunderstanding between the bands' booking agents, no money had been offered and Muse couldn't have played the event anyway since they'd signed exclusivity deals with T In The Park and V2001 that banned them from playing any other major UK event that summer. Still, his first bout of open hostility in the press was confusing and hurtful to Matt. He was used to being thrown out of nightclubs by the neck by angry bouncers or being called names, sure – a few months after this event on his way into the Astoria to see a gig, he'd be called a twat by a random stranger looking for a fight with the tiniest rock star they could find. And he was no stranger to road rage either: he'd regularly borrow his mum's car and face threats from angry motorists. One time he parked on the kerb and a car deliberately scratched against his to point out his mistake; when Matt started swearing at the car, a middle-aged man emerged with a crowbar and set about smashing his headlamps, much to Matt's amusement as he sat in the driver's seat videoing the whole attack.

So everyday threats and violence Matt could laugh off; he was used to it.

And the sneers of the press he shrugged off too, such as that very week when the band were the focus of accusations of selling out when 'Sunburn' appeared as the theme to a TV advert for Apple's new iMac computers, in return for a reported five-figure fee. But concerted hatred from a fellow musician he couldn't understand. That said, he should have taken it as a professional compliment – Jones' snipes were a sign of how important and threatening Muse were becoming to the cosy musical hegemony, of the fear Jones had that Muse had come to burst his lucrative AOR rock bubble.

The Stereophonics' drummer, Stuart Cable, approached Chris in a German hotel some weeks later to apologise on Kelly's behalf, saying that the singer was under a lot of stress to promote his album, but by then Muse had far more pressing things to worry about. Because they were about to come under fire from harsh criticism far closer to home.

★ ★ ★

Befitting a man of unusual mental processes, Matt Bellamy had difficulty listening to music. He didn't like having other people's unwanted music playing around him, on radios or at parties, preferring to pull on a pair of headphones and "disappear". And he had a similar aversion to hearing his own music in public; by the summer of 2001 he'd only actually heard *Origin Of Symmetry* a couple of times, and then only when other people had put it on in his presence, something that made him feel most uncomfortable.

And he wasn't alone in the opinion. While 'Plug In Baby' had been a hit in the UK, US radio had failed to pick up on the track, and the mumblings coming from the Maverick camp were worrisome to say the least. They thought the single was too histrionic, had too much falsetto, and that the album was lacking in singles and wasn't radio-friendly enough. The label even went as far as to tell the band to re-record the song without the falsetto vocal, to which came Muse's curt and prompt response: "Stick it up your arse, you fat cunt". Further pressure from the label for the band to remix or even re-record the entire album caused even more friction, probably not helped by Matt telling the press that he still hadn't met Madonna after 18 months on her label, but that when he sells 10 million albums and develops a body like Ricky Martin's she'd probably give him a blow job. With the label refusing to back down and the band plain insulted by their demands to compromise their music for the radio plays*, Maverick closed discussions by refusing to release *Origin Of Symmetry* in the United States and, bar a few contractual wranglings, Muse would leave the label a short while later. System Of A Down's Serj Tankian stepped in to try to license the album to his own Serjical Strike label but failed; *Origin . . .* wouldn't get a proper US release for another four years and Matt's brother never did get his Madonna autograph.

More fool Maverick, you might argue, since *Origin Of Symmetry* was released in the UK on July 17 to a startlingly positive critical reception from most quarters. *NME*, praising the ambition, reinvention and sheer neo-classical rock violence of the record, awarded *Origin . . .* a rare 9 out of 10, while other reviewers finally began to dismiss the Radiohead comparisons, finding the band to have more in common with Jeff Buckley, Jacques Brel and the *Doctor Who* theme than Thom Yorke's lot. While there was some sniping among the internet-based reviewers (perhaps considering themselves bastions of all things futuristic), the mainstream music press had reversed its usual tendency of enthusiastically plugging a band's debut album only to go lukewarm on its second; they had tried to knock them down only to watch them steadfastly build up. And Matt must have felt a certain satisfaction at the *Kerrang!* reviewer's comment that 'Hyper Music' featured a solo "worthy of Tom Morello himself".

If *Origin . . .* felt to the reviewers like more of a unified album than *Showbiz*, it was reflected in the artwork. In an attempt to emulate the universal symmetry that inspired the title and the continuity within the songs themselves, Muse asked 12 different artists to design a sleeve based only on the title, the idea being that each of the artworks would be radically different but linked by a kind of 11th dimensional theoretical thinking, random works that all have the same origin.

The front cover bore the work by William Eager, a drawing of a barren white wasteland – not too dissimilar to the landscape from Matt's hallucinations – dotted with huge, metal, alien antennae in the shape of rugby goal posts. Other works included Darren Gibbs' drawing of a queue of identical men (worker drones?) waiting to enter a plain white cube/workplace; a negative of an Eastern goddess surrounded by scrawlings of modern

* Although it should be pointed out that 'New Born''s six minutes were cut by 90 seconds for a 'radio edit' on its release.

horrors including tanks, plane crashes, terrorist gunmen and overturned police cars by Austin, which seemed to blame ancient religion for the terrors of today; Leo Marcantonio's block drawing in red, white and black, ironically resembling the later cover for Coldplay's *X&Y* album; Tony Oladipo's portrayal of a robot band playing for a gang of fighting humans; an invasion of smiley orange aliens over 70s Tokyo by Butch Gordon; Tim Berry's dual works of a decaying discotheque sign and an industrialised and technology-blighted suburban barbeque; Simon Earith's photo of a fighter jet as if seen in the rear-view mirror of another plane, complete with the superimposed legend 'OBJECTS ARE CLOSER THAN THEY APPEAR'; obtuse surrealist attempts from Marilyn Patridean and David Foldvari; and the minimalist Soviet Youth space-cadet advert of Adam Cruickshank's contribution, which was featured on the single sleeve of 'New Born'. While the pieces were all unique in vision, collectively they created the impression of a world made worse by technological advances and mired in drudgery and fear. The three-word title, it seemed, had prompted in the artists the same ideas as it had in the band.

When Muse received the news that their second album had not only made the Top 40 (which *Showbiz* had pointedly failed to do) but was resting a week after release at number three in the UK charts (and would go on to match the sales of *Showbiz* within four months), they were in the middle of their second summer of festival dates. A rather more leisurely foray than that of the previous year – they'd played a total of 57 festivals in 2000, thanks to their inability to say no to any gig they were offered – they played 19 shows between June and September, starting two days after Brixton with two shows in Ireland as part of the Heineken Green Energy Show festival, Switzerland's Sound Arena Rock Festival and, on June 24, their second appearance at BBC Radio 1's One Big Sunday. After the disastrous shambles of their truncated set at the previous year's shindig, this two-song set – at Manchester's Heaton Park, alongside the likes of Wyclef Jean and Usher – was thankfully live, and the Manchester crowd lapped up 'Plug In Baby' while the balloon launch during 'New Born' was perfect for a summer festival crowd. Finishing by 4 p.m., the band hot-footed it to London that same day to play 'Bliss' at Abbey Road studios for BBC Choice radio.

Then they hit the festival circuit in earnest, switching the set around to begin with 'Citizen Erased' and end with the balloon-festooned 'Bliss' for five festivals around France: Les Folies De Maubuege in Lille, Festival Les Insolents at Quimper, Le Rock Dans Tous Ses Etats in Evreux, Mimes' Antic Aren in Nimes and La Route De Rock in Saint-Malo, notable for a near legendary final-chord riot that saw Matt's red Iceman guitar hurled into the moshpit and Chris rugby-tackling Dom off the top of his shattered drum kit. Along the way they took in Belgium's Rock Werchter and Pukkelpop events, Germany's Haldern Festival, Holland's Lowlands, Independent Days in Bologna, Italy and Scotland's T In The Park, where they awkwardly shared a bill with Stereophonics. They even slotted in another week in their beloved Japan, playing two shows in Osaka and Tokyo and visiting more Shinto shrines, where Matt, ever the sacrilegious master of mayhem, found great hilarity in throwing holy water in Dom's face.

With *Origin* . . . creeping towards its chart-smashing release it was a high-spirited and celebratory jaunt, capped by Muse's first outdoor festival headlining sets at V2001 in Stafford and Chelmsford, where they headlined the second stage, and at Switzerland's Winterthur festival, where they were top of the bill. Feeling as though they'd cracked the Big League at last, Muse hit a playful and destructive high: at V Dom spent the afternoon hijacking the backstage buggies used to ferry bands from the Portakabin dressing rooms to the stage and back, and drove them around the backstage area like a madman, crashing through entire tables laden with drinks. At one festival, standing in the wings just as Slipknot took the stage (Muse were spotting a lot of Slipknot T-shirts at the front of their shows, a sign that they were connecting with the 'alienated' teen-metal contingent as well as the indie-rock kids), singer Corey Taylor stopped right in front of Dom to let out a primal pre-gig roar, which Dom found so hilarious he stole Taylor's trademark mask after the gig in order to wear it and do an uncanny and hilarious impression of the moment all the way to the next festival. That mask, if Dom kept hold of it, probably wasn't too popular at the masked parties.

As the festival season drew to a close, Taste Media/Mushroom consolidated Muse's chart successes of the summer with the release of 'Bliss' on August 20 – *Origin* . . .'s most obvious single choice after 'Plug In Baby' and a stout live favourite among the balloon-popping masses. The by now regulation 2CD package came backed with the video and a 'making of' – another David Slade production, featuring a scarlet-haired Matt falling through the centre of a futuristic mecha-planet, emerging from the other side and falling all the way to the edge of the universe, where he dissolves into a gas.* The package also included live versions of 'Screenager' and 'New Born' (from the Paradiso and a BBC Maida Vale session respectively) and two new tracks – a synthesiser and theremin instrumental called 'The Gallery' (possibly a pun on the cheesy synth music that used to accompany a section called 'The Gallery' on children's art programme *Take Hart*) and an acoustic take on 'Hyper Music' entitled 'Hyper Chondriac Music'. Hitting number 19 in the UK – an impressive placing for a third single from an album – its charting was marked by Muse returning to London to accept their second award, for Best British Band at that year's *Kerrang!* awards. Fittingly, considering the histrionic and operatic elements of the latest material, with its tongue firmly in its cheek the magazine arranged for Brain May to present the award to Muse, and played Queen's 'We Will Rock You' over the speakers as they stepped up to collect the gong. The band saw the Queen connection as no slight, however; Matt far preferred to emulate Freddie Mercury's hyper-real stage persona than the dull everyman guitar bands trudging sullenly around him in the indie Big League.

And astutely, the press began to take a much greater interest in these normal Devon outsider kids-turned-freaky-haired sci-fi nutters. With their ascent into the Top 10 and rumours of hedonistic tour parties flying thick and fast, the press interest around Muse increased tenfold by September and plenty more nuggets of band trivia emerged. They claimed they'd grown out of their inhibitions on *Origin . . .*, a result of hearing a huge amount of different music, as they were often introduced to classic bands like Captain Beefheart by John Leckie after recording sessions. Dom joked that he kicks Matt in the balls to help him reach the high notes, while Matt believed it's more to do with having small lungs and vocal chords. Matt was bemused by the pleasure that people seem to get out of shaking his hand at meet-and-greets. Chris was really quiet but occasionally got caught acting out little plays to himself. Matt would like to go to classical music concerts but can never get tickets as *Guardian* readers have bought them all 10 years before, and anyway he didn't have the right clothes (he

* This video was made entirely with miniature models and with Matt falling in a harness, not utilising the CGI effects that many suspected.

wore silk shirts specially made for him in Japan). Matt's worst habits were pacing up and down a lot and mild Tourette's; Chris' was heavy drinking, yet somehow he always managed to look like a teddy bear in the mornings. Matt hated 'normalness', doing what everybody else does, and was glad to be detached from it. Musically, Chris was into metal and The Beach Boys; Dom preferred Buddy Miles and The Aphex Twin and Matt was listening to the new Weezer album. They all loved dEus because they cram everything from the blues to disco into the same track. Matt was making music in order to leave something behind when he's gone. Almost all of the songs on *Origin . . .* were about some kind of change or transit: Matt had purposefully lost all of his friends and his girlfriend* as part of a cleansing need to move on as a person. Chris had a lot of shoes thrown at him onstage. If they'd wanted to sell millions they would have made *Origin . . .* an acoustic album. Contrary to popular belief Matt didn't feel 'tortured'; in fact, music put him in a state of utmost contentment. Chris would never follow his bandmates' lead and move to London as he wanted to "watch my boy grow". Matt was seriously thinking about building a cult and leading them to mass suicide (joke).

And more of Matt's bizarre theories came out that September. He'd compare mankind, dimensionally speaking, to a worm crawling across a piece of paper (an image from *The Elegant Universe* used to illustrate beings only aware of two dimensions). He'd claim he can connect with past versions of himself via meditation. He repeated his belief that the brain can absorb people's personalities; that you download a part of your soul or energy force into everyone you meet. And he'd talk about mysterious catacombs in Iraq where he believed you could find tablets predating language, made up of an ancient kind of computer language and star charts, and whoever owns them owns the truth of human existence. These were put there, he claimed, by aliens from the 12th planet, called Nibiru, a massive geothermal meteorite containing super-intelligent extraterrestrial life that orbits the sun every 3,200 years, on an elliptical orbit. When it gets close enough to our planet – it's only near Earth for around 200 years at a time, apparently, and due to approach again soon – they fly over and visit us. In fact, the human race itself was created by these aliens cloning

* Matt never spoke to his girlfriend after they split up.

themselves with apes or Neanderthals to a fifth of their intelligence 300,000 years ago, in order to make a race of subordinate beings to mine the planet for them – after all, we do only use one fifth of our brains and this certainly explains the human conflict between higher intelligence and animalistic instinct. It was an idea he'd picked up from reading *The 12th Planet* by Zecharia Sitchin, a writer who'd served as Colin Powell's main advisor for 20 years. Matt admitted he found the book pretty boring and read only two or three chapters, making up the rest of the story himself.

Sci-fi fantasies, random waffle and trivial titbits; it was the time of unimportant things. An innocent time when such ephemera was of interest, before grander concerns gripped the globe. For only a week after these interviews, Matt's prediction that the world's fear was about to erupt in an extremely negative way was about to come tragically true.

* * *

There are surely few remote corners of Western society and the arts that weren't deeply affected by the events of September 11, 2001, but Muse were closer than most.

On September 10, Muse were in Manhattan, playing a gig back at the Mercury Lounge as part of a short US tour at the behest of Maverick (they were still in the middle of the wrangling over the US release of *Origin Of Symmetry*, and keen to pay their dues in the country that had signed them first). Straight after the gig the band packed up and flew to Boston that night. If they'd booked a flight the following morning, of course, they'd still have been lodged on the Lower East Side, a few short miles from Ground Zero, when the planes hit.

With all air traffic over the US grounded for three days, Muse were stranded in Boston for some time after their gig there, witness to the sweeping fear, raging paranoia and talk of a War On Terror that gripped America so vehemently that week, and still does to this day. To Matt, this was his premonition proved right; that the fear building in the subconscious of society had found its tragic release and the world now trembled beneath a shadowy threat, emanating from the Al Qaida caves and US Senate building alike. His inquisitive distrust of the mainstream media would lead him over the coming months and years to scour the internet for hidden details and become embroiled in the conspiracy theories behind the terrorist attacks. The suggestion that one of the hijacker's passports had survived the inferno when the black-box recorder of the plane had melted seemed ludicrous; the rumours that six of the alleged hijackers were still alive intrigued him; the lack of an independent investigation rang alarms in him; and the whole idea that such a complex operation was carried out by such a lo-fi organisation as Al Qaida – rather than, say, the efficiently organised groups of people who stood to make vast amounts of money out of the subsequent wars it prompted – seemed so unlikely to Matt. Who was really behind it, how much had the US really known about it beforehand, how had it really happened and why? It was an event shrouded in mystery, political spin, hidden agendas, inconsistencies and half-truths, which sharpened his suspicion of media brainwashing and his distrust of what the news was telling him. It turned his mind from the galactical to the political, and such thinking would have a profound effect on Muse's next batch of material.

At the time, however, the band's reactions to the tragedy were as confused as anyone's, but since they couldn't leave Boston to continue their US tour they wasted no time in finding a studio in town in which to record the demos for two new tracks, an instant response to the massive shift in global feeling. The short, punchy and poppy 'In Your World' took a sympathetic tone in line with the mourning attitude of the week: "In your world/Nobody's dying alone" sang Bellamy, wrapping 9/11 references into a song that could easily pass as one of his trademark relationship trauma tales (it was certainly far more upbeat than most post-9/11 tributes). But the RATM-apeing hardcore of 'Dead Star' was far more accusatory, focusing on the hysteria sweeping America that week and the hypocrisy of Americans blaming other countries when they themselves were to culpable: "Shame on you for thinking you're an exception/We're all to blame/Crashing down to Earth/Wasting and burning out/Fading like a dead star/Harm is coming your way". The song read almost like a condemnation of America, Matt mocking the country for not seeing the potential consequences of an international attitude that mirrored the flagrant idiocy and bullishness he'd witnessed first-hand at Woodstock. Bold as the statement here was (and not necessarily caring what America thought of them for the time being, since things were falling apart with Maverick), the band were sensible enough not to release the songs for a full nine months.

Chapter Five

Two weeks later, with Muse having finally extricated themselves from America, I joined them again in what used to be the theological opposite of the US – Moscow – and found them far from dragged down by the yoke of global mourning but in sprightly mood. Matt had spent the flight from London telling the rest of the band to fear the worst; Muse had sold next to no records in Russia and Matt was convinced they'd arrive to widespread indifference or even hostility, playing to a couple of hundred people at most. But the Russian music market is deceptive – largely based around the black market, bands can have massive fanbases there while selling very few records; sales of 100,000 would mean that roughly three times that number owned pirated copies of your album. Plus, the cancellation of many international trips by bands in the wake of September 11 meant that anticipation of their visit was at fever pitch. Where Muse expected a nation shrugging its bear-like shoulders, they found pandemonium.

The first signs of it came that afternoon, during a photoshoot in Red Square. Nobody knew Matt, Dom and Chris would be there at that time, yet within 10 minutes of the first flashbulb everyone under 25 in the square had recognised them and was hotly pursuing them out of the area and into the people carriers. And the gig rammed the point home. Rather than playing a 100-capacity club, the show was at the 10,000-capacity Lukhniki Sports Palace, a crumbling old building on the outskirts of the city housing a massive sports complex. Treated to a legendary bout of Musemania, the crowd were a frenzy of roars and moshing, despite a high-profile presence of armed security guards enforcing bizarre gig rules (for instance, fans were stopped from leaving the auditorium for 15 minutes after the band had finished by gun-wielding policemen). And the scenes after the show were sheer madness – the crush through the mauling crowd from the stage door to the people carriers ready to whisk us to the VIP room of a central, mafia-owned nightclub (complete with metal detectors at the entrance) for late drinks was the closest to full-on Beatlemania that this writer has ever witnessed. And the party in Dom's room that night seemed more like an attempt at the world record for squeezing as many vodka-drenched girls into one hotel room as possible. So rammed was the room, in fact, that Matt eased the crush by ferrying girls around the hotel corridors in pairs, for what purpose we can only surmise.

Russia, it appeared, was the new Japan, and without even trying Muse were among the first new bands of the decade to break it.

★   ★   ★

Back in Europe that autumn, Muse reached a zenith on several fronts.

There was a zenith in sales: four months after its release, *Origin . . .* had hit the 200,000 sales mark, already outselling the 180,000 shifted units of *Showbiz* (although some sources were quoting *Showbiz* as having sold several million worldwide), and fast on its way to being declared platinum in the UK (300,000 sales).

There was a zenith in mood, as Muse's most celebratory year approached its conclusion on a tour taking in clutches of shows in the UK, Belgium, Holland, France, Spain, Italy, Austria and Germany, with no sign of the party abating. At Plymouth's Pavilions they debuted 'In Your World' and 'Dead Star' to a rapturous response and the songs became fixed live favourites for the rest of the year, with 'Dead Star' usually following the introductory tape of Tom Waits' spooky spoken-word slasher tune 'What's He Building?', a tale of a neighbour's ominously secret DIY project full of talk of poisons and chainsaws and low moans and formalde-hyde. At several shows, Matt began throwing out rose petals from the sleeves of his Japanese silk shirts into the crowd. And at the 6,000-seater Palavobis arena in Milan, the band took great pleasure in spraying the crowd with champagne at the end of the show, before disappearing for an after-show that found them acting as weird human art installations, semi-naked and wrapped in blue neon lights with chains attached, which party guests were invited to pull. It was the mask idea taken to its most hilarious and ludicrous extreme by a band knowing they were on the cusp of greatness; in fact, the masks themselves had gone by now, replaced with novelty hats – Dom's new blue hair was crushed beneath a cowboy hat, Chris sported a fetching sombrero, and Matt had procured himself a French riot police helmet complete with visor.

And there were the French zeniths; the chain of venues that Muse played in Lille and Montpellier on the way to two nights at the 7,000-capacity Zenith venue in Paris.

The Paris Zenith shows were a landmark in Muse's career. Though the venues they'd been playing had been steadily increasing in size and they had occasionally headlined mammoth gigs in unexpected places

(Moscow, for instance) and at festivals, these shows on October 28 and 29 (a combined capacity of 14,000 over the two nights) and the show they'd announced that November at London's 12,500-capacity Docklands Arena, marked their first tentative step into the arena circuit, trying the big sheds on for size. To all outside observers they were always meant to be an arena band, but for Muse themselves it was a leap of faith and one that, finding the French shows selling out swiftly*, they wanted to document. So plans were put in place for the filming of one of their first arena shows – they thought the Docklands Arena wasn't quite glamorous enough and wanted to honour France as the territory where they first broke big (and which had snapped up the tickets for the Zenith shows quickest), so opted to film both nights at the Zenith to compile into their first-ever DVD release.

It would be no ordinary DVD though: with Muse believing their live work to be as important as their recordings, they wanted no shoddy output, so 28 cameras would be used to allow the production company, Mission TV, to play around with some groundbreaking visual ideas. And it was to be no ordinary show – for their first proper arena sets, Muse deemed it necessary to bring in big screens for the first time to display visual accompaniment to the songs (albeit very basic visuals compared with later shows; these were swirling stars and shapes interspersed with footage of the band streamed from the cameras) and show the faces of the band to the fans at the back of the hall. Backstage before the show, while coming up with some lighting ideas involving casting huge shadows across the backdrop as Muse took the stage, Matt suggested that they arrive onstage by bursting through the big screens, only to be told that was a terrible idea due to the cost of the screen fabric. Sure enough, his mischievous nature sniffing out a challenge, as the final burst of stage destruction on the last night reached its peak, Matt pierced the fabric of the nearest screen with the head of his guitar, tore it wide open and clambered through, eventually wearing the entire screen around his neck like an enormous ruff.

The Zenith gigs were astonishing examples of Muse's development into one of the UK's biggest rock prospects; truly the band stepped into the arena circuit like they already owned the place. To Waits' terrifying deadpan, strobed silhouettes of Matt, Dom and Chris flashed 20 ft high on the backdrop before 'Dead Star''s pummelling RATM riff blasted and the

* The Docklands Arena show didn't sell out, deflating the band's then rising ego.

stage was strafed in spotlights, lighting Matt, with his hair spiked like a Martian punk and a camera strapped to the front of his guitar to film his flaming fretwork. Throughout the shows, Muse were consummate rock showmen: Matt, spinning, twirling and bunny-jumping all the way, threw *Phantom Of The Opera* poses as the church organs erupted in 'Megalomania', lobbed guitars into amps or thin air during 'Uno' and 'Agitated', flung ticker tape from his sleeves during the megaphone section of 'Feeling Good', and finger-tapped the entire solo of 'In Your World' without plucking a single string. Dom was a tsunami of sticksmanship, breaking out the bone xylophone for 'Screensaver', and when Chris wasn't supplying lead-heavy bass lines he was playing guitar arpeggios on 'Unintended' while operating the synth backing on foot pedals.

The Zenith shows also marked the first professionally filmed introduction of a new member of Muse – Matt's tarnished silver Manson guitar. As a regular patron at Manson's Guitars in Exeter, Matt was keen to have the owner, Hugh Manson, build a special guitar for him. So that year, with a bit of cash behind him at last, Matt phoned Manson requesting a special design built to specifications that the two of them drew out in pencil, so that it was precisely the right size; a few weeks later Manson called Matt into the shop to see the half-finished instrument, designed to make the neck easily replaceable if Matt were to snap it (which he has twice) and plated in aluminium, which Manson was planning to spend two weeks smoothing down to remove the rough file marks. Matt took one look at the guitar, declared, "I love the finish! It's so industrial!" and took it home that day. Nicknamed the DeLorean after the time-travelling car in *Back To The Future*, it was the first of many guitar designs, each more technically advanced than the last, that the two would develop together.

At the Zenith, as the band closed 'Bliss' with a frenzy of balloon bursting with the necks of their guitars, a vault by Matt over the drum kit worthy of an Olympic high jumper, more sprayed champagne and a band pile-up in the middle of the stage, their status as the new young pretenders of enormo-rock was assured, although which form they'd take in the future was uncertain. It was a set of two halves – the first 45 minutes of sprawling, riff-heavy prog metal (lifted largely from *Origin . . .*) was a display of the heaviness and non-conformism they'd intended to achieve with their second album, featuring enough monolithic bass and thunderous rhythms for them to morph into a Tool or a RATM in the future. The latter portion of the show, however, was all ravenous pop hooks disguised as expansive volcanic hardcore, a more accurate prediction of where their music would expand next. But for the moment, Muse teetered on the pinnacle of success, unsure if they would fall on the side of metal mayhem or diamond-drilled melodicism.

Seven UK dates (of roughly 5,000 people per night), two TV appearances (on Germany's MTV *Spin Rockstars* and BBC2's prestigious *Later . . . With Jools Holland*) and one attendance of their first MTV Europe Awards (in Frankfurt, where they won nothing) later, Muse rolled up at the Docklands Arena – their biggest headline show to date – in the flashiest possible circumstances. The gig wasn't sold out and tout tickets were going cheap, but enough cash had rolled in by now for Matt to treat himself to another boy's toy. Taking advantage of the nearby Lotus showroom, he drove directly onto the arena's floor through the huge load-in doors for soundcheck in a brand spanking new Lotus Elise.

The gig, although set in a cavernous metal packing crate of a venue and feeling half-full due to the site's draconian fire restrictions, which keep capacity on floor level to a minimum (rather than lack of ticket sales), was as sensational as the Zenith, an extravaganza where the flash and flam almost threatened to upstage the trashing of the gear and the moon balloons that were released from nets in the rafters, a sign of the stature Muse had reached, of the huge scale they'd finally – rightfully – achieved.

Like the campest of closet cases finally coming clean, Muse had come out as the finest of arena bands. And getting there faster than Coldplay or any of their contemporaries – faster and with more onward momentum in fact than any band since Oasis – they were clearly bound for even greater things.

* * *

Muse's most successful year yet ended on a multitude of highs. On November 19, the week after the Docklands show, they released the double A-side single 'Hyper Music/Feeling Good'.* The band intended it

---

* Each of the two CD versions led with one of the A-side tracks and was backed with its own video plus a live version of the other A-side; each had a new track too – 'Feeling Good' boasted Muse's cover of The Smiths' 'Please Please Please Let Me Get What I Want', which would go on to be used on the soundtrack to *Not Another Teen Movie*, while 'Hyper Music' came with extra track 'Shine', a bastardisation of the arpeggios from 'Bliss' and 'Falling Away With You'.

as a light-side/dark-side summation of their album – one track is the ulti-mate in positivity, the other the most vicious song they'd yet released, about wanting to destroy a loved one entirely. Both songs received equal attention, billing and plugging. They both had videos made for them (with the budget of one promo): 'Hyper Music' was accompanied by a visceral and violent live performance (with Chris resplendent in a Russian hoodie) in a bare red-and-black room that ultimately fills with moshing fans roped in from the websites; 'Feeling Good' came with a promo filmed at the same time with the same backdrop, only this time they played the song in a storm of rose petals to an audience of warp-faced, wall-climbing mutants, perhaps jarring somewhat with the feel-good factor of the song. Both were aired on *Later . . . With Jools Holland* and both were plugged with equal ferocity to radio, yet it was (ironically?) the 'up' song that received the most attention. 'Feeling Good' hit heavy rotation on radio and dragged 'Hyper Music' kicking and screaming to number 11 in the charts, equal to 'Plug In Baby', their highest position yet.

Suddenly Muse 'owned' 'Feeling Good' in the same way Oasis 'owned' 'I Am The Walrus' or Boyzone 'owned' 'Words'. Such was the record's crossover popularity that Nescafé used it to soundtrack their latest TV advert without the band's permission, and Muse's lawyers were quick to enforce their copyright and have it taken off the advert. A wily Nescafé, however, simply hired session musicians to re-record the song for them-selves, not in the manner of Nina Simone's original but in a faintly cheesy rip-off of Muse's version. Only the truly pug-eared wouldn't have been able to tell the difference, but still it was an underhand jab.

A largely unconcerned Muse, however, finished their laugh-a-minute 2001 touring schedule back in Japan, having sauna parties with fans and trying out a whole new format for live shows. Feeling that they could only try to surprise audiences that hadn't seen them before, they played Tokyo's Zepp, Nagoya's Bottom Line and Osaka's Imperial Hall in two halves – the first half was played acoustically and the second half a full electric set. The idea was that by covering up all of their gear for the first half the audience would assume that's what they were always like live, hence a mind-blowing surprise when they pulled off the covers, turned on the blinding lights, unleashed the balloons and set about destroying the stage during the second half. The traditionally subdued Japanese crowds were suitably awestruck; these gigs were some of Muse's wildest.

The final show of the year closed with 'Bliss' extended to nearly 10 minutes of rampant feedback improvisation, the drum kit in pieces, the stage mobbed, crew, cameramen and band in a heap on the drum riser, Chris spraying champagne over all and sundry, Matt trying to hang off a balloon that popped in his hands and Dom diving into the crowd to have his shirt nearly ripped from his back. When he finally managed to claw his way back on stage, he turned and gave a modest Japanese bow and left the stage to an uproar.

There was only one way Muse could top that. In the very last moments of 2001, as New Year's Eve approached the midnight hour, Chris became a father again, to a daughter, Ava. It seemed like Muse's celebrations would never end.

And yet, in a little over a year, things would get nigh on apocalyptic.

GLEN ROWE

How did the Origin . . . *stage show come about?*
"They saw the whole production thing as something really precious, and they wouldn't at that stage just turn up and do a show. They really wanted the production, and the lighting guy, Ollie Metcalfe, is a fucking genius even back then when he was a real young kid. They were always trying to think of really great ideas to do with no money, and that was how the whole balloon thing came about. I came to talk to Ollie about how we wanted some strange shapes on stage. We had big witches' hats that we had lights underneath. Because they were a three piece there was always space on stage, and Matt always wanted to fill things out. I remember seeing the balls for the first time. We did production rehearsals at the Great Hall in Exeter and there they were. The reason we got into it was because we wanted the projections to be on something spherical, so we had some really simple gobos [a lighting template] under the balloons so that everything felt very 3D. It looked amazing. In production rehearsals we were going through setting the backline and it was almost comical – one of them on stage left just burst. We were like, 'If this happens at a gig we are going to look like such cunts.' And then Matt's idea was maybe we fill them up with bits of paper or something, so if they do burst by accident then at least it looks like we did it on purpose. And then we took them on

tour and it got boring because they never burst! None of them ever burst onstage. They were just giant balloons projecting these gobos, so these patterns would just move around."

When did you start doing that?
"End of *Showbiz* was the witches' hats and *Origin* . . . was the globes, the balloons. Trying to find people who sold these weather balloons was almost impossible. In the early days they were just giant balloons, and then we found a place that did weather balloons. And then on one tour we got stuck and couldn't get any for ages. It just shows the fragile environment; there was a rubber shortage in the trees they'd been getting them from so they couldn't make them, and we were going everywhere trying to buy these giant balloons all over the world. I remember phoning stupid countries trying to explain what we were looking for, and it ended up getting a bit too confusing. Some poor rubber tree in Thailand is probably weakened to this day. We did buy a lot of balloons. Then the whole idea came – it was either my idea or Tom Kirk's. Tom is without a doubt the fourth member of the band and he's not someone to be taken lightly, he's a massive part of their whole thing, and it was either my idea or his to throw them into the crowd and let the crowd go fucking mental with them. And then it's so funny, because having the times when the balloons wouldn't burst, by the end of the tour we would be fashioning long strips of bamboo wire with sharpened edges, lurking like aborigines behind the guitar racks and bursting the confetti over the drums. It was trying to do a huge production show with no budget. The band always wanted to put their money back into touring and doing the live show. It was all they cared about; even in small venues where they wouldn't let you throw the balloons around we'd be trying to think of other ways to make the show look good. That's when Matt said, 'Give me some of that extra confetti', and in 'Feeling Good' he'd always have some in his pocket that he'd throw around. It always looked so epic, just him on the piano throwing that single handful of confetti. It would just rain over him really slowly. They were real visionaries. From the earliest of stages they were really trying to push it."

Did you just have a massive box of balloons you carried around the world, or did you just try to get them in every single place?
"We'd try to buy them en masse and figure out how many we'd need per

show. Then it got ridiculous and we were ordering 800 at a time. 'What, you want 800 seven-foot balloons?' 'Yes'. 'What are you gonna do with 800 seven-foot balloons?' 'Well it's a long story, but there is some tree in Thailand that's a bit sick at the moment . . .' There would be a flight case with nothing but balloons. One of Tom's jobs was to put the confetti in the fucking balloons and blow them all up. A 45-foot production truck that had all of our gear in it would be emptied and then it would be full of balloons, because it takes hours to blow them up. I have so many funny memories of walking round with the band at festivals and seeing Tom with his shirt off, chatting up some local helpers. I thought it was so sweet because he was like the balloon maker at a party and everyone got really excited about the balloons. I remember having to say to the security guards all over the world, 'Here's what will happen, when this moment comes we're all going to stand in a line, I'll lead out and we'll walk out into the front and only from the front will we throw the balloons, we don't throw them from the side', and they all got so excited. By the time they got around in front of the crowd they'd be like (mimes randomly throwing balloons). I'd be having to wrestle the security guards! The whole idea was that if you're in the crowd you see the band and from the same place all of a sudden these balloons pop up, so it looked like they were being fired out from some missile thing but it wasn't, it was just big fat roadies and overzealous security guards, who got overexcited because they were getting to play with the balloons for a little while."

And the legendary parties?
"I was brought into the back lounge of the bus and the three of them sat there and said to me, 'Our live shows are fucking great – it's your job to make our after-show parties as memorable as the gigs.' So I'd be renting makeshift bars and Matt would always opt to be the barman. It was funny. I'd phone venues saying, 'We need an amazing after-show room that's not the dressing room with cocktail makers and kegs of beer.' It was a shame we didn't start doing the massive after-show parties a year before we did, because we had about six to eight months of amazing parties that were insane, really funny. I'll be honest with you, there were times I would get the after-show passes made up, give them to each member of the crew and put their initials on the top right-hand corner, I'd give each member of the crew 10 passes to see which member of the crew could get the hottest girl

back. It was a bit Aerosmith. It was hilarious. People must've thought I was mental, they'd turn up at the parties and I'd go, 'Welcome to the party, enjoy yourselves, but hang on, can I see your pass?' Whoever we thought had the hottest girl, we'd say it was their birthday and get people to sing happy birthday, and the girls would give them a kiss. Matt would always commandeer the bar because he felt like he was giving something. He was really good at it, he really held his own as this guy who felt very confident in this area of 'whatever you want!' He was very candid, taking photographs and talking to people's brothers on the phone. It was that really exciting stage where they weren't superstars, they were just a great band. He relished those moments. He'd sit there talking to these girls' brothers, all the while checking out the ladies. Obviously Chris, the most monogamous man on the planet, would just sit there and get pissed up with the crew."

How did Chris deal with it?
"My heart often went out to Chris. The band would have parties on the buses and there'd be girls and boys running round the bus having a laugh, and Chris would be like, 'Fucking hell, I just wanna watch a DVD and relax.' So it'd be a case of, 'Well, come and sit in the crew bus.' Sometimes he felt a little bit alienated from the big party thing, but Chris would always be one of the first to have a party and get boozing. Chris drinks with the best of them, always has, always will."

Dom was the band's ladies man from the start, right?
"A phenomenal ladies man. He's one of my best mates on the planet and I love him but he's such a charmer. Women can't help but fall at his feet because he's so sweet and inoffensive. Dom was lapping it up and Matt had broken up with his girlfriend on one of the dates. He met Gaia at a show very briefly in Rome, but it was in Rimini that it happened. It was a venue called Velvet. Matt had been in a bit of a funny mood and I saw this unbelievably beautiful girl who security were trying to push out, so I ran out and said, 'She's with us.' I didn't have a spare laminate for her so I put her on a stool at the side of the stage while I went to find her one. I found out later that he'd met her the night before and thought she was amazing and beautiful. After soundcheck they disappeared off to a lake on one of those little pedalos, and I think he fell in love with her at that very

moment. That show was amazing. It was one of my favourite memories of my career. We had a mental party that night, it was literally girls fingering girls, it was so sexy! It was a real debauched night, everyone went mental. Y'know when you're a kid and you hear about the greatest summer party, you go to a house party and somehow everything's amazing? It was that night, in Rimini."

What about the masks?

"We'd send Tom out to go to local shops. We'd theme masked parties. It got to the point where we had the idea of having the whole masquerade thing. Matt still felt that it was a bit of an autograph session, so if everyone wears masks then no one knows who anybody is. We ended the tour with ginormous bass cab flight cases full of after show party costumes. In Japan we'd get superhero costumes and get big fat roadies to squeeze into these tiny costumes. There was a woman from the record label who was so funny; she got into the party spirit, she'd buy these oversized costumes and we'd walk around these bizarre venues in Velcro suits, five fat roadies walking round with Velcro suits on. It got really quite edgy. There was one venue in Germany where we walked into the room and it was really weird, with just rope lights in the floor. Matt went in earlier and gaffer-taped a chair to the wall. A chair suspended from the ceiling with gaffer. It was like being on tour with your mates. We ended up so close. It was the only time in 12 years that I've ever had post-tour blues. You didn't want it to end. And they were fucking long tours as well. I didn't go home to my flat once in three months. The band had this appetite for never coming off the road. It was the greatest time."

Were you Muse's mystery breakdancer?

"I remember doing 'Bliss' on a TV show and it was on Matt's birthday. For his birthday present, I think we did it on *Top Of The Pops*, he dared me to come on and breakdance in the middle, so I came on and did a windmill. I doubt I can still do it now. Once I did it, he wanted me to do it on every fucking TV show, and him and Chris would always bundle me and we'd end up doing loads of TV shows where the three of us are having a fight while Dom was at the back finishing off the song. Professionally, as he would."

What was the most amount of damage they caused onstage?
"They never completely did a Nirvana to annihilate the stage, but they came close. I think the last date, in Japan on the last day of the 'Origin Of Chaos' tour – we nicknamed it the 'Origin Of Chaos' tour for a laugh, and I've since learnt never to give a tour a nickname like that because everything that could go wrong fucking went wrong. The last day of the Japanese tour, which I think might have been the last date of that album, they smashed everything to fucking smithereens. It was amazing."

How much did that cost you?
"Oh, fuckin' thousands. The money they could have spent on new gear. We were buying guitars a day for Matt because on the *Origin* . . . tour we'd strap a pencil camera [to Matt's guitar]; the whole idea was like CCTV footage and we'd do close-ups of each member of the band, and every day he's just smash the guitar up in the same way."

Didn't you lose a lot of money?
"Oh no, when they smash the stuff up it comes out of their own pockets. If Dom broke his drum kit, it's up to him. If Matt broke Dom's drum kit there'd always be an argument. Matt was a little fucker, he'd always be the first person to put a hole in Dom's bass drum. They'd be happily playing away, having a great time, and then Matt would end up [mimes Matt shoving his guitar through the drum kit] and it was always, 'Like that is it?' After a while they learnt to smash up their gear without ruining it all, because after a while they weren't frustrated by their equipment breaking down, it was more of a celebration. I've got great memories of Matt at Pinkpop smashing stuff up and just standing there looking glorious, front and centre of the stage. It was like they'd turned a corner; they were just knocking out timeless tunes."

What were the maddest gigs?
"We got into having security guards on the second album. It was Tony, an SAS guy, because the crowds were absolutely insane. We'd fly into Istanbul and drive out for three hours into the middle of nowhere, and you find out the stage is a makeshift stage with no barriers, just cow gates, and Muse come on and there is a whole surge. I remember really vividly being in the mosh pit in this venue in the middle of fucking nowhere and

looking up at the moon and . . . I'm not a religious man, but I remember thinking, 'No one can die here tonight', and getting really quite emotional about it. Because I knew the songs really well I was commanding the security, [telling them] when there's a guitar riff coming in and everyone would surge to the front. You'd have minutes where you'd have 3,000 people pushing this stupid barrier, and we had about 40 security guards just standing there for the whole 45 minutes of the gigs. It was, in fact still is to this day, one of the most terrifying moments of my life. I remember looking round at Matt and he's going, 'Fine!' We went to a mafia night-club [in Moscow] where the vodka was just non-stop . . . they took us there two or three nights because they wouldn't let us go anywhere else. That was bizarre. Was that the night we pushed all the beds to one side and we totally ruined Dom's room? Weren't we jumping off the wardrobes? They'd run around like schoolboys. Poor Dom, I felt for him back then because it was always his room that got fucking ruined. It was always really shit to stay in a hotel two nights in a row because if you were only staying one night you could get the fuck out of there. I remember Lisa, our agent, ringing up going, 'What were you up to last night?' And I'd go, 'What?' She got really pissed off with me because I'd go, 'That never happened.' I'd have to lie to her and she'd say, 'They're claiming the hotel was smashed to bits', and I'd go, 'Sorry Lisa, it wasn't us', and she'd go and have a fight at the other end. Then I'd leave it a day and go, 'Well, yeah, we had a bit of a party that night . . .'

"One of my favourite memories of Brixton was that I had to take the band to go and do some fucking chart show or something in the morning, and they were really pissed off cos they didn't really get to soundcheck, but they thought, 'You know, we've been on tour, it's fine, we'll be fine.' Matt had said he wanted one stack of amps and Paul English [sound man] though Matt wanted a big Marshall row, a stack of amps, and the first Matt sees of Brixton Academy is when he walks onstage and he sees a row of Marshall amps; we got loads of dummy amps made, so it was one amp that worked and the rest were fucking dummies to make it look big. Paul thought that's what Matt meant, but Matt just meant one stack to make it look really sparse, so he hated it. At this point I walk up behind and I'm thinking, 'Oh this is a good view, I can stand behind this big stack of amps, it's safe here.' Next thing I know Matt walks over and kicks the whole fucking wall down on my head. Luckily I was hit by a dummy cab, fucking knocked my head. As it all falls down, Matt sees me rolling behind the amps going, 'Fucking hell', and he goes, 'Sorry mate', and turns his back as though it was meant to happen and just carries on playing. It's brilliant, he didn't even stop, just kept playing the riff.

"And then there was the *Pepsi Chart Show*. The band would absolutely hate doing mimes so I would beg with the TV pop shows to let them play live. That's why I ended up breakdancing; in fact it got to the point that I was breakdancing so much we even got a write-up in a magazine saying, 'Catch Muse on TV to see their mysterious breakdancer.' It got to the point where people were expecting us to pull up and fucking breakdance on every TV show, and they wouldn't do it unless something funny happened. So we did the *Pepsi Chart Show*, which was terrible, it looked so cheap and shit. So I spoke to the record company and said we were only going to do this if I could take the guys to Spearmint Rhino beforehand. So we arranged some VIP treatment and there we are, minutes away from doing the show, enjoying the wonders of beautiful women. It's ace. It's almost safe to take your missus cos it's beautiful, beautiful women on poles doing amazing stuff, and it's just one of those mad memories of eating steak and fish and good food, not cheap food, while having naked girls walking around you saying, 'Do you want a lap dance?' Me and Matt had a lap dance by different girls at the same time while chewing the food before going to do the *Pepsi Chart Show*, it was ace. That was the ignition paper for going to every great lap-dance club in the world, really. In Moscow there was a club called Golden Girls where me, Matt and Dom all thought that we'd met our future wives. They were just beauty personified. That set the real penchant for going to strip clubs in every town we turned up to. Strip clubs are somewhere you can go and you're never unfaithful to your missus, are you? You have to sit on your hands and someone rubs their leg on you and that's about as far as it gets. So it became like a nice safe thing to do. Chris would come but wouldn't allow himself any lapdances, but he would say, 'You know what, it's all right, I can go and look at tits.'"

How was it headlining V2001?

"The V headline felt like the beginning of the step up. Coldplay had played earlier in the day and were still in awe of Muse, they were like, 'Muse are the best band in the world.' Coldplay had just given each of their crew a

20-grand bonus. They basically just gave them the fee for working V. They were like, 'Thanks for working with us, here's 20 grand.' That's why people do V – for the money. So Coldplay come off and we're hanging out and Chris Martin at that point is a real bona fide pop star – he had big hits with 'Yellow' and 'Trouble' – and he wanted to come and watch the set, so I said, 'Yeah of course, jump in the van.' So we jump in the van, drive round to behind the stage and everyone's in fucking hysterics cos Chris is a really funny guy, and he's got the band cracking up laughing, and I told the crew that Chris Martin's going to introduce the band. And Chris walks out and the place goes absolutely spine-tinglingly mad. He's got his hood up, I remember his words. He said, 'Hello, I'm Chris from the band Coldplay, this is the greatest live band in the world, will you please welcome Muse.' They weren't exactly giving him a standing ovation because they were already standing up but the level got bigger. It was just amazing. The band walked on and it was right there that you felt it. Stadium rock, here we come. It was just perfect. It was faultless. The crowd were going nuts, Matt was just amazing and they played an amazing show. It was so funny, we've got it on film somewhere, there was a dinghy and people were in the dinghy being passed over the heads. You look out over this crowd of people and see this fucking dinghy with two blokes in it holding on to the rings for dear life as they're being pushed across over the crowd. Afterwards I begged the promoters to give me a buggy, so I got a buggy back and I ran into all the bands' dressing rooms and pulled out all of their empty booze on the tables, and me and Matt went off for a spin on the buggy and were driving through all the fucking tables. We caused carnage beyond carnage. At one point, Matt tied me to the front of the buggy and I'm driving into tables with champagne bottles stacked high on them, going 'Oh no!' We fucking ruined everything. There were little plastic tables and chairs, we put them all in piles and went driving through them. I remember being smacked on the head by champagne bottles and beer bottles going, 'Fuck, I can feel a lump on my head', but it was just one of those things of how much mentalness can we create? We were there late and all the other bands were gone, everybody had gone. We ended up driving those fucking things into someone's dressing room and smashing walls."

How did it feel to make the step up to arenas?
"They were so excited, because having done the tour with the Chili

Peppers and Foo Fighters, that's what they wanted to be from there on in. They wanted to be as big as the Chili Peppers. They wanted arena rock, but arena rock that was clever. They never sold out Docklands Arena, though Docklands Arena never looked sold out even if it was. Geoff Meall made a deal with them because he wanted no seats on the floor at all, he got them to take them all out. It was the first time Docklands Arena had ever done that. But it felt really exciting, I felt really proud of the band. It wasn't their first arena headline though. Their first was in Lille, just before Docklands. The promoter put us in an arena that could shift really easily. Some arenas, like Wembley, there's the stage at one end and all you can do is blanket off the rest of the seats. With this one the stage moved, so you sold and sold up until the day, when we were like, 'We're gonna cap it at 8,000 people.' That really felt like the beginning of arena rock. I remember Dom's new drum kit arrived that day, a blue sparkle drum kit, and he was so excited. They were sweet, they were always so in love with their instruments. Dominic started building his own drums, he started his own drum company. Matt engineers a guitar that's been copied millions of times across the world now. Chris plays drums in a local band, he's been doing it for a laugh recently. They're so in love with music that they're drowning in music all the time."

SAFTA JAFFERY

How did that Maverick deal fall apart?
"After the first album, *Showbiz*, failed to make any impact in the US, at the time Guy was so convinced that 'Muscle Museum' was gonna be a Number One Modern Rock Song, you couldn't talk him out of it. I remember walking round the building at Maverick when they were setting up the album, and I remember Guy saying to me, 'If anyone in this building tells you that "Muscle Museum" is not gonna be a hit, I want to know because I'm going to fire them.' And I looked at him and he fucking meant it. And the problem was everybody was shit scared of Guy in the building. So when I used to talk to the radio department or the press department and ask them their opinion, they'd go, 'Well what does Guy think?' I'd be like, 'I don't know, but what do you think?' and they'd say, 'What does Guy think?' They were just shit scared of saying something

different to Guy Oseary. And when 'Muscle Museum' didn't happen – even after Maverick managed to secure 55 modern rock stations out of the 80, but they couldn't get KROQ, the most influencial modern rock radio stations based in LA and New York, for all the fucking love and money – and he'd spent over $1 million trying to break that song. So by the time we came back with *Origin* . . ., his power wasn't as great as it had been when we were last there, because the first Alanis record had been and gone, and the new Alanis record hadn't performed so well, so Maverick weren't going through a great time when we delivered *Origin* . . . And he was a lot more coy and conservative. And I said to him 'Look, I've got some great news for new, I've got this song, 'Plug in Baby', which I think is a modern rock smash.' And he listened to it and he said, 'I'm not sure.' I said, 'You've got to be kidding me.' And he said, 'I'm not sure. Can I get it remixed?' I said, 'OK, get it remixed.' So he remixed it, and the new mix had all the fucking guts taken out of the song. All the guitars had been taken off it and it sounded horrible. And I said to him, 'Guy, there's no fucking way you're putting that out. You put that out and I'm gonna find a way off the label.' And he was just desperate, he just didn't believe that 'Plug In Baby' was that song that would get the band on the radio. So he just sat on the record. And in many ways that helped us, because at that time Muse were really fucking happening over here and in mainland Europe and the demand for the band was huge. So Maverick sitting on the fence actually really helped us break them in all those other markets. The nightmare would have been if Maverick had believed in that record and went after it. Because Muse would've had to locate to America, and that would have meant I couldn't have had the band play all the European festivals and all the tours they performed that year. Although the band and Taste owe it to Guy for being the first record company executive to recognise the band's talent and have the belief to invest in them so heavily."

How did the American deal come about after that?
"We managed to walk out of Maverick because I got my US lawyer to exercise this clause that we'd negotiated in the contract. There was this time mechanism that meant that if they hadn't released the album by a certain date then we could walk from the deal. So when we identified that clause, we just kept quiet. My lawyer said, 'Don't say anything, just keep

quiet.' And of course Guy is not a lawyer, so he wasn't aware of that. So after we managed to walk out of that deal and when the band went in to do *Absolution*, I decided that I didn't want go out and get another US deal until the band had delivered the third album, because I wanted to make sure the new label loved the new album. Because I didn't want to have another experience where we sign another US deal before the band make the album and then they turn round and say, 'We don't believe there's a hit here for America.' So we already decided that we'd wait until the album was finished."

How did the band change when Origin Of Symmetry *took off?*
"Obviously it was great to see things were working when we'd worked so hard at it, on both sides, so it was just a great feeling. It's a great feeling to know that you were right. It's a great feeling to be confirmed that you were working with a great band and people were beginning to get it. But the industry was still really far behind the fans. I remember being at the Brit Awards that year when the band performed there for the first time, and everyone was coming up to me and going, 'Bloody hell, they're amazing!' and I was going, 'Yeah I know.' And I wasn't being arrogant, because I did know. And I was just amazed that nobody else fucking knew. I just had a big grin on my face saying, 'Yeah, I know, I know they're great, yeah, cheers, yeah.'"

How did you deal with the bills for the Origin Of Chaos *tour?*
"Well, you know, we built that into the tour budgets. They were a young band, we wanted them to have fun. We didn't want them to start thinking this was gonna be a day job of some sort, we knew the touring was gonna be important. So Dennis and I deliberately stayed in the background. So we left them to it. We kept an eye on them; we were talking to the tour manager on a daily basis. I used to go to the important shows; Dennis went to the other ones."

Chapter Six

TWO THOUSAND AND TWO, and Muse's six months were up. With the first three months of the year pencilled in for writing and demoing new songs for the third album (the diary held no official gig activity at all; their first lengthy gap from touring or recording for around four years), Matt had to put into practice his idea that moving homes every six months would keep his creative juices gushing. Matt, Dom and Tom's flat in London had proved to be little more than a storage space in which they slept on the rare occasions they were home from tour; this time they needed more settled and inspiring surroundings to help the music flow.

Initially, the plan was to move to San Diego, then they plumped for a six-month residency further up America's West Coast in San Francisco. Plans were made, arrangements put in place, visas were looked into, and Muse were all set to make the jump when Tom Kirk suggested an equally huge change of scenery a lot closer to home. He'd found out that a house in Brighton once used by Winston Churchill as a country retreat and a base for his many dogs was available for rent. The idea appealed to the band on many levels: it was near the sea, where they felt at home; it allowed Chris to take breaks home to Teignmouth to visit his ever-expanding family*; it was close enough to London for them to cart down all of their equipment to practise with a full live set-up; and it had that essence of history that was a draw to a band used to taking influence from the classical stars of the 18th century and recording in Charlie Chaplin's old party barge.

The house was beautiful. Sloping lawns dipped down from the conservatory to the badminton court in the grounds, and the place felt more like a mansion than Churchill's old doghouse. So they took up a six-month lease and moved in – Matt, Dom and Tom on a permanent basis; Chris on long periods as sleep-over houseguest.

---

* Although not expanding as fast as he imagined; there was a time when he believed his second child, Ava, would turn out to be twins.

Over their six months of relative stasis in Brighton they watched many changes develop. *Origin . . .* crept up to and passed the platinum mark. Taste Media extricated them from their deal with Maverick and began looking for a replacement deal for Muse in the US. While his bandmates were using their new income to splash out on fast cars and expensive holidays, Chris used his to plan a wedding to his girlfriend, Kelly.

They spent a lot of time recapping on the past few years of touring and thinking about how they might do it differently in future – the masked parties had served their purpose of breaking down band and fan inhibitions for a while but, as the parties got bigger, the fans had gotten younger and the parties had turned into signing sessions, so they decided not to hold them on future tours (besides, "a few things had happened here and there", which made the band realise the dangers of groupiedom, and Matt's old feelings of finding nothing less attractive than a girl wanting to sleep with him because of his onstage persona reared up again). They decided that while working with two producers on *Origin . . .* had served them well, they would rather stick with one producer for the third album in order to achieve a more cohesive collection of songs. And they also looked back on the Docklands show with a sense of awe that they had played an event so big, but felt sorry for the fans at the back who hadn't been able to see anything with such paltry-sized screens and so minimal a light show. If they were going to play such big shows again, they decided, they needed big screens, big effects, a proper arena show. They needed to put on a *spectacular*.

Over the first few months of 2002, between freezing badminton games, jamming sessions and bonding as off-tour mates again rather than tour-bus buddies, some new material began to come together. In the eight months since Matt had met that "special" girl in Rimini in Italy – a psychiatry student called Gaia Polloni – the pair had kept in touch and started dating in earnest, and with Dom also coupling up with a girl from Pennsylvania and Chris recently wed, the new material understandably took on a more upbeat, loved-up feel. In the first half of 2002 eight or nine songs were demo'd at the house in Brighton, some with touches of ABBA about them, some more doomy in tone, but most started life as out-and-out love songs, a drastic shift in the mood of the band; if the *Origin . . .* sessions took place under the imposing shadow of Matt's recent relationship break-up, the third album (at first) basked in the rays of a new contentment.

Not that Muse's idea of a happy song was anywhere near that of, say, Supergrass. Given the freedom of demoing material for the first time, Muse grabbed the chance to experiment with each new track as it presented itself, and many songs changed dramatically over 2002 as they tried out different ways of playing them. Of the songs they worked on during the sessions, 'Butterflies & Hurricanes', premiered on the 2001 tour as an instrumental, began to take on a shifting form all of its own – Matt had begun tinkering with it on a Steinway while stuck in a piano room of a hotel on the *Origin* . . . tour for several hours, building notes over a basic two-note paradiddle until he found himself playing heavy five-note chords that sounded like encroaching storm clouds. It would take some months of evolution and rough live performances in instrumental form before the track would become the pomp-rock behemoth it was destined to be, however, and other, fresher songs were taking shape with more urgency.

A riff inspired by System Of A Down, initially entitled 'New D' or 'De-Tuned Riff', started life on piano in Brighton and joined the ranks of instrumental Muse pieces that, by gradual live exposure, would eventually become world-beating classics as it slowly grew into 'Stockholm Syndrome'. A furious pop-metal racket in the vein of 'In Your World' with working titles 'Action Faust' and 'TSP' (eventually 'The Small Print') leapt to the fore, seemingly a retelling of the Robert Johnson crossroads myth* from the Devil's point of view: "Sell, I'll sell your memories/For £15 a year/But just the good days . . . And be my slave to the grave/I'm a priest God never paid."

Another emerging song, begun before September 11 but seeming to predict the global feeling about the catastrophe in its crunching, doom-laden piano chords and apocalyptic lyrics, was 'Emergency'. Eventually re-named 'Apocalypse Please', it was a tune the band knew had impact – not least for its dark wailing chorus of, "This is the end of the world!" – but at this point weren't quite sure how to arrange for maximum effect. But above them all, one track practically raced to completion – a breezy pop

---

* Itself a paraphrasing of Goethe's 'Faust' or Marlowe's 'Doctor Faustus', in which the titular character makes a pact with the devil in the form of Mephistopheles; the Faust legend was also the subject of a work by Matt's beloved Berlioz in 'The Damnation Of Faust'.

confection with a semi-disco groove linked arms with a funk-metal strut called 'I Want You Now', no doubt in dedication to Matt's new girl-friend. It had started life as a guitar line Matt played during soundchecks on the *Origin* . . . tour, before the guitar line was changed to bass and the melody emerged. It would be several months before Matt's discussions about his girlfriend's course would give him the title 'Hysteria': a defunct psychoanalytical term that originally referred to a state of sexual frustration in women alleviated by the massaging of the genitals to the point of "hysterical paroxysms". For now it was a brilliant new pop song, a poten-tial future single and the first new song to be slotted into the live set; it would be another 18 months before it became the slyest ever reference to the female orgasm in rock.

* * *

Three months of writing and demoing into the new year – with one day out to play 'Plug In Baby' at the Irish Meteor Music Awards in Dublin on March 3 – and Muse were itching to hit the road again. They didn't plan to record any of the new songs until Christmas, and so took the oppor-tunity to play a short tour of Europe to mop up the places they hadn't managed to get to on the *Origin* . . . dates and to take advantage of their higher slots on a number of festival dates over the summer. Pausing only to visit Sawmills to record 'In Your World' and 'Dead Star' with pro-ducer John Cornfield for a double A-side release in June, and for Matt to contract food poisoning from some dodgy oysters and spend a few days prior to the tour vomiting constantly, the band set out to play cities such as Athens, Istanbul, Helsinki, Porto and Lisbon throughout April. It was a chance to road-test 'Hysteria', debuted in Oslo on April 10 and thereafter a live staple for the rest of the year, and to soak up the adoration of territories that had felt a little left out by the *Origin* . . . tour schedules.

At the end of the April tour they stopped off at the BBC's Riverside Studios in Hammersmith to perform a cover of Frankie Valli's standard 'Can't Take My Eyes Off You'* for the *ReCovered* TV show on May 3, before beginning a run of 24 festivals that would take them all the way

---

* The version would appear on the B-side to 'Dead Star/In Your World'.

through to the end of August. Despite their few 'chilled' months in Brighton, there was no let-up in their onstage fire. On May 5 they became the first band to sell out the Dublin Castle in Dublin – once a prison, then the official residency of the Viceroy of England, now a gig venue hired by the Heineken Green Energy Festival for a series of summer shows over the May bank holiday – and Matt celebrated by performing some legendary knee-slides across the slippery stage and improvising lengthy piano pieces when Chris' bass broke and proved to be unrepairable.

Via high-ranking slots at two German festivals (Nurburg's Rock Am Ring and Nuremberg's Rock Im Park) and Holland's Pinkpop, on May 26 Muse returned to Russia to play at the Stunt Festival in Moscow's Krylatskoye Sports Complex, a trip that was extensively documented in a piece Matt wrote for *The Guardian* later that year. Muse had played some strangely named festivals in their time – Festival Insolent, Bizarre Festival, Austria's Two Days A Week – but none had been named so surprisingly appropriately as this one. The Stunt Festival was a day of Moscow's prime nutcases performing the most ridiculous of stunts – throwing themselves into rivers, racing trucks and tractors around dirt tracks and riding motorbikes around inside spherical metal cages. Muse were the only band performing that day and, to celebrate the weirdness of the whole event, they unveiled three new songs on top of 'Hysteria' – 'The Small Print', 'Apocalypse Please' and an instrumental of 'Stockholm Syndrome'. These preening and punchy songs had the effect of tightening the set as the likes of 'Showbiz', 'Megalomania', 'Cave' and 'Agitated' dropped out to make way: a certain amount of sprawl and bluster was replaced with precision and taut bombast, and Muse's set stepped closer to sounding like 90 minutes of masterful rock hits.

Beyond the gig, their second Russian experience turned out to be as strange as the festival itself. Their interview with MTV Russia, far from being held in a shiny modern MTV studio as in most countries, was in a shoebox studio in the style of a budget digital TV operation, and the press conference held in their hotel didn't, as Matt had expected, find them fielding questions about Russian composers such as Rachmaninov or Tchaikovsky, or about how Muse's music straddles the yawning chasm between Russian classical music and rock. Instead they were quizzed on their similarities to Yes, Rush and Queen – 70s prog bands with which Matt was largely unfamiliar, but comparison with whom he saw as a sign of his individual rock showmanship and pizzazz. Most UK bands at the time, after all, were deemed 'boring' by the Euro festival set and granted much lower slots than Muse.

After the Stunt Festival, Muse hung out at trashy nightclubs where the music would regularly halt between songs so that the compere for the evening could hold contests for the clubbers to win vodka. The next day they journeyed north to St Petersburg, where things got a whole lot darker: on the afternoon of their arrival Matt was threatened with a gun by a policeman for whistling in the street, and that evening their requests for their Russian guide to take them to a more 'underground' club than they'd visited in Moscow ended up with the band and crew knocking on the stout metal door of an ex-nuclear bunker. The enormous bouncer didn't want to let them in but, when they explained they were a famous British band, the door swung open and locked behind them, trapping them in a filthy cellar with heroin addicts injecting themselves openly at tables and syringes scattered across the floor. The Muse group had half a drink there before fleeing to a strip bar in town recently frequented by Marilyn Manson.

The next day a dazed and confused Muse played to 3,000 indie kids at the Leningrad Youth Palace, a school-hall type venue where they added the instrumental of 'Butterflies & Hurricanes' to the set plus a fifth new song then called 'Get A Grip', which would end up with the title 'Fury'. Dark, atmospheric and brooding, an instrumental version of the song had been played live as far back as February 2000, but this full version continued Bellamy's anti-religious diatribes: "And we'll pray that there's no God/To punish us and make a fuss". The after-show was just as bewildering and scary as the heroin club the previous night: 50 girls queued up to gain access to Muse's dressing room and the band were swamped with them. One girl gave Matt an intricate oil painting of himself, which had taken her five painstaking months to complete. It was a terrifying image of a naked and bone-skinny Matt with birds perched on his shoulders and a beating, sinewy heart clutched to his groin. The picture understandably freaked Matt out and, stepping out onto the balcony of the dressing room to catch some fresh air for five minutes, he was startled by the screams of 10 girls down below, yelling his name. When he finally escaped the venue that night, Matt assumed he'd managed to lose the painting somewhere along the line, only to arrive at the airport for the flight home to find Dom carrying it around and displaying it to strangers in departures.

* * *

In the weeks off between their summer festival duties, Muse were busy overseeing the piecing together of the footage for the Zenith DVD, to be entitled *Hullabaloo*. The band had come up with the idea for the DVD alongside Taste Media, and they told Taste that they would go along with it only if they had personal control over what went in it. As with their creative output, the band were intent on maintaining control over anything with their logo on it, so they were deeply involved in the production of the DVD, overseeing everything short of counting the final product off the factory line. Matt insisted it should be in 5.1 surround sound as he envisioned DVD as the format that would become the standard for releasing music in the future, and it would be a two-disc package – the first DVD would hold a 19-song live show, compiled from footage filmed over the two nights at Le Zenith, and the second would be a documentary montage of footage filmed over the course of the 2001 world tour by Tom Kirk. It would be accompanied by the dual release of a 2CD album, on which Disc One would compile the B-side tracks used to soundtrack Tom Kirk's documentary and CD2 would feature a live set from the Paris shows. Rewinding from track one, meanwhile, would reveal a hidden track on the CD – Tom Waits' 'What's He Building?'*

As the DVD came together Muse attended almost every day of editing, picking the footage that would make up the documentary part of the package solely between Matt, Dom, Chris and Tom, keeping the footage 'in the family' since they were worried some of it might be a little too near the knuckle for any outside editor to select from. It was there to show the good and bad sides of being on tour, but the band were concerned that Tom might have caught some far more personal and intimate good/bad times on his camera than they wanted the public to witness, so they kept

---

* There were also further incentives for collectors to purchase both releases – the DVD featured live tracks not available on the 12-track live CD and the CD featured an unreleased acoustic version of B-side 'Shine'. The Japanese version of the DVD was another must-have for completists, since it featured additional footage of 'Darkshines' live.

the making of the film close to home. However, the finished product was anything but tame: blurred images of writhing bodies, scenes of wanton stage rampages, fear and loathing in hotel foyers, backstage buddy-fights and bonding fishing trips in faraway climes. While not entirely warts-and-all, it certainly exposed some interesting bulges and bruises.

The DVD itself, on the band's insistence, was a forward-thinking product. With so many cameras trained on the band filming all sorts of extreme close-ups and long shots, DVD options allowed the viewer to zoom in to just the mouth or the microphone during six songs in the show, and each song was edited by director Matt Askem to have its own feel, more like a live performance video than straight gig footage. So close were the band to the making of the DVD and so hard did they push Askem to make it perfect that at one point in production, Askem jokingly offered Matt £500 to fly over the audience of an outdoor Jamiroquai gig in Verona in his paramotor with a camera attached in order to fake an aerial crowd shot for added enormity.

Hullabaloo was designed to put the viewer slap bang in the middle of the Muse live experience and it worked brilliantly, even for Matt himself. His memory was so bad that he simply couldn't remember what happened on stage and had to pinch himself when he came off, so he found watching the finished DVD an other-worldly experience, almost as real as playing the gigs themselves.

The shoot for the *Hullabaloo* cover art – a barely lit shot of the three-piece in white ringmasters' costumes and canes in front of a looming blue balloon, with Matt's hair in the most vicious of spikes – was further oppor-tunity for hi-jinx. Raiding a London studio's costume cupboard, the band played around with all manner of ringmasters' outfits, space helmets and Union Jack high-heeled boots in their search for the perfect look, and with the photo studio filled with their ticker-tape balloons they took the opportunity to play around with them properly, balancing on their canes while doing Charlie Chaplin walks around the set and throwing ticker tape around, three mates having a ball in a fancy-dress cupboard. A playabout sort of day, until Matt went to drive home. It was raining outside and Matt had just had an argument with Gaia on the phone, so he drove home in a bit of a rush to make up. Along the way, a BMW 7 Series pulled up sharply at a set of traffic lights and Matt, going too fast to brake in time, crashed into the back, half of his fresh-from-the-showroom Lotus

Elise sliding right underneath the car in front. The BMW was undamaged but Matt's Lotus was ruined; and any road rage over the accident was instantly defused when Matt jumped out of his car wearing a full white top-hat-and-tails suit and carrying a walking cane. The BMW driver was in stitches as he jotted down Matt's insurance details.

Matt, meanwhile, laughed all the way to the bank to buy himself a new car from the proceeds of *Hullabaloo*; the soundtrack album reached number 10 on its release at the start of July.* The release was preceded by the double A-side single 'Dead Star'/'In Your World' on June 17, released on the now Muse-standard two CDs. The first CD came backed with a grainy black-and-white video for 'Dead Star', filmed on a handicam by Tom Kirk for £50, showing the band performing the song in the basement of the Brighton house, plus 'Futurism', a bonus track on the Japanese version of *Origin Of Symmetry* (it wasn't included on the UK version as it was too difficult to play live) and another song warning of a future society where free thought is disallowed by the powers that be – "a future that won't let you disagree". The second CD featured a video of 'In Your World' taken from the Zenith shows and the Muse cover of 'Can't Take My Eyes Off You' from the BBC *ReCovered* session.

The single was to be Muse's only release to date of lead tracks not featured on any of their albums; a between-album tactic favoured by the likes of The Smiths in the 1980s as a way of bridging the gaps between albums with one-off singles that would later be collected on compilation albums. Muse have only produced one stop-gap single however, and it reached a respectable number 13 that June.

Their work on *Hullabaloo* complete, Muse continued their 2002 festival engagements (with 'Can't Take My Eyes Off You' replacing 'Feeling Good' as the token cover version on occasion) at Italy's Jammin Festival in Imola on an extremely hot June 15. They were fresh-faced since they'd had an early night – Matt was due to meet his girlfriend's father for the first time in Imola; he was planning to tell him he was a composer since Signor Polloni wasn't positively disposed towards rock stars – and an early-morning bout of badminton between knocking around new songs. Yet despite their clear-headedness they slightly messed up the newer tracks

---

* Chart figures for the DVD are unavailable.

they played*, possibly due to the rider featuring two large bottles of vodka alongside bottles of Baileys, Jack Daniel's, various wines and fruit to make cocktails. There were similarly ramshackle scenes at the torrential Eurokeennes festival in Belfort in France, which the band described onstage as "a rehearsal", while on a brief jaunt back to Japan to play at the Fuji Rock festival at the picturesque Naeba ski resort some way up Mount Fuji, Matt fluffed the piano notes to 'Apocalypse Please' so much that he ended up simply hitting random notes towards the end out of frustration with himself. Similarly, at Rock Oz Arenas in Switzerland, Matt made mistakes during the premiere of an epic, synth-based new track called 'Eternally Missed' and remarked "bit rusty that one", earning the song the nickname 'Rusty One'.

Despite claiming that every time they had even a week off the road they found themselves itching to get back out to play again, Muse were obviously exhausted and fraying from too long playing the *Origin . . .* set, and needed some time to themselves to perfect the new material and get their heads together. So, after their festival season took them to such out-of-the-way places as Istanbul, Ostend in Belgium, Montreux in Switzerland, Kristiansand in Norway, Joensuu in Finland and Ringe in Denmark, Muse wound up their last set of live dates of 2002 back at the Carling Weekend at the end of August. Second on the bill on the main stage to their old touring mates Foo Fighters, it was only one slot below their benchmark of truly having 'made it' and, at the Reading date, in torrential rain, the crowd greeted them like headlining heroes and the band responded with a guitar-spinning set worthy of it.

A lean 12-song set of past, present and future hits precision-tooled to send a wet festival crowd into paroxyms, it was also the first time future album track 'Falling Away With You' was ever played as an instrumental – the last time it would ever be played was the next day during an equally riotous set at the Leeds leg of the festival.† Watching from the side of the stage to shelter from the downpour as Glen Rowe, the band's tour manager, dressed as a rather soggy ringmaster, ferried the huge balloons

* On set lists at the time 'Fury' was listed as 'New (Slow And Fat)' but introduced as 'Getting A Grip', 'Apocalypse Please' was called 'New Piano', 'The Small Print' was listed as 'TSP' and 'Stockholm Syndrome' as 'New Riff'.
† It would never be played in full as, according to Chris, "it never worked live".

to the photo-pit and hoofed them into the frothing crowd of 60,000, it definitely looked to this writer that Muse had made it.

Gig-fried and frazzled by the strains of success, Muse left the stage at Leeds tired but triumphant. With *Origin* . . . finally put to rest, remarkably, for a band who'd played pretty much constantly for five years, Muse wouldn't play another note onstage for a full 12 months.

★ ★ ★

For a month in September 2002 Muse split up. Not like that, obviously, but the three went their separate ways for their first extended period of time off since 1998. Dom splashed out on a boating holiday in Switzerland, the first time he ever felt 'rich'. Chris went on holiday too, a more family-orientated affair in Majorca where he and Kelly set to work on a third child. And Matt found his ever-changing mood divided between the personal and the political. Taking the opportunity to spend time with his girlfriend in Italy, he also became fixated with global news – the war in Afghanistan had raged for almost a year already with no sign of the Allied forces uncovering the whereabouts of Osama Bin Laden. No doubt Matt's mind was conjuring entirely different reasons behind the invasion, but the romantic, blissful nature of his relationship, and the downward spiral of the world going to shit on the news, would soon combine in powerful and controversial new theories and lyrics.

It was a threshold for the 24-year-old Bellamy. The *Origin* . . . tour had been a character-changing experience; he'd given so much of himself to press, fans, groupies and media that he'd been left with very little sense of self. He'd changed a lot, and the time off didn't take him back to the off-tour Matt he used to be. Not that he could remember who that person was at all – the 20-year-old he'd been before all of this kicked off was now a shadow, a mystery to him. As a believer in the wasting effects of stagnation, Matt had made a conscious decision when Muse's success had begun to take off to never look back, to let himself become who he was destined to be and to forget the life he had before. So Matt stepped off the *Origin* . . . rollercoaster as a rock star's shell raging against inertia. He needed to re-discover a personal life; he needed to settle down, to have something to remember of these times besides tour buses and recording studios. He'd seen it all, trodden the road to excess, gained a mite of wisdom; now he needed a home, a private life. He would become understandably defensive of this new privacy (otherwise what's the point of having it?) but the odd – very odd – detail would sometimes slip out. In one later interview, for example, Matt would claim that as soon as he gets home he slips into a novelty costume for the whole time he's there. He would never let on what he dresses up as, since he claimed it wasn't necessarily very cool, but he assured the interviewer that he had a very good time.

So changes were afoot in Muse-world. On reconvening, they gave up the Churchill house in Brighton and moved into separate flats in London with their various girlfriends, apart from Chris, who has always remained in Teignmouth. They went to supermarkets, bought furniture and went drinking together as friends, getting to know each other again, finding a different approach to the band. They rented a warehouse space in Hackney, an open-plan loft room once used by metalwork artists, converted part of it into a flat so that Chris could stay there when he was in London, and began rehearsing there four days a week, writing new songs, developing old ones, making demos as they went.

And they got a little bit of their bolshy anti-corporate stance back. When Celine Dion announced that her three-year residency in Las Vegas was to be called 'Muse', the band (who owned worldwide rights to the name for use in any musical context) refused her permission to use it since they thought her music was "offensive".* Later Matt would joke that they could have been Celine's backing band, covering "the Titanic song" in a distinctly Muse fashion and staying in a fancy Vegas hotel.

Their new laid-back attitude felt to Muse like going back to the way the band had been before the year-long tours and record deals; it felt like they could take it easy, take their time. There was no pressure to record anything, they simply rehearsed until they had enough music for an album. For the first time Matt felt less like a control freak in writing these songs; they emerged far more as a collaboration between the three-piece than any of Muse's previous works had, since Matt now felt he could trust other people with his music enough to work together with them. Before, he'd insisted on getting his ideas across through a lack of confidence in those around him; now he could relax and share the burden.

Unsurprisingly, in such a chilled and conducive environment, the

---

* Dion instead decided to call her hugely overpriced Cirque De Soleil extravaganza 'A New Day', ironically one of the lyrics from 'Feeling Good'.

album came to them pretty easily. Three months of rehearsals in the Hackney loft and they felt ready to record some of the songs they were piecing together. The original plan to record with only one producer became more elaborate: they found they had three types of song emerging: classical-influenced piano and string songs to be played largely on acoustic instruments; hard-rock songs; and electronic-based material. They decided to work with three producers, each expert in one of the three styles, so in December 2002 Muse decamped to AIR studios, based in a converted church in Hampstead and owned by ex-Beatle producer George Martin, with Paul Reeve (who they knew was good at recording groups of acoustic instruments) and John Cornfield (who had mixed *Origin . . .*), with the intention of recording five songs in the first of these genres. The plan was to record an uplifting album full of massive orchestration; with their us-against-them mindset kicking in, they wanted to rebuff the critics' jibes about *Origin Of Symmetry* being too over-the-top by making a record even more outrageous and huge. They'd been mocked for being pretentious, ludicrous even, yet their two albums so far had sold a total of 1.5 million worldwide between them, so why not take their ludicrous pretentions to their extremes? And so they set about it: A huge 32-piece orchestra was called in, along with 98 backing vocalists, and 'Butterflies & Hurricanes' and 'Blackout' were given all the orchestral oomph it was possible to give.

Written with the mandolin in mind and influenced by the opera and folk music Matt had been exposed to on his regular trips to Italy to visit Gaia that summer, 'Blackout' was a lush, swoony waltz that would make the perfect soundtrack to an ice-skating routine, and fitted perfectly with Matt's new mindset. "Don't kid yourself/And don't fool yourself/This love's too good to last" he crooned over oodles of orchestral loveliness, a pessimist in love. Matt would later explain that the song is about life being too short, written from the point of view of a lover on their deathbed, looking back at a lifetime of a "love too good to last".

'Butterflies . . .', in contrast, was a cataclysm of optimism. During the Hackney rehearsals it had taken firm shape as a song of two distinct halves, with a romantic sweep of astonishingly accomplished Busby Berkeley piano in the middle – a section of the song that would stun audiences for years to come with its almost throwaway proof of Matt's extraordinary virtuosity on the ivories. And it would become a standout on Muse's third album: a head-on collision of molten rock guitars and brooding slasher-movie strings, with Matt wailing one of his most heart-wrenching and positive choruses yet – "Best, you've got to be the best/You've got to change the world/And use this chance to be heard/ Your time is now". A song about trying to find the strength to get through any hardship thrown at you, it also provided Muse's hardest-hitting crescendo; as the classical interlude burst into the final, explosive chorus, on full volume it was enough to blow the listener's teeth clear through the back of their head. To give an idea of how overblown the recording sessions became, 'Butterflies & Hurricanes' ended up with 48 backing tracks of Matt's vocals – a veritable opera of Bellamys – all because Dom would repeatedly ask Matt, "Can we get away with this?" as the layers of orchestral bombast were layered on ever thicker, to which Matt would always reply, "Of course we can!" and ladle on yet more.*

The experience would be Matt's highlight of the recording process, but not necessarily the most successful. Not all the five songs worked out so perfectly with the orchestration and choirs. 'Apocalypse Please' somehow felt weaker with strings on it, and 'Eternally Missed' found the orchestration too much to bear. By the time five songs were completed, the overwhelming nature of the backing was making Muse lose their minds. With only two and a half songs working, they decided to scrap all but 'Blackout' and 'Hurricanes . . .' from the sessions and re-record 'Apocalypse Please' in more stripped-down form in the new year.

The uplifting and love-swathed album they'd planned wasn't quite coming together that way (in fact, on album three Muse discovered that the songs that turned out best were the ones where they got to the end having forgotten what they'd set out to do in the first place), so Muse agreed to take a break over Christmas and rethink their approach. They needed to get away from London for a start – the streets were full of protests against America's proposed war on Iraq and the studio hours were restrictive, the city 'hectic'. They opted to start the New Year recording at Grouse Lodge Studios in West Meath, Ireland, for a severe change of pace and the chance to give more time to the more experimental new songs. They also decided

---

* As the recording sessions for Muse's third album moved around the globe, further changes were made to 'Butterflies & Hurricanes'; at one point it featured bongos while at another it sounded not unlike the soundtrack to West End show *Stomp*.

to turn to a producer they'd never worked with before, a guy called Rich Costey. He'd been their choice to work with on the rockier new songs since they had been impressed by his mixing work on albums by Audioslave, The Mars Volta and their adored Rage Against The Machine. Plus, he'd sent them some of his gentler work with the likes of Fiona Apple and Philip Glass in an attempt to convince them that they should work with him for the whole album. He had drive, ambition, vision and allegedly some rather strange studio practices; he was a very Muse sort of producer.

The changes in the Muse camp around this time didn't stop at the approach to their music: there were changes in the Muse engine room, too. Tom Kirk was brought in as media manager since he had such a close and trusting relationship with the band. The band's accountant, Anthony Addis, was given the position of their manager, while Alex Wall took over the day-to-day running of the band's affairs. Dennis Smith and Safta Jaffery agreed to relinquish their management roles, although the band were still signed to Taste Media for the remainder of their six-album deal.* On the press side, the band's representation was switched from Mel Brown's Impressive company to the highly respected Hall Or Nothing, key players in the success of Manic Street Preachers, Radiohead and – oh yes – Stereophonics.

That Christmas, Matt would treat himself to a few new toys. Going by the philosophy that if you play an old Fender you're competing with Hendrix whereas if you invent your own guitars you're only competing with yourself, with Hugh Manson as his guitar-design testing board he made more and more outrageous technological demands to see what Manson could come up with. He asked for guitars that provided extra feedback, pitch-shifting and phasing, even a 'theremin' guitar with a touch-sensitive pitch shifter like a mouse pad and a proximity-sensitive tone expression unit rather like an e-bow. Over that Christmas and the coming years, Manson dutifully pieced the requested guitars together using some revolutionary designs. When Matt asked him to build him a guitar with a whammy pedal built into it, for example, the design seemed

* The split between Muse and Taste Media was rather more acrimonious than this, however. As Safta Jaffery discusses later, there were hurtful accusations made on both sides and much recourse to legal representation before a final agreement was reached, although no issues ever reached the courtroom.

impossible, since whammy pedals require so much battery power that Matt would have to play it wearing a battery backpack. So Hugh replaced the pedal with a MIDI controller that required much less battery power, the first time any such combination had been tried before – the guitar became known as Matt's Black Manson. Matt also picked up a seven-string guitar that Manson had made for a jazz musician who no longer wanted it, and had Manson make him a guitar with tremelo on and the same mirrored finish as his Silver Manson. The design for this Chrome Manson almost went horribly wrong, as Manson didn't have time to chrome-plate it properly and there was bubbling in the top-plate. So, improvising on the spot, he raced to a nearby scrapyard and bought some World War II rivets from an aeroplane, drilled the rivets into the guitar surface so it looked like sheet metal, and sprayed the whole thing to resemble a chunk of burned wing from a B52 bomber. Matt adored it.

As the years went on Hugh would find himself inspired by ideas for Matt's guitars – a few years later, in 2006, he came up with the notion of putting lasers in a guitar while driving past Heathrow one night and seeing the planes coming in with their headlights on. The design for Matt's Laser Manson involved Manson jumping on a plate of mirrored glass until it cracked, sticking it on the front of the guitar and putting thinner on the wood inside, to destroy the back of the mirror so it looked older. The more Matt played his Laser Manson the more lasers would come on – the guitar made its live debut at Reading Festival that year.

Back in the winter of 2002, however, it wasn't only his approach to making the new album that Matt was rethinking. He was also beginning to rethink his approach to the world. He began to make more effort to see his family, realising that many years had flown by as the tours had rolled into one another and he'd not been in touch enough; as he'd strode into adulthood on the top of the Muse battle-tank, his independence had been important to him, made him feel stronger because he felt as if he was on his own, but his experiences of the closeness of Italian families made him miss the paternal influence in his own life.

The closeness of family was driven home to him sharply that Christmas. Arriving in Italy to spend the holiday with his girlfriend's parents, Matt found himself at an intense family event and he felt like the outsider, that he didn't belong there. It all got too much; taking his leave, Matt drove up into the mountains by himself, parked in the most deserted spot he could find and sat there in the midst of his first-ever white Christmas, contemplating the darkness and light in his life, the pristine snow-white peace beyond the windscreen and the gathering storms of war on the horizon. On his personal level it was undoubtedly the best of times; on a global scale it was among the worst.

And perhaps, as he set off into the snowy hinterland, the crunch of his feet on the fresh-laid ice sounded like the march of jackboots.

PAUL REEVE

What did you work on with Muse around the release of Hullabaloo?

"I didn't really stop working with them from when we went in with 'The Muse EP'. A lot of people forget *Hullabaloo* – it's a DVD of the gig and the other CD is a collection of the best B-sides that we recorded over that period. We only ever recorded one or two things together, so we never did a whole album's worth but we probably did 20 or 30 recordings in that time. I personally think there's something about the *Absolution* collection of B-sides that is really quite special. I did some work with them involving radio, on-the-hoof production. I didn't have anything to do with *Origin Of Symmetry*, but during that time I was doing the B-sides and Matt was experimenting with different producers."

You were a kind of producer on hand?

"Yes, I think that's about right. The band felt very comfortable with me, there was no fear from my point of view of putting ideas across and there was no fear from their point of view of telling me to fuck off, and vice versa. Whenever I speak to the band we still have that, which is great. I didn't go on the road, but every few months we'd go in the studio and do a new batch of B-sides."

They did a lot of growing up over the Origin Of Symmetry *tour – were they different people every time you saw them?*

"Yes. I don't see how you could fail to be. If you go through an experience like that and remain unchanged there's something wrong. But fundamentally they're still the same people. Chris especially is a very rooted chap in a lot of ways, a very earthy chap, and he's probably changed the least. On the whole they've changed for the better. People say fame spoils people, but fame is an experience and so is success, and if you don't take something from it, what's the fucking point? Matt certainly has a hugely eclectic collection of interests. He's got a very healthy relationship, in my opinion, with paranoia and conspiracy, and he's used his wealth and opportunity to mine that and expand his mind, which I think is the sort of thing I'd be trying to do if I had that sort of success. They have changed, but in an interesting and positive way."

Were there any sparks of magic in the studio?
"We recorded things like 'Niche' – if you knew it you'd be an anorak – basically there's no singing in it, it's a pseudo jazz piece like The Beatles might do on *Abbey Road*. Personally, my favourite records are things like *Abbey Road* . . . this whole little journey, this montage of creations that sit next to each other. I'm certainly not laying claim to it, but any creative input I did have would have been to try to move it towards something more experimental. I did have a conversation with Matt once, the last time I recorded a vocal with him, and I said, 'You've been working with other people, is everything cool?' And he said, 'I wouldn't worry Paul, every time we push new boundaries it's with you.' I took that as a huge compliment and still do."

Is that why they chose you to start work on Absolution*?*
"I think so. We started off talking about the whole album being almost a concept album. I was doing a lot of mental-health work at the time and – it was only talk – but we were going to do it along the lines of madness and insanity, mine that vein. Obviously there are still some elements of that. What's left of that is things like 'Butterflies & Hurricanes', and I do really like grandiosity in music. I remember Matt phoning me up when they were deciding who they were going to do the record with and saying, 'It came to me in the night, I nearly scratched it into my fucking arm! Cornhill for the sound and Reeve for the emotion of it!' It was a very typical Matt bold moment, and that is how we started the record. There were other things afoot; certainly there was an eye on the American market so an American producer would have been a sensible choice. So they did a couple of tracks with us and then went to the States to work with Costey and stayed there."

Were the huge orchestras too much for some of the tracks?
"It went successfully. Only one bit of music that was started didn't make it to the record. I personally think that 'Blackout' is their most classy piece of work, I love things like that. Usually, if you go to a session and there are string players, they're on the whole quite snooty. They think they're really above it, they think they'll do it through a lack of something proper to do. Muse weren't particularly well-known at the time, but Matt sat down and did this pseudo-Rachmaninov bit on the piano and their jaws just dropped! This whole orchestra was staring at him in absolute awe. That was a lovely moment, because up until then there was always quite a divide in the sessions between the 'proper musicians' and the band, and that put paid to that. I found it a very creative time, very exciting. We worked with a string arranger called Audrey Riley, who's really quite exceptionally talented, and she and Matt worked together on the string arrangements. Part of the beauty of something like 'Butterflies & Hurricanes' was that we weren't really supposed to have any boundaries, it was supposed to be that big, and I think we achieved that."

Do you agree that those songs were the showpieces of the album?
"I like to think so! I'm glad somebody else goes along with it. The thing I never really understood about 'Butterflies . . .' was why it wasn't a Bond song."

What happened with 'Apocalypse Please' in that session?
"I remember a piece of music not working; we recorded something that wasn't quite the right tempo. John and I put it back together at a different tempo, because you can do that with technology, as an experiment to see if it worked, and it didn't. They didn't have budgets like they've got now, they had quite a tight budget. What we really should have done was go back and do it from scratch, but we didn't have the budget or the opportunity to do that. That's my memory of the song that got away. I thought it was called 'Eternally Missed', which went on some Japanese thing."

SAFTA JAFFERY

How did the management structure change at this point?
"I think by the time the band had done the third album, Anthony Addis

was getting more and more involved. It was our recommendation to bring in someone like Anthony as a business manager to deal with all the touring side. When Dennis and I managed the band we never commissioned it, we did it for free. Because we had the recording and publishing rights, we decided from the beginning that we wouldn't charge them for management. So we decided that the band needed to bring in a business manager to look after the touring, because that was the main activity and, as the tours got bigger, it was the part of our life that was the busiest. You can imagine after a tour you get all these receipts and bills, particularly when you're working on the day-to-day marketing, promotion, planning tours and videos. So Anthony Addis was confirmed as the band's business manager; he was an experienced accountant who wanted to be involved and was excited about the band. I think that was just a gradual evolution and he took it all over eventually.

GLEN ROWE

I have a vivid memory of you wandering around at Reading 2002 dressed as a ringmaster, trailing a stream of huge balloons behind you.
The whole ringmaster thing . . . Matt always found it funny that my dad was a wrestler and they'd take the piss out of that whole 'ladies and gentle-men!' thing, so after they did the photoshoot for *Hullabaloo*, Matt dared me to get up there as a ringmaster every day and do the whole boxers speech. He always said, 'We're from Teignmouth and we're called Muse' and he always giggled because you can't say that with a rock'n'roll conviction can you? Like, 'Ladies and gentlemen! From Teignmouth, Devon . . . Muse!'

"I can also remember the run-up to Reading and being told that there's a £1,000 fine every minute you're late going over, and Muse were the fucking kings of going on late or overrunning their set, because they'd smash everything up and take the piss. In the run-up to it I spent three shows, I think one was in Germany, with a stopwatch writing down the very minute and second when a song started and finished. I've still got that somewhere actually. It's fascinating how long there was in between each song, down to the last second before they started the next, and it somehow magically came to being the perfect amount of time. It was like one of those weird things where you couldn't have rehearsed it to be like that. That was literally the last show before. The two before were safe, but they wanted to add a song, and I'm like, 'Fucking hell', you know? Talk about giving me a heart attack. We'd had two festivals before that where we were lower down the bill so we didn't get as much time – it was the last festival before Reading, and it was the only time we could run a set with the correct amount of time and breaks when things happen. It was just magical when somehow they managed to make the set, like, 35 seconds short of being the exact amount of time. It couldn't have been more perfect. So [at Reading] we were getting the band ready and I always had a strict routine. I'd get them in the dressing room, lock the door and just me and the band were allowed in just to vibe it up and talk about the show, and that was the point that the heavens opened. It fucking pissed it down. So instead of us being in the dressing room, Matt at the last minute had a change of heart and wanted to use the bus as a dressing room. So I'm running from the fucking dressing room to the bus, pulling towels and things on to the bus. Matt had this really cute black, red and white elephant belt. I think a fan might have bought it for him, I don't even know where it came from, but for some reason every time he wore that belt we had amazing shows. Now, he couldn't find the belt and we're in the bus, seconds before we're supposed to be called on, looking for it. I always did this little thing – Matt would take his top off and I'd put his in-ears in and I'd tape up the in-ears to his back with micropore tape, and every time I'd fucking bum him, and at that point he just lost it, he started laughing his head off, because in all the chaos I still remembered to give him one last bum. He lost his belt, it was fucking pouring down with rain, we were going to be on late now, and there I was trying to get changed as well cos I was in the fucking stupid outfit with a wig. They insisted on the wig cos they said it made me look more German. I remember trying to put the fucking wig on, and the hat on, trying to get them ready, and as we came out of the bus it was fucking tipping it down, and we were laughing as we walked up to the stage. I remember looking round to them as the rain was pouring down and all of a sudden I was given the microphone to start the introduction and I looked at my stopwatch and we were already late. I couldn't tell them we were late, it was their big moment, I think we were two minutes late before we even got to the stage. Knowing that we were seconds away from it being perfect I started to panic. Then all of a sudden, I think that was the first time in my life I felt how they would feel when I had to walk out and introduce them in the spotlight. I remember walking into the spotlight and seeing all the pizza and noodle bars and the fucking umbrellas. You just look out and see the rain lashing down and the fucking umbrellas everywhere, it was just unbelievable, and it felt like time had stopped. Then, when I started the introduction, I looked back and Matt and Dom were giggling, and as soon as I saw that out of the corner of my eye I knew it would be that magical moment, and that's when they rose to fucking superstardom. Even though they were shitting themselves, they took some perverse enjoyment out of seeing me dressed up like a twat going on stage introducing them in a big 1960s boxer announcement thing. Before they walked on I just knew they'd done it. It was blind faith, and I remember them walking on stage and when Matt put his hand up, everything at that moment just all came together, and they were the greatest band on the fucking planet. All the other tents were empty, everyone was there. I ripped the wig off, and I remember running through the rain dressed as a dickhead round to the front-of-house tower, but I couldn't get there. Even at the sides where you walk round, it was fucking chock-a-block. It seemed like half of England had turned up to Reading at that moment to watch Muse. It was so emotional."

So you would always introduce the band all dressed up?
"All the time, yeah. All over the world. I didn't give a shit. I found out very early on, anything to make the band giggle. If you keep Matt laughing he is unstoppable. He said to me, 'Glen, as long as you make this fun and exciting I will stay on the road – you could make a load of money if we stay on the road, but you've got to make it fun.' To this day those words rattle around my head with all the bands I work with. 'Fucking hell, he said something really poignant, as a kid, to me.' That is so true, isn't it? I was tour manager and production manager, and it's hard enough doing those two roles for a band that's lunar bound without having to think of things to do on days off as well. Chartering fishing boats in northern Finland. We had a holiday in Japan and we took them to a really posh golf course, and they were literally taking up turf and, like kids, just going for the ball, getting really frustrated. There's these big business guys walking around doing their lunch and talks, and there's the three Muse boys from Devon just laughing and not giving a shit, Dom using right-handed golf

clubs left-handed, so you had no idea where the ball was. Their spirit for adventure is epic, and to this day I catch up with them on tour and they're always doing something mental. They went shark diving in South Africa, always making the most of every country they get to, to do something more bonkers than the last time. Fishing, scuba diving. I tried to get them into fine art. I remember being somewhere in Europe and trying to explain to the promoter's rep that I want to get a nude model to come in and to rent loads of easels. I wanted the vision of the band sitting round with, hopefully, some fat naked man with a beard. It was always that thing of trying to keep it exciting for them and failing miserably."

When Matt started getting the Manson guitars, he suddenly stopped smashing them up so regularly, didn't he?
"Yeah, funny that isn't it? Weird guitars that are costing about three and a half grand each. There were some tears in Russia or somewhere in the Eastern bloc where he smashed his favourite guitar. I think we nicknamed it the De Lorean. It was a silver one and it was like something from *Back To The Future*. When he showed it to us the first time, we'd never seen anything like it. And I think it still is one of his favourite guitars, but then we were spending £150 quid a guitar a day because he just smashed them to bits. After every show on every day for two years, it mounts up."

Chapter Seven

CRUNCH. Crunch. Crunch. Crunch. It began with the stout march of military boot heel on gravel and sand. An ominous artillery thrum struck up overhead and then came the explosions, crashing like hammered piano chords all around, killing children, maiming civilians, thrusting the world ever deeper into the dark.

Before the UN weapons inspectors had fully completed their investigations, against the wishes of many major NATO members including France, Germany, Canada and Russia and millions of protestors worldwide, and illegally in the eyes of the UN Charter, the coalition forces of the US, UK, Spain and Australia marched into Iraq on March 20, 2003 under the banner of Operation Iraqi Freedom. Over the course of the next five years somewhere between 150,000 and 1,000,000 people would lose their lives, depending on whose estimates you believe.

From the recording studio, Matt Bellamy watched the war unfold on the news every day with a growing sense of dread, panic and powerlessness. George Bush, with no proof and in contradiction of the information he'd been supplied by the weapons inspectors and the CIA, might have managed to convince a sizeable percentage of America that Iraq possessed weapons of mass destruction and the capability of launching them, posing an immediate threat to the US – indeed, so blindly did the American populus believe whatever their President told them that many were convinced that Saddam Hussein was directly responsible for the September 11 attacks. But Matt saw through the smokescreens; while many protesters persuasively proclaimed the war was solely waged in order to rob Iraq of its oil, Matt saw a US nation in the hands of a warmonger wanting to build an empire, and his recent reading helped him strip away a further layer. He didn't merely see Bush as a grand conspirator, purposefully ignoring warnings of the 9/11 attacks and cynically manipulating rumours and false information into a cause for warfare, he saw him as a puppet, a yes man to a higher, more sinister authority.

Matt had been reading about the Trilateral Commission, a shadowy organisation set up in 1973 and consisting of the most powerful people in Europe, America and East Asia – bankers, politicians, academics, labour union leaders, spin doctors and CEOs of oil, energy, pharmaceutical and media companies. Members gaining positions in the governments of their respective countries were forced to leave the organisation, but Matt believed they were still pulling the strings and making the most important global decisions. It was these men with their Masonic handshakes and secret dealings who were truly ruling the world, even down to deciding which politicians running for public office would get the most media coverage. Although he felt betrayed by Tony Blair over the invasion, feeling that the UK no longer had a leader they could trust, he believed that the UK wasn't quite as controlled since the Prime Minister had to answer quick-fire questions at Prime Minister's Question Time, but he believed Bush's press conferences were pre-arranged; anyone asking anything out of line wouldn't be allowed to attend again. At the time the war broke out, in fact, Muse were in the middle of recording a song that would eventually have a video based on the Commission – it was called 'Time Is Running Out' and its promo would feature a dimly lit Dr Strangelove-style room inhabited by war-cabinet types shuffling papers, answering phones and clicking pens in unison, running the world from behind closed doors.* Ruling, if you will, by secrecy.

Watching the death toll rise day by day on the news, sensing a growing atmosphere of doom enveloping the globe, and with his scientific reading leading him to believe that we're only 400 years away from the next ice age, Matt realised that his upbeat album about homely matters was going to have to change. The global mood needed to be reflected, documented; the state of humanity had to be exposed. And who better to do it than a band whose music couldn't help but be influenced by world events, whose new album already opened with the lines, "Declare this an emergency/Come on and spread a sense of urgency" before the same song climaxed with the words, "This is the end of the world."

---

* Although they spend most of their time dancing or stripping to their underwear; the band later claimed that the 'Time Is Running Out' video, shot by John Hillcoat, was one of the most enjoyable to make, as there were other performers on set besides themselves and they had to perform the song at double speed to help the dancers keep time.

After all, if his vote meant nothing, the marchers were being ignored and the wheels of war were going to roll on against everyone's will, what else could he possibly do?

In the wake of world events that harsh March morning, Muse's third album was going to have to don a much darker cloak.

* * *

By the outbreak of war in March around half of the new album (which had a working title of 'The Smallprint') was complete, largely recorded at Grouse Lodge Studios with Rich Costey, who would, as he'd requested, end up producing almost all of the record, even re-recording some of the orchestral material in a more toned-down manner. Grouse Lodge was an old, converted farmhouse building with scattered farm equipment lying around, and Muse, as usual, brought their environment onto the record. The second verse of 'Time Is Running Out', for instance, features the sound of a wagon wheel, which Matt and Dom found while out on a walk, being hit in time with the snare drum and the band clicking their fingers and slapping their laps. They also recorded the sound of a piece of equipment used for turning corks, which made a metallic sound when twisted, while the drums on 'Apocalypse Please' were recorded by Dom in the studio's swimming pool, lying on lilos wearing only a nappy. Muse also tried to record the sound of Dom's cymbals underwater to create a gong effect, but gave up after several hours when they couldn't get a decent sound out of it. The pool room acoustics gave the track added reverb and hugeness, and the band went on to add layer after layer of percussion in the farm's huge barns to give the song an over-produced, aggressive feel, complete with sinister marching sounds at the start, made by the band crunching around the studio's gravel garden. Finally, 'Apocalypse Please' was fulfilling its mighty potential.

Friendly, bespectacled and deemed a genius by the band before record-ing was complete, Costey, like Leckie before him, turned out to be a producer with his own formidable idiosyncrasies. With an intricate, minimalist, almost perfectionist approach, he'd go to great technical lengths to achieve the desired result. He'd painstakingly measure out with mathematical precision up to 20 mikes on the speaker cabinets with tape measures and spirit levels in order to achieve perfect 'phase'. He also dug out a sound-morphing computer programme that can mix two sounds together to make a new one at the precise midpoint between the two – put in the sound of, say, a car engine and then a guitar and the programme would recreate it using its internal synthesisers and give you the exact middle sound between the two. Muse used the programme to input a guitar and a synthesiser played through a wah-wah pedal, to create the synth-guitar for the odd-sounding riff on 'Stockholm Syndrome'.

Costey's attention to detail rubbed off on Matt, too – previously he'd layered his guitars a lot in recording in order to make them sound beefier, but playing the songs live he found he was simplifying the guitar parts on 'Citizen Erased' and 'Micro Cuts' and that the songs sounded sharper and more effective. So this time, in order to get one guitar part to stand out on each song, he stripped back his backline set-up – he'd built up his 'rig' to an unnecessarily cumbersome three-amp behemoth that was becoming increasingly annoying to cart around the world – and worked out the guitar parts before recording them. Using mainly his Black Manson (as it sounded best in the studio) plus a semi-acoustic he borrowed from Costey* and a rare Aloha Stratocaster, which he bought for a couple of hundred pounds from a guitar-tech friend who had a basement full of 'dodgy' guitars (it was actually worth 10 times more), Matt became as pernickety about his riffs as his producer was about the mikes. For 'Time Is Running Out', for instance, he broke the chords down to their individual notes and recorded them individually, then built the chords up again from the six different tracks. Matt also rediscovered the whammy arm on 'Absolution', which he hadn't used for years – he used it in solos on 'The Small Print' and 'Thoughts Of A Dying Atheist'.

Costey was also suspicious of the thinking behind the Iraq invasion and would regale the band daily with jaded information about America and world politics. So as the new record took a sudden shift of mood halfway through – suddenly having to be more important, to mean more in the current political climate – so did the tone of the recordings themselves. Aware that he now had to make a record of cultural import, the most vital album of his life, Matt changed the tone of the lyrics to reflect the mistrust he felt in the government, the protests going on in London, the helplessness of the common man in such times and the fear of the end of the

---

* This was the same kind of guitar that Kurt Cobain played in the video for Nirvana's 'Come As You Are'.

world. He'd been too shy to be this openly bleak before, to starkly point out that we're all getting older and we're all going to die, but linking world events with more personal themes, such as his previous relationship coming to an end and his own mortality – what one might think on one's death-bed looking back at your life and deciding whether you are happy with what you've achieved or pissed off by it all – the record became about the end of things (relationships, trust, life, the world) and the positive energies you must find to survive such traumatic events. It was a record about the dark times Matt believed we would see within our life-times, and some notes on how to get through them with a little joy in your heart, without resigning yourself to the gloom.

The atmosphere in the studio altered as well: Matt began to have massive mood swings, switching between extremes of doubt and con-fidence in his ability to live up to the task of creating something of great importance. There were times when the band and Costey would look at each other and wonder what the hell they were doing; moments of hollowness and stark doubt, usually immediately followed by bursts of positivity and assurance. Matt even started having recurring nightmares about being hung upside down and beaten on his feet.

The mania around the recording sessions reached its peak as the main chunk of recording finished at Grouse Lodge and the band returned to their Hackney rehearsal space to decide which song would be the first single. Initially they considered 'The Small Print', since it was a classic Muse pop single, but as talk grew of the possibility of an internet-only release they decided they could take more of a risk on one of the album's heavier, more in-your-face tracks and opted for the black, metallic 'Stockholm Syndrome' as the album's first release, since at six minutes long it wouldn't be a prime candidate for a normal single release. The title was a phrase coined by criminologist Nils Bejerot following a case he studied on the Norrmalmstorg robbery on the Kreditbank in Stockholm in 1973, in which robbers held bank workers hostage for five days, after which the hostages became emotionally attached to their captors, resisted rescue and even defended them on their release, raising money to help with their defence. One victim even got engaged to one of their captors while they were in prison; another changed his name to that of one of the robbers and disappeared. Bejerot suggested that this psychological phenomenon came about when someone is simultaneously shown kindness and has their life threatened by the same controlling figure. To Muse this was a prime metaphor for the tense pleasure of being the weaker half of a one-sided relationship, or a masochistic captive in a world spinning out of control.

The band recorded the video themselves, with Tom Kirk directing – inspired by the film *Predator* they hired several thermal imaging cameras, worth £30,000 each, and used them to film themselves getting up to various heat-based pranks. Dom was filmed lighting a fart over a pool table while Matt threw cold water over himself to make it look as if his body was dissolving, and used ice cubes to write 'FUCK' on his chest; via thermal imaging, it looked as though he was scratching the word into his bare chest (a shot that was never removed from the TV version of the video) or burrowing into his own rib cage.

Nightmarish visions indeed, but if Muse were truly going to sum up the times they needed to dive into the belly of the beast. When Costey suggested that they should record the last batch of backing vocals and mix the album on the same desk that The Beach Boys had made *Pet Sounds* on, they jumped at the chance to finish the album in America – the poisonous heart of the onrushing darkness.

* * *

The Standard Hotel on Sunset Strip in Los Angeles is a monument to faded glamour. The foyer, once an ultra-modern Sixties throwback of deep shag carpeting, spherical seats hung from chains in the ceiling and overhanging lamps fit for a Bond villain's lair, is now a little grubby and frayed around the edges, much like the ex-models who frequent it and its blue-grassed poolside bar, surgically enhanced facsimiles of their former selves. Tedious electro-lounge tunes pump inconsequentially from decks by the concierge desk, and the hotel's main selling point – the Perspex box behind the reception desk in which girls in bikinis are paid to lounge provocatively – has become a dull cliché, more often than not inhabited by starving students working hurriedly on dissertations or checking their Facebook pages. Of all of the trendy hotel hang-outs on the Strip – the Sky Bar at the Mondrian, the Whiskey at the Sunset Marquis, the Chateau Marmont bar, the Standard is the place that got saggy the quickest – it's a fashionista hang-out where the slightly-less-than-beautiful people go to try hard to be cool.

No wonder Matt, looking around the place one night and finding himself desperate not to fit in to a fashionista scene he saw as something not to aspire to, decided to lose his own cool as quickly as possible. So he dropped onto his front on the thick grey carpet and went for a swim.

The seven weeks that Muse spent hanging out on the Sunset Strip – first lodged in apartments out of town then moving to the Standard after a few weeks to be closer to the studio – were far from spent under the yoke of wartime depression. No, chilled and unpressured at last, they had a whale of a time, playing table tennis at the Standard's poolside tables, hiring fast cars to push to the limit, boy-racer style, on the coast road between LA and San Francisco*, and hanging out with Serj Tankian at gigs by The Mars Volta, The Cave-In or The Coral, or at regular scenester Strip hang-outs like On The Rox, The Cat & Fiddle and The Rainbow. With such a small profile in the US, since *Origin . . .* hadn't yet been released there, they weren't bothered by autograph hunters or stalkerish fans; the only time they even got a hint that anyone in America might know who they were was when a bad remix of 'Muscle Museum' crept out of the Standard bar's PA.

Recording took place at Cello Studios, a one-storey building a mile down the Strip from the Standard. A highly respected studio, it had seen the cream of the 50s and 60s artists through its doors since opening in 1961 – Frank Sinatra, Nat King Cole, Dean Martin, Ray Charles, Elton John, The Rolling Stones, Eric Clapton and The Beach Boys. The Chili Peppers had a permanent set-up at the studio and, while Muse were there Tom Petty was recording in the room next door. Though they were keeping socialising to a minimum during their stay – and Matt notably stayed in to watch Larry Clark's film *Kids* on the night of one of his bandmates' biggest booze-ups in LA – Muse were, spiritually speaking, mingling with legends.

It was, if anything, America's lack of concern about the Iraq war that disturbed Matt most. In the UK he'd seen demonstrations and marches and the war was on everybody's lips; in America a populus who could barely point at 'overseas' on a map kept eating their burgers and driving

---

* These cars were totalled by valets who crashed them while racing them around the Standard's car park.

their SUVs, too scared to raise an objection.* In such an environment, various songs on the new album – 'Apocalypse Please', 'Time Is Running Out', 'Ruled By Secrecy' – gained a new importance, and the album earned the title *Absolution*, as in the listener being absolved of multifarious sins of the world by the power of music. To Matt, music was replacing faith in people, and listening to it was the only thing that made him feel that there was an underlying force for good in humanity. What's more, the purpose of *Absolution* was no longer just to document the state of the world but to open America's eyes to the mess of their own making.

To which end he began talking to visiting journalists about George Bush's time as Governor of Texas, and how this supposedly 'Christian' man would never be going to Heaven since he'd personally approved the execution of 152 people, more than any Texan Governor before him. He also, in his inimitable mad-scientist way, came up with a typical Bellamy method to retire from society. He was thinking about buying an island and an oxygen machine and living underwater with, bizarrely, Kleenex boxes on his feet. Alternatively, he'd suggest that we need to use up all of the natural resources on this planet in order to gain the means to escape it before it crashes into the sun and goes supernova. Matt's solutions to the world's troubles, it seems, were as extreme as its problems.

He also uncovered the thinking behind 'Apocalypse Please' in order to open people's minds to the possibilities behind the headlines. After 9/11 and as the Iraq war increased the risk of terrorist attack in all the nations involved in the invasion, religious fundamentalism was the greatest fear hanging over the Western world, pushing us all to the brink of disaster. But 'Apocalypse Please' posited a fresh perspective: from the point of view of a religious fantasist calling for his God to come down and solve the world's problems ("It's time we saw a miracle/Come on it's time for something Biblical/To pull us through"), it argued that the belief in traditional religious ideas such as the apocalypse inevitably led to believers wanting to validate their faith by making them come true. It also explored the idea that inaccuracies in the translations or interpreta-tions of ancient prophecies or religious texts lead to their erroneous

* This writer, at around the same time, made the mistake of loudly proclaiming his support for France's anti-Iraq war stance in a bar in America; the reaction couldn't have been worse if I'd openly wiped my backside with the Stars and Stripes.

re-enactment, i.e. that both America and Islam were making decisions and carrying out actions that would cause the deaths of thousands of people based on stories that were little more than improvisations made up on the spot by storytellers thousands of years ago. As an example Matt would claim that Jesus wasn't Jewish, a contention he claimed the Spanish Inquisition had tried to suppress for centuries but that had recently come to light, and that he didn't die on the cross but was taken down and resuscitated – a word derived from the same Hebrew word as 'resurrected'. He'd also argue that if Judaism stated that the Messiah was to be sent from Heaven to solve the problems of the world then Jesus can't have been the Messiah because he hadn't solved those problems. In fact, fascinated by the idea that the most important religion in the Western world was heavily influenced by Eastern thinking, Matt would point to the seemingly disparate religious theories that (a) the Buddhists would send three 'wise men' out to search for the chosen one, (b) three 'wise men' supposedly attended the birth of Jesus and (c) Jesus disappeared for several years of his life only to return suddenly preaching some very Buddhist-sounding philosophies Matt reached what was, to him, the logical conclusion. Quite obviously, Jesus was a Buddhist.

'Apocalypse Please' would play a pivotal role in the album. As the opening track, it would set the grand and doomy scene for the rest of the record and all of the songs to follow would have a link with it in one way or another. *Absolution* would be a record about relationships: between you and your God, you and your girlfriend, you and your captor, you and the music. As with the artwork for *Origin . . .*, its songs would be intimately linked with each other in a kind of modern, progressive concept-album kind of way, and 'Apocalypse Please' was to represent the musical mothership.

And so, as the height of summer crept upon them and the death toll clicked ever higher, Muse completed their recordings in LA and returned to the UK in July to put the finishing touches to *Absolution*, oversee the birth of Chris' third child (he'd put out one 'release' per album, he'd joke), buy their first suits for his wedding that December, splash out on fast cars (Dom bought an Audi TT, Chris a Jaguar XJS, Matt, already owning his Lexus, instead bought himself a thumb-print coded PalmPilot) and prepare themselves for the promotional onslaught to come. Unlike the nervousness they felt upon unleashing *Origin . . .* on the press and public for fear of how it might be received, this time they knew they had a masterpiece under their belts, so they went back to their constituencies and prepared themselves for superstardom.

* * *

On July 7, 'Stockholm Syndrome' was the first song from *Absolution* to be released for public consumption. In a revolutionary move unprecedented from a major rock band, and predicting perhaps the decline of CD sales and the downfall of the traditional record company release plan, it was only available as a one-track download from Muse's official website at the cost of £1. They'd wanted to give the song away for free – a tactic that artists like Prince would employ to great success several years later – but Taste Media/Mushroom wouldn't let them. Mushroom, coincidentally, was then in the process of being bought by Warner Brothers for a reported £15 million, and label head Korda Marshall would go to Warners sub-label EastWest as managing director, as would Muse, complete with their Taste Media deal. Ironies piled up: Muse transferring to a subsidiary of Warners in the same year that Warners purchased Maverick meant that the band and their album were reunited in America, allowing it a proper release, and Marshall's first signing for EastWest would be The Darkness, a rather more comical pastiche of Queen than he'd previously signed up.

Although there was no such thing as a download chart in July 2003, internet-only sales of 'Stockholm Syndrome' would have been sufficient, if transposed to the official chart, to have pushed the song to number three. For such a raging, horse-scaring scree-fest of chainsaw synth guitars and bludgeoning, psychopathic bass it was, indeed, the quietest major hit single of the year. It would go on to become the biggest-selling download single to date.

On September 8 the first 'proper' single from *Absolution* was put out: the far more radio-friendly (and allegedly Michael Jackson-inspired) 'Time Is Running Out'.* While the video depicted the synchronised dance moves of the military and business elite in a Dr Strangelove bunker, the song itself was more personal, about being suffocated and subjugated by a partner, a religion or society itself. No longer needing the added chart

---

* Jacko influence or not, it would certainly provide the funky bass blueprint for later hit 'Supermassive Black Hole'.

push of 2CDs in the wake of 'Stockholm Syndrome''s success, 'Time . . .' came on one CD (although, for those fans addicted to the multiple format, there was a DVD available too, featuring the single, its video and a 'making of' the video), backed with the video and a politically minded new song called 'The Groove'.

If 'Stockholm Syndrome' had been Muse brutally beating down the comeback door with guitars made of pneumatic drills and screaming through the holes – a majestically tuneful take on the heads-down riff metal of RATM or Metallica – 'Time Is Running Out', charting at number eight in the UK, was the pop hit that would see them welcomed into the hearts of the pogo-pop kids as warmly as into those of the heavy rock crowd. With quite possibly the most credible double-punch cross-over pairing of singles in recent memory, Muse were back with the biggest of bangs.

And it was only going to get better.

Absolution was unveiled to the press not in a gimmicky plastic box (*Origin* . . .'s press copies had come pressed between another clear Perspex square, this time held together with two screws and attended by the necessary plastic screwdriver), but at a full press preview at London's Planetarium a month before its release. Several hundred journalists, PRs, band associates and interested parties were wined and nibbled and ushered into the Planetarium's auditorium, where the record was played via an impressive sound system, accompanied by the Planetarium's ceiling star show. The preview was perhaps inspired by Pink Floyd, who premiered *Dark Side Of The Moon* at the Planetarium in 1973, sending cardboard cut-outs of themselves, but there was perhaps no better way to first experience the likes of 'Sing For Absolution', 'Blackout' or 'Butterflies & Hurricanes' than while whizzing through the galaxy on a close-up, dot-matrix tour of the planets. Even more fittingly, when the album outran the length of the star-show, the projectionist was forced to revert to the Planetarium's only other projections, those of ghosts, ghouls and grave-yards; the viewer sped down into bottomless graves and into a fiery under-world just as Bellamy's voice was wailing, demonically, "And be my slave to the grave" or, "It scares the hell out of me/The end is all I can see". The evening was capped, after the album preview and drinks with the band in Madam Toussaud's next door, by guests being forced to leave the venue at the end of the party through the barely lit Chamber Of Horrors waxwork exhibition in the basement of the building; it was a journey made all the more terrifying by the fact that Muse had hired actors dressed as zombies to lurk chained to the walls around every corner, leaping out at you as you passed.

Absolution, we discovered that day, was an astounding achievement. It began with the stout march of military boot heel on gravel, explosive piano chords and drums rolling like Panzers; the fire-and-brimstone preacherman scream sermon of 'Apocalypse Please', setting a dark and powerful mood of Book Of Revelations bombast and operatic bluster for the album as a whole, a much harder record than Muse had planned. Its funky pop foil came next as a counterbalance – 'Time Is Running Out' gave proof that Muse hadn't drifted off into some deranged musical dimension full of Ring Cycles and burning Brunhildes, but were still firmly tethered to their melodic rock roots.

The lilting music-box piano ballad, 'Sing For Absolution', followed – according to Dom it was the defining song behind the title in that it was about the act of writing music and singing it, and finding absolution from the sins of humanity by doing so. The lyrics, however, read like a love poem to a dead lover: "Lips are turning blue/A kiss that can't renew/ I only dream of you/My beautiful". Matt would refer to it as being oppressive and gothic in sound, but as it built to a soaring crescendo it emerged as one of the most honest and emotional Muse songs to date. And the perfect way to lull the listener into a false sense of security before whacking them in the chops with the all-out sonic assault of 'Stockholm Syndrome'.

Following the loud/quiet pattern synonymous with much great alternative guitar music, 'Falling Away With You' crept out from behind the armoured skirts of 'Stockholm Syndrome', a sweetly plucked and perfectly poised piece of balladry about a crumbling relationship that necessarily burst into a chorus of stereophonic electro fluster, which sounded like the gathered demons of a past affair nagging on Matt's mind in the form of splintered Genesis synthensisers. It gave way to a brooding 37-second chunk of rumbling cinematic mood music called 'Interlude', which acted as a break between the album's two 'acts' and replicated the chord sequence for Samual Barber's 'Adagio For Strings', before 'Hysteria' catapulted us back into the fizzing world of metatronic space pop with a hell of a bang. A song about constantly straining for something tantalisingly out of reach, which may have been why it was adopted as the intro music for the eternal nearly-men of NHL ice hockey, the Washington Capitals, later that year.

A modern classical masterpiece for choir, orchestra and mandolin, 'Blackout' contended for Muse's most beautiful song and was the first *Absolution* song to concern the deathbed reminiscences of a protagonist facing the final blackout. Such ideas came from Matt's belief that the Western world is a bad place to die, scared of the idea of being put in an old people's home and forgotten about as he gradually disintegrates, older and slower but still thinking just as sharply. The pessimism and languor of 'Blackout' needed a counterpoint too, and it came in the awe-inspiring form of 'Butterflies & Hurricanes', the other orchestral behemoth on the record and a message of faith, hope, courage and self-belief in the face of global and personal adversity. As possibly Muse's best song yet, it bestrode the centre-point of *Absolution* like the finely chiselled musical equivalent of the Colossus Of Rhodes, pronouncing the record's genius solely by dint of its own magnificence. It was Dom's choice for the next single despite its length and bombast – he wanted to simply hand it to the record label and say, "Deal with it."

Its testament to the strength of the tunes and the abundance of potential singles on *Absolution* that the band's first choice as a chart hit, 'The Small Print', would never see a single release but instead be relegated to the closing chapters of the album; another sensational hardcore pop moment amid a cornucopia of thrills. A song as much indebted to Goethe as to Rage Against The Machine and Audioslave, its pummelling bass attack and stratospheric hookline were prime Muse, and prompted much debate as to its meaning among their internet fanbase. There was the updating of the Robert Johnson myth already discussed, the cynicism of the music industry or governments blinding the public to what's really happening with media 'small print': "It'll make you insane/And I'm bending the truth". And it's a testament to the impeccable quality of the songwriting throughout that a charmingly disco, electronic love song like 'Endlessly' sounds in this company like throwaway filler.

Prompting some confusion among obsessive fans, since its title was originally used as a working title for 'Megalomania' on *Origin . . .*, 'Thoughts Of A Dying Atheist' was originally the second song on the album, about your life flashing before your eyes at the moment of death. Zipping along with an ironic vim and vigour (considering its subject matter), it was one of *Absolution*'s most plainly catchy songs, and caused much debate about Matt's religious status. He'd never been christened (nor were his parents) and he'd often espoused religious suspicions akin to atheism, but he also claimed around this time that he wished he was religious but that all of the information available on all the world's religions made it impossible to commit yourself solely to a single faith, as that meant shutting yourself off from all the others.

Matt himself has said that the lyrics to 'Thoughts Of A Dying Atheist' evolved to tell the story of an office drone who'd gone insane and torn his workmates to pieces with his bare hands, then goes home to his wife to face the end of his sanity, but this explanation seems to fit far better with the final song on the album, 'Ruled By Secrecy', where the central character may have been driven insane by not knowing who was really in control of his life ("Repress and restrain/Steal the pressure and the pain/Wash the blood off your hands/This time she won't understand"). With a title taken from conspiracy theorist Jim Marrs' book 'Rule By Secrecy', which details the formation and influence of the Trilateral Commission and traces the history of secret societies back through history, via the Illuminati and Knights Templar, to a link with the ancient pyramids and the Iraqi alien tablets (the book was no doubt a huge influence on some of the theories Matt was taking on at this time), the song was a classic Muse album closer in the vein of 'Megalomania'. Sinister, moody and smouldering, it inevitably bursts into vampiric slashes of piano melodrama on its way to a climactic cry of "no one knows who's in control", a lost and desperate end to an album posing many questions but offering only self-belief as an answer.

Nonetheless, the attendant journalists scuttled back to their magazines to tell of a modern rock classic on the horizon. *Absolution* was not only their best record so far but a turning point for Muse – those who had dismissed them as Radiohead copyists had no musical plagiarism to mock on this record, and even their most ardent doubters had to admit that the songs were as strong as on any album in living memory. The patchy prog poseurs had delivered an album that, unlike the billowing-at-the-seams *Origin Of Symmetry*, effortlessly melded their classical pretentions with hard-rock clout and a futuristic electronic nous. It was Muse fulfilling all of the potential they'd ever shown; the multi-faceted future rock butterfly finally emerging from the prog-metal cocoon.

In 2003, alternative music was a lo-fi affair – The Strokes and The White Stripes had rejuvenated the fine art of the tight pop song and inspired a generation of tinny melodic leanness, a mantle taken on by The Libertines in the UK. Bands in their wake only stretched their ambitions to encompass taking crack with Pete Doherty in Whitechapel, recording at Hackney's Toe Rag Studios on antique 1960s tape machines, or emulating Jack White's ragged blues. In the hardcore scene, bands like Tool, System Of A Down, The Mars Volta and Cave-In were making similarly expansive music as Muse were but it was far more aimless, progressive and jazz-inspired and lacked Muse's melodic bite, while everything in indie rock was taut and jagged and hungry and punk and over inside two and a half minutes. *Absolution* was the polar opposite of such an approach, a welcome explosion of pompous theatrics in a musical landscape full of sweaty garage bands in girls' trousers. And its acceptance by the public marked it as a truly important record, a defining force in uncertain times.

Muse knew that they'd made their best record – their most honest and coherent – and they themselves were the only judges that mattered to them. They'd been outsiders from the start, never fitting into any scene, and if the press had trashed the album as out-of-touch or ludicrous they'd have been happy to go back to playing the Barfly circuit. Which is perhaps why Matt couldn't quite believe how good the reviews were. *Absolution* was a critical sensation, receiving gushing reviews everywhere from *NME* and *The Fly* to the broadsheets, typically latching onto a band once they'd done the music-press treadmill and were poised for massive crossover success. They were no longer being dismissed as a band for teenage goths or space geeks; now Muse were a band who could appeal to fans of metal, indie, pop, classical music and even a bit of AOR funk.

The artwork for *Absolution* was typically apt, mysterious and thought-provoking; full of clues to the meaning of the album. It featured a man in a grey stone quarry staring upwards, surrounded by the shadows of hairless, androgynous humanoid figures floating in rigid squadron formation in the sky above him. Whether these figures represented righteous humans ascending to Heaven at the event of the Apocalypse, as the Book Of Revelations predicts, alien beings floating over earth, angels, demons or some new form of life, is open to interpretation, but the striking nature of the image is the result of Muse hiring Storm Thorgerson for the first time –

a designer famous for having created legendary artwork for almost every Pink Floyd album, together with sleeves for The Mars Volta, Peter Gabriel and Led Zeppelin, either with his collective, Hipgnosis, or solo after the design studio dissolved in 1983. His work is notoriously grand and detailed and almost always surreal – for the sleeve for Pink Floyd's *A Momentary Lapse Of Reason* album he arranged for a half-mile stretch of hospital beds, each with different coloured bedsheets, to be arranged in a meandering line along a beach – and the shoot for *Absolution* was no different. The concept came from Muse spotting the basic design on Storm's website and asking if he could do the shot for real. The picture was taken by photographer Robert Truman in a gravel pit in Essex, with various models and children playing the role of the earthbound human*, and the shadows were actually real – Thorgerson refuses to say how the shot was achieved but admits it was a difficult one to arrange, as there was very little sunlight and a strong midday sun was essential for it to work. The finished product, Thorgerson declared, felt rather magical to him, reminding him of a children's illustration by Maurice Sendak because of its fairy-tale connotations.

The combination of eye-grabbing artwork and heart-bursting music sent *Absolution* straight to number one in the UK charts on its September 22 release on Taste Media/EastWest records. Over the coming weeks, as it was released in other territories, it hit number one in France and Iceland as well as number two in Holland and Belgium, the third place slot in Switzerland, number four in Italy, five in Austria and Norway and was Top 20 in Spain, Denmark, Germany, Australia and Finland. In the first week of release in the UK it sold 71,000 copies, making it by far Muse's fastest-selling record yet. Although the band weren't quite satisfied. They might have sold 71,000 in a week, they noted, but Dido's album had sold 71,000 on the first day.

But if they wanted big numbers, they only had to look as far as the ticket sales. Figures came in for the upcoming 'Absolution' tour and they were staggering: Muse were selling out 20,000-capacity arenas all over Europe.

The road, albeit a far wider one than ever before, was beckoning . . .

* * *

* Several variations on the shot were used for the vinyl, DVD, posters and adverts.

Maybe it was the nerves. Maybe it was the reception. Maybe it was the sight of so many crammed-in faces. Or maybe he'd just forgotten how to be a pop star after so many months sitting in studios or temporary flats watching BBC News 24. But as 'Hysteria' crumbled to a close at the Melkweg in Amsterdam in front of 800 fan-club members, Matt himself crumbled into hysterics. He doubled up with laughter, partly at the way that the crowd was singing along to every word of a song that hadn't even been released yet, as they would for all five of the seven new songs that hadn't yet been released as singles*, and partly because he found himself wondering why everyone was looking at him.

It was the first night of a five-date promotional tour of Muse's key European fanbase cities – Amsterdam, Brussels, Cologne, Paris and Milan – and, although all of the shows were fan-club only gigs of around 500–800 avid fanatics with tickets given away on their website, Muse were nervous about getting the new songs right, particularly as the tour started only a matter of weeks before *Absolution* was to be released and they really wanted to impress their fans. Some songs ('Thoughts Of A Dying Atheist', 'Sing For Absolution', 'Time Is Running Out') they'd never played live before, and the tension was released in anti-guitar violence. Before the show that September 3 Matt had bruised his ribs and, by smashing his guitar against them at the end of a shaky but vital 11-song set, he damaged his chest – not the best move at the very start of an *Absolution* tour that would stretch on around the globe for the next 16 months.

This time, though, Muse had decided on a different modus operandi on tour. They'd become a bit sick and tired of the Groundhog Day nature of touring – turning up in a different city every day without ever leaving the backstage area and seeing anything of the world. They wanted more to remember about their lives than playing gigs and sitting in dressing rooms doing interviews, so this time they had a plan. They struck a deal with the record company that they would do a promotional tour to get all of the interviews in Europe out of the way before the tour kicked in in earnest, so that their days before the gigs would be free for sightseeing

---

* The set list, as on most nights of this five-date tour, featured 'Hysteria', 'Butterflies & Hurricanes', 'Sing For Absolution', 'Blackout', 'Time Is Running Out', 'Thoughts Of A Dying Atheist' and 'Stockholm Syndrome', alongside older tracks 'New Born', 'Plug In Baby', 'Bliss' and 'Citizen Erased'.

around cities they'd visited four or five times already but never really seen, or visiting loved ones. In return for doing this the label agreed to put on the five free fan-club shows (footnote: fans could get free tickets from the Muse website by answering the following questions: (a) Which Stanley Kubrick film inspired the set design for Muse's latest video 'Time Is Running Out'? and (b) What is the release date of Muse's new album 'Absolution'?), to make the promotional tour that much more bearable and let them road-test the new material.

Matt was particularly keen on the new, looser touring schedule. He felt as if he'd grown up a little and calmed down. He no longer felt the need to indulge in hedonistic mask parties or wild tours as, he claimed, those things only happen when you've just lost all of your friends – and the plot – and start talking to strangers too much. This time they claimed the tour would be more about golf, museums and girlfriends. So while Dom was now seeing a girl based in New York* and Chris had almost perfected his routine of seeing his family in Teignmouth as often as possible, Matt – now comfortable in a long-term relationship, as single life didn't suit him; he needed someone to spend all of his time with in order to be himself – wanted to see his Italian girlfriend of 18 months as much as possible, going so far as to drive across Europe after gigs to get to wherever she might be. Although coy when asked about the possibility of marriage, he loved nothing more than getting out of England, visiting Italy, eating lots of pasta and scuba diving with Gaia, an interest that almost cost him his life on one trip when the instructor took a liking to his girlfriend. Matt was swimming 18 feet underwater when his air suddenly cut out making him feel as if he was breathing through a tiny straw. Panicking, he grabbed the fin of a nearby instructor and they shared his air to reach the surface, only to find that the lothario instructor had filled Matt's oxygen tank to only 50 per cent.

The day after the Amsterdam Melkweg show, Muse were up at 10 a.m. for their busiest day of interviews ever. From 10 a.m. to 6 p.m. they conducted interviews in the 12th-century church in the middle of the red light district surrounded by graves, which they found rather morbid; at

---

* They'd been together for four months by that September and Dom thought he might be in love, although he was apparently haunted by a comment in a music magazine about a passionate clinch he'd had with another girl back when he was single.

one point Matt found himself playing one of the biggest church organs in Europe for the MTV cameras. The following night at the futuristic glitz palace Ancienne Belgique in Brussels, they were teased back onstage after the same 11-song set for a three-song encore of 'Muscle Museum', 'Micro Cuts' and 'The Small Print', as they were again in Cologne.

The show for 700 fans at the Trabendo venue in an arts complex in the suburb of Paris was the most memorable, however, though not for the right reasons. The Muse lighting rig turned out to be too big for the venue and a short way into the set a fuse blew, casting the gig into darkness. It was repaired after two minutes but blew again, leaving a 20-minute delay in the dark while technicians scurried feverishly around and Muse – with Matt wearing trousers so long they had to be turned up six inches – brought out shot glasses and bottles of wine and spirits for the crowd, apologising to them for not being able to play an acoustic set in the meantime since the microphones had gone down as well. By the time they got the power up and running again, nerves were so frayed and so much alcohol had been necked that Matt ended the set by trashing the drum kit and lobbing his guitar directly into Dom's face. Dom remembers crashing backwards off his drum stool, half-blind, and opening his eyes to see blood all over the riser; he had a huge gash in his eyelid. The band ferried him directly to hospital for a tetanus shot in the rear, to the guffaws of his bandmates.

The final European fan-club show, in Milan on September 15, was filmed by MTV as the climax of the first MTV Muse Day – an entire 24 hours of programming devoted to the band, including the additional footage from the *Hullabaloo* DVD, a 'Making Of *Absolution*' film and a live set from Leeds University; a sign of the stature and importance they were achieving in the rock community. The next day, they came back to London to play two radio shows (a Radio One show for Zane Lowe's programme at Maida Vale studios, where 'The Groove' received its live debut, and a set at Islington Academy for XFM) and attend their first ever Q Awards, where they picked up the inaugural award for Innovation In Music and got up to their usual havoc. At the after-show, Dom managed to spill his glass of wine over Dexy's Midnight Runners, while Matt wangled an invitation from Lemmy of Motörhead to attend his gig at Hammersmith Apollo. Rubbing shoulders with, and spilling booze over, the giants indeed.

The promotional interviews[*] cast a much calmer, self-assured Muse into the papers and magazines. Matt talked at length about Sitchin's 12th planet nearing Earth and about the onrushing ice age, and the idea that we're absorbing the Earth's resources so quickly that evolution can't keep up with the changes we'd need to make to our forms in order to survive once the resources run out; therefore, he hoped we'd find another inhabitable planet nearby with unlimited resources. But galactic notions aside, there was much sense and clarity spoken.

Matt had been listening to a lot of Berlioz and Debussy with the ambition of incorporating the feelings they stirred in him into rock music, and felt that he'd achieved it with *Absolution*. The band have their own on-tour personalities when they're in 'travel mode'. Dom was amazed that Muse had lasted another year, as he is every year. The reason they'd stuck at the band was through the fear of having to get proper jobs. Matt liked the idea of buying a small farm, growing vegetables and having lots of kids, since he'd not taken any drugs for two years and was much more at peace with himself. The band were thinking about hiring a supertanker and sailing it around Britain's ports, playing gigs on it and then sailing on to the next town. They'd given the money they received from Nestlé for the unauthorised use of 'Feeling Good' to Oxfam and local Devon charities. Dom fancied Pink; Matt preferred Norah Jones. They thought that people who didn't like them were probably offended by their lack of shame. Dom's most memorable part of the year was swimming with sharks in the Bahamas; Matt's was driving down to Big Sur while in LA and meeting a park ranger, who invited him and his girlfriend down to a beach where there were thousands of elephant seals during mating season fighting over mates and having sex. Matt didn't get recognised often but still considered his life nerve-racking. Dom recalled being given a bottle of port by the record label in Porto and drinking the entire thing as if it was wine; he threw it all up in bed in a spew of purest black. Chris agreed with his bandmates that religion and the Bible were irrelevant: the Bible was mere fantasy and religion was being used for both good and evil ends. They

---

[*] Of which I conducted the first that year, joining the band at the Science Museum in London in August where we went on a 3D space simulator, in which you are cast as an astronaut trying to save the Earth from an asteroid; in the simulation the Earth is saved but Matt, in typically apocalyptic mood, thought it would have been a better experience if you'd made a mistake and had to watch the Earth explode from a spaceship.

were all very pleased to hear that Michael Stipe had described them as the future of rock. Matt thought that his lyrics had evolved because he now wanted to share his emotions with his audience in order not to feel alone. His latest reading was a book on Alaska exploring the depleting oil reserves there, which George Bush was trying to claim for himself, and claimed that there was around 50 years' worth of oil left in the world, so Matt thought that it wouldn't be too long before there would be no justification for oil wars, there would simply be all-out survival-instinct fighting.

The book also introduced him to another important Alaskan feature: the HAARP installation, a mysterious, pylon-festooned governmental complex the purpose of which was the cause of some debate in conspiracy theory circles. An attempt to control the weather? A secret spying base? A transmitter for mind-control rays? To Matt's probing mind it was a subject of increasing fascination . . .

* * *

Muse's three-month European jaunt at the end of 2003 felt like the Ever-Expanding Tour, as if the venues were exploding day by day. After the micro-tour of fan-club only gigs in tiny venues, the first week of shows in Europe took in 1,000–2,000 capacity venues in Scandinavia and Germany from October 11, mid-sized shows to perfect the new set list. Muse had a good 90 minutes of mind-blowing rock music up their sleeves now: with the likes of 'Bliss', 'Endlessly', 'The Small Print' and 'Sing For Absolution' floating around the set for the first few dates until they found their natural place in the gig, the shows would open with the march of 'Apocalypse Please' and take in early showings of 'Hysteria', 'New Born', 'Micro Cuts' and 'Thoughts Of A Dying Atheist', before hitting a mid-section of 'Citizen Erased', 'Space Dementia', 'Feeling Good' and 'Butterflies & Hurricanes' and a pre-encore run of the big hits, 'Sunburn', 'Muscle Museum', 'Time Is Running Out' and 'Plug In Baby'. The encore would find the balloons released during an elegiac 'Blackout', while 'Stockholm Syndrome' set the stage for the final equipment mash-up. Teasingly, this section of the tour also featured the premiere of a new goth-metal hellfire instrumental tentatively titled 'Take A Bow'.

Muse also played two shows at a tiny venue on the Grosse Freiheit in Hamburg, the street lined with bars, clubs and strip joints where The Beatles cut their teeth in pre-fame days, and both gigs ended with a free-form jam and a classic example of the band smashing their gear and rolling around on the stage in fits of hysterics.

At some point during the drive from Hamburg to Berlin for their gig at the 3,000-capacity Columbia Halle on October 21, Muse stepped up to arena status. They arrived to find themselves staying in the upmarket Adlon Hotel (where Michael Jackson had dangled his baby from a window and Boris Becker and Rutger Hauer were currently in residence) and the venue swarming with juggernauts, tour buses, video crews and two tour managers – a total crew of 28 people plus local caterers, riggers and roadies. There were even Muse beach towels on sale at the merchandise stall. It was the first time the full production of the *Absolution* tour was performed, the show they'd spent a full week devising with Tom Kirk after the Docklands Arena gig to make sure everyone in the venue got their money's worth. The stage set featured three massive screens across the back of the stage, a large riser for Chris to look moody on and leap off from whenever the need took him, and a light-up upright silver piano nicknamed The Dalek for Matt. Apparently, when Matt first explained what he wanted for the keyboard, the rather hippyish computer programmer went and had a long lie down to perform yoga for three hours, before returning with plans for a keyboard with a computer built into it so that every key was linked to a light on the front in the style of the spaceship from *Close Encounters Of The Third Kind*. At various points in the tour Matt would consider playing the five-note refrain from the film to see if anyone would get the joke. He also considered going onstage in a vampire cape and fake fangs in reference to the more Dracula-esque parts of the set, but bottled out at the last minute.

On the screens during the set would appear suitably grandiose images: the Milky Way, a sunset, robots, thermo images of the band, mountain ranges, the moon whizzing by, clouds racing, an orchestra for 'Butterflies & Hurricanes', the flying souls of the *Absolution* sleeve. Small black balloons would descend on the crowd during 'Time Is Running Out'; large white ones during 'Blackout'. The bigger shows would see stage-side cannons fire blasts of confetti into the crowd at the close of 'Stockholm Syndrome'. They'd looked into the possibility of hiring pyrotechnics and glitter bombs for the shows but these had been too expensive; as it was they'd massively overspent on the stage show in order to justify playing much bigger venues. With their website costing them an arm and a leg to run and an office in London to maintain as well, they only made money on the tour by selling vastly more tickets than they or anyone else ever thought they would. And all of that money was saved to pay for further touring. So they decided to simply play 'Take A Bow' instead; it was, after all, pyrotechnics enough.

The Berlin show was, Matt later claimed, a messy flurry of mistakes and technical problems – so fraught was the gig that they didn't even play the encore. Plus, Dom was a little befuddled as he'd left all his clothes in a bin liner in Hamburg and they'd disappeared, presumably thrown out with the rubbish, leaving him with only the clothes on his back to last him the entire tour. Thankfully, at the after-show at the Columbia Halle's upstairs balcony, a lackey turned up with the bin liner intact.

Now playing to an average of 8,000 people per night, the tour rolled on through Europe, Muse living up to their plan of sightseeing during the day and wowing huge crowds after dark. On days off in Germany they visited the Nuremburg war museum and went go-karting on good courses they'd heard about; in Florence on October 28, before a storming gig at the Sashall, they took up an invitation to visit the Mayor of Florence's house (on his daughter's insistence) and ended up getting a guided tour of the tunnels underneath the palace. At the Geneva Arena on a Sunday, 10,000 Swiss rockers were driven wild by Matt knee-sliding through the confetti from the cannons, one of them giving Matt another life-size oil painting of himself, while at Lyon's Halle Tony Garnier on November 10 they played their biggest show yet to 17,000 screaming fans, an audience they found overwhelming and scary to play for, knowing that only a year earlier they'd played the town to a crowd of 6,000. They celebrated by using a day off in Angers to partake of the refined art of wine-tasting in the country, attacking all 36 variations on offer at a country fair with vigour, swallowing rather than spitting and marking each sample out of 10.

Stopping off in Marseilles to play 'Uno' for the last time during their set at the 8,500-capacity Dome, they moved on to Barcelona where, before the show at the Razzmatazz club, they visited the Sagrada Familia, the huge and unfinished cathedral designed by the brilliant surrealist architect Antoni Gaudí. Matt was fascinated by the project, by the imagination and cartoonish flourishes that would festoon the 500 ft central spire, which is yet to be built; Matt found an artistic connection with the cathedral's over-the-top grandeur and scale, the way that Gaudí got away with being so individualistic on such a massive canvas. He bought a book on the cathedral and flicked through it all day; he felt it was what *Absolution* might look like if it was a church.

The next day, they flew to Madrid to play 'Time Is Running Out' on a TV pop show, without realising they'd be playing their dark and deviant rock song to a studio full of pre-teens. To make it more palatable for the kiddie crowd, Matt played the song as happily and smiley-faced as he could before finishing with a knee-slide that sent him crashing into the youngsters, thankfully avoiding arrest for crushing a minor. The next day, they took a day off in Spain to travel to Figueres to visit Salvador Dali's house, which they would describe as "surreal".

By the time Muse's most holiday-like tour of Europe, taking in Belgium, Holland, Germany, France, Italy, Switzerland, Austria and Spain, had reached its biggest gig – at the Palais Omnisports de Paris-Bercy in Paris, a headlining set at the enormous 20,000-capacity venue where the band had once opened for Red Hot Chili Peppers – *Absolution* had reached the one million sales mark. Reviewing the show for *NME,* after a spectacular gig awash with ticker tape and molten rock fury, I joined the band backstage and alongside them made my second Muse freedom dash through the clamouring arms at the stage door. They had by now almost perfected their exit strategy; hysteria had well and truly taken grip.

And as Muse returned to the UK to have a day off to go off-roading in Range Rovers at Northolt in north London (where Dom was apparently the most reckless driver) in preparation for their first arena tour of their home country, 'Hysteria' took a grip on the charts, too. Released as a single on December 1, it was backed with a live version of the track and sporadic live favourite 'Eternally Missed', and bolstered with a DVD of various cuts of the video, live footage from MTV and a 'making of' the video. The 'Hysteria' video was notable as the first Muse promo not to feature the band, since Matt didn't think his acting skills were up to the main role; instead it focuses on actor Justin Theroux playing a man who wakes up in a trashed hotel room with no memory of what had happened there, only to discover via handycam footage that he'd picked up a prosti-tute and trashed the room himself after attacking her.[*] Directed by Matt

* Fan sites have pointed out the shot-by-shot similarities to footage from the movie *Pink Floyd: The Wall*, which included a very similar room-trashing scene starring Bob Geldof.

Kirby, the video was simply titled 'Rage'. A 7″ release of the song, backed with 'Eternally Missed', featured a sleeve design by Adam Falkus, who had won a competition to design the artwork. Ironically, the song was released the day Muse played their most violently received set since Woodstock, at Cardiff International Arena, where huge slam circles opened up before them and all-out fighting broke out in the moshpit; looking down, they could see both joy and agony at the same time, the most insane crowd they'd ever played to. Perhaps tapping into this bloodthirsty carnage via the controversial video, 'Hysteria' reached number 17.

The December arena tour wended its way around the nation's hugest sheds, playing not just to adoring rock or indie kids but to the Radio One-listening masses who only go to one gig a year, and whole families making a night out of it. The numbers seemed huge – 10,000 people in the Nottingham Ice Centre Arena, 12,300 in Wembley Arena, the same at the Birmingham NEC, a whopping 19,000 in the Manchester Evening News Arena. And the shows were blistering triumphs all, the step up to the arena league made with confidence and panache.

Muse's final gig of 2003, aside from a TV recording for Jo Whiley's *Live Lounge* in London three days before Christmas, took them to Iceland for the first time on December 10 to play the 6,000-capacity Laugardalshöll venue in Reykjavik – not the biggest show on the tour but, considering that the city only has a population of 120,000 and all of the tickets were snapped up within an hour by fans queuing overnight, a special one. With the phrase 'end of tour . . . finally' scrawled on the end of the set lists that night and the biggest cloakroom in the world (apparently) rammed with 6,000 of the heftiest winter coats, Muse rocked one in 25 of Reykjavik's populus with 90 minutes of volcanic pomp rock, Matt doing triple pirouettes around the stage wearing balloon track-suit bottoms and Aladdin slippers in a Christmassy pantomime, end-of-year fancy-dress fashion. The next day, free of live engagements for a whole month, they hired out skidoos and went bombing around glaciers before going diving in the Blue Lagoon. Then they went home to marry Chris off.

And hey, you had to give them their chance to blow off steam. Because in 2004 the road would be long, and it would contain many a tragic, painful and violent turn.

GLEN ROWE

What was your involvement in Absolution?

"I remember going to Grouse Lodge. Matt was really obsessed with the doomsday theories at that point. Grouse Lodge is only about an hour from Dublin, but they'd never bother going to Dublin. There's a bar in the studio where you can pour your own pints and they'd just entertain themselves by doing things like that. Before that, to write all the songs, we rented an apartment facility in Hackney. A girl who used to work for the band years before called Kate Lauren lent Matt a white baby grand piano, and that's where he wrote a song called 'Milky Piano'. It had all their gear set up all the time and a little living area and a pool table. I remember taking the guys to Ikea! They had the real notion of finding somewhere where they could write and record at four o'clock in the morning if they wanted to. Matt was up in north London, so was Dom, Chris was actually living in this space and Paul Reeve would come up as well. It was a fucking dream, because it was really secure and really posh as well. It had an inflatable bedroom. Chris wanted to have some sort of privacy, so we bought him an inflatable room! We pumped it up for Chris to have his bed in, so he could have some walls and some solace from everyone else. They really lost themselves there.

"They'd spend so long getting excited about grooves. I remember 'Time Is Running Out' coming out of nowhere. Things like 'Stockholm Syndrome' – I remember Matt sitting on a drum riser somewhere in Spain playing the bass riff on his guitar. You just thought it was Matt noodling, but within three minutes he'd got the riff and out of nothing the song came. I've never seen a bush fire start, but I'd imagine it's just like that. It was insane. Dom and Chris have telepathy that's insane. 'Time Is Running Out' happened in seconds. I never heard Matt sing any vocal lines for that album, ever, until I heard the album. Matt hated singing, he'd do it all in his head. In fact Dom and Chris, up to that point, had never heard him sing in a studio. Everyone would leave. I remember there were Radio One sessions where they kicked me out. I was quite angry with them because I was knackered, I'd done a long day, got them to Radio One, set up all the stuff and they went, 'Glen, can you go now, mate?' 'Can't I just fucking sit here for an hour? I'm knackered!' When it's a full live thing it's different, but when he's playing the tracks and having to sing, he doesn't like it. We came up with a really amazing notion of recording songs in pods, and getting a mixer so the guys could go to any radio station and give them a live recorded version instead of doing acoustic versions, because they hated them. Then, literally on the day I was about to spend a load of money to buy all this gear, Dom phoned me up and went, 'Glen, of course we can't do it – Matt's just pointed out that if we're all recording with our in-ears, someone will be able to hear Matt singing on his own. It can't happen.'"

Was there a lot of apocalyptic talk?
"He told me about how mankind ruins nature, that if you have an estuary, mankind will go to these areas like ants, ruin what's around it and then go more inland to find the things they need to pull in. He gave me night-mares once talking about the disease of mankind. He was the first person who talked about Utopia to me, going, 'How would you feel about start-ing your own Utopia in another country, just us on a fucking island where we'd fish for our dinner?' His mind was really fast thinking about the decay of modern mankind. It freaked me out a little bit because what he read about was really quite true, that mankind is raping the planet for what it is good for and soon we'll eat ourselves out of house and home. He'd never lecture you about it, he'd always tell you about it very matter-of-factly. That was what scared me about it. He's a very, very smart boy."

The tour for Absolution *was a much bigger production.*
"There was the Dalek, the piano thing. Then there was the first bit of staging where Chris could walk on top of the amps, the drum riser, the moving plasmas. That tour was when it all became very grown-up, and the band would start leading a very different life. It gets to that sad moment when it would never go back to being how it was. The band were on their trajectory and everybody else would have to catch up. Different hotels to the crew in different parts of the city. There were no after-show parties. There were meet and greets that were very formal and very few and far between. It all became much more about the show, because by that point hysteria was everywhere, every show they played, they didn't have to do anything. . . ."

I remember coming out of the stage door at a couple of shows with you and the band and having to run the gauntlet of clutching arms trying to get to the car. Was there a lot of that going on?

"Yeah, Muse fans would turn up, and even if they couldn't get into the gig they'd just hang out, and there would be times afterwards when we were getting out and people would just be there. That's when we went from one security guard to two or three. Because there was a need as soon as they'd accelerated into arena rock, fully. The freight of the gear from country to country wasn't just a few bits, it was fucking everything goes, you know? Tons and tons of gear. That's when it became a bit stale really."

The experience of it?

"Yeah, everything became the same. It was literally a case of get back to the hotel, chill out. Dom had a girlfriend, everyone was loved up then. Chris had his third kid in between *Origin Of Symmetry* and *Absolution*. There'd be a lot of travel days because the band would often have to travel the day of the gig, turn up, not bother soundchecking and just go straight in for the night. It all started turning into the same thing. I stopped working with them because I knew that if I didn't, my life would always be with Muse until the day I died. I remember having this horrible meeting with Matt and Dom and saying, because I'd started my own production company by that point, 'I need time to be here.' I'd met my girlfriend, whom I've now married and had my kid with, and I felt we'd all move on to the next thing, and all they're gonna be from here on upwards is a fucking massive, massive band. It was that awful thing of, 'Do I want to do that for the rest of my life? No.' Well, I can't say it ever stopped being fun, because it was always fun, but for me, it felt my time had come to an end and since Muse I haven't really tour-managed for any long period of time for any band. I can't do it any more"

Did they ruin you?

"They broke me! It made me feel like I was never going to get that time back ever again, and it was magical. Since then I've worked with some huge bands and some lovely bands, but nothing will ever replace my time with Muse. To this day I have the band asking me to come back to it, and I'm so emotionally proud that they've turned into what they turned into, because they've become what they were always going to be, and they never took their eye off the ball. But if I hadn't got out then, then today I'd be on my way to Portugal to do a show tomorrow! I still see the guys all the time and we're still really good mates, but it was really uncomfortable for a while because they felt that I'd walked away from them. But I hadn't walked away from them, I'd walked away from that entity. They were never gonna stop! In the beginning I signed up to do three weeks of dates. Four years later you go, 'Jesus Christ, what happened?'"

SAFTA JAFFERY

"When *Absolution* was finished I then went back to the States and started shopping it, and again the competition got down to Columbia and Warner Bros. And Columbia were so keen to sign Muse that they sent this deal memo that was absolutely ridiculous, I mean the advance that they were willing to pay was just huge. But by that time the band had been talking with and started a relationship with Cliff Bernstein & Peter Mench at Q-Prime, and part of the thinking when I was trying to shop the third album was that all the US labels wanted to bring in an American manager. And because Q-Prime had the relationship with Warner Bros, that's where the deal ended up. But the deal with Columbia was a better one in comparison. But I think they did find the right home in the end."

How did your working relationship with Muse end?
"After the third album Mushroom had sold the company to Warners and the whole vibe over there went weird with us, because Warners were really jealous that we held all the rights. There were a lot of disagreements once that process happened because they weren't used to people having the freedom we had been afforded while working with Mushroom. Korda completely trusted us and had left us alone while at Mushroom, but once he was at Warners, he changed and sided with the label. Taste made all the creative decisions with the band and we delivered everything from the recordings, videos, the artwork. When it came to Warners, they weren't used to working like that – they had all these in-house departments that they wanted us to work with and we didn't want to, because we already had independent teams set up that had worked really well. So I think in the end it was really a sort of gradual evolution, as the band were already

platinum status and all the real groundwork had already been laid. Because all the licence deals I did had been three-album deals, once the band had delivered *Absolution*, all those deals were up. None of those labels had options on the band so we were free to sign with anyone for the next album(s). So we signed them to Warners worldwide, that's what the band wanted. We sat down with the band and they believed that they'd out-grown us. They felt that Dennis and I had done our bit, they'd become a very successful band, *Absolution* was number one in all those territories, it was a great album, we'd achieved our goals."

Was there any bad feeling?

"The band had become global rock stars and as the territorial three-album licence deals had now come to an end and with Taste having no further contractual obligations to any of the labels including Warner, and with Taste still having ownership to a further three albums in their contract with Muse. So if the band could be free of Taste, that would be a very desirable outcome. The new management had sensed this opportunity and pursued accordingly, with Taste out of the way the band could sign a direct worldwide deal with Warners. Which is of course exactly what they did. The new regime wanted to take over from Taste and finally after much deliberation did so."

But what about the band? Did you lose contact with them?

"Yes, I think I did. I think the problem is when a band gets to the size that Muse had become, unfortunately there are so many people that come out of the woodwork who think they know better, and so many lawyers get involved, and there was some confusion going on with our contract with the band, there was some bad advice given by our lawyers, but in the end the final outcome was probably the right one. I still speak to Anthony, I'm still the publisher, we're all continuing with our lives. It's just one of those things. But I hope the band would be the first to admit that had it not been for the belief, support and guidance that Dennis and I gave, they would never have developed and achieved the level of success in the way they did."

How do you look back at it now?

"I see it as a major achievement. I'm very proud of what we managed to achieve. At the time when I was doing those territorial deals, people were saying, 'You're making mistakes, it's not gonna work, it's gonna be messy.' We were the complete underdogs. In many ways that worked for us, being the underdogs, because everyone expected us to trip up and fall over. At every stage of the game everybody so underestimated us. They just thought, 'Who are these guys, who the hell are they? What have they done before? Nothing. So why should they have the glory?' There were always all these darts and daggers being thrown at us, as I used to say in those days. Warners at the end just wanted to own the rights to the band. Am I bitter about it? No, because the guy at Warners that eventually negotiated the deal with me, I actually just had lunch with last week. We're still very good friends. It's just business, it's the way the music business is."

Chapter Eight

HAVING made their name with an album musing over the above, the below and the earthly tumult in between, the year that would see Muse sway between Heaven and Hell at sometimes hourly intervals began in something approaching paradise.

The Big Day Out festival is a touring collective of bands in the style of America's Lollopalooza, which travels the major arenas and stadiums of Australia every January. Not so much a festival, in fact, than a touring beach holiday, since almost every day Muse – joining the revolving tour line-up in 2004 alongside Metallica, The Mars Volta, Dandy Warhols, The Strokes and Hoodoo Gurus – found themselves within a short drive of a beach and with a daily supply of free beer. And they made the most of it. By day they'd surf and drink their way along the coast of Australia; by night, after playing their truncated late-afternoon set of 11 songs, rotating the songs from their arena tour every night, they'd crack open the lagers and hang out with The Strokes. Matt found himself taken with The Strokes' way with a simple catchy song, and began thinking about writing such a stripped-back beast himself, the kind of song you hear once and think you've known your whole life. They also made friends with Lars Ulrich of Metallica, who found much to admire in Muse's wild and raucous sets. He even turned the rest of his band on to their music and, by the halfway point of the Big Day Out tour, Muse would come offstage to find Metallica seated in a practice area set up in a tent by the side of the stage, warming up by playing 'New Born'.

In fact, the only band that Muse met on the tour with whom they didn't find some kind of bond were their labelmates at EastWest, The Darkness. Now thankfully defunct, this ageing bunch of novelty rock chancers, who peddled a hackneyed tongue-in-cheek brand of hair rock and brazenly wore Freddie Mercury catsuits in blatant copyism, were becoming rapidly popular among the nostalgia rock crowd, selling 1.2 million copies of their debut album, *Permission To Land*, since July 2003, and moving up festival

219

bills with alarming speed. They were also, unsurprisingly perhaps, looking like the UK's most likely new band to break the States (along with Wales' Lostprophets, who were selling well in the US), since ridiculous hair rock had never really gone out of fashion in brain-dead Middle America and was met with a knowing sense of kitsch in LA. Considering them to be the sort of band that might well come along and steal Muse's pomp-rock crown, in a regional Spanish radio interview Matt had been asked about them and told the interviewer that he considered them to be a joke band. Taking himself far more seriously than anyone else did, singer Justin Hawkins approached Matt at one of the Big Day Out shows to challenge him about it (after a pleasant chat), to which Matt could only utter a surprised, "Aren't you a joke band?"

Interspersed with two full Muse shows at Sydney's Metro theatre and Melbourne's Hi-Fi Bar And Ballroom, both of which sold out quickly, the Big Day Out tour took them from the Ericsson Stadium in Auckland, New Zealand (where Matt wore a white lab coat onstage for the first time), through Queensland's Parklands and two days in Sydney at the Showground and the Olympic Park in front of 40,000 people per day. It wound up a week later via showgrounds in Melbourne, Adelaide and Perth and an appearance on Channel V's *What U Want* show, playing *Absolution*'s three singles. Whichever way the water went down the plughole, Muse's brilliance went down equally as ecstatically and, before the year was out, Muse would be back in Australia for their own sold-out tour. The southern hemisphere fell for Muse just as heavily as the northern one.

Stopping off on their way home from Australia to play seven sizeable venues in Japan – two each in Tokyo and Osaka and one each in Nagoya, Hiroshima and Fukuoka – Muse were back in England in time for rehearsals for their performance at the Brit Awards on February 17. Receiving their first Brit nomination for Best Rock Act, at a show renowned for over-the-top stage sets (that year Beyoncé Knowles performed in £250,000 worth of diamonds, while presenter Cat Deeley arrived onstage straddling a gigantic bottle of champagne), they performed 'Hysteria' on a bare stage dressed in black, since their label had decided to spend all of their money on a flashy futuristic stage show for The Darkness to match their silver sequinned trousers. Muse didn't win their award, while The Darkness picked up three Brits, but for all the flash and expense of Hawkins' performance, it was Muse's sparse brilliance that stole the show.

Matt demonstrates why he needs a crane for a microphone stand,
The Brits Are Coming showcase, Clapham Grand, November 26, 2003.
(LFI)

Revisiting Teignmouth Community College, July 2004.
(MID-DEVON ADVERTISER SERIES)

Proud alumni of TCC, Muse are reunited with former music teacher, Jill Bird. July 2004.
(MID-DEVON ADVERTISER SERIES)

Jester Matt and his Silver Manson do their
bit for Live 8, Paris, July 2, 2005.
(SIPA PRESS/REX FEATURES)

Dom fumes over the previous night's poker
game, Curiosa Festival, Atlanta, July 29, 2004.
(CHRIS MCKAY/RETNA)

Muse moodiness, New York, May 27, 2006.
(DAVID GOLDMAN/RETNA)

Futurism in collapse – Matt playing his in-guitar neon Kaos pad onstage
at Gampel Open Air Festival, Switzerland, August 18, 2006.
(OLIVIER MAIRE/EPA/CORBIS)

Hilarity at the puniness of their 2006 Mercury Music Prize consolation gonk.
(JM ENTERNATIONAL/REDFERNS)

More impressed with actually winning 'Best Alternative Band'
at MTV Europe Music Awards in Denmark, 2006.
(ALEX GRIMM/REUTERS/CORBIS)

"I want to bungee jump onto the stage from the arch, but health and safety might have
something to say about that...", Wembley Stadium press conference, December 4, 2006.
(ANTHONY HARVEY/WIREIMAGE.COM)

Matt as Gandolf, trying out the destructive
powers of the Brit for 'Best Live Act',
Valentine's Day 2007.
(DAVE HOGAN/GETTY IMAGES)

Hugh Manson showing off the M One D One
MIDI guitar he made for Matt.
(TIM STARK)

The Sensory blitzkrieg that was Muse at Wembley Stadium,
June 16, 2007. HAARP never rocked so hard.
(BRIAN RASIC/REX FEATURES)

Madison Square Garden, NY, August 6, 2007.
(LUCAS JACKSON/REUTERS/CORBIS)

Preparing for the author's most recent
interview, *NME* Awards, February 28, 2008.
(DAVE HOGAN/GETTY IMAGES)

Cowboy Chris playing for the Sultan at Dubai
Desert Rock Festival, March 2008.
(AWAIS BUTT)

Shortly after "firing up the beast" of the Royal Albert Hall's organ, April 12, 2008.

Undaunted, and with a tweak of the set list that saw 'Dead Star' and 'Fury' return and 'Apocalypse Please' shift to open the encore, Muse set out for a sporadic month of touring around Ireland, France, Spain and Italy, playing to around 8,000 people a night in places such as the Zenith arenas in Orleans, Toulouse and Rouen in France, and 14,000 at the Palacio de Vistalegre in Madrid eight days after the terrorist bombings on the Madrid railway system (Q magazine reviewed the show under the headline 'How Muse Saved Madrid'). The gigs led up to a long-awaited project for Muse: the American invasion.

With their US activity largely put on hold during their difficulties with and eventual dislocation from Maverick, Taste Media had negotiated them a deal with a new US label – Warners – keen to release *Absolution* in America that February. And that meant finally dedicating the many months of touring the vast territory that it takes to break the States (unless you're The Darkness). It was a huge undertaking; the band and Taste Media knew that despite half a million sales of *Showbiz* in the US, which guaranteed they'd be taken seriously Stateside, their profile in America had fallen far behind that in Europe, with the lack of release for *Origin Of Symmetry* meaning they would have to start from scratch, playing tiny clubs across the country to build up a fanbase. So they treated the USA as a totally different concern from the rest of the world and staggered their touring there; the USA was a mistress to be courted sporadically but at length over the course of most of 2004.

And it was a courtship, like all of the most chivalric, that would not come without its wounds.

* * *

Matt Bellamy honestly didn't know what had hit him. Nor, really, did he know where he was. The onstage disorientation had started to kick in after a few months on the road – the dizziness that came over him when the bar lights were dim and the music was loud, the feeling that he didn't know his own name and was surrounded by strangers. And, finding himself playing tiny, 300-capacity bars but now with an arena-sized ego and sense of stagecraft, his antics were too big for the stages; he'd knee-slide into amps or throw guitars hard into low ceilings and too-close drum kits, losing the plot like a full-grown tiger in a cage meant for a cub.

And on the second date of their American tour, in the Cotton Club in Atlanta on April 9, the inevitable happened.

Halfway through 'Citizen Erased', the fifth song of the set, Matt got excited and tripped over himself on the cramped stage. He felt no pain from the fall but, when he recovered and tried to sing into the mike, he found his mouth full of liquid; he spat it out and watched a stream of blood cover the microphone. Unknowingly, during his fall he'd rammed his guitar head straight into his jaw, spearing himself. He leant across to a roadie and pointed at his face; in the light, the roadie later commented, it looked like there was water pouring from his mouth. When Matt rushed off to throw up backstage before being taken to hospital for stitches (where he stayed for five hours), Dom remembers looking up and seeing the stage as a "gorefest".

The next day's show at the Kyber club in Philadelphia was cancelled but, with the help of heavy-duty prescription painkillers and a short rest, Matt was well enough to continue the tour four days later at the 550-capacity Bowery Ballroom in Manhattan. For the next week until the stitches were removed in Montreal on April 18, every time he sang he could feel them stretching around his wound until they began to grow into his lip.

Clearly putting their lives on the line in the name of rock, Muse went down a storm in America that spring, taking off quicker there than any band since, perhaps, Coldplay. As they were a techno-savvy futuristic-style band, the US internet community had latched onto them despite their absence from the record stores, and *Origin . . .* had been something of a web favourite, to the point where crowds at the US shows were singing all the words to songs that hadn't been released in America yet. Sure enough, as they moved on to playing the 1,000-capacity Cabaret club in Montreal, fans had begun travelling from entirely different states to catch them, Union Jacks started cropping up on regular occasions, and once again Muse were met with a fandom bordering on the obsessive wherever they turned. It seemed there was no territory immune to their dark appeal and sense of outsider belonging, and that maybe their stance on the Iraqi war, which was so boldly writ across *Absolution*, and its attendant press cuttings was making them popular with the more intelligent anti-war minority in the US. Their music was meaningful enough to strike chords in the darkest of climes, and yet elaborate and other-worldly enough to act as an escapist thrill.

It was an impression Matt certainly didn't quash with his interviews around this tour. He spoke about his need to suppress extreme feelings, like the desire to get a gun and shoot anyone who annoyed him. He talked of his fear of death, which struck him every time his aeroplane took off. And he expanded on his theory of the human race being cloned to mine the Earth for Sitchin's alien race to include the existence of minotaurs, who had once been part of the same cloning programme, hence the legends often found them placed in labyrinthine mines.*

Muse's American tour, besides a slew of more improvised and spontaneous sets than the arena set-up had allowed them, also saw them slide into a new, dangerous addiction: gambling. In his few weeks off in London, Matt had started frequenting a semi-legal poker club in Clerkenwell Road to play for small stakes for fun, and the game had become something of an obsession. He'd begun waking up and going to bed shuffling cards, even perfecting under-the-leg shuffles. Poker became a regular post-gig pastime; in Montreal the band stayed up gambling until 6 a.m. after the gig and, finding themselves with a few days off mid-tour, they took the opportunity to fly to Las Vegas to indulge in their new addiction. And this itself led to another new interest, as the band rolled out of a casino one morning for a helicopter ride to the Grand Canyon, their first ever ride in a helicopter. Seeing his bandmates hungover as hell, Dom asked the pilot to pull off as many roller-coaster-style drops and leaps as he could, until Matt threw up all over the cabin. Dom and Matt were hooked: they wobbled gingerly off of the copter, determined to get lessons to fly one themselves. Indeed, as soon as they were back home they booked joint lessons but, as Matt found with his paramotor, there'd sadly not be time to reach any level of expertise.

Buoyed by their positive American experience, which took in an appearance at the none-more-hot Coachella Festival in California, and a gig at San Diego's Brick By Brick club that ended with Matt throwing his Black Manson guitar away into a dumpster (it was swiftly stolen by a passing fan), Muse returned to the UK on May 11 to prepare for their biggest and most rewarding challenge yet. Where there used to be an endless succession of mid-afternoon festival shows across Europe stretching through the summer, in 2004 there were 26 festival dates booked

---

* Matt also happily admitted that he liked to talk about such outlandish things because it made boring interviews more interesting, and he felt as if he should be himself even if it did mean talking a load of rubbish to journalists.

for them, several of them being their first main-stage headlining slots.

And one more than any other would be both the proudest and most tragic of Muse's career.

* * *

On June 27, 2004, the Muse got the apocalypse they'd been asking for.

In rainy years the Glastonbury festival is often transformed into Somerset's biggest swamp; in 2004 it was more like a lake. After a scorching Thursday welcomed revellers into the Vale Of Avalon, word spread of a storm that was forecast for that evening. Those of us who stayed up all night – as is the tradition at Glastonbury – were relieved to hear some thunder in the distance at around dawn, which swiftly faded into the distance. The bad weather, we sighed with relief, had thankfully passed us by.

Then, at 8 a.m. on Friday June 25, the heavens gushed open. In the space of a few hours Worthy Farm experienced heavier rainfall than in its entire history, and the Great Glasto Flood was widespread. Entire sections of the campsite were totally submerged, the last few pairs of Wellington boots were selling at premium prices, and festival goers were seen literally canoeing around the site. Conditions were possibly the worst that the festival had ever experienced; many campers who couldn't cope with the mud, overflowing toilets and inability to sit down anywhere on site for three days gave up and went home, while those who braved the inclemency were seen through the flurry by main-stage headline performances by Oasis, who put in a workmanlike set on the Friday night, and Paul McCartney, who wowed the biggest audience of the weekend with a pyrotechnic display of stone-cold classics from The Beatles and Wings back catalogues on Saturday evening.

For Muse, the festival was a huge event and a massive honour to play. It was their first main-stage headline set in the UK and many had questioned the organiser's decision to book them as the headliners on the final day of the festival, suggesting that Michael and Emily Eavis had taken a huge risk on a band untried in such a prestigious slot. Those of us who had seen them blow the roofs off arenas for the previous 10 months were certain they'd be the band of the weekend, but there were many unconverted Glastonbury goers who believed that Muse simply weren't ready for such a vital slot, and would undoubtedly make fools of themselves on the Sunday night.

Muse arrived at Glastonbury buzzing from a run of festival sets around

Europe at which they'd taken either the headline or high-on-the-bill slots. They'd been third on the bill at Nurburgring's Rack Am Ring and Nuremburg's Rock Im Park, and top of the bill at Bologna's Flippaut and Holland's Pinkpop. They'd also won over a hard-rock crowd of Korn and Linkin Park fans at the metal festival Superbock Superrock in Lisbon, Portugal, on Matt's birthday on June 9, where they took the opportunity to play five separate riff 'songs' in a row for a metal crowd. Two weeks before Glastonbury they'd also attempted a failed day of sightseeing at the Colosseum (the queue was too long) and Vatican (Dom wasn't allowed in as he was wearing 80s running shorts), before a gig at the Stadio Centrale Del Tennis in Rome, a classical monument to Mussolini on the Tiber's banks, built by the dictator himself – an obelisk in the venue's entrance plaza is carved with his name. At dinner that day, Matt ordered a plate of pasta and tomato that was so delicious and simple that it literally brought him to tears.

All of this was in the wake of further chart successes – on May 17, 'Sing For Absolution' had been released as a single, with a mere one extra track – live favourite and *Absolution* offcut 'Fury' – and had hit number 16 in the UK charts. The single's main additional selling point, in fact, was its stunning video, featured on the DVD single release.* Their most elaborate and no doubt expensive promo film so far, it was a sci-fi story inspired by Matt's idea of having to evacuate a planet approaching an ice age to find a new one to mine for resources (or possibly by our trip to the space simulator at the Science Museum the previous August).

In the heavily CGI'd video, Matt, Dom and Chris play astronauts launched into the galaxy from a futuristic planet that is attempting to bomb the encroaching glaciers in order to transport cryogenically frozen people to a new planetary home. Breaking through a wormhole, they find themselves in an asteroid storm and collide with rocks that send them crashing onto a dead red planet. The viewer might think they'd started off from a future Earth and crashed on Mars, but the final shot, in homage to the ending of *Planet Of The Apes*, shows the three of them stranded amid the ancient wreckage of the Houses Of Parliament. As they commented at the time, for all the numerous times they'd turned down TV shows and

* Along with the song, a 'making of' the video and backstage footage entitled 'The Big Day Off' were included; this showed the band on a day trip to Piha Beach near Auckland.

teenage magazine interviews, when they were offered the chance to jump into spacesuits and fly spaceships around they leapt at the opportunity.

So Muse reached Glastonbury on a high – it was close to their home county of Devon so was attended by many members of their family and friends, and they'd been looking forward to the show for months, hoping to catch Morrissey at the end of the day but sad to be missing the last-ever gig by Orbital, which was taking place on the second stage at the same time as their set. Preview interviews caught the band in jubilant mood as they expounded on their festival trivia: the worst thing Dom had ever eaten at a festival was a dirty schnitzel in Germany; Matt once had a painful shiatsu massage; if it rained, they said, they'd arrive by helicopter half an hour before their set, but suggested the crowd should go with it, get naked, put on stupid hats, swim in the mud and roll their mates down hills in the portaloos before hugging them. Essential festival kit? For Matt it was black bin-liners to use as shoes or a rudimentary lavatory; for Dom it was a drum kit.

But for all their excitement and playfulness, they knew there was serious business at hand. Glastonbury tickets that year had sold out before any of the acts had been announced, so they wouldn't be playing to a dedicated Muse crowd – in fact, with the weather the way it was they expected around 4,000 Muse fans to stick around in their wellies and the rest to go home before they took the stage. And they weren't too far wrong – although a healthy crowd stayed to watch their set the audience was certainly depleted from previous nights, and those that were there needed to be hugely impressed in order to keep them from leaping in their cars and fleeing towards a dry bed. Muse had to go out there, win over the doubters and blow the mud from the ears of the slosh-weary. And they wholeheartedly succeeded on both counts.

Muse, in short, gave the performance of their lives. In the white lab coat from the Big Day Out, and looking like a space-rock sorcerer, Matt twirled, spun and balanced his Silver Manson on his head mid-solo like a perfectly poised whirling dervish. Chris provided the meatiest bass rumbles he'd ever wrenched from his instrument, and Dom pummelled out beats to drown out even Friday's thunderstorm. The towering rendition of 'Apocalypse Please' was deemed so hyper-charged that the Glastonbury live version was released a month later as a one-track download, with proceeds going to Oxfam, and reached number 10 in the first-ever download chart. Organiser Emily Eavis would describe it as the best set of the weekend, and Muse, who had gone into the gig feeling like underdogs, emerged as Glastonbury's conquering heroes.

From the very first note of 'Hysteria' they knew the gig was going to be a sensation, and as the balloons bounced joyously to the end of 'Blackout' and the confetti cannons were charged for a mud-thickening second encore of 'Stockholm Syndrome', Matt made a rare public announcement of more than five or six words. "Thank you very much for staying out in all the mud and everything," he told the crowd, "this has been the best gig of our lives."

An hour after they left the stage, however, it became the most devastating night of the band's career.

As the post-gig family celebrations took place in Muse's backstage Portakabin, Dom's father, Bill, aged 62, collapsed from a heart attack, was rushed to the on-site medical centre and died there. It was a horrendous and tragic end to what had been the most ecstatic of nights, and doubly difficult for Dom since his touring schedule had made it hard for him to see his family for some time. It was, he would later admit, both the best and the worst day of his life.

Muse's next live appointment, at the Lazzaretto in Bergamo, Italy, was cancelled, and a statement issued that the band would appreciate the press respecting their privacy. For almost a week they holed up in Devon, Dom to mourn his father and Matt and Chris to support their friend and his family. It was a week of deep understanding and consideration between the three; they talked about stopping touring altogether, and Dom considered leaving the band to be with his family. But his closest friends convinced him to get out and play, thereby finding the positive side of the tragedy through the thing he enjoyed doing most. It was, after all, what his dad would've wanted. Within a week Dom had decided he wanted to be back out on the road, and the band continued their festival dates with a headline set at Switzerland's St Gallen festival and appearances at Belgium's Werchter and Roskilde in Denmark, before Dom was afforded another week off to gather his thoughts and mourn in earnest.

Those three festival dates in the immediate aftermath of Bill Howard's death were strange and difficult for the band.* The tragedy brought them

---

* The death of Dom's father was the first story about Muse ever to appear in the tabloid newspapers.

closer as friends, made them more appreciative of and understanding towards each other. It made them realise that the cliché was true: you really don't know what you've got until it's gone, and that went for parents, friends and each other. They'd come close to losing Dom as a bandmate and maybe the band falling apart altogether, and that reminded them of the basic pleasure of playing their music; how much they appreciated being able to play onstage for so many people. From a terribly sad event Muse gained much strength within themselves, forged new bonds, learnt a new openness and positivity towards each other, became an ever-more solid unit.

By the time they'd regrouped and played their hearts out as headliners of that year's T In The Park festival in Balado Park, Kinross, Muse had become invincible.

Although there would be still more agonies before the tour was out.

* * *

Chris Wolstenholme honestly didn't know what had hit him. As he picked himself up from the ground and hobbled back into position it turned out to have been a sliding tackle by one of The Cooper Temple Clause, whom Muse had challenged to a game of five-a-side football between soundchecks. The two bands were touring America together as part of the Curiosa tour in July and August, a 13-date rolling festival around the middle of America organised and curated by headliners The Cure and made up of two stages populated by bands with whom The Cure felt a kinship or fondness.

Having reached the tour via eight festival dates in Europe in July – including the Oxegen festival in Ireland where 'Apocalypse Please' had been cut from the set due to local heroes Ash overrunning their set, and the Santiago de Compostela shindig in Spain where Dom had greeted the crowd with the immortal and embarrassing Spinal Tap gaff "hello San Diego!" – Muse were playing on the second stage alongside The Coopers, ex-Hole and Smashing Pumpkins bassist Melissa Auf Der Maur and grunge rockers Thursday, while the main stage throbbed to the post-rock miserablisms of Interpol and Mogwai and the incongruous cowbell dance stylings of The Rapture. Muse had bonded with The Cure themselves over Texas Hold Em poker – Matt had won $400 from singer Robert Smith one night, largely because Smith was so drunk he became a very bad bluffer, not realising that Matt was holding four aces – and The Cooper Temple Clause over football.

So as Chris picked himself up on the patch of wasteland outside the venue in Detroit, 10 dates into the Curiosa jaunt, and brushed himself off, he didn't think too much of the ache in his wrist. It was just another on-the-road Muse injury, like the bruises Matt had given Dom in Toronto the night before by throwing his guitar at him. He happily played the day's gig – a six-song, half-hour set of solid rock hits – drank the night away at the after show party that the band had resurrected on the Curiosa tour and went to bed with the throb in his arm a mere afterthought.

It was only when Matt was woken up in the middle of the night by a naked Chris pacing up and down the tour-bus corridor, swearing to himself and holding a wrist swollen to twice its size, that Muse collectively sat up, looked at a diary that told them that they were due to headline the V Festival in England in 11 days' time and thought, "Jesus, we've blown it."

Drastic action was called for. With Chris' arm in plaster the band dropped out of the last three dates of the Curiosa tour and rushed home to put a safety net in place. They contacted a mate called Morgan Nichols, originally in The Senseless Things back when Muse were teenage fraggle fans and then bass player in The Streets, and set about teaching him their entire headlining set on the bass in a matter of 10 days.

Hence V2004 was a strange and subdued experience for Chris. He was still on stage, prodding out the odd keyboard line in front of 50,000 screaming Muse fans at both nights of the festival (the first at the Chelmsford site on August 21), but he couldn't enjoy the gigs since he found himself frustratingly listening to Nichols playing his bass parts and wincing at even the tiniest fluff or mistake. Despite having a fourth member for these and the next two festival shows before the end of August, Muse claimed they felt somehow incomplete. At those two festival dates, at Austria's Two Days A Week and France's Rock en Seine, Chris struggled through as much of the show as he could on the bass, with Nichols on hand to take over whenever it got too much.

The first time Chris made it through an entire set on the bass was a few days later at the opening show of their first sold-out tour of Australia. The gig was in the Metropolis club in Perth, a larger venue than they'd planned to play since the original gig had sold out within a day. On their first visit to the Metropolis' glorified community hall to play in 2000 they'd pulled in an audience of 10; this time the queue was around the block, in the rain, from 8.30 a.m. on the day of the show. The gig was a stormer and, with three days off in Perth to follow, Muse partied so hard that, through a combination of jet-lag and late drinking, they barely slept for around 72 hours. During one particularly arduous bout of insomnia, Chris remembers watching the movie version of *Starsky & Hutch* in his hotel room at 5 a.m.

Understandably, once they hit Adelaide – Australia's fifth biggest city, known as the City Of Churches since, well, there are so many churches there – for the second show of the Australian tour, Muse decided to go on a health kick. Tony, the bodyguard hired for them by Anthony Addis since they had become an arena band and therefore 'proper' pop stars, acted as their personal trainer, too. The first time he took them to a gym, however, it was almost too much for the jet-lagged young souls – their tour manager threw up after 20 minutes of cycling, and Chris very nearly followed suit.

It was his digestive system that was almost the undoing of Matt, though. Having consumed an entire leg of goat over dinner in an Argentinian restaurant on their last night in Perth, the set at Barton Theatre in Adelaide in front of 200 fans was cut short halfway through as Matt had to race off-stage in desperate need for the lavatory, leaving his bandmates to jam away for several long minutes until he returned, relieved. Dom later joked that such behaviour was acceptable at small club shows, but at an arena show they'd have made him go onstage in a nappy.

Picking up a platinum disc for Australian sales of *Absolution* along the way and upgrading venues as demand permitted – in Brisbane an extra night was added at the downtown Arena venue when the first advertised date sold out in an hour, and by the time Muse arrived, both dates had been upgraded to the 5,000-capacity River Stage – the band wrapped up a rampantly successful tour at the St James Theatre in Auckland on September 14, flying home for a few days' rest before their third US jaunt of the year. A mammoth leg of their American invasion, this three-month stint Stateside would take in 38 shows in almost as many cities the length and breadth of the US and Canada, from Nashville to Milwaukee, Portland to Albuquerque, Palm Beach to Tucson. Despite having been so successful in every other territory, it shows Muse's dedication to world domination that they were prepared to play chicken shacks in Middle American towns for such lengths of time (and with such arduous drives between cities; the 15-hour overnight stretch from Pittsburgh to Detroit was fairly average) in order to get their music heard.

As they arrived in California on September 18 to play a five-song showcase for KROQ radio's Inland Invasion event, 'Butterflies & Hurricanes' was just hitting US college radio and getting rotated far more heavily than any Muse track before. The single, released on September 20 in the UK*, was a sure-fire hit back home, reaching number 14 thanks to the employing of even more new technology: the single came with U-MYX software on the disc, which allowed the listener to remix the song themselves or to turn off chosen instruments and play along with the track (there was a prize for the best remix fans sent in). But America was slowly waking up to their brilliance, and Muse were relishing the challenge; in Europe they felt like old men playing the enormodomes, while playing clubs of 200 people in a country where they'd sold a mere 200,000 copies of *Absolution* (barely a drop in the ocean in such a vast territory; it had sold 1.5 million worldwide by this point) made them feel young and up-and-coming again.

In San Francisco three days later Matt also found himself reverting to being a quivering fanboy when he spotted a childhood hero on the street. He'd become drinking buddies with Dave Grohl of course, but the first time he saw Nirvana's only other surviving member, Krist Novoselic, having his shoes shined on the streets of San Francisco, all he could do was sit at the same shining stand and have his own boots buffed, too scared to say anything to the lanky grunge bassman.

The tour was another messy explosion of big egos in small venues. After a warm-up including four days' glugging mojitos at the exclusive poolside A-list hangout The Sky Bar at LA's ultra-swish Mondrian hotel, and two festival dates alongside Morrissey, The Yeah Yeah Yeahs and Franz Ferdinand, in San Francisco Muse played the 2,200-seater Warfield Theatre – a step up from the 200-capacity club they'd played there in May. After the set they sloped off to a loft party downtown held by the

---

* Backed on CD by a BBC2 acoustic session of 'Sing For Absolution' and on vinyl by 'Butterflies & Hurricanes' live from Glastonbury; there was also an accompanying DVD single released. EastWest Records had been rebranded as Atlantic by this point, to which label the single was attributed.

support band, where Dom jammed the night away on bongos and Matt found himself cornered by a dotcom millionaire from Scarborough. The next night at the University Of California's Freedom Hall in Davis, near Sacramento, they played to 2,000 partying college kids, Matt throwing all his best Marty McFly knee-slides until he managed to headbutt his guitar and left the stage with a lightning-flash cut on his forehead. Another battle scar in the War On America.

As the tour rolled on through the American heartland and on to Canada, the obsessive tribes gathered. Tattooed rock heads and black-haired, mascara-clad teenagers were the core of them, along with the more hardcore followers. One 20-year-old Iraqi girl had written to Matt to tell him about her experiences of growing up exposed to torture and imprisonment at every turn, and how his music had helped her; he'd written back to show his appreciation but didn't expect the girl to show up for every date of the Canadian leg of the tour.

By the time they reached Salt Lake City on October 22 – a month into the tour and the day before Chris, who'd been playing every gig in his plaster cast, would injure his finger during the first song at McEwan's Ball in Calgary and be reduced to playing with a pick for the first time in a decade – all those hours on a cramped tour bus had started to pay dividends. The first glimmer of new material was allowed into the set in the form of 'New One (DES)' as the set list proclaimed it.* While hardly a potential comeback single, it was a rock song in keeping with Muse's lyrical themes, full of satellites and the need to rocket through the universe, and Matt referred to it in a blog on Muse's official fan message board as 'The Church Of The Sub-Genius', stating "the 33 randomised guitar overdubs on church of sub genius . . . have a high chance of making it" onto the fourth album. The name 'Church Of The Sub-Genius' came from what Matt described as a "weird slacker cult"; a religious group founded in Dallas in 1979 and prevalent on the internet in the 90s, publishing humorous and satirical articles. However, by the time it came to disc the song would be renamed 'Glorious'.

---

* The song would eventually become the bonus track on the Japanese release of *Black Holes And Revelations*, and there has been much debate among Muse's internet fanbase as to the meaning of (DES); some believe it to stand for Data Encryption Standard, an American governmental cipher used to encode classified information, others thought it referred to Des, the band's keyboard technician.

They played in Halloween masks in London, Ontario on October 31, with Dom as Gandalf. They let a couple onstage to get engaged at the first of two 2,300-seater shows at LA's Wiltern Theatre. They took to attaching pins to the ends of their guitars to help them pop the never ending onslaught of balloons that made it onstage in the closing moments of the dozens of closed-in US theatre shows. At some point on the tour they were informed that they'd been named Best Alternative Act at the MTV Europe awards. And 36 gigs after they'd arrived in the US, with their crowds building city by city, something truly magical happened. One morning, Dom woke up on the tour bus to hear Matt playing a new riff in the back lounge. It was like no riff he'd ever heard Matt play before; heavy, bold and galloping, it sounded to Dom like a herd of wild desert horses stampeding out of Matt's guitar. He sat up and opened the blinds of the tour bus to find they were out in the middle of the Arizona desert with nothing but cacti, rocks and sand as far as the eye could see. The riff fitted perfectly with the surroundings, as if the desert itself had seeped into the song. A song that would eventually be called 'Knights Of Cydonia'.

On December 14, after playing their last US date in Tucson, Arizona, Muse flew back to the UK with more than just a few cowboy hats and ponchos as remembrance of their visit to America's wild western states. They were enthused by the atmosphere of the country, of the Morricone stand-offs and the Eastwood cigar snarls. They spoke breathlessly to journalists about their new material sounding like The Strokes and Calexico, like epic country & western music that put them in mind of a man riding a horse through Mexico playing a trumpet and being shot by bandits. It was, they claimed, a bit flamenco, a bit Kill Bill, a bit Tex Mex, a bit Tom Waits. They spoke of one new song of such an epic, widescreen hue that they had no idea how they were going to record it, but were determined that when it was done it would make people think of knights in sombreros riding through the deserts of alien planets.

The hugeness of all things American had clearly rubbed off on Muse. In interviews that December, Matt claimed that the band would be the next Bon Jovi-style stadium rock act, complete with enormous video screens and lighters-aloft sections of the set – possibly even long hair and cowboy boots. He talked of getting a full cast of supporting dancers, a full orchestra and stage sets, and doing the show in scenes like a West End musical. He'd already worked out the plot to Muse: The Musical – it would be about a futuristic Lone Ranger travelling around the universe on a mission to prevent the end of the world.

The next step up on that road to global enormity was imminent. On December 19 and 20, Muse played what many thought to be astronomically huge gigs for them: two nights at the Earls Court Exhibition Centre in London to a total of 36,000 fans. The significance of the gigs can't be underestimated: there is no bigger indoor venue in the UK and to sell out a second night there due to 'unbelievable' demand is to prove yourself to be ready to burst into the stadiums. It's a venue usually reserved for the highly established likes of Radiohead, Oasis and the massive rock survivors from the 60s and 70s, not a three-piece pop-metal band from Devon on only their third album. Muse had long been Britain's best alternative rock band, now it was official: they were also the biggest.

Having seen at the Docklands Arena the dampening effect that a cavernous metal shed of a venue could have on the impact of their show, Muse set about doing everything in their power to make the gig as huge as the hall. They made plans to use a brand new breed of sound system one step beyond surround-sound, and looked into the design of such a thing only to be told that such a system hadn't properly been invented yet. There were flaws in the design and the PA company, who initially agreed to provide the system, eventually backed down, unwilling to risk staging their first-ever concert from the future.

So Muse had to up their game, performance-wise. They hired in some of the pyrotechnic gimmickry they hadn't been able to afford for their previous arena shows – a stage-front rank of CO2 flume jets were launched during 'Butterflies & Hurricanes', and more explosive ticker-tape cannons were rolled in to reach every inch of the venue. Wearing a shiny red coat on the first night and a stark black one on the second, Matt opened each gig by running around backstage with a TV camera linked to the stage screens, accosting security guards, making devil horn signs in front of the lens and racing along the front row filming the most ardent fans, while Dom and Chris played an instrumental filler called 'Dracula Mountain'. On the second night he did all of this while wearing a monkey glove puppet, which he made dance for the cameras before joining the band onstage to rocket into 'Hysteria'. On both nights, as 'The Small Print' skidded to a violent close, Matt beat his guitar into the stage until it was little more than a wreck of wood and metal, and then threw it into the crowd. On the first night they premiered a new song called 'Crying Shame', an upbeat pop number that fans bootlegged to death, speculating that it might be the first single from the next album. However, Matt told XFM the next day that he thought the song went down "like a ton of bricks" on its first performance and it was dropped the following night until they got it right.

Nonetheless, as the glow of 17,000 mobile phones lit the balloons and the confetti bombs showered the crowd in the closest they'd get to a white Christmas, Muse bowed out of 2004 with an almighty bang. In the previous 14 months they'd sold 900,000 records in the UK alone and had played to 1.4 million people worldwide. They'd survived tragedy and triumph in equal measure and come out of it closer and more confident than ever.

It was undeniable: Muse were now supermassive.

★   ★   ★

For the first three months of 2005, Muse chased that alien Lone Ranger as he tried to lasso them some new songs. Holed up in a rehearsal studio in London, they worked on their mariachi-metal new tracks, Matt becoming more and more obsessed with writing Dick Dale surf-guitar tunes and two and a half minute pop bombs (he also expressed a desire around this time to buy a house in the spring and travel barren landscapes to observe the activities of whales). By the beginning of April they'd worked up five or six new songs; when they were offered the chance to hop on a month's tour around the Midwest of America with jag-pop urch rockers Razorlight in support, they leapt at it. Here was an opportunity to kill two birds with one stone: to build on their good groundwork in America, particularly in the heartland hick towns that many tours fail to reach, and to try out a few new songs in the country that inspired their epic atmospheres.

Though Muse had a good seven or eight years' of live experience on Razorlight, the bands were on a roughly equal footing in America – Razorlight were beginning to garner some rabid attention thanks to their immediate and accessible new-wave guitar pop in the vein of Television, and their singer Johnny Borrell's cocky habit of proclaiming himself a genius in the press. Within two years Razorlight would be wowing the

US on the hugely influential David Letterman show with their knowingly unpatriotic song 'America' but, for the time being, in the eyes of the kids snapping up tickets for the 22-date MTVU Campus Invasion Tour, hitting universities and colleges across the Midwest, these were two damn fine rising bands on a pretty awesome bill, dude.

Kicking off at the Auditorium Field at Boca Raton in Florida, Muse introduced two impressive new songs. The first would eventually settle, after much reworking and several months under the title 'Demonocracy', on the name 'Assassin'. Built on a bedrock of Mexican flamenco metal (possibly inspired by the Armenian metal guitar work of Daron Malakian from System Of A Down), it was Muse's most vitriolic and political song to date, blatantly advocating violent revolution over a snarl of a verse, a soaring chorus hook and a nod to Rachmaninov's 'Prelude In G Minor'. Underneath its heady riff, Chris could be heard to grumble, "Aim, shoot, kill your leaders."

The second, meanwhile, was a Suede-esque swagger of slinky drums and seductive vocals that would come to be called 'Exo-Politics', although over the course of the month's tour it would go by many bizarre names. At the first few shows on the Campus Invasion Tour the set list marked 'Assassin' and 'Exo-Politics' as 'New D (Easy Tiger)' and 'The Other New One' respectively. As the tour went on, however, these two songs took ever more outlandish names on the set lists. 'Assassin' was, by turns, 'Debase Mason's Grog', 'Cold Aqua Tomato', 'Moniker Probes', 'Majestic Blue', 'Arty Seige', 'Starship Crowds' and 'Evaluating Mortals'. 'Exo-Politics' went by the names 'Codebreak Shy Outsider', 'Timescale Keeper', 'Unpacked Residents', 'Auditory Masks', 'ABA', 'Preservable Heat', 'Harem Meeting' and 'Obtain Drowsy Powders'. It looked to the passing set-list snatcher like the work of bored and playful minds on tour, but more probing and illuminated Muse fans – regulars on the fansites where hints were being dropped by Muse's entourage about hidden meanings to the names – began delving deeper.

The presence of the word 'Codebreak' was a major clue: these were anagrams, clues and ciphers. Some were nods to previous internet babble about hidden meanings to otherwise innocuous Muse set-list abbreviations: 'Codebreak Shy Outsider' was an anagram of 'Des is our keyboard tech'. But knowing that their fans were avidly scouring every scrap of information about the band for secrets and veiled information, they decided to give them a whole tour's worth of hidden meanings to play with.*

While the labyrinthine web of clues and ciphers they weaved was far too elaborate to fully unravel here (and apologies if I'm erroneous on the true cryptographic path, since I didn't solve each step myself at the time), the central route went roughly like this – on the list from Philadelphia's Liacouras Centre gig, 'Debase Mason's Grog' deciphered to 'Messageboard Song', a clue that they were writing secret messages to their messageboard fanbase, the first being 'Codebreak Shy Outsider' on the same set list. Next, in Buffalo, New York, 'Cold Aqua Tomato' was an anagram of Matt's old email address, while 'Timescale Keeper' told players to 'keep email secret'. Someone obviously didn't, since the next night in East Lansing, Missouri, came the disappointed 'Moniker Probes' ('broken promises') and the saucy 'Unpacked Residents' ('send naked pictures'). Then the game really kicked in: 'Swiss Rhapsody' (a title used in place of 'Crying Shame') translated as 'Password is shy', while 'Majestic Blue' was 'email subject'. Anyone emailing the address with the subject title of 'shy' received a seemingly unintelligible reply – unless they'd also worked out that 'Preservable Heat' from the Cleveland show was an anagram of 'reverse alphabet', the code needed to decipher the email. The email gave the location of the prize – a bike that the band had been using to keep fit on tour, which Matt had left hanging from an abandoned railway bridge when the tour passed through Amhurst, Missouri.

There were four bikes in all, left at specific locations along the route of the tour, often near the headquarters of secret societies such as the Illuminati, and each more fiendishly difficult to trace the clues to. Deciphering 'Obtain Drowsy Powders' ('write password on body') and 'Starship Crowds' ('password Christ') would mean anyone writing 'Christ' on themselves and emailing a photo of it to the inbox would be directed by encrypted email to a second bike. A third required the player to merge 'Harem Meeting' with 'Evaluating Mortals' and somehow come up with 'Get M-Three Naval Enigma Simulator', a downloadable program that, upon the user entering the code 'ABA', gave you the encryption code for the next directional email. It was enough to make the heads of the

---

* Before we go into the solutions, new players might like to cover up the following pages, go back to the titles and try to work it out for themselves.

protagonists of *The Da Vinci Code* explode, but the grand prize was won by the clever Muse-ite who worked out the near impossible anagram to 'Auditory Masks': 'RAK Studios May'. Simply by turning up they won themselves one of Muse's signed guitars.

It was an ingenious game (run largely by Tom Kirk), not just to kill time on the long drives across America by concocting such wild-goose chases but to forge a bond with their most devoted fans, reward them for their intense attention and teach them to always think beyond what you might at first be shown. Indeed, many fans were driven half insane by not being able to work out the anagram to the song title that ended almost every set list on the tour: 'Dealer's Choice'. That's because it wasn't an anagram at all – it referred to the poker practice of the dealer of each hand choosing the variation of poker to be played that hand, meaning that the band would take turns to choose the opening song of the encore.

Through Louisville, Kentucky, Columbus, Ohio, Kansas City and countless other middle-of-nowhere towns, the tour wound its way to a close at the heady student town of Austin, Texas on May 7, after which Muse returned home to resume their rehearsals and plot the course of their fourth album. For a year and a week they would work, being drawn away from rehearsal room or studio only once to play a live set. And with good cause too: on July 2, 2005, Sir Bob Geldof organised the Live 8 event to raise awareness of Third World debt on the eve of the G8 summit in Gleneagles, Scotland, where leaders of the eight major economic powers would meet to discuss just such problems.

With a chance to stand up for the downtrodden masses against sinister groups of untrustworthy politicians – a cause close to Matt's heart, having written an entire album about it – Muse obviously couldn't turn down the offer to play. But being comfortable by now in their off-road personalities, Muse were pleased to avoid the publicity circus of the London concert, the fulcrum of the whole event, and instead moved out of the Hyde Park running order a week before the event to play in Paris at the Versailles Palace (original home of King Louis XIV, the extravagant Sun King, and therefore a slightly ironic place to hold a Make Poverty History show) to a crowd of 150,000 instead. Given four songs to play, as opposed to the two or three afforded to stage-mates such as Placebo, Shakira, Dido and Craig David, they launched a ferocious – if somewhat shambolic – 17-minute assault on 'Hysteria', 'Bliss', 'Time Is Running Out' and 'Plug In Baby', with Matt in a top hat with a bizarre bib effect and Dom revealing a new-found taste for bright pink trousers. It was a laid back day with little in the way of TV or press commotion and few political activists, and Muse took the opportunity to have a bit of a laugh at the end of 18 months of almost continual touring.

And then, having finally laid the *Absolution* tour to a right royal rest, Muse set about uncovering newer revelations.

CHRIS WOLSTENHOLME

"We got offered the headline slot [at Glastonbury], which scared the shit out of us to start with because we didn't think we were big enough to do it. The day was a bit shit to be honest, it was muddy and it was miserable and you could tell it was the end of the festival, the crowd were kind of jaded. We saw this during the day and we thought, 'This is going to be fucking tragic', but it was completely the opposite. It's an honour to play there, with all the history of bands that've played there before. I remember seeing those flags waving all over the place. You do that and think, 'We've fucking made it.' But for all the highs there's always the lows, but you get through that."

DOMINIC HOWARD

"Obviously Glastonbury was a big one. That was the first time I went, 'We've actually made it.' The band had got to a point that I didn't think we'd get to. And coming from the West Country it meant a lot to play there. Headlining Glastonbury was amazing but tragic at the same time. I still remember the gig as being a real achievement. It's one of the worst things you can imagine in the world but I still remember the gig as being a really positive thing, and you have to try to draw some positivity from extremely negative situations."

MATT BELLAMY

"That was really tough. It was overwhelming, that whole night in general. It's difficult to describe the ups and downs of it and how surreal both extremes were, and how close together they happened. It was particularly tough obviously for Dom but, if there's anything good to come out it, it's that his dad was there for probably the best moment we've ever had. It was an important moment for us and it brought us back down to earth as a band, brought us closer together and influenced how we saw the future. It made us realise we shouldn't tour ourselves to death, it made us realise we'd spent way too many years away from family and friends with just us and a few crew guys and whoever we meet on the road. There does come a time when you're gonna lose it completely, or you're gonna go home for a while and go back to what you used to be before it all happened."

"I'm sure we go through cycles, like having a great time then getting fucking jaded and then having a darkly good time, when you're having these jaded parties and vibes and it's just a bit dark. It seems to constantly go in that cycle. So in April of the [*Absolution*] tour, it got a bit dark. You find yourself throwing yourself around into various situations, drinking a bit and not looking after yourself, and laughing at that and enjoying that. You think, 'I'm fucked and I don't care, it's quite cool.' But with the second coming of that cycle, we were like, 'Oh God, we're going down-hill again, we need to go home and not book a tour for a long time.' It's nothing to do with music and it's nothing to do with each other, it's just the road in general. Three albums pretty much back to back."

GLEN ROWE

"Dom's dad, Bill, was always laughing. That's my memory of him, he'd always laugh at the funny things that everyone got up to and he was always easy to make laugh. He always made you feel good about yourself; he'd always laugh at your jokes or laugh at something that you thought was funny."

Was there a discussion about the band not carrying on around then?
"[Dom] didn't take a lot of time out because he felt that the band was his way to escape the sadness of his dad's death. But there was a time – it was only a tiny, short time – when Dom didn't know if he wanted to do it any more. He didn't know what was next, and then none of them knew what was next. Chris's dad died when he was very young, so Chris had sort of

grown up and missed his father. Matt's parents divorced when he was very young but Dom's family were like a solid unit, so when that was lost, I'd say there were a definite couple of days of . . . not uncertainty about the band, but uncertainty about who they wanted to be and what they wanted to do."

Was there ever a real possibility they might not carry on?

"I don't think so. I think it was grief and absolute shock. They were obsessed with Reading, because that's where they first went camping and had a laugh, but Glastonbury was their local festival that they'd always tied to. They were so happy when they walked offstage. All the crew said it was just the grimmest thing; in fact, some of the crew didn't know until a couple of days later. The death just wiped Glastonbury away then. Dom's girlfriend at the time was amazing; she was over from America to see Glastonbury. But his sister was travelling in Australia and she was on the aeroplane due back two days after Glastonbury, so however the times worked out, he'd died while she was already en route back to England, so she was unobtainable. So Dom had to drive to Heathrow to go and pick up his sister and tell her their dad had died. It doesn't get any worse than that, does it? And then that was that same Christmas that Tom's sister died in a car crash, and that overwhelmed the band with tragedy. Dom convinced me to go snowboarding with them – we were gonna go for New Year's Eve. But I'd been away a lot so I decided not to go. I remember getting a text in the afternoon from Tom saying, 'Been in a car crash, Helen didn't make it.' My first instinct was that Helen didn't make it to France where they were going skiing, but then I thought, 'Oh my God, it isn't that, he's been in a fucking car crash and his sister's died.' Helen was always there from the beginning of the band's conception, and was at all those local gigs and saw the band becoming the thing they are. So the Helen Foundation was founded, which they have supported through bits and pieces, sponsoring kids and arts."

DOMINIC HOWARD

"Some of the smallest gigs we did were [in 2004] in the States. We went from headlining Glastonbury to doing 400-people gigs in the States and it felt like being a new band again. It felt really good, really refreshing. You could feel the energy in the room. It was great for us, because we'd been touring for eight or nine months and suddenly we felt like this brand new band. I think we can adapt to any situation like that. We weren't doing the typical arena-headlining set list, it was a lot more rock, but it worked. I think it's good when you can hear something that's too big for the room. But the shows were rubbish. I looked at some footage of us at Wembley Arena and I thought, 'Fuck, we're quite good', but then I looked at stuff later on and you can tell we're tired and jaded."

MATT BELLAMY

"We went from playing these massive arenas in Europe to playing to 200 people in some pokey hole again. At first it was really cool, but we'd run on there and try to do our usual stage moves and the whole thing fell apart. I smashed my face in and had to get stitches in my lip. That's the price of getting too comfortable on large stages. But it was good to be treated like a new band over there and get that feeling of being discovered again. We went from playing smaller venues to finishing up playing 3,000-capacity venues again. It's not many bands that get that feeling twice."

CHRIS WOLSTENHOLME

"The worst gig for me was when we did V, that was tough. I just didn't want to be there and in a way I wasn't. It was upsetting, because you take it for granted that you can do this every night and then suddenly you can't, and I was a lot more gutted than I thought I'd be. I was kinda playing keyboards for those two gigs and I thought it'd be a laugh at first, like, 'Ah, these'll be easy gigs, I'll just fuck around and play some keyboards', but when we started playing I was thinking, 'This isn't right at all.' We'd literally had about four days to rehearse and we couldn't cancel V – it was such a big gig. It was awful. The day before we were close to saying we can't do it."

Chapter Nine

THERE were many tips that Matt Bellamy learnt from reading nuclear survival handbook *Dare To Prepare*. Water purification was one: in the event of a nuclear catastrophe uncontaminated water will be in desperately short supply, so the clued-up survivor will have set up a purification system. Lots of big dustbins filled with rocks, soil and purification tablets with holes in the bottom so that impurities can be filtered through it and come out clean. You'd also need to live in a house with a large cellar full of guns, tinned beans and dried pasta. If you were to fill up silver bin-liners with such foodstuffs, keep a nitrogen tank in the basement, pump nitrogen into the bin-liners and seal it up, that food would last for a decade.

And most importantly, location location location. Since America is the most likely target for terrorist attacks and Britain and Spain not far behind, you'd need to be elsewhere; somewhere on mainland Europe that was isolated and remote. Matt had already made steps towards his future safety by June 2005 by relocating from London to Italy, buying a villa near Moltrasio* some miles outside of Milan for him and Gaia. Matt loved the area as he'd spent a lot of time there visiting Gaia over the previous couple of years, since she'd finished her psychology course in London and moved back to Italy to begin a doctorate at a hospital there. And it was an immensely picturesque spot; all of the villas are built into the mountains overlooking Lake Como and George Clooney was regularly to be spotted hanging out there, spending time on his huge and heavily defended yacht. Matt's villa was once owned by Sicilian composer Vincenzo Bellini, Frank Sinatra used to holiday there and, showing the origin of some kind of Muse symmetry, Winston Churchill used it as a retreat when he needed to take a break from the stresses and strains of World War II and paint a landscape or two.

* Also the location of a planet called Naboo in the Star Wars film *Attack Of The Clones*.

Matt settled into Italian life by first overcoming his massive arachno-phobia – the area was crawling with spiders, and Matt would find millipedes the size of his hand in his own bed when he was getting into it every night – learning the local language and letting Gaia help him develop a more chic style of dress; black shirts with white braces would become Matt's new look. Then it was time to get musical: the building came with a massive, cave-like cellar, which Matt set about converting into a studio for the band to record in. Unfortunately, despite builders' promises it would be completed by September, it wasn't ready in time for them to begin recording their fourth album that autumn, so Muse were forced to seek out another, equally remote locale. Somewhere away from the influence of friends or colleagues that would give them the distance they needed to expand their musical horizons in whichever way they were drawn, to reinvent the way they played as a three-piece and, crucially, to not get bombed when World War III kicked in.

Chateau Miraval in Provence, France is a 17th-century castle cut off from the world among sloping gardens and acres of fresh vines. The site was originally a monastery and it was apparently used as a hiding place by the Knights Templar (and still haunted by their ghosts) and, looking even deeper into the region's mythical history, a safe house for Mary Magdelene after the death of Jesus. Owned by the Orsini family for centuries after-wards, it eventually became one of the region's most celebrated vineyards, producing fine wine from 1850 to the present day. A recording studio had been built by jazz pianist Jacques Loussier in the chateau and used during the 70s and 80s by the likes of Sting, The Cranberries and Sade – it was also where Pink Floyd recorded their sprawling masterpiece of bleakness and isolationism, *The Wall*, and perhaps the darkness around that record and the dissolving of the band in the immediate aftermath rubbed off on the studio itself, because it had fallen out of use for some years by 2005. At that time the chateau was primarily a very successful wine-making concern.

For Muse, however, the place was ideal. After checking it out by himself, Matt convinced the rest of the band it was the perfect place to write and record, and the three of them set about convincing the chateau's owners to reopen the studio for them to record there. Reluctantly they agreed (although Muse would feel constantly unwelcome there; the rather petulant owner would constantly interrupt them during writing or recording) and Muse moved in for two months that September, brimming with ideas and excitement about the possible new directions they might try. They stuck to the rule that if they started a track and it sounded anything like something they'd done before, they'd simply abandon the song and try something new.

With the over-the-top lyrics Matt was writing to 'Take A Bow' (working title 'Hex') prompting them to go equally over-the-top musically, and with time restraints and worries about being able to play the new material live put aside, Muse felt extremely loose and free to rebuild the band in whichever form they liked, making music for themselves as in the pre-*Showbiz* days. Nothing was too cheesy or too silly to try; they were unafraid of heading down any path available. So, recording their rehearsals as demos in the live room while preparations were made for more formal recordings as soon as the songs took shape (to allow a seamless transition from rehearsal to recording, or so the plan went), they exploded with ideas for an album with the working title of 'Equilibrium', recording a huge amount of material without anything ever being properly finished. They recreated an entire "drunken military marching band" for one track, and eight-minute songs were the norm as the band found themselves with a plethora of new directions but no idea which of them was good, or which to take to end up with a coherent finished album. They were taking on the influence of the galloping arpeggios of southern European folk music from Sicily and Naples, the original source of Mexican mariachi music they realised, and roped in a chain-smoking trumpet player called Franco, whom they met in a bar, to play an introductory tootle to 'Knights Of Cydonia', a song that was growing into a megalithic beast since Matt wanted to inject it with the space-age Joe Meek surf guitar of his father's hit, 'Telstar'. As a tribute to his dad's greatest musical achievement, Matt tried to get the opening guitar part to sound exactly like the clavioline on 'Telstar', a long outmoded, battery-powered, monophonic, portable keyboard instrument, and he was also after the Wild West atmospherics of the Clint Eastwood movie soundtracks that were a regular studio favourite. The band were throwing so much at the tune – trumpets, explosions, the sound of stampeding horses, vocoder sections, huge metal outros – that it was threatening to approach 20 minutes in length.

Elsewhere, there was much experimentation underway. The band would have 'lab days', in which they'd bring out the old musical equipment they'd bought from eBay before the sessions and spend days reading the manuals to try to get them to work in different and interesting ways. One such instrument was the Buchla 200e, a deviously difficult synthesiser to play that was designed by pioneering synth engineer Don Buchla in the 70s. Thanks to Buchla's methods of routing voltage through unusual places to make his synths – named things like Science Of Uncertainty – work, it took a week of lab days to understand it, yet Matt persevered, and the Buchla 200e would go on to be the first noise the listener heard on *Black Holes And Revelations*.

After a few weeks of musical splurge, drinking fine wine and exploring their own parameters as a band, Muse took a look at the material they'd recorded and simply didn't understand it. It was unfocused and weird – classical jazz pieces merging into Bond themes, 10-minute piano interludes like the centrepiece of 'Butterflies & Hurricanes' stretched out to interminable length, or skronk-rock jams on the furthest boundaries of contemporary electronica. It was more the result of them trying to expand their horizons as a band than record any complete songs and it simply didn't make any sort of sense; none of it fitted together. They considered making it a double album for a while, or even a triple album, with the first disc containing a devolution of rock music in a progressive jazz style, the third consisting of all the strange synth twiddles they'd laid down, and a proper rock record sandwiched in between. And some of the songs had simply become too swamped down in their own influences: a track tentatively titled 'Supermassive Black Hole' was turning out to be the most difficult Muse song to get right. They'd taken such disparate influences, from RATM riffs to Belgian rock from dEus, Millionaire and Soulwax to bits of Kanye West, Prince funk and chunks of electronica, and the whole thing just didn't hang together as a cohesive song. It was their attempt at fusing Belgian rock with James Brown or Solomon Burke, but they needed to take a break from it, approach it from a more vibrant, urban sort of direction. So Muse were caught between the shallow pop side of their nature, which was throwing up some of their best pop hooks yet, and their tendency to wallow in long-winded conceptual pieces that might well have seen the album turn into a prog jazz opus of four long tracks spread over 90 minutes. Rather like the recent work of The Mars Volta. They were in the grip, indeed, of the less than legendary 'difficult fourth album'.

Plus, the isolation of Chateau Miraval was making them lose their minds. With no mobile phone reception, no internet or TV, not so much as a text message for two months, they were completely cut off from society. The satellite dish they hired in order to get more eBay instruments and check emails was ludicrously slow, to the point of uselessness; until Rich Costey arrived a few weeks into rehearsals to oversee recording*, the three of them really were on their own. At first they'd used the remote location as a playground: they went ghost-hunting in the catacombs under the castle, studied the dead bats they found lying around with the faces of Satan, and tormented the local wildlife. They played badminton with live hornets for shuttlecocks and, finding a praying mantis in the undergrowth near the studio, they tied it to a rocket with a camera attachment that can be built from a kit in order to take pictures from high above and launched it into the air, filming it all the way.† They swam in the chateau's pool, helped make the wine and began a new jazz side-project, playing their hits in a jazz style for their own entertainment.

But as the weeks wore on, the vibes got darker, fear began to encroach on their cut-off world. Chris would go running along the vineyard's driveway, but after an hour he'd yet to reach the gates since the drive was five miles long; it made him feel trapped and dislocated, like Forrest Gump starring in *The Shining*. And Matt's lyrical themes were reflecting a far more introverted mindset: he was looking inside himself and reading *Crossing The Rubicon* by Michael C. Ruppert, an ex-LAPD narcotics investigator who has turned his hand to exposing governmental conspiracies. *Crossing The Rubicon*, named after an idiom for going past the point of no return (originating from Julius Caesar crossing the river Rubicon in 49BC as a deliberate act of war against Rome) details America's growing need to wage war in the face of an unprecedented economic crisis brought on by the depletion of global supplies of oil. It posits that the oil age is coming to an end as oil fields run dry, and the US economy, hugely dependant on its continuation, will be brought to its knees by the crisis, forcing it into ever more draconian and unthinkable methods of warfare, population control and repression as

---

* Not exactly someone who'd be bringing the most positive news of global developments.
† They felt guilty for torturing the poor thing the second they'd shot it into space, but when it landed, the insect hopped off the rocket and crawled away, so they consoled themselves with the probability that they'd expanded its universe or at least sent it on a brief holiday.

industrial civilisation grinds squealing to a halt. Ruppert doesn't stop there; his book goes on to assert that since the decline of America's manufacturing industry, the entire US economy relies on covert dealings in guns and drugs from opium and coca fields run by CIA-sponsored warlords, and that Wall Street is just one big laundering system for illegal firearms and narcotics profits. We're talking widespread, desperate and uncontrolled fighting over the last remaining oil reserves, nuclear retaliations, starvation, disease and death: an end of days.

These were the sort of topics Matt brought to the dinner table each night at Chateau Miraval. The Iraqi War, the truth of who was really behind 9/11, the inevitability of an impending World War III, martial law creeping in, the one-world government being manipulated by MI6 or the FBI, brainwashings, his future vision of a world reduced to tribes squabbling between each other over the crudest of resources, like in *Mad Max*. They grew beards, stockpiled firewood, became fearful, indulged their paranoia, considered buying livestock so they could live off the land when the end of the world came, wondered if it might have already happened but they were too cut off for the news to have reached them yet. Matt began to worry for his own mental health, since the paranoia he was experiencing seemed to match exactly the symptoms of the schizophrenics that his girlfriend was working with in the Italian hospital, and his lyrics were taking on ever more reclusive themes, full of anger at his powerless-ness in the face of being so manipulated. He envisioned an album about humanity waking up and taking control of its destiny from its shadowy puppet masters. These would be songs about personal and political revela-tions, dragged from the blackest holes of his imagination.

If they had stayed any longer in Miraval, however, they'd have ended up with a very dark, very long and very wearying progressive rock album indeed.

No, to complete *Black Holes And Revelations*, Muse need to rejoin the human race.

*   *   *

In New York City Muse came alive again. Rejuvenated by the sudden closeness of bodies and the bustle of an extant civilisation, by day they and Costey – a NYC resident – would hammer away at recordings beneath the grand wooden ceilings of Avatar Studios in midtown Manhattan, where everyone from David Bowie, U2 and Iggy Pop to Celine Dion, Britney Spears and The Last Shadow Puppets had recorded, or at the Electric Lady studios in Greenwich Village, opened by Jimi Hendrix in 1970 and decorated like a psychedelic spaceship, which suited Muse down to the ground. And by night they would dance; Matt knew an NYC DJ who played at a Lower East Side bar a couple of nights a week, and she would take the band out on the downtown club scene, near where they were staying. She taught Matt the rudiments of DJing and, while the concepts of cross-fading or scratching were beyond him, Matt took to it with a louche passion, playing Depeche Mode, Beck and Eurythmics songs and smoking nonchalantly; girls would come and tell him how much they enjoyed his set, and Matt would accept the acclaim for other people's music with a wry shrug. Far from a civilisation in crisis, in Manhattan Muse found a society dancing its life away, and the positivity rubbed off on them.

With the studio soundtrack now bopping along to R&B and electropop, and the likes of David Bowie popping into the studio during the recording of 'Take A Bow' to say hello to Costey ("The last time I was in here I was recording something with John Lennon," the Thin White Duke told an awestruck Muse), they found it impossible to stay dark in a busy city full of thousands of people. The grooves they found on the dance-floor instantly lightened the vibes of the music they were making; the obtuse electro experiments they'd started at Miraval suddenly began to make sense, and adding the Lower East Side groove to 'Supermassive Black Hole' seemed to galvanise the song instantly. Where once they had a disjointed gaggle of ideas and influences, they suddenly had one of their greatest electro-rock tunes yet, and the most un-Muse Muse song they'd ever created. In the New York clubs they noticed the merging of electronica and guitar music in the works of American dance-floor-friendly bands like The Rapture and !!!, and happily soaked in the influence of it, got (as it were) a groove on. In New York City, Muse dived hungrily into the shifting waters between dance and rock, and there they found pearls.

Between October and late December 2005[*], with a taut, fresh and more

---

[*] During which time a DVD of 12 songs from their legendary Glastonbury performance, plus bonus extras of six live videos from Wembley Arena, Earls Court and their American tours of 2004/5, was released under the title *Absolution Tour* on December 12.

decisive approach to the record kicking in, the album tightened itself up considerably. They'd left Miraval with full takes of 18 to 20 songs that had been written, but only two completed tracks – 'Take A Bow' and 'Invincible'. Many of the takes were re-recorded amid the steam and essence of New York, and the bulk of the record was completed by the time they flew home for Christmas. So pleased were they with the way the record was progressing, in fact, that they decided to give themselves the boldest of deadlines – they booked themselves in to headline the main stage at the Carling Weekend 2006, that dream slot from so many years ago.

A resoundingly upbeat and successful year like 2005, however, would not end without tragedy touching the lives of Muse once more. On Boxing Day that year, while driving home from a Christmas break with her boyfriend and Tom Kirk in the car, Tom's sister Helen Kirk – an actress and long-term friend of the band – was startled by a car overtaking her and swerved into the path of an oncoming Volkswagen. While Tom and Helen's boyfriend survived, Helen was killed, aged 24. Hence the celebrations that would usually accompany New Year and Chris' daughter Ava's birthday were overshadowed by Helen's funeral, which the band all attended. They would honour her by becoming patrons of the Helen Foundation, a charity to help aspiring actors and artists, running competitions in aid of the charity and dedicating their forthcoming album to her with the sleeve note, 'In memory of Helen Kirk 1981–2005'.

* * *

Muse's fourth album was completed over four or five weeks early in 2006 at Officine Meccaniche studios in Milan, with the band staying at Matt's villa; the villa's basement studio still wasn't finished, and wouldn't be until September according to the remarkably unrushed builders, whom Matt would often find lounging by his pool when he popped down to check on their progress. After some final vocal tracking in Italy they completed the record with their greatest sense of achievement yet; on previous albums they'd come out of the studio feeling compromised, but this time, after their hardest bout of recording and the greatest amount of musical soul-searching so far, they felt as if they'd got it right. Nonetheless, they were uncertain that the record would hang together until mixing was completed at London's Townhouse Studios; it was only hearing the whole thing in the context of a completed album that they became amazed at the way they had stretched their boundaries, at the huge variety of musical styles they had mastered. Even the harshest critics – themselves – were silenced; they'd made a great album.

Black Holes And Revelations was not just a great album, it was truly universal. If the socio-political subtexts of *Absolution* had been buried somewhat under Matt's swathes of quasi-religious tub-thumping and personal confusion about the future, here was a more solid and direct dissection of the ills of the world and the fears of the common man, wrapped in sparkling electronic rock hooks. Taking the role of the man at the very bottom of the pyramid of global control, in these songs Matt looked upwards at the selfish, insane few deciding the fate of the angry, helpless many, and roared his ladylike lungs out.

Discussions were heated over which song should open *Black Holes And Revelations*. Some thought starting with 'Knights Of Cydonia' would be the boldest statement of intent and the most startling way to introduce listeners to the all-new, all-huge Muse sound; others that such a move would be career suicide. Instead the band plumped for 'Take A Bow', a song equally gargantuan in scale – one long rising build to a crescendo without a quantifiable verse or chorus, inspired by Palestrina's choral music – but a good two minutes shorter than 'Cydonia' and providing more of a bridge with *Absolution*. It had been written at the tail end of the previous album sessions and shared its apocalyptic feel, with its stomping guitar riffs like marching Godzillas and Matt's cry of, "You will burn in Hell for your sins". Rather than bewailing some nonexistent and ineffectual deity as in 'Apocalypse Please', though, this was a more political damnation, pointing the finger at corrupt politicians and world leaders who were lying to their populations, abusing their power and making decisions they would never have to pay the consequences for, Matt claiming that retribution was on its way in this life or the next. With its revolutionary theme and electronic introductory surge before the gigantic guitars descended, it was the perfect bridge between the pomp and austerity of *Absolution* and the politicised electro-fripperies of New Muse.

Compared on occasion with Philip Glass due to its intense filmic atmosphere, 'Take A Bow' was Muse's most over-the-top blowout yet, originally a classical piano piece that developed techno sections and metal waltzes until it represented the evolution of music itself. And while Muse followers might have thought it another, more transparent attack on the Trilateral Commission than the likes of 'Ruled By Secrecy', in fact Matt had uncovered an even older group of puppet masters to aim at; the Bilderberg Group, a collection of 130 of the most powerful people in the world who had been meeting since 1954, including bankers, defence experts, press barons, prime ministers, royalty and international financiers. Slowly, through song, Matt was peeling back the veils on the men who really controlled our lives, exposing the hidden demonocracy that, to Matt, bordered on fascism.

Thankfully the song ended in the key of B, the same key of 'Starlight', and Matt was free from political bombast for a few tracks to indulge his other musical passion – love songs with vaguely sci-fi imagery slapped all over them. 'Starlight' was about being away from home and missing the ones you love, only told from the perspective of an astronaut being fired away into the unknown, possibly for the rest of his life, on a mission to uncover some revelations about the nature of black holes (since the song's chorus includes the album's title). The subtext was obvious – by losing touch with home you lose touch with who you actually are – but to the casual listener (of whom there would be millions) this paled into insignificance next to the sheer jubilance of the tune. From the opening bass buzz, the drumbeat designed for arenas to clap along to and a sparkling space-age piano*, this was part The Strokes' '12:51', part Abba space synths, part stalling spaceship noises and all classic pop hit; a song that felt like being rocketed into the ether at the speed of light with every croon of, "I just wanted to hold you in my arms". Originally written in a rehearsal room way back in late 2004, it was first recorded as a slow and mellow number in Miraval, but thankfully the New York dance floors inspired Muse to give it some funked-up glam oomph, and it's been grooving in the indie nation's hearts ever since.

As has 'Supermassive Black Hole', that trickiest of beasts to perfect but the song from *Black Holes . . .* with the most glittering chart potential once Muse got it right. The sort of R&B-meets-rock amalgam of dEus, Beck, Justin Timberlake and Franz Ferdinand, which they'd tried numerous times before but had failed to make work, this time it clicked magically.

---

* The final piano sound on the track was created by plucking the piano strings with guitar picks, dropping forks on them and smearing them with putty.

Taking the metaphor of the enormous black hole in the centre of the universe left by the Big Bang, into which the entire universe will one day be sucked again, to represent a destructive relationship you can't escape, the song had the stomp of an android army, the spooky falsetto pop nous of an undead Prince and the metal-clad funk of that 30 ft statue of Michael Jackson coming to life. In its Miraval form it sounded like an experiment that they didn't know if they'd want to include on the album; in its finished state it was a shoo-in for the first single.

'Map Of The Problematique' was indeed problematic; one of the electronic songs born from mucking about with synthesisers and rhythmical keyboard patches that didn't work in Miraval but came into its own in the urban dance sprawl of Manhattan. Muse considered it their ode to the rave scene since the piano part is pure acid house, but it actually resembled the late 80s electronic goth of Depeche Mode or the pioneering indie-techno work of New Order more than any pure dance record. The title, however, carried the main thrust of the album; this is an optimistic record inspiring us all to face the problems of the world and a will to fight against being downtrodden, just as 'Butterflies & Hurricanes' had before it. It refers to a book called *Limits To Growth*, commissioned by the Group Of Rome in 1972, outlining a 'map of the problematique' that laid out the global problems that are likely to arise in the future as a result of soaring world populations and dwindling natural resources (which the book predicted would all have been exhausted by 2070*), plus some methods of altering those outcomes. That said, the title seems to be a theoretical totem with little to do with the actual lyric, which finds Matt lost in a storm of desolation and despair brought on by loneliness, unless this is a character caught up in the "fear and panic" of a human race struggling to survive. Internet fans have also suggested that "fear and panic in the air" is a reference to the moons of Mars, Phobos and Deimos, the Greek gods of fear and panic. Fittingly, the song was to be used in the trailers for 2006 movie *Children Of Men*, in which society is driven to violence and desperation by the sudden and inexplicable inability of women to conceive children. Just one of the possible unexpected catastrophes Matt might have envisioned for us all.

---

* The book also claimed that oil reserves would run out by 1992, but admitted that its predictions were based on trends of consumption that might change in the future.

Matt would describe the central pairing of 'Soldier's Poem' and 'Invincible' as negative and positive sides of the same song, the heart of the album, one about losing hope, the next about finding it in yourself. 'Soldier's Poem' started life as a track considered for inclusion on *Absolution* in a far more heavy and epic style, but turned out to be one of the songs that would benefit from the isolation and paranoia of Miraval. Inspired by Elvis Presley's '(I Can't Help) Falling In Love With You', Matt completely rewrote the lyrics and arrangement and it was recorded at Avatar with just four microphones, Matt playing an old acoustic guitar, Chris on an upright bass and Dom tapping away at a beaten up old drum kit, taking on the tones of 40s and 50s swing music while also recalling the brevity and lush harmonies of prime Beach Boys over a gently arpeggio-style melody. While reminiscent of 'Blackout', the new stylistic approach, along with the electronic elements of 'Starlight', 'Supermassive . . .' and 'Map Of The Problematique', pointed listeners to a whole new experimental Muse, but the title was deceptive. It wasn't specifically about the Iraq War as many originally thought, but a song of sympathy for the men who think they're fighting for a good cause when they're actually unthinking pawns in unjust wars, wherever they may be. Written from the perspective of a soldier in prison who has been abandoned by a disintegrating country, it's a damning message to the people back home who sent him there.

Its breathtaking counterpoint, 'Invincible', was ironically born in the most down-to-earth of circumstances: staying in some hideous, TV-less motel in a snow-smothered small town in the Great Lakes area of America during their Campus Invasion tour in 2005, the band decided to spend a day off fishing on the lakes and hired a boat, only to have the heavens open while they were still reeling them in. Brought down by illness thanks to the exposure and seasickness, Matt was so bored in the motel afterwards that he wrote the optimistic-sounding intro of the song to cheer himself up. It was recorded in a fit of pique one day at Miraval because the band were so frustrated that they hadn't been able to record 'Take A Bow' successfully; 'Invincible' came out almost entirely live and complete, bristling with energy. Still, the band thought it one of the weaker tracks of the sessions until Matt started playing the solo; one of the most incredible and intricate pieces of virtuosity ever recorded outside of the show-offish hair-metal genre, it sounded like it was being played by a five-armed alien guitar god. With the added sound of an approaching army of drummers (produced by setting up a microphone at an open window and marching towards it, drumming) and Matt's sumptuous guitar atmospherics* adding depth, it became an album highpoint, a stirring reveille of a torch song that took the military theme of the previous track and turned it into a song of immense comfort and belief.

The lyrics went through various stages; 'Invincible' began as a far more political song, an all-out riot starter calling for the burning down of Parliament, then Matt scrapped the lyrics and made it a guileless love song. It ended up somewhere between the two; a song aware of struggles ahead and fundamental changes that need to be made to society, but knowing that those changes need to be made by a group rather than any one individual.

The Parliament-burner in Matt had to come out somewhere though, and here it came, roaring through 'Assassin' with a Molotov cocktail in each hand, yelling, "The time has come for you/To shoot your leaders down/And join forces underground". Matt would claim this was a character study of a 'terrorist' (he didn't like to use the word in relation to the song, saying the protagonist didn't fit the 'classic' model of terrorism) driven to the brink and ready to shoot the President, but the anger and passion in the delivery suggested a firm personal belief in revolt. When Matt had spoken before about finding the strength to tackle the approaching world problems, 'Assassin''s entreaty for us to "destroy demonocracy" felt like his most direct instruction on how best to save the world. And it was *Black Holes And Revelations*' most direct metal song too; the Deftones-esque chunder, influenced by underground US noise duo Lightning Bolt, kept them nailed to their freak-out hard-rock roots, while all around it was going electro-flamenco-funk crazy.

The New York funk returned for 'Exo-Politics': having worked the song out almost completely on the Campus Invasion tour, Muse went into the studio with the song largely finished, needing only the odd experimental studio tweak – the drums, for example, were recorded in the studio's lift shaft, and cheesy spaceship noises were slipped onto the backing

---

* Played using the Kaoss pad, which Hugh Manson had built into a guitar for Matt, so that he was essentially playing a theremin inside his guitar; this was also employed on the intro to 'Exo-Politics'.

track. The song's meaning, on the other hand, had become vastly different from the fairly innocuous version performed in the US in 2005. Partly driven by his readings on the HAARP installation, Matt had come across the theory that a massive media and government conspiracy was afoot. Over the next 10 years, went the theory, films and media would make the public more and more aware of the possibility of alien life in our galaxy, to the degree that politicians involved in exopolitics – a new branch of political relations that deals with the socio-political connotations of any past, present or future contact with extraterrestrials* – would soon be advocating the introduction of high-grade weaponry into space in case the Earth were ever to come under attack from alien invaders (referred to in the song as 'Zetas'). Along the lines of Ronald Reagan's Star Wars, these massive-budget military programmes, conspiracy theorists thought, would just be a cover to get practically undetectable weapons pointing at far more terrestrial enemies, since future wars between countries would most likely be fought in space. Alternatively, the satellites could be used to beam mind-control frequencies towards Earth.

Pretty head-spinning stuff, but *Black Holes . . .* had even wilder cards up its sleeves. The final three songs on the record could be seen as an epic triptych of spaghetti Western storytelling. 'City Of Delusion' revisited the violent revolution theme of 'Assassin' but this time in a flurry of flamenco guitars, Arabian strings and mariachi trumpet interludes, casting Matt as a kind of Wild West Che Guevara. It was actually the oldest song on *Black Holes . . .*, having been written during a soundcheck in Japan three years earlier. It almost didn't make it onto the album, but Matt had met a string arranger in Italy who was an aficionado of Arabian music, and asked him to come up with an arrangement for the track; his Turkish take on the song was its saving grace.

Acting as a smoky interlude between '. . . Delusion' and the final prog rampage, 'Hoodoo' was an intangible waft of Spanish guitar and sultry strings that eventually charged into a tumult of violins, piano and operatic largesse before sinking back into the jazz lounge. An unnecessary fancy, but one with an essential role in the record: it seemed to mean next to nothing, a relief after all the sinister theories and soapbox politics that had

---

* Matt may well have come to learn about exopolitics through another of *Rule By Secrecy* author Jim Marrs' books, *Alien Agenda*.

gone before it, and it gave us a bit of a breather, which we were damn well going to need.

The hum of an alien levitation ray. A snort and gallop of Apocalyptic horses. A rising siren. And then a climactic drum roll and a falsetto choir of angels, cowboys, Martians or banshees. Even before the rumbling 'Telstar'-meets-*Dr Who* stampede of 'Knights Of Cydonia' sets off in earnest the song is Muse's most ludicrous, epic, progressive and cinematic moment yet, not least for its title. Matt would expound several different ideas about the origins of our solar system while trying to explain the song, but essentially it came back to Sitchin's suggestions of a link between the positioning of the great pyramids at Giza and in North Africa, which, when viewed from above, appear to form a gigantic star map of the Orion nebula*, and what appeared to be very similar pyramid formations on an area of Mars known as Cydonia. The area also appeared to contain what looked like a human face and signs of what once might have been pockets of water, evidence that there had once been life on Mars.

More recent Martian probes have proved the face to be a trick of the light on rocks, but Matt was drawn to the idea that this story was just a NASA cover-up to conceal the notion that building had occurred on the planet by some ancient civilisation, mirroring the Earthly pyramids in order to point to our creators in the sky with obelisks. He'd heard rumours of Earth and Mars once being the same distance from the Sun, back when the Earth was a smaller globe that would eventually expand so that oceans would fill the gaps between the continents.† Mars could support life but Earth couldn't and the song imagines a fantasy Martian landscape of people fighting a great war with phaser guns, until a time when Venus entered the solar system as a comet and sucked all of the water out of Mars, leaving the planet uninhabitable so that the Martian armies had to relocate to the nearby Earth.

Of course, within hours of elaborating on these topics with the stoniest of faces to one interviewer, Matt would be telling another that the title was intended as a joke, and that they make music in the same way that Monty Python made comedy. But whether you embrace the sci-fi

---

* Matt would also claim that Washington in the USA is laid out in the same formation.
† He rubbishes the idea of there once being one solid mass of land known as Pangea, which shifted apart to create the different continents.

nerdiness and Yes-style fantasy elements of it or not, it's nonetheless a spectacular piece of rock frivolity. While the music reflects the space-age Western concept, the lyric about fools becoming leaders fits in more tightly with the anti-Governmental stance of the album's previous tracks. But when the final riff descends, precision aimed at causing maximum devastation in any festival moshpit, all talk of prog indulgence was blown out of the water by Muse's most powerful rock outro; a kind of Cloverfield version of 'Bohemian Rhapsody'. It was, Chris would later state, 40 years of rock history crammed into six minutes. That the American label would see fit to release it as their first single from the album in the US seemed both insane and hilarious; that it would totally break Muse in the States, hitting number 10 in the Modern Rock chart, was nothing short of incredible.

And there *Black Holes And Revelations* inevitably ended, with no grander statements to make, no more subversive politics to expound and no heavier it could get. A revelation in itself, it saw Muse mastering new genres that enriched their sound and sped them off into thrilling new musical terrains – R&B, funk, flamenco, mariachi. It made them not only one of the UK's biggest rock bands, but also its most experimental and adventurous, a sure sign of a long and fruitful future that would never see them sink into a formulaic furrow like so many major rock bands, releasing similar-sounding records until the fanbase got bored.

It needed a sleeve of equally epic scope of course, and so Storm Thorgerson was called in again, this time coming up with the concept of the Four Horsemen Of The Apocalypse seated around a table on a barren red Martian landscape. Shot in Spain, half a mile from the Spanish Air Force's prime bombing test area, Storm represented the Horsemen by the different coloured horses on the table in front of them, far too small for the Horsemen to ride, to signify that the sins of the riders had far outgrown their steeds. The pale horse represented Death, the red one was war, the black horse was famine and the white horse was that of the Antichrist, and the Horsemen each wore a suit representing an ailment of humanity. For these Storm envisioned a very modern Apocalypse, with the four Horsemen standing for greed, paranoia, religious intolerance and narcissism; you'll note that greed has more horses than the others.

The artwork for the sleeve booklet was equally significant and thought-provoking: there was a photo of the HAARP installation in Alaska; the

M87 elliptical galaxy in Virgo, which caught Matt's imagination since it throws out a plume of matter which is probably emerging from a supermassive black hole; and a shifting blue aeroplane with seemingly no aeroplane to have made it, a reference to the secret hypersonic aircraft the Aurora. A mass of hints, clues and hidden meanings, *Black Holes & Revelations* was a rich seam for the obsessive mind to mine.

Now, ironically for a record so steeped in secrets, all they had to do was keep it to themselves for a few months.

* * *

Security around the release of *Black Holes And Revelations* was akin to a rock Fort Knox. With major records regularly leaking onto the internet before release and the labels convincing themselves this was having a dramatic effect on sales, all sorts of ploys and tricks were invented to restrict access to pre-release music by the biggest bands to reviewers only. At the very least CDs were watermarked so that they could be traced if they appeared online, and such discs were invariably packaged in yellow and black diagonally striped cardboard (so as to imply heavy security *a la* police lines), with warnings of dire consequences should the music be leaked. Other measures included reviewers being allowed to hear the records only under supervision in the label's offices or being invited to group playbacks (such as the one for Radiohead's *Kid A*, during which the playing of hangman was widespread and one journalist fell asleep).

Hired to write Muse's press biography for the *Black Holes And Revelations* campaign, I was one of the first to hear the record outside of close band associates and management, and the copy I was given (which still listed 'Take A Bow' as 'Hex' and 'Assassin' as 'Demonocracy') in March 2006 came attached to a contract I was required to sign, which pretty much gave Muse the right to remove my internal organs and feed them to hyenas if the music appeared online. Using the most modern security methods possible, when the record was finally released to the press it came inside a set of MP3 player headphones that would only play *Black Holes . . .* at the flick of a switch and out of which (they thought) the tracks couldn't be downloaded.

Yet a fanbase as rabid as Muse's was by this point (and as technologically cunning) would go to any lengths to hear the music as soon as possible. Making their first live appearance since Live 8 ten months before at Radio

One's One Big Weekend show at Dundee's Camperdown Park on May 13, Muse premiered three songs from *Black Holes . . .* alongside a smattering of classics in their seven-song set – 'Starlight', 'Supermassive Black Hole' and 'Knights Of Cydonia'. Muse were overwhelmed to see the crowd go crazy to 'Knights . . .', pleased that they had got such a seemingly indigestible track on first listen and that the riff at the end had gone down so well. Then, within a few weeks, they were shocked to find that a version of 'Knights . . .' had appeared on the internet, but certainly not being played by Muse. From that one performance, a fan had learnt to play the song with frightening accuracy and recorded their own version for public release.

Although finding the band a bit rusty after so long off the road, the Camperdown Park show, performing alongside Razorlight, Bloc Party, Primal Scream and Dirty Pretty Things, was memorable for several other reasons. First, in figuring out how to play their new songs live, Muse realised that they couldn't be performed as a three-piece so they hired a fourth member, Morgan Nicholls, who'd played bass for them while Chris' wrist had healed in 2004, to play additional keyboard parts and do all the Kraftwerk-style knob-twiddling. It also saw the arrival of a brand new and very expensive transparent acrylic drum kit for Dom – after Matt had gone so far as to have his guitars specially designed by Hugh Manson to look increasingly like spacecraft (this gig saw Matt unveil the Kaoss Manson for the first time, distinguished by its glowing X-Y touch pad), Dom wanted his own futuristic trademark instrument. Thus ended the days when Matt could happily trash Dom's kit at the end of gigs, knowing he could easily pick up an identical one on the way to the next gig.

A mimed performance of 'Supermassive Black Hole' the next day on the *Quelli Che il Calcio* show in Milan was possibly the downfall of all their security measures. Within days of the performance a good quality version of the song was being circulated online*, and Muse's paymasters had no option but to release their perfect-quality version of the song as a download in order to wrong-foot the pirates – they reasoned that they might lose a fair few chart-eligible sales from the move, but knew that Muse's fans had built up such a buzz around the track that they'd probably download it illegally anyway. Hence the song was made available for

---

* It's uncertain if this came from the TV recording.

download purchase (along with a ringtone) at the very second it received its first radio play, and it hung around at the bottom end of the charts (which now allowed for downloads to be included) for six weeks until the full release on June 19 – backed with 2005 live favourite 'Crying Shame'.

If the Muse fanbase had long since downloaded the track, intense national radio play of 'Supermassive . . .' had found a huge crossover audience, its funk grooves and Beck falsettos clicking with daytime radio listeners who might well have been totally unaware they were a hard-rock band at all. There was also a slightly disturbing video, filmed in LA that April by Floria Sigismondi – the band had been taken with her videos for Marilyn Manson and The White Stripes' 'Blue Orchid', and hired her to film a promo that featured dancers in full-body Lycra suits covering even their faces while the band, all in black, had images of their faces projected onto their own full-face masks. Confusing and macabre; yet the song shot to number four in the UK, despite its internet leaking. No longer were Muse reliant on a cultish fanbase snapping up several formats of every single each to get them anywhere near the Top 10; now they'd truly smashed into the mainstream.

Inevitably, a mono version of the full album leaked onto the net on June 7, sounding as though it was recorded from one of the headphone MP3s. But there were too many pre-release plans in place for Muse to drop everything and rush the album onto the shelves. They had a series of seven TV, radio and internet showcases to fulfil throughout June at the likes of TRL in Padua, Canal+ in Paris and, back in London, an AOL gig in Covent Garden Hospital, T4, *Top Of The Pops* and *Friday Night With Jonathan Ross*. They had a proper warm-up gig at Rolling Stone in Milan the day the album leaked, where they would play 'Invincible' and 'Map Of The Problematique' live for the first time. And they had a fan-club-only show booked at the Shepherd's Bush Empire on June 28, with tickets given away free on the official Muse website as a thank you to their most loyal followers. Close as they were to their online communities, it was a show of immense importance to Muse and, frankly, only an act of God would prevent them from playing it . . .

* * *

Germany's Hurricane Festival in 2006 certainly lived up to its name. After their first full live festival appearance of the year, headlining the

Southside Festival in Neuhausen ob Eck the night before, had gone with only a few hiccups – Matt messed up the intro to 'New Born' and the outro to 'Stockholm Syndrome', and the megaphone hadn't worked on 'Feeling Good' – Muse arrived for their slot at Hurricane ready to take on the world. Unfortunately the world had other ideas. As the band walked to the stage for their headline set the sky suddenly turned black with storm clouds, strong winds tore the back of the stage clean off and eight inches of rain fell on the site at Scheessel, near Hamburg, inside 30 minutes, in a thunderstorm of Biblical proportions. Although the band were prepared to carry on regardless, the performance was pulled by organisers on safety grounds and the band evacuated, as Muse's crew battled with tarpaulins and guy-ropes in an attempt to save the storm-battered equipment. The heavens, it seemed, were keen to give Muse their Apocalypse at last.

With some of their gear rendered useless by the storm damage, Muse weren't sure how much of it would actually work when they walked onstage for their 'Empire Strikes Back' fan-club-only show at Shepherd's Bush Empire. It was a vital gig for the band; not only would much of the new album be performed (eight of the album's songs got an airing) for their most avid fans and the whole thing be filmed for broadcast on MTV, but it was also the unveiling of the stage set they'd trawl across the world's festival circuit to the Carling Weekend. For the first time they'd had enough of a gap between the end of recording and the start of touring to really plan out their stage show. Three large dot-matrix screens flanked the stage, showing highly polished visuals to match the songs: spectacular fire-works at the climax of 'Invincible'; marching and pole-dancing robots for 'Supermassive Black Hole'; galaxies racing by at warp-speed for 'Starlight'. Black boxes twinkled out bursts of light and a row of transparent tubes laced with glowing neon coils ranked the back of the stage like mad scientists' test tubes, which Matt – clad that night in black shirt, white braces and smatters of red in his hair – had originally planned to fill with mannequins to make them look like cybernetic wombs, until the band decided that it would look a bit naff. The whole stage gave the impression of a kitch 60s vision of a future spaceship control bridge.

Rain damage notwithstanding, the show was a triumph; opening with 'Take A Bow', Muse slotted classics like 'Bliss', 'Hysteria', 'New Born' and 'Plug In Baby' between showcases of *Black Holes* . . . tracks, which the crowd unsurprisingly knew all of the words to. A piano was wheeled out for 'Feeling Good' and Matt's solo take on 'Soldier's Poem', and 'Knights Of Cydonia', an anthem already becoming famed as a formidable slayer of festivals, was received as wildly indoors as it was out. Matt ended the song in foetal position, kissing the stage.

As *Black Holes And Revelations* inched its way towards release and Muse set out to regain their gig legs and hone their new set list across a flurry of European festival headline slots – Rock Werchter in Germany, Eurockeennes in France, Quart in Norway, among others – the first interviews about the record, conducted that May and June, began to appear. And with them, amid much talk of Martian pyramids and government conspiracies, came Matt's political ideas, let loose by the record's political openness and honesty.

He believed we were only months away from World War III. That democracy was a lie and the news is orchestrated to create a false reality in which we live like prisoners; that the difference between ordinary life and the reality of the world is as stark as that depicted in *The Matrix*. That being 'ordinary' means being part of the system that enslaves you from your schooling; you're taken away from your parents at your most impressionable age, fed with lies that make you think that Western civilisation is just, moral and stable when it clearly isn't, and emerge as a slave to the banks. In fact, to break himself out of such a bond, Matt kept most of his money in cash, bought physical objects with it or gave it away. He'd been reading *Synthetic Terror* by Webster Tarpley (not one for lightweight chick-lit this lad; indeed, he felt sure he was already on an FBI list simply based on the books he'd ordered from Amazon), which claimed that there was a massive suppression of what was really going on, that 'false flag' operations were underway under which governments assist, orchestrate or even completely make up terrorist events in order to convince populations to back their military manoeuvres. He considered September 11 to fall into such a category, obviously an inside job that was either allowed to happen or made to happen as part of a conspiracy entitled Project For The New American Century: a plan compiled by neo-con right-wing writers in the 1990s that stated that America needed a Pearl Harbour-level event to justify invading the Middle East, and which George Bush's policies appeared to be following to the letter. He thought we'd soon all be microchipped, that ID cards were just the first step to a true Big Brother society. He claimed there were simple solutions to the world's energy problems but that the energy companies had bought them and suppressed knowledge of them.

On occasion, his behaviour tripped over into the seriously paranoid. He'd claim that The Beatles were the front for a think-tank being used to brainwash the youth of America. He'd wear amulets to interviews, claiming they'd been made for him by a scientist to protect him from electromagnetic waves; he didn't know how they worked, but radiation pictures of people wearing them had revealed an invisible shield around the wearer. And with a straight face he'd recommend reading snooker commentator-turned-mystic visionary David Icke's book *Tales From The Timeloop*, saying that the first half of the book consisted of conspiracy theories that made a lot of sense, but even he might baulk at Icke's assertion that George Bush is related to Queen Elizabeth II via a reptilian bloodline that stretches back thousands of years to the reign of the lizard people on Earth.

Matt knew exactly what he was doing in cultivating his image as rock's premier madcap mind; a few weeks later, during a long stint of press interviews in New York, a very tired Matt needed some time off, so he convinced the label representatives looking after him that he'd heard a meteorite was about to wipe out Manhattan with a gigantic tsunami, and so he couldn't leave his hotel room for 48 hours. And when he eventually did, he insisted on doing an entire day's worth of press interviews in a helicopter over the city in case the wave hit.

And with the press interest even more feverish around *Black Holes . . .* than ever before, vast amounts of news trivia flooded from the pages. The conspiracy theories had prompted hundreds of new-age types with crystals and tarot cards to start coming to Muse gigs. Matt liked the idea of a trip to Mars to record an album at zero gravity, and had even got in touch with a friend of his who funded the X Prize (a foundation offering million dollar rewards for innovations that benefit humanity) to enquire about getting one of the first tickets on Virgin Galactic. Dom was just back from a holiday on the Virgin Islands and hadn't spent more than three days in Teignmouth in about 10 years. He had a piano piece similar to one of Matt's as a ringtone; Matt's answerphone featured fart noises and he'd had to change his phone number since Italian fans had found out where he lived. Chris had recently been mobbed by seven-year-old fans while picking his kids up from school. Despite a volatile relationship that saw them split up almost every day, Matt was madly in love with his girlfriend of three years and was considering getting married underwater. He was frustrated by the TV series *Lost* but had been amazed by his first-ever stadium gig, watching U2 in Milan. They hadn't played poker together since one mammoth game after which the band didn't speak to each other for three days. They had a collective nervous tic that makes them yawn a lot before gigs, and they often ended up giggling like schoolboys over the ridiculousness of what they do. Matt had nine points on his licence for illegal right turns, owned two classic American cars as they were so cheap to insure (although he drove his girlfriend's Beetle when in Italy) and couldn't live without lemon tea. They'd recently stopped using false names when checking in to hotels: Matt went by Hector Berlioz while Dom's favourite name used to be Sergio Georgini, the name made up by David Brent in *The Office* when his boss asks him who designed his leather jacket. Matt liked The Strokes because he thought they sounded like Muse. Dom wanted to get into diving; Matt wanted a scooter to help him get around the huge venues they were playing these days. They thought they were the most unique band in the UK and peerless in the current rock scene; they agreed they might well be the best live band on this arm of the Milky Way, but wouldn't go as far as to claim the whole universe as there might be some seriously weird shit out there.

Innocuous snippets in the grand conspiratorial scheme of course, but every little helped. By the time *Black Holes . . .* was released on Warner Bros records in the UK* on July 3, 2006, its predecessor *Absolution* had sold a massive 2.8 million copies worldwide. But even this was about to be dwarfed. *Black Holes . . .* sold 100,000 copies in the UK in its first week of release and spent two weeks at the number one position. Over its staggered release it would reach number one in seven countries, including Australia and Ireland, and go Top 10 in every territory it was released in

* Warner Brothers had purchased the worldwide rights to a Muse album release for the first time, since in August 2005, after Korda Marshall moved from EastWest/Atlantic to their parent company (Warners) as MD and took Muse with him, Safta Jaffery and Dennis Smith had sold the rights to release the remaining three studio albums in their six-album contract to Warners for an undisclosed but substantial sum. Warners therefore released the record on its various global subsidiaries, thereby giving the band their biggest ever worldwide push.

except for Belgium, where it charted at number 11. An astonishing achievement, but there was one country where Muse felt it the most.

* * *

The day that Muse stepped onstage at the San Francisco Design Centre to begin their first sold-out tour of the USA and Canada, covering 15 dates in the major cities across the continent from July 18 to early August, was something of a minor victory for the UK. Thom Yorke from Radiohead's debut solo album, *The Eraser*, had been expected to do well and had lived up to expectations, charting at number two in the *Billboard* chart, but another UK act had snuck into the Top 10 that week, making it the first week for over a year that more than one UK act had debuted in the US Top 10. For there at number nine in the chart compiled for the biggest music territory on Earth sat Muse's *Black Holes & Revelations*, with sales of 48,000 in the first week. Bearing in mind that *Absolution* had charted in the US at number 107 in 2004, and the previous year's release of *Origin Of Symmetry* hadn't fared much better, Muse's seven years of sporadically struggling to break America had made them an overnight sensation.

The gigs reflected their stature as the new Great British Hope. On July 19 Muse played their biggest American headline show yet at the 5,700-seater Greek Theatre in LA, and the starlight well and truly shone. Justin Timberlake, Haley Joel Osment from *The Sixth Sense* and Paris Hilton all blagged their way into the gig to watch a typically barnstorming Muse performance involving Matt playing the entire 'Plug In Baby' solo with his guitar on his head. Not that Muse were impressed by the atten-dance of the glitterati; when Paris Hilton requested an audience with the band backstage they turned her down, claiming they'd hired a private jet in order to play in Toulouse that night.* Haley Joel Osment, meanwhile, was so overwhelmed by the gig that he managed to flip his 1999 Saturn car over after hitting a pillar on his way home from the venue.

With 'Take A Bow', 'Knights Of Cydonia' or 'Map Of The Problematique' at the top of the list, Muse honed a devastating set over their month touring the US. The typical running order for the US shows

---

* Strangely, there is no record of a Toulouse gig at this time and Muse were certainly back in America to play at the San Diego Soma on July 21, a gig attended by the man who'd proposed onstage at Muse's previous San Diego show.

was 'Take A Bow', 'Hysteria', 'Map Of The Problematique', 'New Born', 'Assassin', 'Butterflies & Hurricanes', 'Supermassive Black Hole', 'Sunburn', 'Soldier's Poem', 'Starlight', 'Invincible', 'Plug In Baby', 'City Of Delusion', 'Stockholm Syndrome', 'Time Is Running Out' and 'Knights Of Cydonia', although 'Apocalypse Please', 'Hoodoo', 'Forced In' and 'Bliss' made sporadic appearances. Through Denver's Fillmore Auditorium, Chicago's Aragon Ballroom, Detroit's State Theatre, Toronto's Docks Concert Theatre (where Dom, Chris and Tom Kirk found a go-kart track next to the venue and raced around it to the cheers of the fans queuing to get into the gig) and New York's Hammerstein Ballroom, they wowed around 4,000 US fans every night before heading off to Japan to play the Summer Sonic festival over two stadium dates, supporting Linkin Park and above My Chemical Romance. In Japan, *Black Holes . . .* had already sold twice as many copies as *Absolution*'s two-year total inside a month and, now comfortable with the hassle and hectic pace of Japan, the band wanted to celebrate, so girlfriends and family were brought along (Dom was keen to treat his mum to the trip as he'd had to miss her 60th birthday the day Muse had played in Montreal), ancient shrines in Kyoto were visited, Osaka's Bar Rock was plundered for its finest booze alongside Lostprophets, and the brightest canary yellow trousers were donned by Dom for the duration.

A shame, then, that the gigs weren't as enjoyable. At the first night in Osaka's WTC Stadium (essentially a car park surrounded by a plasterboard fence) on August 12, Matt suffered several guitar malfunctions and ended up sliding his guitar across the stage at a tech, dropping 'Map Of The Problematique' from the set list and leaving the stage early. In the rather subdued people-carrier back to the hotel afterwards, swamped by fans taking pictures through the windows with their mobile phones, he'd comment that it was as close to a bad Muse show as he could remember playing. The next night at Tokyo's Marine Stadium went better, but even then calamity almost struck the band. A few hours after they left the stage an earthquake hit the arena, another attempt by the rock Gods to smite these Earthly heathens.

Four more European festival shows – at Austria's Frequency Festival, Switzerland's Open Air Festival, Holland's Lowlands and the Eden Project in Cornwall, close enough to Sawmills for locals to claim they could hear 'Supermassive Black Hole' – and Muse were set to kick over another career milestone, possibly the most momentous one yet.

After a fault-blighted show to 16,500 Scots at Edinburgh's Meadow-bank Stadium on August 24 (which, from the stage, Matt put down to having a new guitar tech), Muse travelled south to prepare for their legendary headlining slots at the Carling Weekend. The other 2006 head-liners would pull off their own stunts at the event – Franz Ferdinand filled the stage with drummers, and Pearl Jam, um, wore interesting shirts – but Muse had put by far the most planning into their show. After all, this was where the dream was born, watching Rage Against The Machine at the Reading Festival, so they had to make it special. They'd wanted a giant robot onstage (management refused). They'd asked permission to drop a million giant balloons or hang a spotlight spaceship from a helicopter over the crowd (the promoters wouldn't allow it on safety grounds). So failing that, they made do with every stadium pyrotechnic they could get their hands on: stage-front flumes of flame, which burnt Chris' face when they went off, a fountain of fireworks from the backdrop and a huge screen the breadth of the enormous stage. When an almighty thunderstorm broke out during Muse's set at the next night's show in Leeds, many thought it was part of the special effects.* At the Reading site there was much talk of the Saturday night line-up being a battle between Muse and the Arctic Monkeys, playing before them, as to who would take the crown of the Band Of The Festival. One look at Muse's firework receipt alone would've told you that the Arctic Monkeys were going to get blown so far off the stage they wouldn't need to hire a tour bus back to Leeds.

Matt spent the day before the Reading show in London's Hyde Park, reading the newspaper, calming his nerves by the Serpentine, forgetting he was to play the gig of his life to 50,000 Reading kids that night. Come nightfall, however, he rocked the field from its roots. Opening with 'Knights Of Cydonia' for maximum mosh effect, finishing with 'Take A Bow' for the ultimate operatic climax, and with Matt clad in a T-shirt reading 'Google Video: Terror Storm' in reference to a controversial documentary by US film-maker Alex Jones positing the possibilities of terrorist acts as inside jobs, Muse delivered the knockout rock punch

---

* Muse didn't play an encore at Leeds as they hated the idea of people standing around in the torrential rain; still, at least the crowd was greeted with the slapstick sight of Matt getting his white braces caught in the piano stool after 'Feeling Good'.

of the weekend. *NME* would declare it the gig of the Millennium and Matt would know how they felt; he was so buzzing from the set that he couldn't bring himself to leave the stage before the second encore of 'Time Is Running Out', 'Stockholm Syndrome' and 'Take A Bow' but stayed to soak up the applause.

And as Muse finally did leave the stage, having fulfilled their ultimate dream of headlining the main stage at Reading, you can bet Dom asked Matt, in time-honoured Muse tradition, if they'd made it yet.

And Matt will have had to reply that they had. Muse had definitely made it.

Now they just had to make it even bigger.

MATT BELLAMY

London, Spring 2006

How was Miraval?

"It was quite secluded and cut off and it was wine season, which was nice. It's a Knights Templar settlement as well, and we saw some of the secret tunnels they used to have. There were a load of unusual bats that lived in there as well that kept coming in during the night; you don't hear them, they just flap around. One of them crashed on the table tennis table and I got to look at his face. Have you ever seen a bat up close? It's sick. It looks like the Devil. Dom read *The Da Vinci Code* while we were down there and we figured we should have a bit of a hunt around for the Grail, get out the old fire on a stick and do a bit of Indiana Jones; the only problem is all the secret passages are waist high in water, so we didn't venture too deep. It reminded me, if anything, of Devon. Most of the writing process started out there, being a quieter place and truly cut off from the lifestyle we had, being on the road all the time. It was going back to a simpler way of life, and that was the influence of what happened at Glastonbury.

"We didn't really have any TV in the French studio, we just had the internet. So we listened to internet radio, which was interesting because we'd be listening to radio from India or Iran or places you'd never heard from before. We spent a while listening to and experiencing other music. Living in northern Italy as well, I met some guy, a violin player called

Mauro, who introduced me to some south Italian music from the 19th and 20th centuries, a mix of the Middle East with the West, and I found that an interesting concept in general. When people hear Ennio Morricone they associate that with Clint Eastwood shooting a gun, and I used to as well, but I realised that south Italian music makes you think about elements of deserts. I found that interesting, not just for reasons of what was going on in the world, and that was one thing I found that was new.

"I think the south European elements definitely came from being in France and going back and forth, because it was only a few hours' drive from where I was living in Italy. The last three songs on the album would definitely have not happened if it wasn't for being there. The heat as well – it was the first time we'd ever really worked in the sun, that was a different experience. And going to New York had an opposing influence. If we'd stayed in France for the whole album it probably would've ended up real prog. Songs like 'Knights Of Cydonia' would've been 20 minutes long. Going to New York for some reason tightened everything up and it got more groove orientated. Songs like 'Starlight' and 'Supermassive Black Hole' and 'Synthetic Dreams' [eventually retitled 'Map Of The Problematique'], they all had grooves that radically changed when we went to New York, I don't know if that was the vibe of the city or what. That was a good contrast, because we were going up the wall a bit being so cut off towards the end. It was important because it helped us to absorb some of the influences and get removed from our past and from any expectations; all of the unusual elements were constructed at Miraval but the main recording was in New York. Hendrix's ghost was hanging around and Bowie came in for a day and said hello. It was something to do with John Lennon's 50th whatever, he came in and it was good to get the nod of approval from the old boy. We had a shaker part planned and an acoustic part, but we thought if he was coming in to listen to it, to try to get him to play something would've been a little bit in bad taste."

By starting the record with 'Take A Bow', were you trying to carry on where Absolution *left off?*
"Originally that song was going to be the ending of the album, but we thought it'd be good to start with the most over-the-top we've gone, lyrically and musically. The whole thing is just one big build from start to finish and it ends, to me, with a ridiculous climax. It's like an ending – it's

easy for us to go a lot of other places after that because in some ways it's a conclusion to the last album. There are elements that've been influenced by the identity card stuff and there's definitely a connection to Revelations with that. It talks about a time when people will not be able to purchase anything without a number or exist without a number. There's definitely a mood for this with the identity card thing – instead of going for a job interview they'll just swipe you. They'll get your medical history, your financial history, the lot. To relate it to the song, that's one of the reasons why Hell would come up, connected to Revelations, but that song would be aimed at the people in charge, the movers and shakers in arms deals and energy deals and pharmaceutical deals."

The themes that come up seem to be war, death, rebellion, lies, fighting, doom . . .
"The usual vibe, innit? There's definitely a bit of New World Order. There's a feeling of powerlessness of the small man, a bit of, 'Fucking hell, what power do any of us have over anything any more? And are our governments actually doing anything?' I don't know. I don't even know what I'm voting for any more, when I'm voting. It's that things are moving in a direction of, I wouldn't say apocalyptic proportions, but big change proportions. A whole load of things which, if you add them all together, add up to the feeling that something's gonna happen in the next 10 years. The fears and hopes associated with that are definitely coming out – this is the first album where I've started to believe we're heading in that direction. You've got the climate change, the oil crisis, wars happening all over the place and no one really knows why they're happening – obviously some of them are happening for oil or whatever. But there seems like an orchestrated chaos that's been deliberately created for some purpose. I'm not the sort of person to say, 'We've got to change this', it's too late."

Is 'Assassin' a rebellion song?
"I think so. I think we're approaching that time. If you look at those protests in France, the size and level of protest doesn't really relate to what they're protesting about. I think there's something underneath that people are feeling, particularly the younger generation. We feel like we've been born into some pre-created situation where we don't actually have any control over anything. We've got an ageing population as well, and that

control factor grates a little bit. I feel, through this album, that I'm feeling pessimistic and frustrated about it all, but at the same time I'm not against revolutionary moves and I wouldn't be ashamed to have incited a small riot, if it's for a good cause."

What sparked such anarchic ideas?
"It depends how deep you want to go – if you want to get into stuff outside the planet . . . reading books about the energy crisis got it going a bit. I read a few books about survival – I got this book called *Dare To Prepare*, which shows you how to store food for 12 years and purify water of uranium, all this kind of stuff, so I know how to do all that stuff now. That got me heading down a dangerous road – obviously climate change is a big issue, I look into weather situations and there are some people who believe that weather is being controlled already. There's this big storm that was moving around and you could see these two huge forks came in and tickled a huge hurricane and moved it towards the sea. There are definitely some funny things going on. Weather control, pandemics, all that stuff. You can look at it all and get overwhelmed with fear or you can look at it all and say it's all being orchestrated as a way to keep people down. Or you can think, 'Fuck that, let's get pissed.' As a band, we do mix those three responses to those things. First you get this desire to fight and change, second you get the urge to point out to everyone that we're all fucked, and third you want to get pissed and have a laugh and forget about it all, just smash up your guitar and have a laugh. You can hear all of those responses on this album."

How long before Muse stop being a band and become a military movement? Could you ever become Chairman Matt?
"I hope not, I definitely don't want to be one of those spokesman types. I find that embarrassing and cringeworthy when you see the usual suspects; everyone knows who they are, preaching and trying to come across as world-changing types. To me, the fact that these individuals can acquire £400 million is the problem with the Earth. For these people to be talking about problems, I find it uncomfortable, embarrassing and hypocritical to the extreme, so I certainly hope I don't fall into that category."

'Starlight' appears to be using space as a metaphor for an emotional vacuum.
"The space thing is there because, one, it's clearly where we came from,

and two, it's clearly where we're going. Just the amount of bad knowledge we get taught in school about space – look at the Earth, y'know. Everyone thinks the Earth was once Pangea, one big lump of land on one side. Bollocks. The Earth is growing. It's a swelling sphere. If you look at the continents they fit together on all sides, and if you crush the Earth down to a small ball all the continents fit together and there's no water. The reason why there's water is because as it grew the continents ripped apart at the sections and collected gasses and stuff. There's loads of stuff like that to do with space that are core things that we think are right but aren't right. That's the basis of a lot of things in our lives – we think things are one way but they could be a much more weird or radical way. Also, all the religions on this Earth are basically interpretations of various interactions with aliens that have happened over the past few hundred thousand years. I think we are from space, our home is not just this little bundle."

Religion is just down to a fear of death, surely.
"No one can say that's 100 per cent right and fear is a big [element], but also not knowing what is possible in the way of cross-pollination – I want to believe that. It's more interesting. It's just better than believing it's all come out of nothing, out of fear. In that case it's fucking boring. I think there's definitely a possibility of cross-pollination."

What is the 'Supermassive Black Hole'?
"That's this thing in the centre of the galaxy that's sucking all the stars and planets in. It's a pretty cheap song really, it's pretty basic. I've got a girl-friend at the moment and we're having trouble, we're fighting all the time and you think, 'How long can this go on, fighting constantly?' It's all right for three or four years, but that song could be a little bit about why I'm drawn to that battle with a woman. Why am I fucking banging my head against the wall? There must be something behind it."

'Map Of The Problematique' sounds like Depeche Mode doing a Queen cover for a Bond soundtrack.
"That's kind of a feeling, towards the end of a tour, when no matter how many people are around you've got that loneliness starting to creep in, you get a blur of shit around you and you want to get away from it all."

The centerpiece of the album seems to be two war songs – 'Soldier's Poem' and 'Invincible', which deals with war in the sense of a relationship.

"Originally those were kind of almost one song – it's the heart of the album, someone losing hope to the extreme. You could say 'Soldier's Poem' from the perspective of a soldier feeling that they're fighting for no good reason, and that the people they're fighting for don't give a shit and the country they're fighting for doesn't give a shit. That must be a pretty tough place to be. Most wars are about natural resources and the country they're fighting on behalf of doesn't really care, the people they're fighting to liberate don't really care or they hate them, the governments don't really care if they live or die. That seemed like a good subject matter to deal with – losing hope and giving up. The next song is almost fantastical optimism, a strange, almost dream-like optimism. Those songs are connected in that way, one's going right downhill and the other's coming right up."

What is 'Exo-politics'?

"That's about the possibility of an orchestrated alien invasion created by the New World Order. There are some people who think that in the next 10 years there'll be an orchestrated alien invasion. Not an invasion, but aliens will appear. Not appear, but there'll be discussions about it. There have already been Exo-politics discussions going on in Canada by this guy who used to be the defence minister there, he's already discussing the possibility of having weapons in space to protect against aliens coming in. You can look at it two ways. One, there could be aliens and they could be coming and we need to make weapons; or two, it's orchestrated because the government needs an excuse to increase its military budgets. In America they're running out of excuses to increase their military budgets because all their black ops, all their secret stuff, is funded by the military, and they want as much budget as they can because that's where most of the secret stuff is going on. So if you see any reference in the news about the possibility of aliens or the possibility of putting weapons in space you have to ask yourself, are they inventing this because they want to make more weapons or is this real? Either way it's fucking scary."

What about 'City Of Delusion'?

"It's about multiculturalism and the good side and the bad side to that."

And 'Hoodoo'?

"That's casting the mind back to old relationships from the past. It's the first time I can really look back on the first relationship I had like it's a forgotten thing. It's really weird when you start to forget that kind of stuff, and I think it's talking about how someone can come in and out of your life like that and have a massive impact and then it's gone. The song is about missed opportunities if you like."

'Knights Of Cydonia'?

"It's trying to be objective about the rise and fall of civilisations, how they've come and gone. It's part of a cycle. If you look at the past it's always been that way but, by the end of the song, it's about let's stop it happening, let's not let it happen this time. That song is a bit of a personal number for me because its quite influenced by dad's band . . . It touches something a bit deeper for me personally. In particular with the guitar bit at the beginning, it's a bit more of a wink towards the Joe Meek connection. Just because I never really contemplated that when I was growing up, especially the first few years in the band, I never really acknowledged what my dad did. I think that song was a connection to that. When we were making the album, that was one we were all really into because it was so weird and ridiculous, and we thought it might do no harm to stick something like that out. Some of the other songs, like 'Supermassive . . .' or 'Starlight', are a bit more straight down the line, a bit more vertical. It's nice to have different songs on the album like 'Take a Bow' or 'Knights . . .' which are a bit more out there."

DOMINIC HOWARD

London, Spring 2006

"Writing, you show who you really are, and it's amazing to realise that you can be travelling around the world with each other in the back of a bus but people can change without you really knowing it. So it was really good to get together and open up a lot. We've ended up being a lot closer and opening up musically. A lot of our albums have branched off into different areas, but this one is way more extreme. We tried loads of different ways of playing the songs, taking radical left turns all the time, seeing what feels right to play. You can feel a bit of discomfort if something isn't correct. It was a lot more rock from start to finish when we started it. It's a weird one, because it doesn't show one direction of the band, it shows a mix of what we're capable of doing. [On] the last album, we reached a point of coming close to a typical identity for the band and this time round there are definitely elements of that identity but there are also a lot of other things. We've branched out even more."

Did you have much material to work with?

"We thought about doing a double album – we had about 18 or 20 songs and we thought maybe we should do two. But the more you work on songs the more you get drawn to various songs. Once we thought we wanted to do a very diverse album, then we realised that if we do a double album it wasn't going to be very diverse. We got in a whole load of vintage jazz instruments and started applying that way of playing to a whole bunch of songs . . . and old songs for a laugh while we were at it. By the end of it we were saying, 'Right, let's become a jazz band!' We could do a whole jazz album as a piano three-piece and I really want to do that, play a couple of nights at Ronnie Scott's."

How claustrophobic did recording get?

"You're so far away from everything that it almost inspires more fear. You're talking about how we're going to survive when World War Three happens. Then all of a sudden we were in a club in New York, dancing."

CHRIS WOLSTENHOLME

London, Spring 2006

"Last time it was fairly obvious what the record was going to be like but this time it wasn't, purely because there was so much. It was important for us to give each song a fair amount of attention, because in the past there have been songs that didn't quite make the album that you listen back to and think, 'If we'd had time to finish that it would've been great.' Usually we're in a rush because we've got a tour booked, but this time we wanted to make sure we had time to work on all the songs. It feels like there's absolutely no bullshit on this album at all."

GLEN ROWE

"The making of the last record was weird, because I put them in a rehearsal studio underneath my office in Putney and they were never there! I'd go downstairs and they'd be sitting around, saying, 'We're stuck, we're talking.' They'd have rehearsal sessions that wouldn't really amount to anything; they'd just chat about stuff and they were asking me about, 'What shall we call our record label?' – because at that point they were going through the whole thing with Warners, and by the time they got to Miraval they hadn't got any ideas, it was still in discussion mode. I can remember Matt saying to me, 'What do you think about a Western song, but with eighties disco?' I was like: 'Sounds ace!' But I'm not a visionary, I can't hear or imagine what someone's gonna do with that. But he was like, 'Ennio Morricone and some fucking big disco beats!' His vision was there, and he said to me, 'We want to make an album where every song is a different emotion, a different thing.' I'm like, 'Aren't there only three emotions?' You know, how many emotions are there? They talked themselves around for so long, and then Dom hurt his finger, then me and him did the London to Brighton bike ride, because it was the first Father's Day after his dad had died, so we did it for charity. I hadn't ridden a bike since years before; that little fucker had been riding to the rehearsal studio, 20 miles a day, just to get himself fit. I remember feeling like some old bloke with his young whippersnapper brother who would ride on ahead and have to wait for me to catch him up! London to Brighton on the hottest day since 1964! Got there, had a couple of pints, then we got a taxi back and went to see Mötley Crüe, then we went for a curry. It was just an amazing day. And I thought it was the perfect, fitting way to celebrate his dad's life by doing something fucking bonkers. It was very emotional – there were a few times on the bike when I looked at Dominic and I felt for him. He was actually doing something for himself."

What was the atmosphere like at Miraval?

"It was bleak, but I was only down at the start of the recording and me and Dom were nerding out about drums, and we were trying to put drums outside to see how they sounded. By the way it sounds terrible. Don't ever bother, it just sounds so shit, it's not the way to record drums. And then I left them all set up and ready to have a great time and make the most amazing album, but not a lot happened. It was a bit bleak, it was a bit weird, they were just talking. They talked about ending the band or they talked about what life would be like after Muse."

Was that a serious discussion?

"I don't think it will ever end. I think they're intelligent guys who might think it can't last forever, but I can't see it ever stopping. I think they just had to check, 'Where are we? What are we doing? Are we doing the right thing? Is this how to do it next?'"

What can you remember about Reading?

"I remember watching Arctic Monkeys, who just looked a shower of shit in comparison! [Muse] were made for that day. That was when I could see the spoils of fame. Matt had his own bus. I phoned him up to find out where he was and he was in Hyde Park! It was really weird; he didn't come down till the last minute. Chris had his own tour bus with his family and his nanny, I was on his bus fighting with his little kids, seeing the spoils of what it's like to come to a festival with your own hotel! Dom was in the band bus, which carried just Dom and Morgan and Tom and a few bits and pieces, but if Matt had turned up in his bus it would have been three empty vessels. But Chris, he just turned up and it was like the gentleman had arrived with his family in tow and it was just a normal day. I remember the vibe was really funny. They were just laughing, no nerves. Then Matt turned up, a little bit nervous, and I left them to it. He said, 'No, no, it's all right, come back in, it's just a gig, isn't it.' It was really exciting, but they were trying to get their heads around the fact that they were now headlining the Reading Festival. And it was a 10 out of 10. Just absolutely incredible. The set list just built and built and built and got mental. It was actually one of my favourite Muse shows ever."

Chapter Nine

MATT BELLAMY

Madrid, October 2006
(Printed by kind permission of IPC Media)

How was Reading?

"It was good, an important moment for us because being from the West Country we didn't come to London very much; we'd go to festivals because you get to see all the bands you want to see in quite a short time. I went to Reading about four or five times as a punter and the same with Glastonbury, but with Reading I remember seeing bands like Rage Against The Machine and thinking, 'I really wanna get up there and do that.' So playing that gig was a really good moment for knowing what it feels like to be in the crowd and onstage at the same time. I knew exactly what it was like being out watching a band play, so whilst I was playing I was remembering that feeling."

Having headlined the Carling Weekend, are you no longer rock's outsiders?

"I think we're kind of outsiders, but if we were ever going to become a big band or a well-known band it would always have to be on our own terms. I don't think we'd ever wanna latch on to what's fashionable at the time or pretend you're in with some kind of group of bands. If a band gets well known it's nice to have done it in that way, create your own world. Live music has kicked off again and it's a really good time for British music, but I'm proud of the fact that there are no other bands that sound like us out there."

You seem to have broken down the barriers and united the warring indie tribes this year.

"I was into rave in the early 90s, I was out there to The Orb holding the glowsticks and that's starting to happen again, and I quite like that vibe, that it's happening again with live bands playing like the Klaxons, but I also like really hard, raw earnest rock like Rage Against The Machine and then I'm also into stuff like Franz, this arty, angular guitar work. I'm not sure what's made us that broad-minded when it comes to music. With the myspace generation there are so many bands that feel they have to create such a tight niche image-wise and music-wise to get any attention. They think, 'That's what we are, let's do that over and over again as much as possible and exaggerate it and put the image together that makes it look as strong as possible.' Bands are fashioning themselves, doing the record company's job better than the record companies ever did. So you're getting these up-and-coming bands that are marketing experts before they've even written a song because of the amount of time they've spent on the internet, understanding how to build a niche."

What do you think about the state of music at the moment?
"You can judge the health [of current music] by people's willingness to go and see live music, and live music is becoming bigger than it ever has been. All the festivals sell out before anyone even knows who's playing and a lot of bands are playing the bigger concerts; next year we might start seeing people other than U2 playing stadiums for the first time in a long time. It's about time a couple of other bands start getting up to that realm. In the 80s and early 90s the stadium vibe and big live music seemed to be declining a bit, but it feels like it's really coming back. That's a healthy sign because that's what I care about, concerts, live music. To me that's what it's really all about . . . I've always cared about playing the big old gigs, I've always looked forward to that, and I think it's about time for a good few bands that could take to that realm apart from the old classics like U2 and Bon Jovi. It'd be nice to see a new generation of big live acts coming through. I see people's will to go and see bands and get out there, fucking get out of the house, stop watching TV and stop sitting at home doing nothing."

Chapter Ten

"**Y**OU see this?" Matt Bellamy gestures towards the floor of Madrid's Palacio Deportes arena to where his crew are frantically trying to piece together the stage set, with only two hours to go until doors open and not even a glimmer of a chance of starting soundcheck anytime soon. "This is what it was supposed to be like at nine o'clock this morning . . ."

Five p.m. on October 27, 2006, and Matt Bellamy and I retired to the stalls of the Palacio Deportes to conduct an interview for *NME* to preview Muse's forthcoming UK arena tour, centred light-heartedly around his various conspiracy theories. We discussed Sitchin's 12th Planet and how it might explain the huge gap in fossil records between Neanderthal and man, the 9/11 set-up possibilities, the lizard people from another dimension and their ability to easily possess those of a royal bloodline, the Cydonian star maps and various political corruptions.

Matt, ever the eccentric rock star in orange pyjama-style trousers and angular Japanese sunglasses, vented his frustration at the joke he saw as 'democracy', showed suspicion at the news that North Korea had tested nuclear weapons at all and expressed the forthright view that civil war, throwing Molotov cocktails at politicians and burning down the Houses of Parliament were the only reasonable ways forward. His theory was that a revolution of the mind had to take place before any physical action, that people needed to see the newspapers as mere propaganda and their leaders as puppets serving darker world forces. He wouldn't lead a revolution, he claimed, but he'd certainly follow one.

We also chatted about the five-week, 17-date North American tour Muse had just completed*; heading Stateside after the Carling Weekend via a few festival dates in Istanbul and Verona, it had been their biggest US

---

* Morgan Nichols hadn't been able to participate in this tour as he didn't have a US work visa; it also featured the band performing 'Muscle Museum' for the first time in several years.

tour yet, playing 5,000-capacity venues everywhere from Columbus, Ohio to Grand Prairie, Texas and beyond. There was talk of Chris almost getting hit in the face by a bottle at a festival in the middle of the desert near Tucson, Arizona; at the KFMA Fall Ball festival at Tucson Electric Park, shoes and bottles had been flying stageward from the very start of Muse's set, and the band pulled the gig halfway through 'Forced In' when they noticed security beating up members of what appeared to be a line of bikers in the front row, leaving one man with a bloodied, busted face. And on a lighter note, there was the party they'd held in the desert outside Las Vegas after a show at the Hard Rock Hotel – they'd met someone who had a load of mushrooms on them and the band hadn't touched the drug since the *Origin Of Symmetry* tour so, since America was now the place they came to party hard because the European shows were too big to allow for messy nights, they felt it was time to indulge. Hiring a bouncy castle, they decamped to the desert with all-girl LA support act The Like, whom they convinced to dress as aliens and Red Riding Hoods, along with a whole host of other girls, for a surreal blowout that reminded Matt of *Twin Peaks*, so unsure was he of how much of it had been real. Was there really a member of Vegas show-group The Blue Man Group there? Or had that actually been a real blue man? Whatever, the party had spilt over onto the last show of the tour in Seattle's Paramount Theatre, where The Like dressed as aliens once more and invaded the stage during 'Forced In'; two of the girls performed a bizarre dance routine involving the wheelbarrow, breakdancing and making out with each other, while the third lobbed an inflatable dinghy into the crowd, jumped in and rowed away across the moshpit.

Other topics came up: the huge downer they felt the day after the monumental highs of Reading when, still buzzing from blowing the rest of the festival off the stage, they had to go to Abbey Road to film three songs for Channel 4's *Live From Abbey Road* programme to no audience; Muse's liking for the Klaxons; the mainstream acceptance associated with the nomination of *Black Holes And Revelations* for the Mercury Prize; the ginger one from Girls Aloud winking at Matt at the Q Awards; the appearance of the 'Starlight' single* at number 13 in the charts in September; Matt's mistrust

---

* Accompanied by a video of the band playing on an oil tanker off the coast of Los Angeles and backed with the bass-heavy 'Easily', which had previously been leaked on various

of My Chemical Romance for being overly styled (a quote Muse later requested be taken out of the interview as there was a chance they'd be touring with MCR in 2007). And of course the new stage show that their road crew, when they weren't flashing their arses on the big screens, were trying and failing to squeeze into the venue at that very moment.

America had seen the four-screen giant-Slinkys set, but almost as soon as they were offstage at the Carling Weekend Muse were working on a brand new, even more impressive stage design. With 14 arena shows booked across the UK in November, including an amazing three-night run at Wembley Arena, Muse wanted to put on a completely different show to the one they'd taken to the festivals – with up to 20 songs per night planned, the gig needed to be as spectacular as it would be long. So the six weeks before the first European show that autumn were spent frantically putting the concept together. Becoming a little obsessed with America's $30 million HAARP installation in Alaska – the mysterious centre that the US government claimed to be a method of communicating with submarines or spacecraft, but experts suspect might be a new form of weapon, America's attempt to tap into the ionosphere in order to control the weather or our minds – the band attempted to recreate the installation onstage. Huge pylons either side of the stage were linked with drooping neon 'beams', a full dot-matrix screen spanned the entire length of the stage, and Matt's new guitar rig was so powerful it could practically burst thunderclouds – when he first plugged it in to test it at his Italian villa, he caused a blackout all over the village.

And there, as its centrepiece, was a new drum riser designed to resemble the satellite with which the installation might be communicating. Unfortunately, no human stage was big enough to fit any wings on the thing so the resultant, screen-covered contraption was described variously as a massive neon blender or a futuristic funnel, but the effect was still fairly stunning. Each night at the start of the gig, in the dark, Dom would crawl into the satellite and begin drumming just as the riser lifted apart to reveal him. In Madrid, Matt joked that he was desperate for the thing to get stuck one night so that Dom would have to stay in there until the venue had emptied before he could clamber out.

Muse fan sites in encoded 20-second chunks by a 'Mr X', whom Matt later revealed was a record label employee.

Most of the money the band would make from the tour had been spent on the set design, but even this wasn't enough for Matt; he'd originally wanted an extra pylon planted out in the middle of the auditorium with wires linking it to the stage, but he was told that would cost an extra £1 million, so he abandoned the idea. He'd also suggested the possibility of staging an alien invasion during the gig by flying an inflatable UFO over the crowd that would land on the band and 'abduct' them off the stage, but this too was deemed unworkable. Nonetheless, the stage set took five lorries and dozens of stagehands to transport from its first appearance at the Bizkaia Arena in Bilbao in Spain, on October 24, around Europe and the UK, so teething problems were to be expected. That day they'd arrived at the venue to find that the lighting rig simply wouldn't fit. Muse, it seemed, had finally outgrown the arena circuit.

There was only one place to go next, I pointed out to him. Stadiums.

He looked around at the expensive tons of technical wizardry being constructed for his benefit, at his whim. He wondered for a moment at how far he'd already come; from the pub back-rooms of Teignmouth to such elaborate flamboyancies of hydraulic drum risers, fireworks, steam jets and bouncing plastic globes. He shrugged sagely. "I don't know about that," he said, pretending to mull over the idea for the very first time. "But it's probably about time a new generation of bands started playing stadiums."

Heaven knows how he managed to suppress a snigger.

★ ★ ★

On December 4, 2006, at a pitch-side press conference at the £575 million new national stadium at Wembley, which was finally reaching completion nearly three years late, Muse announced that they would be the first band to headline the newly built venue when it opened the following summer. At a capacity of 90,000 it was one of the largest stadiums in Europe, and far and away Muse's biggest show ever. They'd been turned on to the idea of playing stadiums during that year's Summer Sonic festival in Osaka; the coliseum shape of a stadium appealed to the band, rather than the flat-lying festival environment, and there seemed to be so much more potential for putting on a show there, rather than turning up at a festival with a big box of lights. That year Muse had been offered various options of putting on their own festival, at Hyde Park or in Milton Keynes, but manager

Chapter Ten

Anthony Addis had heard that Wembley stadium had to be finished in time for the 2007 FA Cup Final and the decision was made. After huge shows planned there by Bon Jovi, The Rolling Stones, Take That and Robbie Williams had all been relocated because the stadium's construction was delayed, the Wembley people wanted a UK band to open the stadium rather than the usual dinosaurs, and Muse were the right band with the right breakthrough album at the right time. George Michael would be the first solo artist to play the new Wembley Stadium, but Muse would be the first full band to really put its still-drying foundations to the test.

Walking into the place for the first time gave Muse mixed feelings: fear, apprehension of being able to sell it out or play a show worthy of such a vast arena, excitement at what they might be able to do with the space, and sheer awe at its size. Only Chris had been to the old Wembley Stadium, to watch England and Brazil draw 1–1 in 1992, and it was far bigger than any of them could have expected. Dom, for one, hadn't slept properly since the day they decided to do the gig. It was what Matt might describe in poker parlance as an all-in move.

Still, they remained optimistic and light-hearted during the conference. Matt reckoned that while they were relishing the idea of playing there, it wasn't such a big deal; if they messed it up they could always go home and become painters and decorators again. He claimed he'd like to take to the stage by bungee jumping off the stadium's enormous new overhead arch, but health and safety rules might stop him. In later interviews, Matt would say that they'd probably blow all the money from the gig on putting on the best show possible, which was in the spirit of the event, and Dom would reveal that the band had watched DVDs of Queen playing the stadium in 1986 to glean some handy tips, even going so far as to corner drummer Roger Taylor at a glitzy event to ask him his advice. He'd told Dom not to bother, it was shit and everyone was so far away you couldn't see anything. Muse booked the gigs anyway.

At 9 a.m. on the morning of December 9, 90,000 tickets were put on sale for Muse's show at Wembley Stadium on June 16, 2007. By 9.45 a.m. every one had been sold. Fans parading their purchases on the fan sites found that rather than being among the heartened many, those with tickets were the lucky few. Demand far outstretched a single date at Wembley, and online auction site eBay was flooded with hundreds of pairs of tickets for the event. On a tour bus just outside Munich, Dom was nudged out of a restless semi-sleep and informed that the first Wembley gig had sold out, that a second one, on June 17, had already been put on sale and that it was selling as fast as the first. The sleep he fell back into was far sounder than the one from which he had awoken.

It was the end of an incredible year for Muse. Only a week earlier they'd seen the single release of 'Knights Of Cydonia' – a song unthinkable as a single until it had been such a massive hit in the US – reach number 10 in a busy pre-Christmas UK chart, backed with a live version of 'Supermassive Black Hole' on the CD format and an extended version of 'Assassin' on the vinyl release, dubbed 'Grand Omega Bosses Edit' in a nod to the cryptology competition from 2005 (it was an anagram of 'Messageboard Song', the name 'Assassin' went by for the 2005 tour). The video was as elaborate, cheesy and hilarious as the song, following a 'man with no name' as, taking Matt's vision for the song extremely literally, he rode through a spaghetti western landscape on horses, motorbikes and unicorns, shooting space-age laser guns and pulling *Matrix* karate moves as he went. Sci-fi movie references abounded – *Star Wars* holograms of the band, massive silver robots, the top half of the Statue Of Liberty poking out of the sand – and indeed a competition was run on Muse's official website for entrants to name all 15 of the sci-fi movies referenced in the video. Perhaps, at such a festive time of year, the promo struck a chord with the national mood of novelty and ridiculousness.

What's more, the end-of-year polls and awards had begun rolling in. Muse had picked up Best Alternative Act at the MTV Europe awards in November, unaware that they were even nominated until the day before (the band performed 'Starlight' at the November 2 ceremony, using the biggest laser the show had ever seen). In a poll of *NME*'s 100 Greatest British Albums Ever, *Absolution* had rolled in at number 21, while *Black Holes And Revelations* sat pretty at number three in the magazine's Albums Of 2006 poll, and equally high on most other music magazine's lists. They'd been shortlisted alongside Radiohead and The Clash for XFM's Hall Of Fame, Siobhan Grogan of the *Daily Mirror* included their Shepherd's Bush Empire show among her top five gigs of the year, and even the white-van man readers of the *Daily Star* voted them Best Live Act in the paper's year-end round-up. *Record Collector* magazine, meanwhile, re-evaluated the other end of the band's canon, valuing a copy of

'Showbiz' at £80, while the limited, numbered vinyl run of 1,500 of 'The Muse EP' was fetching up to £200. The magazine argued that Muse were developing a grip on the collector's market not seen since Queen in the 1980s.

Press acceptance was never Muse's standard of success of course; they judged themselves by the levels of rapture in the faces in the crowd. And that winter's arena tour had floored more Muse fans than ever before. From the Patinoire Meriadeck in Bordeaux on Halloween, when Dom had dressed in a full-body Spiderman suit throughout and Chris had briefly worn a teddy bear's head, through those three sold-out nights at Wembley Arena, and onwards through other European arenas right up until December 19, Muse played their HAARP to dizzying effect. Revealed from behind a large black drape with Matt often clad in a flowing wizard's coat or his tight red track suit, thrusting his guitar in his groin like an android sex toy and knee-sliding across stages highly polished for the purpose, the show was a sensory blitzkrieg. Stars exploded, galaxies raced by, robot armies marched directly into camera, dark cities of delusion rose from celestial space dust, balloon worlds fell from the sky, heavenly steam and hellfire burst from the stage and up to 19,000 people every night roared along to the greatest rock spectacular of the modern age.

And even under such technological pressure, no two sets were ever the same. Belfast's Odyssey Arena got a surprise 'Muscle Museum' in the encore; *Manchester Evening News* Arena got a trumpeter called Dan joining the band for opener 'Knights Of Cydonia', the first UK performance of 'City Of Delusion', the last (to date) of 'Showbiz' and a guitar thrown into the crowd at the end; Nottingham's National Ice Arena got a six-song encore including 'Sunburn'; while the second night at Wembley got *Black Holes And Revelations* performed in its entirety as the first 11 songs and two encores of classics, the first of songs from *Showbiz* and *Origin . . .* and the second of *Absolution* hits. The final Wembley show, as if to make it up to anyone who missed the previous night, had Chris go to kick one of the inflatable balloons only for it to become attached to the top of his head for several minutes like the hugest of bobble hats. Everywhere got riffs tacked to the beginning or end of songs nodding to Muse's heroes – Dylan's 'Maggie's Farm', 'RATM's 'Killing In The Name' or 'Township Rebellion', Queen's 'I Want To Break Free', Led Zeppelin's 'Heartbreaker'.

Through Berlin and Hamburg, Rome and Milan, Geneva, Vienna, Munich and Dusseldorf, two sold-out nights at the massive Bercy in Paris and more, Muse's unstoppable march of delectable devastation left a trail of blown minds, frazzled eyeballs and warmed hearts across Europe. It climaxed with a 20-song set on December 19 at Antwerp's Sportspaleis Merksem – capacity 21,000 – with Dom in his Spiderman suit once more, the 'Bliss' balloons released halfway through and the Christmas party at the end of the universe raging on well past curfew.

For once, no tragedy marred Muse's Christmas in 2006. As Dom and Chris headed back to Teignmouth to spend the holiday with their families and Matt raced off to the Alps for skiing, their heads were no doubt filled with the Saturday afternoon lead-ups to FA Cup finals of their youths.

And Muse's road to Wembley would be just as winding.

★ ★ ★

Like all the most seasoned travellers, Muse were excited by the exotic and unknown. And now, as a bona fide stadium concern, they decided that 2007 would be the year they ventured from the well-trodden tour path and explored less-travelled territories. And before hooking once more on to the Big Day Out tour across Australia and New Zealand, they started as they meant to continue, with their first-ever show in Singapore, at Fort Canning Park on January 16, to 6,500 fans who rarely see Western bands coming to play their country. Demand was so high for the shows that the promoter was forced to raise the venue's capacity by 1,000 to accommodate the audience. And while the rock kids of Singapore took advantage of the (late-running) metal-pop thrills, Muse took advantage of the nation's fine silk, buying up several rolls of it to act as decoration in the dressing rooms for the rest of the year.

The Big Day Out Tour of 2007 saw Muse play as second headliners for the three-week run beneath Tool, and with the impressive likes of My Chemical Romance, The Killers, The Streets and Trivium in support. Between festival dates Muse would play their own headline shows at Sydney's 5,000-seater Hordern Pavillion and Melbourne's even larger Festival Hall. *Black Holes . . .* had hit number one in Australia in its first week of release, and Muse were a big deal down under by now: Matt would regularly be woken up by legions of fans knocking on his hotel door in the middle of the night. And at the Big Day Out dates the summer party was in full swing – while Morgan Nicholls became renowned as a one-man after-show, hopping between Muse and his old band The Streets, Matt was loving the sunny days off and, finding himself unable to sleep because of the time difference, indulged in an all-night party after the show at Gold Coast in Queensland, which ended with him swimming in the sea at dawn. The band also got friendly with Las Vegas indie showmen The Killers, spending many small hours discussing the Mayan calendar, which predicted the end of mankind in mid-2007. Matt was so convincing in his arguments that the end of the world might indeed by nigh that Killers singer Brandon Flowers suggested that they shouldn't play at Wembley at all, but instead go on an extended holiday around every continent, running up debts they'll never have to repay. Strangely, Muse opted to stick to their original plan.

Flames were shot from a 'Hand Of God' atop the main stage at the Sydney Showground, problematic guitars were switched seamlessly and Muse completed the Big Day Out tour on February 4 with a hearty "Hello Adelaide!" from Dom – a glorious ending to the tour, if they hadn't been in Perth at the time. They flew back to England to attend the Valentine's Day Brit Awards at Earls Court, where they'd been nominated for Best Album, Best Group and Best Live Act; the tabloids had fanfared them as the band with the most Brits nominations that year. But even as they stepped up to the podium to accept the award for Best Live Act with minimal fuss and speech, humbled by the realisation of how far they'd come, their minds were already on the girder arch; the very next day, after Matt had spent the night celebrating Valentine's Day with Gaia, Muse convened to start working on another new design, this time for the huge Wembley Stadium stage. Rebuilding the entire arena show from scratch for the second time in a year (they were so keen to give their fans value for money that the idea of repeating themselves was anathema; they wanted to play every show like it was their last), a whole host of tricks and treats came up, and on February 16 Muse met with architects from construction company Stageco to discuss the design of the stage (there was talk of a second stage somewhere in the stadium, to be lit by helicopters) and with Brent Council's health and safety officials to go over their proposals. Many didn't make the grade: they wouldn't be allowed to fly a blimp over the stadium with the gig projected onto the underside so that all of London could watch the show; they couldn't beam searchlights or lasers from helicopters above the crowd in case anybody was blinded; and the inflat-able alien invasion idea was a total non-starter, as were Matt's suggestions for the band to arrive onstage in jet packs or descending from a giant zeppelin.

Muse's Wembley plans might have been brought solidly back down to Earth, but they were determined to make it stratospheric. There was talk of the most revolutionary stage ever devised, possibly with the entire floor of the stage as a gigantic screen beaming the show to the heavens, or with a hidden message built into the very design and construction. As so many people would be looking downwards at the show, they wanted it to face up, and to consume the entire stadium. They wanted no less than the greatest show on Earth.

The band themselves were extremely hands-on in the organisation and conceptual planning of the Wembley shows. While Matt was put in charge of putting together the visual and stage ideas, Dom was charged with finding the support bands. Muse wanted the two gigs to work as mini-festivals, with an impressive supporting line-up worthy of such a monumental event. So a shortlist was drawn up of bands Muse wanted to play with, the criteria focused more on whether they were nice people to hang out with than whether the music necessarily fitted in with Muse's. Lily Allen, Wolfmother and Bloc Party were all approached by Dom, and electro-rave flavours of the month Klaxons revealed that January that they'd turned down a slot when Dom had approached them at a bar simply because they were a bit drunk, and had it in the back of their heads that their manager had told them they shouldn't be supporting anyone any more. They quickly retracted their refusal but it was too late: other acts had already snapped up the slots, including Carl Barât from The Libertines' new combo Dirty Pretty Things, Scottish rockers Biffy Clyro and their Big Day Out 2007 tourmates My Chemical Romance and The Streets.

Their heads spinning with possibilities, and concerns about how long they could stretch their set for – the longest set they'd ever played before was one hour and 45 minutes in Antwerp at the end of the 2006 arena tour, but they were confident they could stretch it to two hours with a slower, chilled-out section – Muse boarded a flight to Jakarta, Indonesia on February 22 to begin the next step of their off-road tour adventures. For the first time the band ventured into even more exotic climes, playing their first gigs in Malaysia, Taiwan, China and South Korea on the way to an eight-gig tour of Japan in March. Without ever having set foot in these countries before, Muse arrived to find they were playing to 7,000 people in Jakarta's Istora Senayan arena, 10,000 in the Stadium Negara in Kuala Lumpur, and many more in Hong Kong, Seoul and Taipei City. Between songs Dom would read out local phrases from phonetic prompt cards, which the band would often sabotage so that he'd tell 10,000 screaming Malaysians that, "I've got a nice bum", or collect awards – the *NME* award for Best Band was presented to him onstage during the intro of 'Stockholm Syndrome' at Taipei City's Chung Shan Soccer Field on February 28, while he simultaneously recorded a filmed acceptance speech saying, "Shit, I'm knackered. This is very kind, it means a lot to us, seriously. I must go as I have to play a fat riff".*

The costs of getting the band and their stage set (the test-tubes show rather than the full satellite extravaganza) to the Far East meant that Muse only broke even on these dates, but they made the sacrifice in the cause of exploring unfamiliar territories and having a bit of a laugh there, although Muse's quest for larks almost fatally backfired in Indonesia. If it wasn't bad enough that the band's tour manager was robbed by three ladyboys in a lift in Jakarta, Dom's hunt for an ecstasy pill led him to get in a cab to the city's ghetto, where the car pulled up at a rubbish-festooned shack and was instantly surrounded by beggars beating on the car windows and bonnet, rabid and angry. The car screeched away and not a second too soon. The taxi driver explained that if the mob had managed to wrench open the doors of the car then Dom would have been robbed and shot in the street.

In Hong Kong, meanwhile, Muse were adopted after the show by a journalist who was acting as if he owned the city. Dragging them off to his favourite bars and hang-outs that night he became increasingly over-excited, drunk and troublesome, culminating in the final bar when, draining his drink, he gave a satisfied look of smugness and tossed the empty glass across the room. A grand statement of rock'n'roll excess, he might have thought, except that the glass smashed on the back of one of the mountainous security guards who by now accompanied Muse everywhere they went. Never the most forgiving types at the best of times, Muse's bodyguards gave the journalist a hefty beating for his arrogance.

* Matt also won Sexiest Man at the 2007 *NME* Awards.

Onward through Japan rolled the *Black Holes . . .* tour (they played their longest ever set at Tokyo's International Forum – 23 songs over almost two hours, including the first outing of 'Sing For Absolution' for two years), still facing nine months before Muse's next bout of decent time off. Their month back in the UK after Japan was spent finalising details for Wembley and filming a video for the next single – 'Invincible', released on April 9.* Sticking to their end of the world theme, the 'Invincible' video featured the band on a carnival tunnel of love ride, which carries them through the history of the planet. Playing the song in a floating carriage, they sail past cartoonish felt re-creations of prehistoric times, ancient Greece, Viking invasions, industrialisation, World War II, a futuristic cityscape and finally, following a cartoon World Trade Centre attack, scenes of cuddly global chaos where robotic mega-mice bite buildings in half and alien spacecraft obliterate the toy mankind. It was a *Sesame Street* apocalypse, brought to you by the letters W and W and the number three.

Not everyone shared Muse's light-hearted approach to international conflagration, however. On April 7, Matt reached the departure gate for his flight to San Francisco for three gigs in the US and Mexico as a warm-up to a six-week American arena jaunt supporting My Chemical Romance. According to airport protocol, the official at the desk asked him what he intended to do in America, and Matt jokingly replied that they weren't to worry, he wasn't going to be working illegally or making bombs. Now airport security personnel, like traffic wardens and angry rhinos, aren't renowned for their sense of humour, and Matt was duly reprimanded for making bad jokes, but let on the plane. A few minutes later, however, he was hauled off again by even more officious officials, taken to an interrogation room and questioned over his opinion of American people and his attitude towards the country before being allowed to fly. Matt could only count himself lucky he didn't have a copy of *Black Holes . . .* in his luggage or he'd have been banned from America as an insurrectionary influence. And you imagine he would've kept his in-flight reading to himself too: around this time he was studying methods of mind control from Kathleen Taylor's *Brainwashing: The Science Of Thought*

---

* Backed with a Simian Mobile Disco remix of 'Knights Of Cydonia' on the CD and 'Glorious' on the vinyl, it made number 21 in the UK.

Control, wishing he'd have read it when he was a teenager so he could have discussed it with the Jehovah's Witnesses who'd come calling.

In America by this point Muse were being managed by Q Prime, the same company that had built the Red Hot Chili Peppers up from funk-rock frat-boy favourites to global superstars, and their influence certainly showed that spring. If their San Francisco show at the 7,000-seater Bill Graham Civic Auditorium was their biggest US gig so far, the next day they eclipsed it almost threefold. At LA's Inglewood Forum, slap bang in the middle of South Central's gangland and where Quentin Tarantino's *Pulp Fiction* movie was set, Muse performed to a sold-out crowd of 18,000 – the equal of most shows they'd played so far in Europe and an 'exceptional' achievement according to editor-in-chief of concert information company Pollstar, who likened the level of Muse's support in America to that of Depeche Mode's in the 1980s. And the band carried the achievement well, rampaging ferociously through 20 songs, despite the fact that only the night before Chris had been vomiting between the encores due to a chest infection.

LA was the 111th gig of the *Black Holes . . .* tour and by this point the band and crew were like a well-drilled machine. By day they would perform meet-and-greets at the regional radio stations, sometimes getting talked into go-karting, paintballing or even shooting sessions with the local DJs. On days off they'd then head off for skiing or fishing trips arranged by their tour manager; on gig days, around soundcheck, they would relax in their dressing room draped with Singapore silk, with masseurs at their beck and call, while their tour manager would deal with their laundry issues – they demanded disposable socks and pants on every rider to minimise laundry, and Matt would often be seen wearing the same v-necked T-shirt for three days' running. It was here that Chris would generally phone home twice a day, running up phone bills that went directly to the band's accountant and would be described as 'painful'. And after the show they drank until dawn: in LA, Matt's late-night session at the hotel bar ended at 5 a.m. with threats from the hotel staff of a call to the sheriff, while in Mexico on April 12 Dom was up until 8 a.m. drinking so heavily that he failed to notice the 6.3 Richter-scale earthquake that hit Mexico City that night, the third Act Of God that had failed to smite the *Black Holes . . .* tour.

Mexico itself was a strange experience for Muse. With corruption so rife in the country that the police had demanded a sizeable portion of the profits from the band's gig at the 22,000-capacity Palacio de los Deportes, so in return Muse had made their own demands; they wanted a police escort wherever they went in the city. The time they most needed protection, though, was in the venue itself; the crowd barriers here were so frail and flimsy that at the most relaxed of concerts they were known to collapse every other night. During Muse's set they broke twice.

Bizarrely, for a touring party that consisted of three 50-foot trucks, hundreds of lights and a very flustered guitar tech dealing with eight very unique guitars, the rest of Muse's American tour was spent supporting My Chemical Romance, playing a mere seven or eight songs a night over 45 minutes around an American arena circuit they were very close to headlining themselves. Despite Matt's slight diss of MCR as being too heavily styled in *NME* the previous year (although they were never mentioned by name), the two bands clearly shared a young, disaffected and passionate fanbase, and developed a healthy mutual respect over the course of the tour. MCR would watch Muse's gig from the wings every night, and Matt found himself enjoying the showmanship of the MCR circus – a kind of travelling teen-goth musical based on the story of the band's third album, *The Black Parade*. The show roughly followed the tale of a character called 'The Patient' as he dies from cancer in a hospital ward, and his reflections on his life. Matt was familiar with the theme, having explored it himself in 'Thoughts Of A Dying Atheist' and other songs from *Absolution*, and he came to admire the barnstorming quality of the rock-opera concept. That, he figured, was something Muse could adapt to their own purposes.

The tour was to be short-lived, however. Eleven dates into a scheduled 20-show tour, both the Muse and MCR parties, bands and crew, were struck down by a massive outbreak of salmonella poisoning, reportedly caused by some 'bad chicken' that everyone ate in Williamsburg, Vancouver. The final nine dates were postponed by days, then cancelled as the entire tour succumbed to the illness. Apart from Matt; one of the few members of the tour not to fall ill, he flew back to Italy to check up on the builders working on his studio-cum-band accommodation complex (to find them mostly swimming in the lake or sunbathing; Matt's studio seemed to be taking longer to complete than Wembley Stadium) and to put the finishing touches to the gigs of his life. Six more dates were in the tour diary before June 16 – two festivals in Germany and Holland, two headline shows in Luxembourg and Italy, a chance to brush off downbeat classics such as 'Unintended' and 'Blackout' in time to brush them up for the big event. Then they were to headline the first night of the Isle Of Wight Festival on June 9, the most high-profile warm-up gig ever played.

Because just one week later he'd be standing on a hydraulic lift in the dark, stranded out in the middle of a spanking new football pitch, back to back with his two best friends, hearing the geysers of steam set off, the opera strike up and the crowd begin to roar . . .

★ ★ ★

At Wembley Stadium on June 16, 2007, there was a real scent of victory in the air. From the tenth row back in the press block, stage left, you could smell it rising like steam from the crowd, taste it like copper dust in your teeth. There was achievement, unity, celebration. It was a triumph of out-sider culture unlike any rock had seen for decades. Oasis had come here, played drunk and looked like an indie band playing a very big gig; Muse came here to consume the place. Whether you'd followed the band from day one, started a fan site, decoded the cryptology, bought all the formats, learnt all the words, led one of the sing-alongs of Muse songs in Trafalgar Square the previous evening*, carried their amplifiers, tuned their guitars, organised their tours, managed their business deals or, like me, written dozens of gushing reviews and interviews in their honour, that day we could all feel we'd played our part in creating the first of a new generation of stadium bands. Together, it turned out, we really were invincible.

The set alone upstaged the stadium. A cascade of gigantic screens, so ultra-modern that the wind could blow through them, lined the entire length of a stage festooned with industrial side markings, turning the entire stage into one enormous screen. Two gigantic satellite dishes flanked the stage, preparing to beam huge lasers into the stratosphere. A lucky thousand or so gold ticket holders were penned in to a triangular section in front of the stage, edged by what appeared to be trolley tracks and sliced through the centre by a gangway stretching out from the stage to the centre of the stadium. And above it all, up in the stands, those trademark

---

* Hundreds of Muse fans had congregated in Trafalgar Square at 6 p.m. on June 15 to sing Muse songs and raise money for the Helen Foundation, the MS Society and Cancer Research.

white globes had grown to 20 ft in diameter and now rested on platforms like a council of alien brains casting judgement over the beast they had created. That stage took seven trucks to transport and used 10 miles of cabling, yet – believe it or not – it could be erected within three hours flat.

At 8.30 p.m., after Rodrigo y Gabriela, Dirty Pretty Things and The Streets had roused an already excitable crowd into a state of tense anticipation, the steam unleashed, the ticker tape flew and, to the austere and brooding tones of 'Dance Of The Knights' from Prokofiev's *Romeo And Juliet*, Matthew Bellamy, Dominic Howard and Christopher Wolstenholme rose back to back through a platform in the centre of the stadium. Matt wore a red suit, Dom bright green trousers and Chris standard issue black; three ordinary kids from Teignmouth made heroes by the sheer, unignorable force of their passion, power and virtuosity.

Flanked by a troop of stagehands in yellow radioactivity suits and protective face masks, Muse strolled the length of the walkway to the stage, waving, grinning, soaking it all in. Before the gig they'd been unbearably tense, but seeing 90,000 faces beaming back at them dissolved their nerves instantly. They reached the stage, took their places; Matt collected his DeLorean Manson from a radio-controlled robot that would bring him all of his guitars that night. He looked down at his fingers on the strings, picking out the riff from *Close Encounters Of The Third Kind*; they felt like someone else's fingers on someone else's guitar. He felt light-headed, distant, as if he was floating out of his body. He looked back up at the crowd and wondered what the hell he was doing there.

And then the fingers on his guitar hit the first note of 'Knights Of Cydonia'. And the horsemen of the new rock Apocalypse descended.

Muse at Wembley Stadium was not merely a landmark gig for the band, an evolutionary step for new alternative rock bands into the giddy heights of the musical aristocracy or even just the number one best gig ever, as it was voted by readers of *Kerrang!* that year. It was a generation-defining event. 'Hysteria' exploded like an atom bomb. Android armies 50-feet high marched for the duration of 'Supermassive Black Hole'. Fireworks filled the screens at the climax of 'Invincible'. Matt played a transparent piano with light-up strings for 'Feeling Good'. 'Butterflies & Hurricanes' threatened to rattle the Wembley arch from its settings. The opening riff to 'Plug In Baby' finally got a venue worthy of its size. The screens were a pupil-frying mash-up of live action, sensational visuals and lyrical slogans:

"LONELINESS BE OVER" and "NO ONE'S GOING TO TAKE ME ALIVE". And the highlight, for crowd and band, was the heliospheres: during a tender, elegiac 'Blackout', two enormous floating white moons were rolled out down the trolley tracks; suspended by an elastic rope from each was a ballerina in a white body stocking, floating, sweeping, twirling and spiralling 30 feet above the crowd. For Matt it was the perfect performance, the audience watching the ballerinas rather than the band, everyone caught up in the magic and amazement of the scene. It was, Matt would say later, a Mary Poppins moment.

The balloons bounced free for 'Plug In Baby', the riffs blew molten for 'Stockholm Syndrome', Matt's banshee wail was unleashed for 'Micro Cuts', the fire and steam erupted for 'Take A Bow' and, one hour and 50 minutes after they rose from the pits of the Wembley brimstone, Muse were gone, off to celebrate with friends and family and prepare to do it all again (with added 'Bliss') the following night. Governments still betrayed democracy, the media still peddled propaganda, the bombs still fell and the oil barons still scrapped and clawed us all towards disaster. But Muse, with their own dazzling waves of shock and awe, had struck a blow, won 90,000 more hearts and minds.

Hell, when you're shouting this loud, eventually someone at the top of the pyramid is going to hear.

★ ★ ★

And there, for many a lesser band, the story would end. The pinnacle, the pride, the justification of all the hard work. After this, there would only be decline.

But Muse don't think in terms of 'biggest' or 'best'; they think 'bigger', 'better'. For Muse there are no pinnacles, only further peaks to ascend.

Muse are no 'lesser band'.

Stripped back to Dom's satellite and a parade of big screens, the *Black Holes . . .* tour rolled on for a further five months through 2007. Some 60,000 saw them play at the Parc des Princes in Paris a week after Wembley, just as the digital download release of the last single from *Black Holes . . .* – 'Map Of The Problematique'* – hit number 18 in the UK

---

* The only Muse single other than 'Cave' that had no video; the download came backed with a Does It Offend You, Yeah? remix of the song.

charts. A slew of European festivals over the rest of the summer saw them take the headline slots above such acts as Björk, Marilyn Manson, The Beastie Boys, Snow Patrol, Kaiser Chiefs, Razorlight and Kings Of Leon in places such as Belgium, Poland, Denmark, France, Switzerland and Benicàssim in Spain. They sold out the biggest arenas across Europe, playing to 10,000 in Latvia, 16,000 in Nîmes, 18,000 in Monaco and 22,000 in Verona. Fuji Rock in Japan saw their set delayed 20 minutes and Matt arguing with his guitar tech throughout; the show ended with a now rare bout of gear-trashing as Matt pushed over his amp stack and piano, Dom kicked apart his drum kit and Matt's precious Kaoss pad M1D1 Manson guitar met a sticky end, impaled pad-first on a strobe light.*

In July they were invited back to Wembley Stadium to perform at the Live Earth event organised by Al Gore in aid of reversing climate change through carbon-dioxide offsetting. The band refused, however, since they were due to headline the Oxygen festival that day and the only way they could have made the gig was by hiring a private jet from Ireland, and that was deemed totally hypocritical in light of the event itself. Discussions were held with other Oxygen bands about sharing a normal flight but these fell through, so Muse had to decline the offer, claiming that they didn't think carbon dioxide offsetting to be the best way to tackle greenhouse gases anyway. Matt proposed an environmental tax on big businesses to be calculated retrospectively; that way the people who'd caused the problems in the 80s would pay for its solution now.

In August, Muse played that US arena tour they were always meant for; 16 shows on the circuit around which they'd supported My Chemical Romance only months before. The tour took in unthinkably big shows at the 20,000-seater Madison Square Garden in Manhattan and the Red Rocks Ampitheater in Colorado, built into the side of a rust red canyon and made famous by U2's *Under A Blood Red Sky* album. At Toronto's Mississauga Arrow Hall, one of the stage-front steam jets came loose and fired into the crowd, although no one was hurt. Technical problems during their Lollapalooza headline set in Chicago saw Matt running off-stage for 10 seconds between each song. At Arizona's Mesa Ampitheater,

---

* The guitar was replaced quickly, and a new Seattle Manson received its premiere at Seattle's Key Arena the following month, now improved with an automatic tuning system.

Matt played the solo from 'New Born' using a shoe thrown at him from the crowd as a plectrum. And as Muse's most overtly political move yet, an audio recording of a John F Kennedy speech given to the American Newspaper Publisher's Association in 1961 concerning secret societies, was played as an introduction to the show or encore; in it JFK decried communism as a "monolithic and ruthless conspiracy" and claimed "the very word 'secret' is repugnant in a free and open society, and we are as a people inherently and historically opposed to secret societies, to secret oaths and to secret proceedings". It was Muse's way of saying, "Wake up America, you're being lied to."

For the rest of the year, the tour first chased the snow, then the sun. In October, the band shivered through their first Eastern European tour, taking in Bucharest in Romania, Zagreb in Croatia, Kiev in the Ukraine (where Matt smashed his amplifier up so badly that he ended up giving it to fans in the front row), St Petersburg in Russia and Belgrade in Serbia where, the night before the band made a whistle-stop visit to the UK to pick up the Q Award for Best Live Act for the third time, Matt would experience what he'd call his most memorable and depraved night out ever. Details were scant, but he assured us it involved a transsexual called Pete sitting on Dom's lap and a dildo. The imagination, quite frankly, baulks at the challenge.

Back in Moscow to play at the city's Lukhniki Sports Palace for the second time, Muse were met backstage by a group of Russian fans concerned that the girl who had presented Matt with the disturbing oil painting of himself naked had given them a bad impression of the country's hospitality. To make up for it, they gave him a fully functioning and extremely expensive telescope. Matt would use it to study the craters of the moon, amazed at how strong the piece was; he could even see the dust hills thrown up by meteorite strikes.

A sweep through Scandinavia for Matt to ram his Silver Manson into his amp in Stockholm (with the swift replacement of his M1D1 guitar, it seemed that the Manson guitars were suddenly deemed trashable) and Muse finished the year defrosting on the sunny side of the planet. They celebrated supporting their heroes Rage Against The Machine at the Las Vegas Sam Boyd Stadium by getting Dom in his Spiderman suit and having scantily clad policewomen come onstage to spank Morgan Nicholls during 'Supermassive Black Hole', and then it was back to Australia, where 'Starlight' was now a huge radio hit, to round out the year, and their longest tour to date, with a huge arena tour[*], which again wasn't without its mishaps. A collapsed barrier at the Perth Supreme Court Gardens caused a two-hour delay; a piano fault at Melbourne's Rod Laver Arena meant that Matt had to abandon the planned outing of 'Ruled By Secrecy' in favour of 'Apocalypse Please'; and at the same gig, when the balloons were launched during 'Plug In Baby', the band were startled to see that half of them were much smaller than usual, and one in particular was about the size of a beach ball. The shock prompted Matt to yell, "What the fuck is that?" instead of the chorus.

The *Black Holes And Revelations* tour squealed to a halt on December 9 with a headline slot at the KROQ Almost Acoustic Christmas show in LA's Gibson Ampitheatre, complete with a knowing riff on 'The Star Spangled Banner' as a nod from the band to a country that had finally accepted them, Presidential jibes and all.

And that, after 19 months on the road, was it. Muse went home to oversee the completion of their recording studios (Matt), indulge their love of scuba-diving holidays in the Caribbean (Dom), and make a fourth baby (Chris).

And to consider that tricksiest of subjects.

[*] The 13,000-capacity gig at the Sydney Entertainment Centre was double the size of Muse's previous Sydney gig.

Chapter Eleven

"THE future?"

Matt Bellamy pursed his lips, and considered the entire remaining life-span of the human race.

"Well, there's the oil depletion, World War Three . . ."

I stopped him there. No, I explained, I meant what's the future for Muse?

"Oh," Bellamy checked himself, giggling at his reflex ability to slip into the universal catastrophic theme. "We're playing V."

The *NME* Awards, February 28 2008; Matt, Dom and I (Chris had a sore throat so wasn't partaking in interviews that evening) sat down at a busy press bar in the Indigo 2 venue next door to the O2 Arena in the revamped Millenium Dome for an interview for the cover of *NME* to preview the release of the DVD/CD *HAARP* on March 17. The package would consist of a DVD of 20 songs recorded live at the June 17 Wembley Stadium show and a CD of 14 songs from June 16, and Muse had taken as much care and attention over its production as they had with *Hullabaloo*; Matt claimed that since the last tour had mostly consisted of large venues where he couldn't see the fans' faces very well, he'd been insisting the editors put lots of crowd shots in. Another shot that Matt found pride in were those taken from a circling helicopter overhead that showed the grand scale of the event; he picked out one shot where the helicopter camera zoomed right into his upturned face from half a mile up. The DVD would be premiered to competition winners in Vue cinemas around the country in high definition format, perhaps the only proper way to watch such a dazzling technological marvel of the modern rock world.

The three worldly men hitting their thirties that I met that day were unrecognisable from the nervy young kids I'd first interviewed almost a decade before. They lived in three entirely different cities – Dom in London's Belsize Park, Matt in Italy and Chris in the posh side of

Teignmouth – but were affluent enough to consider a flight to Milan no more trouble than a drive to London when band business called. They were still modest men, unaffected by fame, and reasonably settled with allegedly 'boring' home lives to return to at a tour's end, the inverse of Pete Doherty, Matt would argue (although both Matt and Dom around this time would describe their private lives as being 'all over the place').

Dom, once the band's Teignmouth punch-bag, then its Don Juan, was now a scuba fanatic and a 'stadium man' at heart with an exclusive London address and enough airmiles to get him to the world's most exotic climes a few times a year. Chris, adoring of his growing Devon family, was soon to be a dad of four, the fatherly rock at the heart of the band. And Matt had gone through many changes since he'd stuttered nervously into my Dictaphone back in 1999: he'd wiped clean his childhood personality, rejected friends and loved ones, gone wild with rock'n'roll freedom, learnt all manner of dark truths about the world, learnt to put his fears of them into song, discovered the importance of those around him and finally found himself on the other side. Matt Bellamy@2008 was a wealthy and successful rock star who split his time between his villa in Italy and a London flat in the shadow of the US Embassy in Grovesnor Square. He had investments – the Asian market was particularly lucrative for him – but considered this merely an extension of his poker habit. He was considering buying a helicopter but needed a back garden big enough to land it in. He'd stopped stockpiling the latest gadgetry, sold his jet-pack and didn't even have a mobile phone any more since one day he'd decided to turn it off for a few days and had found the resulting peace and quiet utter bliss. He'd learnt a few things about fame: that money merely serves to alienate you from your friends and family; that the bigger the house you live in and the more cars you have in the driveway, the more of a lonely twat you feel; and that home life is everything – he much preferred staying home with Gaia to going out and possibly running into a clingy obsessive (the paparazzi never bothered him as he simply didn't feel part of the *Hello* set). He'd been writing more abstract music which he hoped to use on a film soundtrack at some point, and had spent some time revisiting his interest in contacting the spiritual plane: he'd begun to believe that mediums might be connecting with the memories of dead people which live on inside the living and that Ouija boards might work because they allow us to connect with those memories under a form of self-hypnosis. Hence he'd started trying to contact the ghost of Vincento Bellini – the composer who'd once owned his villa – to help him write songs; at 3 am Matt would turn down the lights and play snippets of new songs on the house piano in hope of making contact. So far, nothing.

Yet of all the changes, the most pleasing was their confident air of achievement, of knowing they were capable of rising to any challenge the world could offer. It wasn't just the immense satisfaction in their eyes at the mention of Wembley, but the small things too. They knew that somewhere out there was a lock-up full of smashed up old Muse equipment that they should one day sign and sell on eBay for charity. They'd heard that the hometown where the mayor had once been photographed throwing their CD in a dustbin was now petitioning to have the town sign changed from 'Teignmouth: Gem Of Devon' to read 'Teignmouth: Home Of Muse'. The plan, it seemed, was only thwarted when someone pointed out that 'MUSE' was an acronym for Medical Urethral Suppository for Erection. Which perhaps showed just how geriatric in soul and body the residents of Teignmouth really were.

That day Muse and I discussed what they'd been up to since the end of the 'Black Holes . . .' tour (sleeping, mostly), their plans for the future (they were still considering touring by ocean liner to play in city docks, or possibly by business zeppelin) and their smattering of upcoming gigs. While recording *Black Holes* . . . they felt they had departed from being a live band altogether, so while writing and recording their next they planned to include a sporadic smattering of gigs through the year in places they'd really like to holiday in. The first of these was a week later in Dubai where they'd play at the Dubai Festival City event above ex-Guns'N'Roses crew Velvet Revolver, then at the end of March they'd fly to South Africa to play at the two dates of My Coke Fest in Cape Town and Johannesburg. In July there was rumour of Muse's first South American dates in Brazil, Colombia, Argentina and Chile, and Matt hinted at a gig in China in October. And then there was their headline slot at the V weekend festival in August, which Matt saw as a less high-pressure show than Reading or Glastonbury and, due to the inordinate fee paid by the promoters to headliners, perhaps a chance to finally make his dream of landing spaceships on the audience's heads a reality.

Beyond that, having reached the heights of stadium performance, Muse promised multiple nights in smaller venues on future tours and with more performers onstage (there'd long been debates about incorporating an orchestra into the live set) to add to the pizzazz. The first evidence of their desire to see the whites of their fans eyes came a mere six weeks later when Muse played a Teenage Cancer Trust concert at London's Royal Albert Hall – organiser Roger Daltrey from The Who had twice asked Muse to play the event and Matt was keen to play since his father had performed at the venue three times with The Tornados and always told Matt it was his favourite place to play. After an unprecedented demand for tickets which saw internet box office Seetickets collapse under the strain and eBay tickets going for £300 each, anticipation for the event among those lucky enough to be attending was perhaps even greater than at Wembley. It was a stripped-down set, in as much as their usual huge screens were reduced to a small four foot strip across the back of the stage showing a thin sliver of their usual visuals, but it packed as great a punch as any arena show. Where most major rock bands would have used the opportunity to try out acoustic versions of their hits with a string quartet in tow, Muse rocked harder than ever and Matt even fired up the RAH's mammoth organ, an instrument stretching the height of the main hall, for the first performance of 'Megalomania' in six years, proclaiming "it'd be rude not to play this beast!". Bombastic, operatic, thrillingly modern: it was as if the band were wrestling the venue itself over which was the grandest. The result was a dead heat.

On Muse's fifth album there was little news at our February 2008 interview. The villa studio was finished at last and the band had a few 'bits and pieces' they'd start working on as soon as they'd got the place ready. There were lots of songs, they said, but no cohesive style as yet. Dom hinted at a possible electronic feel to the record and there'd been word of more experiments in taking apart old instruments to see what noises they'd make. Matt, meanwhile, thought that it was perhaps time for Muse's "silly prog opus" and "at least one fifteen minute space rock solo". He wanted to push the boundaries again to keep their own interest up and he hoped the fans were open to them experimenting musically as he thought Muse could stretch on to infinity. *Supermassive* . . . had opened up a whole world of groove-based dancefloor possibilities for the band which he was keen to explore. What's more Matt suggested that there might not be another conventional album release from Muse.

"I don't think we're going to approach the next album like we're making an album," he said. "I think we're just gonna make a load of music. I'm sure there will be an album format that comes out but we're more open to releasing a few things unconventionally if that appeals at the time. I like the idea of releasing a series of songs, every month or every couple of months just putting songs out there. Almost like making the single a more prominent format, and then every few years doing a 'best of' that period and that would be the album. So in other words throw out songs every couple of months and see how people like them and which-ever ones people like, stick that on a record of eleven tracks."

The immediate future, however, would pan out rather differently.

★ ★ ★

Precisely one year later, at the *NME* Awards 2009 at Brixton Academy, Matt Bellamy's grinning face emerged from the crowd. Whisking his drink away from Muse's table, past those of The Cure, Grace Jones and The Last Shadow Puppets, he strode over trailing an air of triumph.

"We did it."

At first I wasn't sure exactly what he'd done. There'd certainly been no cruise liner tours of the Mediterranean and no Muse zeppelin drifting to Earth blasting out 'Sunburn' in the twelve months since I'd spoken to him last. There'd been no series of singles released as lead-ins to their forth-coming fifth album either. There hadn't even been a Chinese gig – although, after a fault-strewn set for 90,000 Portuguese revellers at Lisbon's Rock In Rio in June 2008 (both Matt's Kaos pedal and guitar strap broke), the South American tour had gone ahead as planned that July. Across the 3,000-plus capacity auditoriums of Monterrey, Guadalajara, Bogota, Buenos Aires, Santiago, Rio De Janeiro, Sau Paulo and Brasilia, Muse had wowed the Latinos with the flags of the home countries draped over Dom's bass drum, Matt wearing a traditional Chilean chupalla hat during 'Feeling Good' in Santiago and rarities such as 'Nishe', 'Dead Star', 'Space Dementia', 'Fury' and 'Apocalypse Please' tossed out with reckless abandon, playful traipses through the more obscure corners of their back catalogue. Such exotic climes encouraged Muse's adventurous bent.

There'd also been no spaceships hovering over the crowds of V*, but

---

* The plan was submitted for a model UFO to fly over the site but rejected by the local authority's Health And Safety department.

the gigs themselves were celestial enough. The spotlight antennas from Wembley, crammed onto a stage that could barely contain them, scanned the crowd like gigantic alien CCTVs: the sunburnt hordes of the Chelmsford leg and the sheet rain-soaked mud monsters of Stafford. And to booming chimes of orchestral doom, Muse took the stage and stole the weekend with a display of riff rock pyrotechnics fit to quake a festival usually synonymous with the AOR plodding of Snow Patrol or Stereophonics. Though the weather Gods objected – high winds at the Marlay Park show earlier that week in Dublin had kept the heliospheres grounded and 'Blackout' out of the set – Muse completed the final 'Black Holes & Revelations' festival gigs as globe-straddling rock Collossi. The Girls Aloud fans didn't know what hit them.

But it was none of this that Matt was boasting about. What had they done exactly?

"The fifteen-minute epic," he grinned, revelling in his own inner ridiculousness. "We've done it. You've got to come out to the studio in Italy and hear it."

If I'd known to what lengths other Muse fans across the world would go to hear a snippet of 'The Resistance', I'd have booked my ticket to Lake Como on the spot.

* * *

On Friday July 10, 2009, some eleven months after their last public transmission was received*, the Muse website was replaced by a clock counting down from 48 hours. The following Monday the site ceased to exist, the second the timer having hit zero. It was replaced by a new official site, and a sister microsite: The United States Of Eurasia. Its front page held a blank map of the Europe, Africa and Asia continents alongside the following message.

PROJECT EURASIA

FLASH BRIEFING DECLASSIFIED AND APPROVED FOR GENERAL RELEASE. PREVIOUS CLASSIFICATION: INDIGO ALPHA SHARD

GEOPOLITICAL EVENTS NOW NECESSITATE ACTIVATION OF THE STANDBY PLAN BRAVO NINER PREVIOUSLY KNOWN AS GRAN AJEDREZ.

---

* Besides the band's numerous updates from the studio on their official website and Matt's regular Twitter messages.

MARKERS INCLUDE REALTIME ASSESSMENT OF POLITICAL AND PUBLIC
SENTIMENT AT -2.57 (KNIGHT INDEX), SOCIO-ECONOMIC INDICATORS
AT (REDACTED), ENERGY STABILITY INDICATORS AT (REDACTED), GLOBAL
MARKET VOLATILITY MARKERS AT [REDACTED] AND SOVEREIGN STATE
MILITARY EFFECTIVENESS AT (REDACTED).

FOR GRAN AJEDREZ TO BE FULLY ACTIVATED, APPROVAL HAS BEEN
GRANTED FOR WIDESPREAD MOBILISATION OF INITIATED
NON-CONVENTIONAL HUMINT RESOURCES.

GRAN AJEDREZ WILL BE ACTIVATED IN A PHASED PROCESS. SUCCESSFUL
ACTIVATION OF EACH PHASE WILL RESULT IN THE UNLOCKING AND
DECRYPTION OF AN AUDIO BRIEFING. THE FULL PROJECT EURASIA/GRAN
AJEDREZ AUDIO BRIEFING WILL BE AVAILABLE FOR DOWNLOAD UPON
SUCCESSFUL ACTIVATION OF ALL PHASES.

PLEASE STAND BY AND COMPLETE THE FOLLOWING FOR PRE-APPROVED
HUMINT RESOURCE MOBILISATION.

Fans completing the accompanying registration form were told that
they had been successfully recruited as an 'ACTIVE HUMINT' and to
stand by for orders. Fansites buzzed with discussion and conjecture. What
did it mean? What was Project Eurasia? How would they be called upon
to play their part in the activation of its phases? For what sort of sinister
intelligence mission had they signed up as agents?

The following morning, Tuesday July 14, Western Europe turned red
on the Eurasian map.

PROJECT EURASIA / GRAN AJEDREZ (BRAVO NINER) IS NOW ACTIVE.

WIDESPREAD MOBILISATION OF INITIATED NON-CONVENTIONAL
HUMINT RESOURCES IS APPROVED.

STAND BY FOR PHASED ACTIVATION OF GRAN AJEDREZ STATIONS.

STATION//FUSE IS NOW INITIATED.

Those that had been following Matt's Twitter messages hinting at a new
coded game had an inkling of what was underway. This was a musical
treasure hunt so elaborate, testing and pan-continental that it would make
the 2005 set-list anagram conundrums look like a Beano sudoku.

Station Fuse was the first to become active. This was a web page
describing itself as 'PROJECT EURASIA INTERNAL DOCUMENTATION ACTIVA-
TION SCENARIO 1/6 – THIS DOCUMENT IS CLASSIFIED INDIGO AMAZON
ZENITH.' The document stated that activation of Station Fuse required the
acquisition of a 'USB ARMING KEYCODE' and instructed players to 'FOLLOW

PROCEDURE TIMATION, CARTESIAN CHI MARKING TO DETERMINE DROP LOCATION GRANDCREW. ON ARRIVAL AT DROP LOCATION GRANDCREW PROVIDE THE VERBAL AUTHENTICATION CODE BILDERBERG GROUP TO DESIGNATED AGENT 978-0465027262. STATION//FUSE WILL BE ACTIVE TO 20090715:1000-1200 LOCAL STATION TIME.' It then directed players to a Youtube channel and a Flikr Project as 'depositories' for photographic or filmic proof of their meeting with said agent and to an audio file of a woman's voice reading out map coordinates in phonetics.

When translated, the coordinates led players to a building on Rue du Perche in Paris. If they arrived there between 10 am and 12 pm, found agent 978-0465027262*, received the USB keycode, took a photo or film of him and uploaded it to the Flikr or Youtube sites they would win two tickets for a Muse gig of their choice and a personal audience with the band (or, as the site called it, 'SUCCESSFUL STATION UNLOCK AND PHOTINT WILL RESULT IN PERSONAL DEBRIEF WITH PROJECT EURASIA ARCHITECTS AND 2X ADMITTANCE TO PROJECT EURASIA (MIKE UNIFORM SIERRA ECHO) RALLY OF AGENT'S CHOICE').

The entering of the USB keycode into the site only 'primed' Station Fuse. Now all of the agents had to work together to unlock the Station. A list of 50 seemingly random phrases were posted with the instruction for the player to decrypt them: 'BECKONS FROZEN FISH', 'I SLUNK INTO FAUNA', 'TEAR UP SEXY OPERA', 'TWO SHY CHICKS' and so on. These, the instruction claimed, were 'NIGHTMARE CLASS ENTITIES ACTING AT ELEVATED LEVELS', and the example given: 'NIGHTMARE CLASS ENTITY CORRUPT AUGURS HAS BEEN IDENTIFIED AS ARCTURUS GROUP.'

So the random phrases were, of course, anagrams of 'ACCREDITED LOBBYING ORGANISATIONS' to the EU at Brussels; answers included Ericsson, Danish Dairy Board, Taxpayers Europe and Olympic Airlines. Once all 50 anagrams had been solved and entered, the first clip of a new Muse song called 'United States Of Eurasia' was unlocked on the site's music page.

Station Fuse was primed and activated. Western Europe turned green on the map; East Europe turned red. Station Charlie had become active.

There were six Stations in all: Fuse, Charlie, October, Umayyad,

---

* This was also the ISBN number for the book *The Grand Chessboard* by Zbigniew Brzezinski.

Doolittle and Buahinia. Players were directed to each by audio files of phonetic coordinates and told to meet a numbered agent there at a specified time, give them a password, photograph them as proof of the meeting for the site, collect their USB keycode and enter it into the site. Station Charlie was a building in Niederbarnimstraße in Berlin, October was a Coffee Bean Café in Moscow, Umayyad a Virgin store in the mall of the Emirates in Dubai, Doolittle the Hibiya Kokaido Public Hall in Tokyo and Buahinia the Fringe Club in Hong Kong. Each Station, once primed, set a second cryptic puzzle and cipher task to all players to unlock the next music clip. Once all six Stations had been unlocked a final Station Colossus was activated via a drop location in New York; the song would not be downloadable, went the message, unless the USA recognized the United States Of Eurasia. Once an American had claimed the New York keycode, 'United States Of Eurasia' was downloaded to all participating 'agents'.*

The song they received for all their brainstorming, insurrectionary spy-speak and international legwork was a sprawling pan-continental epic which owes Muse's greatest debt to Queen so far. Its plaintive piano opening, building to a histrionic, glossy squeal-rock chord at its peak, mirrors 'Bohemian Rhapsody' in style and structure, although fan-sites were quick to liken it also to such disparate sources as Paul McCartney's 'Live And Let Die', Christina Aguilera's 'You're Beautiful' and the *Lawrence Of Arabia* soundtrack. The orchestral centre-piece of the track certainly has an Arabian feel, resembling Ravel's *Bolero* engaged in a dance of the seven veils. The title was taken from Zbigniew Brzezinski's global political analysis *The Grand Chessboard*, in which Polish-born ex-advisor to Jimmy Carter (and, it's rumoured, a man also working with Barack Obama) Brzezinski argues that America is bent on controlling Eurasia in order to gain a stranglehold in its supplies of oil. The book, Matt would later state, has the feel of Stanley Kubrick's strategic war-room comedy *Dr Strangelove*; discussing the fate of Eurasia as if it is a mere playing board for a real-life game of Risk. Linked to the references to Eurasia in George Orwell's vision of the ultimate oppressive society in *Nineteen Eighty-Four*, the song's lyrics seemed to tell the story of this huge land mass united, of a

---

* In addition, during the hunt Muse fans managed to get #USOA to sixth place in Twitter's list of most popular 'trends' and #muse to number nine.

Eurasia vs USA stand-off, of megalomania gone mad. It hinted at a belief that humanity will forever be at war until all concept of 'country' is destroyed and we realize we're all stuck in the same sinking boat.

As if to press home the image of conflict blighting the planet's quintessential beauty, 'United States Of Eurasia' came attached to an outro track entitled 'Collateral Damage'. This found Matt playing Chopin's *Nocturne In E-Flat Major, Op. 9 No. 2* to the accompaniment of strings, birdsong and children's laughter, until the idyllic aural scene is torn apart by the roar of diving bombers.

Behind all this cloak and dagger espionage, all this sound and fury, meanwhile, lurked a band lost in beautiful scenery, literature that skipped between romantic and terrifying and their own hilarious, rampaging musical freedoms.

Behind the scenes, pulling the strings, Muse were having the time of their lives.

★ ★ ★

By the summer of 2008, Matt Bellamy has accumulated three homes. His main residence was the villa nestled in the hills of Lake Como, Lombardy, where the tranquility and scenic wonder of the forests descending to the shores of the great lake had drawn George Clooney, David Beckham and the casts of *Casino Royale* and *Star Wars II: Attack Of The Clones* to its surrounding villas – Daniel Craig's Bond recuperates in one; Anakin Skywalker is married in another. Here he demo'd in his home-built studio he called Studio Bellini, and played piano late into the night, furiously channeling the dead maestro's spirit.

In Italy Matt felt he was losing touch with England, so he immersed himself in BBC World News and had UK newspapers shipped out to him daily. The distance gave him an objectivity as the scandals of 2008 and 2009 unfolded – the banking crisis, the MPs expenses furore, the continuing war in Iraq. The sense of powerlessness he'd always felt in Britain and which had fed the themes of *Absolution* and *Black Holes & Revelations* simply didn't apply to Italy; it was ever more clear to him that the UK needed a change, that its democracy was laughable, its media twisted, its Parliamentary systems outdated – he struggled to believe that not only was the House Of Lords unelected but, indirectly, so was PM Gordon Brown. In his paradisiacal hideway Matt brainwashed himself with the BBC and

John Perkins' book *Confessions Of An Economic Hit Man*, detailing American attempts to snatch other countries' mineral wealth by destabilising their Governments. He also re-read George Orwell's *Nineteen Eighty-Four*, finding inspiration on second reading not in its dystopian politics but in the hope and romance of its central relationship between Winston Smith and Julia. Though Winston and Julia's clandestine affair ultimately leads to their arrest, torture and mutual betrayal in Orwell's novel, Matt found in it a rebellious emotional streak against a totalitarian regime which he believed could be applied to modern society. It all set him thinking: at the core of the electronica, R&B and long, piano-based symphonic prog songs he envisioned for Muse's fifth album could sit the idea of love as a method of resisting or escaping the oppressions and corruptions of the 21st Century Western world. Love, he concluded, equalled freedom; it was the one place Big Brother couldn't watch you.

Then, when staying at his flat in central London, Matt witnessed a different brand of resistance. The nearby US embassy and other embassies in the area were constantly targeted by protestors, some angry and vitriolic, others more light-hearted, in comedy costumes. Suddenly he was caught between two stools: support for the angry and destructive yet non-violent (towards people, at least) G20 protests which he believed was the closest the UK had come to the revolution it so desperately needed, and a wish to see the cheesy costumed protesters exact real change through far more peaceful means.

In Devon, at the house he'd bought for his mother and grandmother and where he'd use a spare room when he was visiting home, Matt reverted to his apocalyptic preparations. Aware that the West Country was traditionally where people had moved in order to be away from major cities in case of nuclear war, he made the house there a living eco-friendly bunker: it was around 40% self-sufficient for vegetables thanks to an allotment beside the building and the larder was stuffed with 50 cans of baked beans – having been told that a blockade of the UK would see us run out of oil in a week and food in a fortnight, and realizing that tinned food would last for two years, Matt had bought up the entire local shop's stock of beans along with an axe to chop firewood. His girlfriend stopped him buying a crossbow, but she couldn't stop him rescuing some chickens from a local battery farm for his own training purposes. After treating them well for the remaining months of 2008, at Christmas he killed them by hand to make dinner for his family. He felt guilt over it but the act brought him closer to real life. To know what it was like to kill animals for food, he believed, might one day be important.

All of this – the redemptive pinprick light of romance in the inky darkness of global and socio-political turmoil, the thin line between protest and revolution, the ascension of superpowers, the survival of humanity – began to colour Matt's vision of the forthcoming album. Not only did he want it (as he thought Muse's fans would) to be bigger and better, even more theatrical, the culmination of everything Muse had learnt about music – every style they'd attempted, every idea they'd forged – but he wanted to make something defiant, a fight back. If *Absolution* and *Black Holes* . . . had been swamped in alien myth, conspiracy and anger, this would be a very real album of resistance to what he called 'the corporate-ocracy'.

And above all else, Muse were determined that *The Resistance* would be a damn good laugh to make.

Initial work on the record began in June 2008; the band convened for loose writing sessions in Studio Bellini along with engineer Mike 'Spike' Stent. As much as they had enjoyed working with Rich Costey and loved his work on *Black Holes* . . . they wanted the new record to be as honest, risk-taking, fun and free of boundaries as it could be, and that meant venturing far out of their comfort zone, answering to no-one, making no compromise to outside forces. It meant producing the record themselves. With their own studio ready in Lake Como they had no time limit, so could relax into the recording. They planned a democratic decision-making process: any musical disputes between two members of the band would be resolved by the third. The approach reminded them of making *Origin Of Symmetry*, the last time they had thrown caution to the wind and fearlessly let themselves get carried to whatever wild zeniths the songs wanted to explore. This was Project Extreme.

By the end of July the band had five or six lyric-less songs underway; hints began to leak out via Dom's posts on the website or press interviews. There was a song which Matt likened to U2's 'New Year's Day' with a bit of glam rock creeping in, and others which he said were funk or R&B. Dom Twittered about "otherworldly disco", "15 minute orchestral monsters" and "things in between". Matt also talked of this orchestral opus, claiming it was like "a slimy opera version" of previous Muse songs. Chris, meanwhile, commented that the first time he heard Matt play some of his new compositions, often performed like Chopin recitals, they confused him. These were more like orchestral pieces than rock songs and few had a familiar beat; they reminded him of Brian Wilson's lost classic *Smile*.

Towards the end of the summer Muse decamped to a huge eco-house by a stream in the Devonshire countryside to rehearse the songs ready for recording. Like a gigantic pale-wood shack with plate glass windows whole storeys high, stuffed with touring gear and with only a poster for Fritz Lang's *Metropolis* as a sign of its space-brained inhabitants, the house was near enough to Teignmouth to ground them in the territory where they first met and recapture the thrill of first starting out, but remote enough not to scare the locals. Muse intended to finish these rehearsals and start recording by September but the intricacies of finishing their mammoth orchestral piece slowed them down into October. Here the tracks were primed; activation would occur back in Italy.

The Officina Mecanique Studios in Milan is an unobtrusive, shabby industrial building from which great beauty emanates. Here, and at Studio Bellini, between October 2008 and the spring of 2009, Muse collected to record *The Resistance*. There was much frivolity: every time they played back the Freddie Mercury wails of 'United States Of Eurasia' they fell on the floor laughing – it reminded Matt of a scene from the scymore-wielding sci-fi classic *Highlander*. But should a song intended to have such a weighty emotional punch have a ridiculous Brian May widdle and Freddie freak-out slapped in the middle of it? An intense discussion decided that they couldn't take it out. The outrageous and over-the-top comedy element of their music was an essential counterpoint to the lyrical heaviness - it was their Monty Python side, these fun, flamboyant flourishes struck with tongues lodged firmly in cheeks. This and the glam rock beat evolving out of a song called 'Uprising' helped to offset the darker elements so that the listener didn't become jaded but excited instead. Daftness and excess were all part of being human and anyway, if they took it out it wouldn't make them laugh anymore, and for them that intrinsically devalued the song. They'd agreed, after all, not to balk at anything weird or hilarious; that was a boundary. They didn't care about getting compared to Queen; in the end no-one else's opinion mattered. They loved it, so it stayed.

Experimentation naturally abounded: they played llamas toenails to recreate the sound of camel hooves, and tinkered with Timbaland style beats and syncopated rhythms. Dom programmed all of the electronic drums; Matt arranged and scored all of the strings for fear of another composer messing with the music. Dom and Chris were initially shocked and flummoxed by Matt's falsetto operatic vocals on the 12-minute orchestral epic he was calling 'Exogenesis'. Matt democratically talked them round to allowing it on the album. As crazy as it seemed, they just had to trust him on this one. Arguments and fights arose often but were resolved quicker than on the *Black Holes . . .* sessions.

The recording sessions crept on through Christmas 2008 and into 2009. Fans were kept in the loop with silent snippets of footage from the studio posted online by Tom Kirk – Matt playing a keyboard wearing a santa hat, Dom playing a snare drum in a field, the full band finger-clicking into a microphone in a toilet. In April there was talk of a studio collaboration with new rave maniacs Does It Offend You, Yeah?, who had mentioned that they might be visiting Studio Bellini, but the collaboration never materialized.* Instead, the last bout of recording took place in Officina Mecanique where 23 classical musicians, having been given only five minutes to sight-read the score, laid down the Arabian strings for 'United States Of Eurasia' while conductor Audrey Riley ran between studio and mixing desk trying to capture an air of Mahler or Bellini's *Casta Diva* and Matt sat hunched over the 100-track mixing desk making corrections to the sheet music as recording went along.

Recording finished by May 2009; by June 23 the record had been mixed in Studio Bellini by Mike Stent and sent for mastering in New York. Muse looked upon their first (almost entirely) home-made record and rejoiced. If they had wanted to push their styles, sounds and ideas beyond all known limits, they'd achieved it. If they'd wanted an album that veered between the sublime and the ridiculous at will, they'd achieved that too. And if they'd wanted to make an album of romance, rebellion and righteousness, well that was *The Resistance*'s hat trick. And where the previous two albums had started with grand building anthems leading nowhere, this time they wanted to start with a bang.

The Resistance opened, sniggering at the activist demo, with that glam rock stomp the band found so amusing. 'Uprising' encapsulated the avid intent and stylistic humour of the sessions. The press would liken it to

* Does It Offend You, Yeah? did, however, remix 'Uprising' for a B-side of the single.

everything from The Sweet's 'Blockbuster', The Glitter Band and Marilyn Manson (for the 70s drum beat) to Jean Michelle Jarre's 'Oxygene 2', The Timelords' 'Doctorin' The Tardis' and the *Dr Who* theme (for the retro-futurist synths). But for Matt it represented those costumed pro-testers outside his London flat; a light-hearted approach to a very serious issue. Envisioning gangs of football hooligans chanting slogans in protest to the banking disaster, he could hear in it the anger of being let down by politicians, bankers and major institutions, a once-bitten determination not to trust the people in power, a cry for public resistance. In September it would be the first official single release from *The Resistance* and its pack-aging would reflect its two-sided nature. The artwork would feature rows of teddy bears in military formation, while Matt's vision for the video had the teddies staging a sinister uprising and causing chaos on a march on Parliament. 'Uprising' was cuddly subversion indeed.

It coupled with the second track 'Resistance' to set the insurrectionary tone of the album. Building from an ethereal electronic buzz, a ghostly operatic hum and a drumbeat reminiscent of 'Map Of The Problematique', it retold the relationship of Winston and Julia from *Nineteen Eighty-Four* as their secret affair is discovered by the Thought Police in what they'd believed to be a safe room in the Proles district. As the sharp-edged chorus line – akin to ELO, Queen or Jeff Wayne's *War Of The Worlds* – breaks into Matt's sumptuous verse like police boots through the door, the lyrics make a plea for the love within to always stand in defiance of oppression. This, apparently, was the tune Matt had previously compared to 'New Year's Day'. Who knows what planet he was on that day?

'Undisclosed Desires' was *The Resistance*'s first Timabaland-inspired R&B track, a song Chris could image people getting drunk to and pulling. It was also, according to Matt, the first "anti-Muse song", since none of the band take up their usual roles on the track: Chris plays a style of slap bass reminiscent of Depeche Mode, Dom programmed electronic drums instead of playing his normal kit and the rest of the song is made up of edited string samples. Matt does nothing on the song but sing; a distinctly personal ode to Gaia that could easily have been sold to Beyonce. It took the funk roots of *Supermassive Black Hole* into new realms of chart-friendliness for Muse, by far the most pop song they'd ever recorded.

Such an uncompromising band could only possibly follow something so personal and groove-based with something global and stately: the slow-burning resplendence of 'United States Of Eurasia/Collateral Damage'. Acting as the album's centerpiece much as 'Butterflies & Hurricanes' did on *Absolution*, it draws the sights out from the minutiae of relationships to take in the grander scale, stamping the album with the jackboot print of the imperialist superpower. If we might have wondered what shadowy oppressor we were being told to resist in the previous songs, it was all here: the land mass of Eurasia being urged to unite against the war-mongering USA. And this was its National Anthem.

The bombers at its close seemed to crash land somewhere between 'Vienna' and 'Barcelona'. Ultravox's greatest moment and Freddie Mercury's histrionic 1987 duet with Montserrat Caballe combined in the crunching backbeat, misty synths and soaring vocals of 'Guiding Light', a song Muse played so loud during recording that you can hear the sound of the neighbours banging on the door towards the end.* The song appears to reflect the end of Winston and Julia's relationship, when they're divided and broken down by the torturers of the Ministry Of Love, left as hollow shells of sheer obedience. As stirring as it sounds, 'Guiding Light' might just be the bleakest moment of *The Resistance*.

Time to fight back. 'Unnatural Selection' finds Matt tearing off his furry animal costume and pushing "beyond peaceful protest". Driven by a Queens Of The Stone Age riff – the most 'rock' track on the record – the song advocates rampage and destruction, commotion and unrest, a demand for the truth. It's here that Matt teeters between peaceful protest, violent revolution and simply running away, and the song reflects his sway – a ravenous punk rock segment gives way to a laid back Led Zeppelin groove before the rock riot wins out in the end.

While the album purposely avoids conspiracy theories in favour of more realistic socio-political world-views – Matt was tired of being painted as a crackpot – 'MK Ultra' is its one slice of political paranoia. Named after Project MK-ULTRA, a secret research program allegedly conducted by the CIA into mind control and interrogation drugs, its protagonist finds his thoughts being hacked from the outside, losing control of his own brain as "the wavelength gently grows". Chris probably didn't help Matt's attempt to be taken more seriously, however, by saying that he thought this

---

* You can also, with close attention, just about hear the stream that Dom recorded the drums beside.

pummelling electro-rocker (in the vein of a keyboards-led 'Assassin') might be about David Icke's lizard royalty.

Some light relief before the mountainous finale came in the form of 'I Belong To You', a jaunty piano piece full of whoops and finger clicks that nodded towards Blur's Britpop peak, Billy Joel, Supertramp and The Beatles in its upbeat swagger. A song of devotion with classical references to pillars being destroyed and crowns worn – Muse couldn't leave it as simple as that. No, mid-way through the first ever mention of their own name in song, 'I Belong To You' breaks into a segment of 'Mon Coeur S'Ouvre A Ta Voix', an aria from Camille Saint-Saëns' opera *Samson And Delilah* performed by the band, choir and orchestra. And if you thought that was extravagant, you hadn't seen nothing yet.

'Exogenesis', a twelve-minute symphony in three parts entitled 'Overture', 'Cross-Pollination' and 'Redemption', had been swirling around Matt's brain for several years, and had held up the *Resistance* writing sessions for some months as he struggled to perfect the arrangement and score. Many times he'd imagined Muse songs performed by a symphony orchestra and large choir; now was his chance to indulge his wildest Berlioz fantasies.

The theory of exogenesis[*], suggests that the universe contains 'seeds' of life throughout and that life on Earth might have spawned from such a seed; that we were 'cross-pollinated' from elsewhere, by a comet perhaps. The song itself imagines an End Of Days scenario when mankind is forced to leave Earth or to send scraps of its DNA to another planet to begin the human race again. Using space imagery to reflect the enormity of the music where a more religious era would have sung Heavenly hosannas, it was more of a classical piece than a song; the band were a backdrop to the strings to the degree that Chris would claim it would work just as well without Muse on it at all.

A swell of strings, a blaze of horns, a rumble of timpani: 'Overture' swept in with all the grace and nimbleness of the most revered Philharmonic. Matt's shrill operatic voice, hitting heights not heard since 'Micro Cuts', was full of questions over an undulating refrain: who are we, where are we, why are we? A languid Floydian guitar solo gave way to 'Cross-Pollination', all stabbing piano chords descending to a maestro's

---

[*] A better known word for what should technically be called panspermia.

flourish. Here the last hopes for humanity break through the planet's toxic clouds, burst free of our atmosphere, head off to "spread our codes", and its soundtrack is suitably florid and evocative, an orchestral orbit achieved. Then the band kick in, Dom's drums thunderous, Chris' bass blasting off to some distant galactic quadrant, before the initial refrain is repeated; destination reached. It could end there, but 'Redemption' strikes up with Bach-esque fragility, the sumptuous and hopeful final part of this cinematic visual journey, representing the new seeds being sewn. Matt would later point out that the final track of each of their albums has hinted at what the next would sound like; if 'Exogenesis' is anything to go by Muse's sixth album can only be a real-life version of the opera from The Fifth Element.

If *The Resistance* was Muse's most uncompromising, challenging and extreme record to date, it still didn't stop it being – in chart terms – their most successful yet. On its release in September 2009 it made number one in 15 countries including the UK, France, Germany, Mexico and Canada, and hit number three in that most insidious of superpowers, the USA. It looked like the most politically docile nation on Earth, the warmongering Great Enemy, had finally got Muse's subversive message.

But before they could go there to expound on it, they had some unfinished business to attend to. Back home.

* * *

Ever since they'd met there as teenagers, Matt and Dom had fantasized about playing a gig at The Den, the patch of greenery pooled in the lap of Teignmouth, the baize of the seafront. So where better for Matt to reconnect with his homeland, to inspire the disenfranchised young souls of their hometown and to premiere *The Resistance* to their home planet?

So on September 4, 2009, 10,000 active Muse agents descended upon The Den for the first rally of Project Eurasia, known by the code name 'A Seaside Rendezvous'. Though the local council had only agreed to license the gig, and a second the next day, on the condition that sound levels didn't exceed 84.1 decibels*, spirits were high – behind the street cordons

---

* Following a council meeting between locals and fans to decide whether the shows should be granted permission – Chris personally appealed to Muse fans to attend the meeting in their support.

and barricades shop-fronts had been decorated with Muse posters and signs reading 'THE BOYS ARE BACK IN TOWN'. The stage was decked out like a gigantic Punch & Judy booth, two enormous Mr Punches peering down on the stage from the speaker fabrics; a circus ringmaster roused the crowd for Muse's entrance. "Hello Teignmouth!" yelled Matt, gesturing nostalgically towards the pier, 'it's wonderful to be here again."

And beneath a full moon strafed with lasers, Muse unleashed *The Resistance* – the majority of the record, excluding only 'Exogenesis', 'MK-Ultra', 'I Belong To You' and 'Guiding Light', interspersed with crowd pleasers* and a couple of rarities – a cover of Hot Butter's 1970s synth hit 'Popcorn' and 'Cave', dedicated to the mayor that had binned their debut album in the local paper a decade before. Towards the end Dom stood on his drum stool to announce how much of a dream it had always been for Muse to play The Den.

And with that, *The Resistance* was set in motion.

After two more relatively low-key warm-up shows in theatres in Paris and Berlin (featuring almost identical set-lists to The Den gigs), several TV and radio sessions to promote the album in France, London and Italy (where the band mimed 'Uprising' on *Quelli che . . . il Calcio* having swapped places, Dom taking up 'vocals' and Matt drumming) and an appearance at the MTV Video Music Awards in New York, Muse joined U2's mammoth 360° world stadium tour as support on its Eastern Seaboard US leg through September and October. As the world's biggest territory crumbling at their feet it was the perfect opportunity to slaughter 60–80,000 American rock fans every night with a tight eight-track set of super-charged hits. From Giants Stadium in New York through Landover, Charlottesville, Raleigh, Atlanta, Tampa, Arlington and Houston, Muse slid down the Eastern curve of the States, playing on a stage U2 had designed for the centre of the stadiums – a 165-foot metallic claw poised over the centre of the pitch like a robotic spider. The central stage gave Muse an idea for the set of their own forthcoming European arena tour – something to represent the totalitarian themes of the album, replete with another outing from the suspended acrobats from the

---

* 'Supermassive Black Hole', 'Starlight, 'Knights Of Cydonia', 'Hysteria', 'New Born', 'Plug In Baby', 'Time Is Running Out, 'Map Of The Problematique', 'Stockholm Syndrome' and, on the second night, 'Feeling Good'.

Wembley shows, perhaps chasing each other through the air but failing to catch each other, Winston and Julia meets Peter and Wendy. Matt set about looking into opera sets and Cirque de Soleil, edgy forms of performance imbibed with drama. The O2 beckoned, 20,000 seats strong. *The Resistance* was going to have to burst it at the beams.

* * *

The lights go down; the lights come on. Lights from the windows of the three grey four-storey tower blocks stretching from stage to ceiling, lodged at one end of the O2 arena this November 12, 2009, encircled by craning faces.* Columns of white figures fade into view, parading the corridors of the towers, marching up their staircases, disappearing into their rafters.

A synth flurry swells, a woman's voice intones "we are the universe destroying itself", the towers' outer sheets drop and Muse have entered the buildings. Suspended twenty feet above the stage in the slim gaps between huge square columns of pixel screens they kick into the 25th Century glam crunch of 'Uprising' as the towers flash neon patterns of authoritarian black and red and Matt shoots lasers from a hand-held mirror. Sans flying dancers, the show doesn't quite live up to Matt's ambitious vision, but the set perfectly conveys the restless, shackled, under-surveillance mood of *The Resistance*: giant monochrome eyes scan the crowd from the screens during 'New Born', 'Map Of The Problematique' is accompanied by visuals of fingerprint and facial scans, 'United States Of Eurasia' opens with a mattress of passport photos of audience members, shot on their way into the arena. We're snapped, scanned and x-rayed at every turn, goes the message, for one clear purpose. The map of Eurasia glows green below the text 'STATUS: DIVIDED, POTENTIAL THREAT: MINIMAL'.

Through the plumes of steam, the swarms of tiny laser insects and the rise and fall of their individual tower platforms, freeing and containing them at will, Muse rock with their trademark magnificent mettle. Chris and Dom play a funk rock mega-jam on a spinning drum riser, Matt's piano is lifted high into the air for 'Feeling Good' and with ferocious fire-ups of 'Plug In Baby', 'Hysteria', 'Stockholm Syndrome' and 'Knights

---

* There was no backdrop to the stage, allowing seats to be sold to the rear and the sides; the O2 was as full as it's capable of being.

Of Cydonia' they prove once again that, though the powers that be may have the strings of our DNA and the distortions of our irises on file, it's Muse that have the access codes to our souls.

The next day Muse announce another date at Wembley Stadium for the summer of 2010. The airborne love affair, we assume, will have to wait until then.

★ ★ ★

And the future?

Back at the NME Awards 2008, Matt was thoughtful for a second.

"I'm sure we're gonna get a kick in the teeth at some point but we've had such a good run that we almost expect to get a kick up the arse and a slap round the face, like 'go back to Devon!'."

The rest of us, however, envision a rather different future. When the international oil crisis breaks out into global conflagration, Muse will be there to wail a magnificent 'I told you so.' When the secret leaders of the world are unmasked and paraded in city squares by the heads of the revolution, Muse will be there to spit most heavily in their faces.

And when the aliens from the geothermal planet Nibiru return from their 3,200 year orbit to collect all of the gold they'd cloned us in order to mine for them, we can hand them the collected works of Muse and know that they'll proudly leave us alone for another 3,200 years, safe in the knowledge that we're doing a damn fine job.

Muse UK Discography

All recordings released on CD unless stated otherwise.

SINGLES

Uno
Taste Media/Mushroom Records (June 14, 1999)
CD: Uno / Jimmy Kane / Forced In
Vinyl 7″: Uno (alternative version) / Agitated

Cave
Taste Media/Mushroom Records (September 6, 1999)
CD 1: Cave / Twin / Cave Remix
CD 2: Cave / Host / Coma
Vinyl 7″: Cave / Cave (instrumental remix)

Muscle Museum
Taste Media/Mushroom Records (November 22, 1999)
CD 1: Muscle Museum / Do We Need This? / Muscle Museum (live acoustic)
CD 2: Muscle Museum (full length version) / Pink Ego Box / Con-science
Vinyl 7″: Muscle Museum / Minimum

Sunburn
Taste Media/Mushroom Records (February 21, 2000)
CD 1: Sunburn (radio edit) / Ashamed / Sunburn (live)
CD 2: Sunburn / Yes Please / Uno (live)
Vinyl 7″: Sunburn / Sunburn (live acoustic)

Unintended
Taste Media/Mushroom Records (May 30, 2000)
CD 1: Unintended / Recess / Falling Down (live acoustic)
CD 2: Unintended / Nishe / Hate This & I'll Love You (live acoustic)
Vinyl 7″: Unintended / Sober (live)

Plug In Baby
Taste Media/Mushroom Records (March 5, 2001)
CD 1: Plug In Baby / Nature_1 / Execution Commentary / Plug In Baby video
CD 2: Plug In Baby / Spiral Static / Bedroom Acoustics
Vinyl 7″: Plug In Baby / Nature_1

New Born
Taste Media/Mushroom Records (June 5, 2001)
CD 1: New Born / Shrinking Universe / Piano thing / New Born video
CD 2: New Born / Map Of Your Head / Plug In Baby (live)
Vinyl 7″: New Born / Shrinking Universe
Vinyl 12″: New Born (Oakenfold Perfecto remix) / Sunburn (Timo Maas'
Sunstroke remix) / Sunburn (Timo Mass' Breakz Again mix)

Bliss
Taste Media/Mushroom Records (August 20, 2001)
CD 1: Bliss / The Gallery / Screenager (live) / Bliss video
CD 2: Bliss / Hyper Chondriac Music / New Born (live) / Making of Bliss video
Vinyl 7″: Bliss / Hyper Chondriac Music

Hyper Music/Feeling Good
Taste Media/Mushroom Records (November 19, 2001)
CD 1: Hyper Music / Feeling Good (live) / Shine / Hyper Music video
CD 2: Feeling Good / Hyper Music (live) / Please Please Please Let Me Get
What I Want / Feeling Good video
Vinyl 7″: Hyper Music / Feeling Good

Dead Star/In Your World
Taste Media/Mushroom Records (July 17, 2002)
CD 1: Dead Star / In Your World (live) / Futurism / Dead Star video
CD 2: In Your World / Dead Star (live) / Can't Take My Eyes Off You /
In Your World video
Vinyl 7″: Dead Star / In Your World

Stockholm Syndrome
Released exclusively on muse.mu (July 14, 2003)
Stockholm Syndrome

Time Is Running Out
Taste Media/EastWest Records (September 8, 2003)
CD: Time Is Running Out / The Groove / Stockholm Syndrome video
Vinyl 7″: Time Is Running Out / The Groove
DVD: Time Is Running Out video / Making Of / Photo gallery

Hysteria
Taste Media/EastWest Records (December 1, 2003)
CD: Hysteria / Eternally Missed
Vinyl 7″: Hysteria / Eternally Missed
DVD: Hysteria – Director Cut (video) / Hysteria (audio) / Hysteria video live
MTV2 / The Making of (video) / Gallery

Sing For Absolution
Taste Media/EastWest Records (May 17, 2004)
CD: Sing For Absolution (Full Length US Remix) / Fury
Vinyl 7″: Sing For Absolution (Full Length US Remix) / Fury
DVD : Sing For Absolution (video) / Sing For Absolution (audio) / The Making
Of (video) / Big Day Off [Behind the scenes from the Big Day Out tour] /
Gallery

Butterflies & Hurricanes
Taste Media/EastWest Records (September 20, 2004)
CD: Butterflies & Hurricanes (Remix full length) / Sing For Absolution (live
acoustic) / U-myx technologie
Vinyl 7″: Butterflies & Hurricanes (Full length) / Butterflies & Hurricanes (live)
DVD: Butterflies & Hurricanes (audio) / Butterflies & Hurricanes (video) /
The Groove in the States / The raw video edit

Supermassive Black Hole
Helium-3 (June 19, 2006)
CD: Supermassive Black Hole / Crying Shame
Vinyl 7″: Supermassive Black Hole / Crying Shame
DVD: Supermassive Black Hole (video) / Making Of / Bonus video / Gallery

Starlight
Helium-3 (September 4, 2006)
CD: Starlight / Easily
Vinyl 7″: Starlight / Supermassive Black Hole (Phones Control Voltage Mix)
DVD: Starlight (audio) / Starlight (video) / Making Of / Gallery / Hidden Track
(audio)

Knights Of Cydonia
Helium-3 (November 27, 2006)
CD: Knights Of Cydonia / Supermassive Black Hole (live)
Vinyl 7″: Knights Of Cydonia / Assassin [Grand Omega Bosses Edit]
DVD: Knights Of Cydonia (audio) / Knights Of Cydonia (video) / Making Of /
Gallery

Invincible
Helium-3 (April 9, 2007)
CD: Invincible / Knights Of Cydonia (Simian Mobile Disco Remix)
Vinyl 7": Invincible / Glorious
DVD: Invincible (audio) / Invincible (video) / Invincible (video – live in Milan)

Map Of The Problematique
Digital release only (June 18, 2007)
Muse.mu exclusive: Map Of The Problematique (Rich Costey Edit) / Map Of The Problematique (live from Wembley Stadium) / Wembley Digital Souvenir Pack
Itunes exclusive: Map Of The Problematique (AOL Session)
Digital: Map Of The Problematique / Map Of The Problematique (Does It Offend You, Yeah? Remix)

Uprising
Warner Brothers WEA458CD (September 7, 2009)
CD: Uprising / Uprising (Does It Offend You Remix)
Vinyl: Uprising / Who Knows Who

Undisclosed Desires
Digital Release only (November 16, 2009)
Undisclosed Desires / Undisclosed Desires (Thin White Duke Remix) / Undisclosed Desires (Thin White Duke Remix Edit)/Undisclosed Desires (The Big Pink Remix)
Promo CD: Undisclosed Desires (Radio Edit)/Undisclosed Desires (Album Version)

EPs

Muse
Dangerous Records (March 1, 1998)
Overdue / Cave / Coma / Escape
Note: Limited & hand-numbered edition (999).

Muscle Museum
Dangerous Records (January 11, 1999)
Muscle Museum / Sober / Uno / Unintended / Instant Messenger / Muscle Museum #2
Note: Limited & hand-numbered edition (999).

Random 1-8

Taste Media/Avex (October 4, 2000)

Host / Coma / Pink Ego Box / Forced In / Agitated / Yes Please / Fillip (live) / Do We Need This? (live) / Sunburn (Timo Maas Sunstroke Mix)

Note: Made for Japanese release.

ALBUMS

Showbiz

Taste Media/Mushroom Records (October 4, 1999)

Sunburn / Muscle Museum / Fillip / Falling Down / Cave / Showbiz / Unintended / Uno / Sober / Escape / Overdue / Hate This & I'll Love You / Spiral Static★

★ *Bonus track on Japanese version only.*

Origin Of Symmetry

Taste Media/Mushroom Records (June 17, 2001) (from Muse website)

New Born / Bliss / Space Dementia / Hyper Music / Plug In Baby / Citizen Erased / Micro Cuts / Screenager / Darkshines / Feeling Good / Megalomania / Futurism★

★ *Bonus track on Japanese version only.*

Hullabaloo Soundtrack

Taste Media/Mushroom Records (June 30, 2002) (from Muse website)

CD1: Forced In / Shrinking Universe / Recess / Yes Please / Map Of Your Head / Nature_1 / Shine (acoustic) / Ashamed / The Gallery / Hyper Chondriac Music

CD2: Dead Star / Micro Cuts / Citizen Erased / Showbiz / Megalomania / Darkshines / Screenager / Space Dementia / In Your World / Muscle Museum / Agitated

Note: Disc 1 includes a selection of B-sides and disc 2 includes live tracks recorded at Le Zénith in Paris on October 28–29, 2001.

Absolution

Taste Media/EastWest Records (September 22, 2003)

Intro / Apocalypse Please / Time Is Running Out / Sing For Absolution / Stockholm Syndrome / Falling Away With You / Interlude / Hysteria / Blackout / Butterflies & Hurricanes / The Small Print / Endlessly / Thoughts Of A Dying Atheist / Ruled By Secrecy / Fury★

★ *Bonus track on Japanese version only.*

Black Holes And Revelations

Helium-3 (July 3, 2006)

Take A Bow / Starlight / Supermassive Black Hole / Map Of The Problematique / Soldier's Poem / Invincible / Assassin / Exo-Politics / City Of Delusion / Hoodoo / Knights Of Cydonia / Glorious★

★ *Bonus track on Japanese version only.*

H.A.A.R.P.

Helium-3 (March 17, 2008)

CD: Intro / Knights Of Cydonia / Hysteria / Supermassive Black Hole / Map Of The Problematique / Butterflies & Hurricanes / Invincible / Starlight / Time Is Running Out / New Born / Unintended / Micro Cuts / Stockholm Syndrome / Take A Bow

DVD: Intro / Knights Of Cydonia / Hysteria / Supermassive Black Hole / Map Of The Problematique / Butterflies & Hurricanes / Hoodoo / Apocalypse Please / Feeling Good / Invincible / Starlight / Improv. / Time Is Running Out / New Born / Soldier's Poem / Unintended / Blackout / Plug In Baby / Stockholm Syndrome / Take A Bow

Note: This is a live CD and DVD release of Muse's concerts at Wembley Stadium, England on June 16 and 17, 2007. The DVD also includes a documentary and pictures of the shows.

The Resistance

Warners Brothers 825646874347 (September 2009)

Uprising / Resistance / Undisclosed Desires / United States of Eurasia (+ Collateral Damage) / Guiding Light / Unnatural Selection / MK Ultra / I Belong To You (+Mon Cœur S'Ouvre à ta Voix) / Exogenesis Symphony: Part 1 Overture / Part 2 Cross-Pollination / Part 3 Redemption

DVDs

Hullabaloo

Taste Media/Mushroom Records (July 1, 2002)

DVD 1: What's He Building (intro) / Dead Star / Micro Cuts / Citizen Erased / Sunburn / Showbiz / Megalomania / Uno / Screenager / Feeling Good / Space Dementia / In Your World / Muscle Museum / Cave / New Born / Hyper Music / Agitated / Unintended / Plug In Baby / Bliss

DVD 2: Documentary / Interactive Discography & videos / Gallery

Note: The first DVD features 90mn live concert recorded on October 28/29 2001 at "le Zénith" in Paris. The second DVD features 40 minutes of unseen offstage footage from around the world including B-sides taken from the *Hullabaloo* soundtrack album.

Absolution Tour

Taste Media/Warner (December 12, 2005)

Hysteria / New Born / Sing For Absolution / Muscle Museum / Apocalypse
Please / Ruled By Secrecy / Sunburn / Butterflies & Hurricanes / Bliss / Time Is
Running Out / Plug In Baby / Blackout

Bonus: Fury (live in Los Angeles) / The Small Print (live at Earls Court) /
Stockholm Syndrome (live at Earls Court) / The Groove in the States (live in
Cincinnati/San Diego)

Hidden Extras: Endlessly (live at Wembley Arena) / Thoughts Of A Dying
Atheist (live at Wembley Arena)

Note: The main set list compiles highlights from their performance on
Glastonbury's Main Stage on June 27, 2004.

Acknowledgements

My primary mission in writing *Out Of This World: The Story Of Muse* was to compile in one place every scrap, sliver and snippet of information available to mankind in the public arena about the rock group Muse. These would be compiled alongside previously unprinted excerpts from the many interviews I'd conducted with the band since 1999, admitting no quotes cut and pasted from Muse's myriad of well-thumbed press clippings. This way, I cunningly plotted, I could write a comprehensive and definitive biography of the band with little or no outside help whatsoever.

In this assumption I was woefully naïve.

As I sliced and diced my way through Muse's history, more and more individuals, like so many new broomsticks in *The Sorcerer's Apprentice*, were called to my assistance. Without any of the aft-mentioned this book would at the very least be riddled with inaccuracies and at most be simply impossible to produce.

As planned, every quote within these pages, except on rare occasions where credited in the text, is taken from interviews conducted by myself between 1999 and 2008, and have previously been unprinted. For the acquisition, transcription and permission to print these I'd like to thank Matt Bellamy, Dominic Howard, Chris Wolstenholme, Glen Rowe, Safta Jaffery, Paul Reeve, Colin Stidworthy, Jack Burkill, Rebecca Dicks, Hannah Ellis-Peterson, Hall Or Nothing PR, Conor McNicholas and IPC Media.

Many millions of words have been written about Muse over the course of their career and the research for this book brought me into contact with the vast majority of them, largely thanks to Amy Vickery and Mel Brown at Impressive PR and Gillian Porter and Terri Hall at Hall Or Nothing PR, who kindly allowed me access to their press archives and photocopiers. Ben Myers' fine Muse biography, *Inside The Muscle Museum*, provided a reference point to ensure I'd missed nothing out, but by far the most detailed and dedicated source of information on the band is to be found online. Sites such as microcuts and musewiki proved utterly invaluable in offering gig-by-gig set lists, song-by-song analysis and eyewitness reports, and so, by inadvertently helping me out with their feverish and honourable devotion to the Muse cause, I must thank the hundreds of fans who update and contribute to these sites daily. Where these sources offered conflicting information I thank Chris, Dom and Matt for clearing up the discrepancies, and for invaluable corrections to the text I thank Safta Jaffery and Taste Media. Special thanks go to Romain Lefebvre and his colleagues at Microcuts for providing the discography.

Many thanks to Chris Charlesworth at Omnibus Press for support and encouragement beyond the call of duty, and finally to Debbie King for putting up with being a Muse widow for the first six months of our relationship. I'll make it up to you in Rio, baby.

ALL LYRICS USED IN THE BOOK HAVE BEEN USED BY THE KIND PERMISSION AND COURTESY OF TASTE MUSIC LIMITED

The publishers are grateful to Taste Media for permission to quote from the following Muse songs: